SOMEONE LIKE ME

SOMEONE LIKE ME

Images for Writing

Fifth Edition

Sheena Gillespie
Linda Stanley

Queensborough Community College
City University of New York

LITTLE, BROWN AND COMPANY

Boston • Toronto

Library of Congress Cataloging in Publication Data
Main entry under title:

Someone like me.

Includes index.
1. College readers.   2. English language—
Rhetoric.   I. Gillespie, Sheena.   II. Stanley,
Linda.
PE1417.S614   1984   808'.0427   83-19564
ISBN 0-316-31368-8

Library of Congress Catalog Card No. 83-19564

ISBN 0-316-31368-8

10   9   8   7   6   5   4   3

HAL

Published simultaneously in Canada
by Little, Brown & Company (Canada) Limited

Printed in the United States of America

Acknowledgments

Photos for Chapters 1, 2, 4, 5, and 6 by Linda Stanley. Photo for Chapter 3
by Arnold Asrelsky.

James Agee, "Knoxville: Summer 1915." Reprinted by permission of Grosset
& Dunlap, Inc. from *A Death in the Family* by James Agee. Copyright © 1957
by The James Agee Trust.

Sherwood Anderson, "Discovery of a Father," From *Sherwood Anderson's
Memoirs,* edited by Ray Lewis White, University of North Carolina Press,
1969. Reprinted by permission of the publisher.

Maya Angelou, "Sister Flowers." From *I Know Why the Caged Bird Sings,* by
Maya Angelou. Copyright © 1969 by Maya Angelou. Reprinted by permission of Random House, Inc.

W. H. Auden, "The Unknown Citizen." Copyright 1940 and renewed 1968
by W. H. Auden. Reprinted from *W. H. Auden, Collected Poems,* edited by

(Continued on page 350)

To Lillian Gillespie McCallum
and Colleen Stanley,
who influenced us to be
"particular" people

 # Preface

Someone Like Me, Fifth Edition, like those preceding it, includes essays, short stories, and poems, all selected in the belief that students become more involved in literature in general and in essay models in particular when they can sense a person behind the pen. Consequently, nearly all the essays are written in the first person—about two-thirds are autobiographical—and they discuss six essential areas of personal experience and ideas: people, places, events and experiences, emotions, choices, and philosophies. As in earlier editions, the short stories and poems develop the thematic thrust as well as the organizational principles of the chapter.

In this edition, we have changed over 40 percent of the selections in a continuing effort to reflect student needs and interests. We have made a concerted effort to use only those writers we like to think of as "classical," whose works are both transcendent and timely and written in a seemingly effortless prose style accessible to every reader. Those writers—both "new" and "old"—who have been added to this edition include George Orwell (represented twice), E. B. White (whose "Once More to the Lake" we have included in several editions and whose "The Geese" we include here for the first time), James Agee, Saul Bellow, Richard Selzer, Elie Wiesel, Loren Eiseley, Lewis Thomas, William Golding, Katherine Anne Porter, and Richard Rodriguez. Writers who have been with us from earlier editions are Sherwood Anderson, Joan Didion, Anne Morrow Lindbergh, Henry David Thoreau, Helen Keller, E. M. Forster, and Plato.

The fifth edition also continues with the inductive approach to the development of writing style that was the major feature of earlier editions. The book directly utilizes essay models to suggest various writing techniques, two of which receive intensive discussion in each chapter following the two lead essays. The book thus combines the features of an essay anthology with many aspects of a rhetoric text. Moreover, thematic units and rhetorical units are synchronized to help the student see the logical need for the various methods of essay development. Good writing techniques, such as creating a subject, generating ideas, composing a thesis statement, organizing the essay, developing paragraphs, and achieving coherence, are also clarified. Both the rhetorical modes and the writing techniques form the basis of the rhetorical sections in each chapter.

Someone Like Me stresses experiential writing throughout but with increasing complexity of thought and experience. At least one essay in each chapter is purely expository, with the majority of the essays in the last three chapters of a transactional nature despite a first person or autobiographical framework. In the early chapters, the essays are autobiographical in purpose; later, they are autobiographical in illustration of an expository point.

The sections on writing techniques and rhetorical modes that follow the lead essays in each chapter have been rearranged, expanded, and new sections added. Specifically, the section on language and tone has been moved from chapter one to chapter five, and a second prewriting section on generating ideas added to chapter one. The rhetorical sections have also been expanded to include ideas from the new research in writing that go far to help the student through the writing process. Each section draws on the essay preceding it as an inductive impetus for rhetorical discussion. Then, the principles of that rhetorical device receive expanded discussion, using the new research and utilizing the other essays in the chapter as further examples. Finally, steps are outlined whereby the student can use the material in writing his or her own essays.

As in earlier editions, we have arranged the chapters to accommodate the instructor who may wish to use the anthology but not the rhetorical sections. Questions after each selection are divided into two sections, "Probing for Meaning" and "Probing for Method." For those instructors who wish to use the rhetorical sections, chapters one through five all contain discussion of two rhetorical devices, and chapter six contains one.

Although we have made every attempt to choose selections that do not have highly sophisticated or technical vocabularies—hence our use of "classical" texts—we have included some essays with relatively abstract language. Questions on vocabulary as well as on comprehension follow each essay.

Finally, each chapter includes suggestions for essay topics in "Topics for Imitation." This section offers two types of writing assignments: one encourages students to develop their own experiences and ideas; the second calls for the critical evaluation of the ideas presented in the chapter selections.

There is also a short biographical section on the writers in the text included at the back, as suggested by the personal nature of the text. We have not placed the biographies at the beginning of the essays to avoid a cluttered look.

For those teachers who find teachers' manuals useful, David Shimkin has prepared one to accompany the Fifth Edition of *Someone Like Me* with "answers" to the questions in the Probing for Meaning and Probing for Method sections, as well as other useful teaching tools and additional writing topics.

We wish to thank those teachers of composition who generously offered suggestions based on their experience with the Fourth Edition:

Robert Achenback, Iowa State University; Ruth Ames, Queensborough Community College; Kenneth Anania, Massosoit Community College; Mary Lee Archer, Victoria College; Leroy Ater, LA Pierce College; E. Morris Azbill, Victoria College; Robert Banfelder, Queensborough Community College; Larry Bronson, Central Michigan University; David Bruner, Iowa State University; Alberto Cacicedo, Massachusetts Bay Community College; Fay Chandler, Pasadena City College; Tony Clark, Paris Junior College; Betty Clement, Paris Junior College; Pansy Collins, Evangel College; Donald Dunlop, Iowa State University; Jack Edwards, Victoria College; Nancy Edwards, Bakersfield College; Samuel Eisenstein, LA City College; Lyon Evans, Iowa State University; David Fear, Valencia Community College; Marco Fraschella, Delta College; Jack Friedman, Queensborough Community College; Geneva Frost, University of Maine at Machias; Margaret Furcron, Rutgers University; Norma Garry, Mercy College; Thomas Gay, Youngstown State University; Harris Green, DeKalb Community College; Kenneth Greenhill, Victoria College; Janet Halbert, Western Texas College; Charlene Hollows, Massachusetts Bay Community College; William Hoopes, College of the Redwoods; Emily Jensen, Lycoming College; William Jones, Rutgers University; Jean Keith, Massachusetts Bay Community College; Barbara Keyser, Baruch

College; Paul Kistel, Pierce College; Margaret Read Lauer, Bloomsburg State College; Bill Lemley, College of the Redwoods; Elaine Levy, Queensborough Community College; Madeleine Lynch, San Joaquin Delta College; Kevin McKenna, Iowa State University; Phyllis Mael, Pasadena City College; Marilyn Maxwell, Massasoit Community College; John McCully, Iowa State University; Karen Mead, Vincennes University; Mary Jane Moffat, Palo Alto Center/Foothill College; Gratia Murphy, Youngstown State University; M. Janice Murphy, Spalding College; Jeanne Nichols, Los Angeles Harbor College; Joyce Pair, DeKalb Community College; Bernon Peacock, DeKalb Community College; Ulrica Bell Perkins, Cerro Coso Community College; Joseph Raia, Miami Dade Community College; Debbie Reynolds, Vincennes University; Janet Ripin, Massasoit Community College; Gary Roseman, DeKalb Community College; Arlyne Samuels, Queensborough Community College; Marta Shapiro, Queensborough Community College; Beth Shelton, Paris Junior College; Steven Sher, Oregon State University; David Shimkin, Queensborough Community College; H. Snelgrove, College of the Redwoods; Carol Sokolowski, Massasoit Community College; Joseph Somoza, New Mexico State University; Paul Strong, Alfred University; Karen Swenson, The City College of New York; Fay Tate, DeKalb Community College; Marilyn Underwood, Victoria Community College; Alice Ventry, Valencia Community College; Kathleen Wallace, Denison University; Anne W. Watts, Morehouse College; Pauline Woodward, Lesley College; Karen Wunsch, Queensborough Community College.

Contents

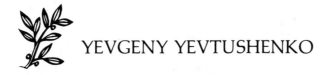

YEVGENY YEVTUSHENKO

People

No people are uninteresting.
Their fate is like the chronicle of planets.

Nothing in them is not particular,
and planet is dissimilar from planet.

And if a man lived in obscurity
making his friends in that obscurity
obscurity is not uninteresting.

To each his world is private,
and in that world one excellent minute.

And in that world one tragic minute.
These are private.

In any man who dies there dies with him
his first snow and kiss and fight.
It goes with him.

They are left books and bridges
and painted canvas and machinery

Whose fate is to survive.
But what has gone is also not nothing:

by the rule of the game something has gone.
Not people die but worlds die in them.

Whom we knew as faulty, the earth's creatures.
Of whom, essentially, what did we know?

Brother of a brother? Friend of friends?
Lover of lover?

We who knew our fathers
in everything, in nothing.

They perish. They cannot be brought back.
The secret worlds are not regenerated.

And every time again and again
I make my lament against destruction.

# Introduction

In his poem "People," Yevtushenko seeks to convey the uniqueness of each individual:

> Nothing in them is not particular,
> and planet is dissimilar from planet.

Paradoxically, however, while people are dissimilar, they also have many qualities in common. In this anthology, you will encounter people who have had experiences, felt emotions, and developed thoughts that are common to all human beings. In reading about them, you will no doubt recognize yourself.

The selections are written by writers of many ethnic backgrounds who have sought to clarify their own experiences and ideas. In each essay, story, and poem, the author has tried to capture in words the meaning of an aspect of his or her life. You may have expressed yourself in another medium: music, painting, or photography. Each attempt by an individual to capture a thought or experience in some concrete way is an indication of a desire to prolong it because of its intellectual or emotional value.

This book offers a new medium through which you can crystallize your thoughts and experiences — the essay. You may feel, like Jonathan Swift, that "there are words enough already," but perhaps by the end of the book you will agree more with Arthur Miller, who has expressed his reason for writing in the following words: "One had to write because other people needed news of the inner world, and without such news they would go mad with the chaos of their lives." You also may have something that other people "need" to know, even if those people are simply your friends. In writing these essays, you will develop your powers of written communication, aided by the rhetorical sections in each chapter.

Most of the essays in the book are autobiographical. The essays you write based on these models will come from your own life experience. You may think that nothing as unusual has happened to you as to them, but you will find as you read their selections that the authors are writing about ordinary people, experiences, and ideas — people like some you have known, experiences similar to those you have had, and ideas that have no doubt occurred to you as well.

Yevtushenko writes that

> In any man who dies there dies with him
> his first snow and kiss and fight.
> It goes with him.
>
> They are left books and bridges
> and painted canvas and machinery
>
> Whose fate is to survive.

We are all captives of time, and in order to bring dimension to our lives, we must think of our experiences and our ideas as significant enough to clarify for ourselves and others.

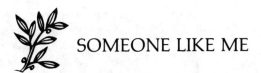 SOMEONE LIKE ME

ONE

 # PEOPLE

"No people are uninteresting"

"He was horribly ashamed of being a tramp, but he had picked up all a tramp's ways," George Orwell writes in his sketch "Paddy the Tramp." In Paddy, you will meet a person on the fringe of society who is bewildered as to how he got there. In Richard Goldstein's "Gear," on the other hand, you will become acquainted with an adolescent struggling with the problems of puberty, desperate for the acceptance of "the kids in the park." Both Paddy and Gear, each in his own way, reinforce Yevtushenko's concept in his poem that "no people are uninteresting."

We are unique, but we are also influenced by those who share our daily lives, and four of the authors in this chapter write about a person who influenced them. The narrator in "Wallace" writes about his fourteen-year-old friend who not only freed him from his fear of teachers but also taught him that they were not infallible. Maya Angelou in "Sister Flowers" writes about the lady who threw her her "first life line."

Two authors write about people who were negative influences. Martin Ralbovsky expresses the fear and hatred he felt for his high school basketball coach in "A Little Foul Play, the Coach's Way," and in "Discovery of a Father," Sherwood Anderson announces that as a child, he did not get that special thing a boy wants from his father.

The short stories dramatize the lives of two or more of Yevtushenko's unique people. Wallace refuses to subscribe to the social code expected of him in his boarding school, and Walter Mitty tries to escape from his boring, frustrating life through extravagant fantasies.

The poems have unlikely subjects for poetry: a grandmother, a secretary, and an anonymous citizen. Poets can
make people interesting. Can you?

Creating an Effective Subject and Generating Ideas

Two of the first steps in writing are to create an effective
subject and then generate ideas about it for your essay. Both
of these steps are part of the prewriting stages of the writing
process; in most cases they are formulated before you put
pen to paper. As you read the essays in this chapter, ask
yourself how the writers went about creating an effective
subject — not only deciding whom to write about but also
choosing what aspects of the person's life and character to
emphasize. How might they have gone about generating material for their essays? Further discussions of these two very
important steps in the writing process can be found following
each of the first two essays in this chapter: *Creating an Effective
Subject* after "Discovery of a Father" on pp. 9–11 and *Generating Ideas* after "Sister Flowers" on pp. 16–18.

 SHERWOOD ANDERSON

Discovery of a Father

You hear it said that fathers want their sons to be what they
feel they cannot themselves be, but I tell you it also works the other
way. A boy wants something very special from his father. I know that
as a small boy I wanted my father to be a certain thing he was not. I
wanted him to be a proud, silent, dignified father. When I was with
other boys and he passed along the street, I wanted to feel a flow of
pride. "There he is. That is my father."

But he wasn't such a one. He couldn't be. It seemed to me then
that he was always showing off. Let's say someone in our town had got
up a show. They were always doing it. The druggist would be in it, the
shoe-store clerk, the horse doctor, and a lot of women and girls. My

father would manage to get the chief comedy part. It was, let's say, a Civil War play and he was a comic Irish soldier. He had to do the most absurd things. They thought he was funny, but I didn't.

I thought he was terrible. I didn't see how mother could stand it. She even laughed with the others. Maybe I would have laughed if it hadn't been my father.

Or there was a parade, the Fourth of July or Decoration Day. He'd be in that, too, right at the front of it, as Grand Marshal or something, on a white horse hired from a livery stable.

He couldn't ride for shucks. He fell off the horse and everyone hooted with laughter, but he didn't care. He even seemed to like it. I remember once when he had done something ridiculous, and right out on Main Street, too. I was with some other boys and they were laughing and shouting at him and he was shouting back and having as good a time as they were. I ran down an alley back of some stores and there in the Presbyterian Church sheds I had a good long cry.

Or I would be in bed at night and father would come home a little lit up and bring some men with him. He was a man who was never alone. Before he went broke, running a harness shop, there were always a lot of men loafing in the shop. He went broke, of course, because he gave too much credit. He couldn't refuse it and I thought he was a fool. I had got to hating him.

There'd be men I didn't think would want to be fooling around with him. There might even be the superintendent of our schools and a quiet man who ran the hardware store. Once I remember there was a white-haired man who was a cashier of the bank. It was a wonder to me they'd want to be seen with such a windbag. That's what I thought he was. I know now what it was that attracted them. It was because life in our town, as in all small towns, was at times pretty dull and he livened it up. He made them laugh. He could tell stories. He'd even get them to singing.

If they didn't come to our house they'd go off, say at night, to where there was a grassy place by a creek. They'd cook food there and drink beer and sit about listening to his stories.

He was always telling stories about himself. He'd say this or that wonderful thing had happened to him. It might be something that made him look like a fool. He didn't care.

If an Irishman came to our house, right away father would say he was Irish. He'd tell what county in Ireland he was born in. He'd tell things that happened there when he was a boy. He'd make it seem so real that, if I hadn't known he was born in southern Ohio, I'd have believed him myself.

If it was a Scotchman the same thing happened. He'd get a burr into his speech. Or he was a German or a Swede. He'd be anything the other man was. I think they all knew he was lying, but they seemed to like him just the same. As a boy that was what I couldn't understand.

And there was mother. How could she stand it? I wanted to ask but never did. She was not the kind you asked such questions.

I'd be upstairs in my bed, in my room above the porch, and father would be telling some of his tales. A lot of father's stories were about the Civil War. To hear him tell it he'd been in about every battle. He'd known Grant, Sherman, Sheridan and I don't know how many others. He'd been particularly intimate with General Grant so that when Grant went East to take charge of all the armies, he took father along.

"I was an orderly at headquarters and Sim Grant said to me, 'Irve,' he said, 'I'm going to take you along with me.' "

It seems he and Grant used to slip off sometimes and have a quiet drink together. That's what my father said. He'd tell about the day Lee surrendered and how, when the great moment came, they couldn't find Grant.

"You know," my father said, "about General Grant's book, his memoirs. You've read of how he said he had a headache and how, when he got word that Lee was ready to call it quits, he was suddenly and miraculously cured.

"Huh," said father. "He was in the woods with me.

"I was in there with my back against a tree. I was pretty well corned. I had got hold of a bottle of pretty good stuff.

"They were looking for Grant. He had got off his horse and come into the woods. He found me. He was covered with mud.

"I had the bottle in my hand. What'd I care? The war was over. I knew we had them licked."

My father said that he was the one who told Grant about Lee. An orderly riding by had told him, because the orderly knew how thick he was with Grant. Grant was embarrassed.

"But, Irve, look at me. I'm all covered with mud," he said to father.

And then, my father said, he and Grant decided to have a drink together. They took a couple of shots and then, because he didn't want Grant to show up potted before the immaculate Lee, he smashed the bottle against the tree.

"Sim Grant's dead now and I wouldn't want it to get out on him," my father said.

That's just one of the kind of things he'd tell. Of course the men knew he was lying, but they seemed to like it just the same.

When we got broke, down and out, do you think he ever brought anything home? Not he. If there wasn't anything to eat in the house, he'd go off visiting around at farmhouses. They all wanted him. Sometimes he'd stay away for weeks, mother working to keep us fed, and then home he'd come bringing, let's say, a ham. He'd got it from some farmer friend. He'd slap it on the table in the kitchen. "You bet I'm going to see that my kids have something to eat," he'd say, and mother would just stand smiling at him. She'd never say a word about all the weeks and months he'd been away, not leaving us a cent for food. Once I heard her speaking to a woman in our street. Maybe the woman had dared to sympathize with her. "Oh," she said, "it's all right. He isn't ever dull like most of the men in this street. Life is never dull when my man is about."

But often I was filled with bitterness, and sometimes I wished he wasn't my father. I'd even invent another man as my father. To protect my mother I'd make up stories of a secret marriage that for some strange reason never got known. As though some man, say the president of a railroad company or maybe a Congressman, had married my mother, thinking his wife was dead and then it turned out she wasn't.

So they had to hush it up but I got born just the same. I wasn't really the son of my father. Somewhere in the world there was a very dignified, quite wonderful man who was really my father. I even made myself half believe these fancies.

And then there came a certain night. He'd been off somewhere for two or three weeks. He found me alone in the house, reading by the kitchen table.

It had been raining and he was very wet. He sat and looked at me for a long time, not saying a word. I was startled, for there was on his face the saddest look I had ever seen. He sat for a time, his clothes dripping. Then he got up.

"Come on with me," he said.

I got up and went with him out of the house. I was filled with wonder but I wasn't afraid. We went along a dirt road that led down into a valley, about a mile out of town, where there was a pond. We walked in silence. The man who was always talking had stopped his talking.

I didn't know what was up and had the queer feeling that I was with a stranger. I don't know whether my father intended it so. I don't think he did.

The pond was quite large. It was still raining hard and there were flashes of lightning followed by thunder. We were on a grassy bank at the pond's edge when my father spoke, and in the darkness and rain his voice sounded strange.

"Take off your clothes," he said. Still filled with wonder, I began to undress. There was a flash of lightning and I saw that he was already naked.

Naked, we went into the pond. Taking my hand he pulled me in. It may be that I was too frightened, too full of a feeling of strangeness, to speak. Before that night my father had never seemed to pay any attention to me.

"And what is he up to now?" I kept asking myself. I did not swim very well, but he put my hand on his shoulder and struck out into the darkness.

He was a man with big shoulders, a powerful swimmer. In the darkness I could feel the movement of his muscles. We swam to the far edge of the pond and then back to where we had left our clothes. The rain continued and the wind blew. Sometimes my father swam on his back and when he did he took my hand in his large powerful one and moved it over so that it rested always on his shoulder. Sometimes there would be a flash of lightning and I could see his face clearly.

It was as it was earlier, in the kitchen, a face filled with sadness. There would be the momentary glimpse of his face and then again the darkness, the wind, and the rain. In me there was a feeling I had never known before.

It was a feeling of closeness. It was something strange. It was as though there were only we two in the world. It was as though I had been jerked suddenly out of myself, out of my world of the schoolboy, out of a world in which I was ashamed of my father.

He had become blood of my blood; he the strong swimmer and I the boy clinging to him in the darkness. We swam in silence and in silence we dressed in our wet clothes, and went home.

There was a lamp lighted in the kitchen and when we came in, the water dripping from us, there was my mother. She smiled at us. I remember that she called us "boys."

"What have you boys been up to," she asked, but my father did not answer. As he had begun the evening's experience with me in silence, so he ended it. He turned and looked at me. Then he went, I thought, with a new and strange dignity out of the room.

I climbed the stairs to my own room, undressed in the darkness and got into bed. I couldn't sleep and did not want to sleep. For the first time I knew that I was the son of my father. He was a story teller as I was to be. It may be that I even laughed a little softly there in the darkness. If I did, I laughed knowing that I would never again be wanting another father.

PROBING FOR MEANING

1. In the first part of the essay, what impression of his father does Anderson create? What examples of his father's behavior are given to achieve this impression?

2. What does the boy discover is different about his father in the swimming scene?

3. Explain the phrase "a face filled with sadness," which appears in the second part of the essay.

4. Anderson recognizes something about himself and his father as a result of this encounter. What does he find out?

5. What kind of man was Anderson's father? Why was he a clown?

Why didn't he support his family? Would a father like Anderson's have embarrassed and angered you if you had been in Anderson's place? How important are the roles that society has given us to play?

Creating an Effective Subject

How did Anderson create an effective subject?   At some point, Anderson decided that his purpose in writing an essay about his father should be quite specific. He decided that his purpose would be to convey his feelings about his father. He therefore limited his subject to that time in their relationship during which he came to understand his father. One event, when they went swimming together one night, served best to indicate what he had learned about his father, and he chose to write nearly half of the essay about this one event. By limiting his account to one dramatic event, Anderson controlled the length of the piece and wrote an absorbing as well as informative essay.

He decided to show us his father in action so that we would understand both his own early hatred and his subsequent admiration of the man. He chose to write an informal, folksy essay filled with conversation and anecdote. His informality and simple vocabulary indicate that his desired audience was the common reader, the majority of Americans, regardless of the level of their education.

Creating an effective subject.   In choosing a subject about which to write, several considerations must be kept in mind: the purpose of your writing, the audience to whom you are writing, your knowledge of your subject, and the proposed length of the piece. Once you have taken these aspects into account, you can begin to formulate an effective subject.

In writing for English classes, your purpose is usually to write an informal, informative essay, and your audience is usually your instructor and your classmates. However, your instructor may also ask you to write an informal letter, a factual report, a scientific research essay, a persuasive editorial, or an informative magazine article. Likewise, you may be asked to write for various audiences during the semester: your peers, an employer, your coworkers, or the readers common to a particular publication such as your college newspaper or a magazine. Should your purpose and your audience vary, your choice or presentation of a subject will also vary. What is suitable to one purpose and one audience is not suitable to another.

For example, as you read the other essays in this chapter, compare them for audience and purpose. You will notice that they were written for widely divergent audiences and with very different purposes. Maya Angelou's informative autobiographical essay, like Sherwood Anderson's, is written for the average person. Martin Ralbovsky's essay focuses not only on himself but also on an aspect of American sports, and he writes for a reader inclined toward athletics and sociology. George Orwell draws a portrait of a person and a lifestyle few of his educated readers will have encountered. Richard Goldstein writes for the "hip" reader, and his purpose is not autobiographical at all; he is classified as one of the "new" journalists who approach their objective subjects as though they were writing biography or even autobiography.

Ralbovsky and Goldstein selected their subjects to suit their purpose and audience. The purpose and audience of Anderson, Angelou, and Orwell, on the other hand, influenced not so much their choice of subject but their presentation of it.

A third consideration in choosing an effective subject is your knowledge of it. You write most easily about what you know best as did Anderson, Angelou, and Ralbovsky. Orwell, however, researched his subject as a journalist would by joining Paddy in his wanderings. Unless you are given an assignment to research your subject, then, choose one with which you are familiar, about which you have knowledge sufficient for your purpose.

A final consideration is length. Most assignments in English classes call for much shorter essays than those written by the professionals in this chapter — usually in the 500- to 1000-word range. You will therefore want to focus more narrowly than they in order not to sacrifice the concreteness of detail which is the mark of any successful essay. It is much more effective to devote full attention to one specific aspect of your subject than to try to tell everything about it in a short space.

Once you have taken into account purpose, audience, your knowledge of the subject, and the length called for, you should be able to shape an effective subject.

Procedures to follow in creating an effective subject.

A. Choose a general topic that interests you and about which you have some knowledge. Think about as many facets of it as you can.

B. Jot down what interests you most about it. Define your purpose.

C. Determine how much writing would be necessary to develop your purpose specifically.

D. If you find that you have too much material for the length of your paper, reexamine your list for an aspect or aspects that you could develop specifically in the allotted space.

E. Once you have limited your general subject to an effective subject, make an exhaustive list of your knowledge about the latter. Make sure that you do not still have too much material to enable you to write a specific paper, or that you have not limited your subject so much that you have left yourself with too little material.

F. Consider your audience. What is your audience most likely to be interested in and know about? If you are writing an informal essay to your instructor and classmates, then consider how the material might best be presented in an essay written for this audience. If you are given the assignment of writing with a different purpose and to a different audience, consider how you should present this material in this context.

G. Phrase a sentence to clarify for yourself exactly what you intend to write about. Be as specific as possible. For example, Anderson's thesis sentence might have been "While for many of my childhood years I was ashamed of my clownish father, I one night came to realize his serious side, which made me proud to be his son."

 MAYA ANGELOU

Sister Flowers

For nearly a year, I sopped around the house, the Store, the school and the church, like an old biscuit, dirty and inedible. Then I met, or rather got to know, the lady who threw me my first life line.

Mrs. Bertha Flowers was the aristocrat of Black Stamps. She had the grace of control to appear warm in the coldest weather, and on the Arkansas summer days it seemed she had a private breeze which swirled around, cooling her. She was thin without the taut look of wiry people, and her printed voile dresses and flowered hats were as right for her as denim overalls for a farmer. She was our side's answer to the richest white woman in town.

Her skin was a rich black that would have peeled like a plum if snagged, but then no one would have thought of getting close enough to Mrs. Flowers to ruffle her dress, let alone snag her skin. She didn't encourage familiarity. She wore gloves too.

I don't think I ever saw Mrs. Flowers laugh, but she smiled often. A slow widening of her thin black lips to show even, small white teeth, then the slow effortless closing. When she chose to smile on me, I always wanted to thank her. The action was go graceful and inclusively benign.

She was one of the few gentlewomen I have ever known, and has remained throughout my life the measure of what a human being can be.

Momma had a strange relationship with her. Most often when she passed on the road in front of the Store, she spoke to Momma in that soft yet carrying voice, "Good day, Mrs. Henderson." Momma responded with "How you, Sister Flowers?"

Mrs. Flowers didn't belong to our church, nor was she

Momma's familiar. Why on earth did she insist on calling her Sister Flowers? Shame made me want to hide my face. Mrs. Flowers deserved better than to be called Sister. Then, Momma left out the verb. Why not ask, "How *are* you, *Mrs*. Flowers?" With the unbalanced passion of the young, I hated her for showing her ignorance to Mrs. Flowers. It didn't occur to me for many years that they were as alike as sisters, separated only by formal education.

Although I was upset, neither of the women was in the least shaken by what I thought an unceremonious greeting. Mrs. Flowers would continue her easy gait up the hill to her little bungalow, and Momma kept on shelling peas or doing whatever had brought her to the front porch.

Occasionally, though, Mrs. Flowers would drift off the road and down to the Store and Momma would say to me, "Sister, you go on and play." As she left I would hear the beginning of an intimate conversation. Momma persistently using the wrong verb, or none at all.

"Brother and Sister Wilcox is sho'ly the meanest — " "Is," Momma? "Is"? Oh, please, not "is," Momma, for two or more. But they talked, and from the side of the building where I waited for the ground to open up and swallow me, I heard the soft-voiced Mrs. Flowers and the textured voice of my grandmother merging and melting. They were interrupted from time to time by giggles that must have come from Mrs. Flowers (Momma never giggled in her life). Then she was gone.

She appealed to me because she was like people I had never met personally. Like women in English novels who walked the moors (whatever they were) with their loyal dogs racing at a respectful distance. Like the women who sat in front of roaring fireplaces, drinking tea incessantly from silver trays full of scones and crumpets. Women who walked over the "heath" and read morocco-bound books and had two last names divided by a hyphen. It would be safe to say that she made me proud to be Negro, just by being herself.

She acted just as refined as whitefolks in the movies and books and she was more beautiful, for none of them could have come near that warm color without looking gray by comparison.

I was fortunate that I never saw her in the company of po-whitefolks. For since they tend to think of their whiteness as an even-izer, I'm certain that I would have had to hear her spoken to commonly as Bertha, and my image of her would have been shattered like the un-mendable Humpty-Dumpty.

One summer afternoon, sweet-milk fresh in my memory, she stopped at the Store to buy provisions. Another Negro woman of her health and age would have been expected to carry the paper sacks home in one hand, but Momma said, "Sister Flowers, I'll send Bailey up to your house with these things."

She smiled that slow dragging smile, "Thank you, Mrs. Henderson. I'd prefer Marguerite, though." My name was beautiful when she said it. "I've been meaning to talk to her, anyway." They gave each other age-group looks.

Momma said, "Well, that's all right then. Sister, go and change your dress. You going to Sister Flowers's."

The chifforobe was a maze. What on earth did one put on to go to Mrs. Flowers' house? I knew I shouldn't put on a Sunday dress. It might be sacrilegious. Certainly not a house dress, since I was already wearing a fresh one. I chose a school dress, naturally. It was formal without suggesting that going to Mrs. Flowers' house was equivalent to attending church.

I trusted myself back into the Store.

"Now, don't you look nice." I had chosen the right thing, for once. . . .

There was a little path beside the rocky road, and Mrs. Flowers walked in front swinging her arms and picking her way over the stones.

She said, without turning her head, to me, "I hear you're doing very good school work, Marguerite, but that it's all written. The teachers report that they have trouble getting you to talk in class." We passed the triangular farm on our left and the path widened to allow us to walk together. I hung back in the separate unasked and unanswerable questions.

"Come and walk along with me, Marguerite." I couldn't have refused even if I wanted to. She pronounced my name so nicely. Or more correctly, she spoke each word with such clarity that I was certain a foreigner who didn't understand English could have understood her.

"Now no one is going to make you talk — possibly no one can. But bear in mind, language is man's way of communicating with his fellow man and it is language alone which separates him from the lower animals." That was a totally new idea to me, and I would need time to think about it.

"Your grandmother says you read a lot. Every chance you get. That's good, but not good enough. Words mean more than what is set down on paper. It takes the human voice to infuse them with the shades of deeper meaning."

I memorized the part about the human voice infusing words. It seemed so valid and poetic.

She said she was going to give me some books and that I not only must read them, I must read them aloud. She suggested that I try to make a sentence sound in as many different ways as possible.

"I'll accept no excuse if you return a book to me that has been badly handled." My imagination boggled at the punishment I would deserve if in fact I did abuse a book of Mrs. Flowers's. Death would be too kind and brief.

The odors in the house surprised me. Somehow I had never

connected Mrs. Flowers with food or eating or any other common experience of common people. There must have been an outhouse, too, but my mind never recorded it.

The sweet scent of vanilla had met us as she opened the door.

"I made tea cookies this morning. You see, I had planned to invite you for cookies and lemonade so we could have this little chat. The lemonade is in the icebox."

It followed that Mrs. Flowers would have ice on an ordinary day, when most families in our town bought ice late on Saturdays only a few times during the summer to be used in the wooden ice-cream freezers.

She took the bags from me and disappeared through the kitchen door. I looked around the room that I had never in my wildest fantasies imagined I would see. Browned photographs leered or threatened from the walls and the white, freshly done curtains pushed against themselves and against the wind. I wanted to gobble up the room entire and take it to Bailey, who would help me analyze and enjoy it.

"Have a seat, Marguerite. Over there by the table." She carried a platter covered with a tea towel. Although she warned that she hadn't tried her hand at baking sweets for some time, I was certain that like everything else about her the cookies would be perfect.

They were flat round wafers, slightly browned on the edges and butter-yellow in the center. With the cold lemonade they were sufficient for childhood's lifelong diet. Remembering my manners, I took nice little lady-like bites off the edges. She said she had made them expressly for me and that she had a few in the kitchen that I could take home to my brother. So I jammed one whole cake in my mouth and the rough crumbs scratched the insides of my jaws, and if I hadn't had to swallow, it would have been a dream come true.

As I ate she began the first of what we later called "my lessons in living." She said that I must always be intolerant of ignorance but understanding of illiteracy. That some people, unable to go to school, were more educated and even more intelligent than college professors. She encouraged me to listen carefully to what country people called mother wit. That in those homely sayings was couched the collective wisdom of generations.

When I finished the cookies she brushed off the table and brought a thick, small book from the bookcase. I had read *A Tale of Two Cities* and found it up to my standards as a romantic novel. She opened the first page and I heard poetry for the first time in my life.

"It was the best of times and the worst of times . . ." Her voice slid in and curved down through and over the words. She was nearly singing. I wanted to look at the pages. Were they the same that I had read? Or were there notes, music, lined on the pages, as in a hymn book? Her sounds began cascading gently. I knew from listening to a thousand preachers that she was nearing the end of her reading, and I hadn't really heard, heard to understand, a single word.

"How do you like that?"

It occurred to me that she expected a response. The sweet vanilla flavor was still on my tongue and her reading was a wonder in my ears. I had to speak.

I said, "Yes, ma'am." It was the least I could do, but it was the most also.

"There's one more thing. Take this book of poems and memorize one for me. Next time you pay me a visit, I want you to recite."

I have tried often to search behind the sophistication of years for the enchantment I so easily found in those gifts. The essence escapes but its aura remains. To be allowed, no, invited, into the private lives of strangers, and to share their joys and fears, was a chance to exchange the Southern bitter wormwood for a cup of mead with Beowulf or a hot cup of tea and milk with Oliver Twist. When I said aloud, "It is a far, far better thing that I do, than I have ever done . . ." tears of love filled my eyes at my selflessness.

On that first day, I ran down the hill and into the road (few cars ever came along it) and had the good sense to stop running before I reached the Store.

I was liked, and what a difference it made. I was respected not as Mrs. Henderson's grandchild or Bailey's sister but for just being Marguerite Johnson.

Childhood's logic never asks to be proved (all conclusions are absolute). I didn't question why Mrs. Flowers had singled me out for attention, nor did it occur to me that Momma might have asked her to give me a little talking to. All I cared about was that she had made tea cookies for *me* and read to *me* from her favorite book. It was enough to prove that she liked me.

PROBING FOR MEANING

1. What is Marguerite like before Sister Flowers takes an interest in her? Why is the attention of Sister Flowers important to her?

2. Marguerite calls Sister Flowers "one of the few gentlewomen" she has ever known. What does she mean? What is it that makes Sister Flowers a gentlewoman in her eyes?

3. What sort of lessons does Sister Flowers give Marguerite? Why does she encourage Marguerite to be "intolerant of ignorance but understanding of illiteracy"? Why does she insist that Marguerite read aloud?

4. After she has grown up what does Marguerite realize about her relationship with Sister Flowers?

5. Marguerite says that Sister Flowers made her "proud to be Negro." How does Sister Flowers do that? Is this the most important thing that Sister Flowers does for Marguerite?

PROBING FOR   1. Why does Angelou choose to write about Sister Flowers? Is there
METHOD   any one sentence that best explains the significance of her subject for her?

2. In what ways does Angelou contrast Momma with Sister Flowers? In what ways does she contrast herself as a child with each woman? How do these contrasts help us to understand "Marguerite" better?

3. Angelou chooses to focus on the first time Marguerite goes to Sister Flowers's house. What do we learn about Marguerite through this experience? What, for example, do we learn about her when Angelou writes that the odors in the house surprised her?

4. Angelou begins the essay by comparing Marguerite to "an old biscuit, dirty and inedible." What does this image tell us about her? How does the image of the tea cookies help us to understand the kind of effect Sister Flowers will have on her?

Generating Ideas

How did Maya Angelou generate ideas?   In writing about Sister Flowers, Angelou is obviously telling about a person she knew as a child. However, she narrates the experience as vividly as though it were taking place in the present. How did she recall the details of Sister Flowers's clothes, her smile, the odor in her house, the appearance of the rooms? Angelou might have kept a diary to furnish these telling details, but no doubt her main source was her memory. Through meditation-like concentration on remembering her encounters with Sister Flowers or perhaps by helping memories to emerge by free writing, she was able to recreate for us the acute feelings and keen sense impressions of a childhood experience.

Generating ideas.   Once you have chosen an effective subject, you may still be left with the question "What do I write about my subject?" You may have jotted down ideas in thinking about your subject but know that you lack the concrete detail important to a good essay.

Various methods of generating ideas may help you find something to write about your subject. If you are writing a personal essay, for example, you may want to try freewriting about your subject. Freewriting means writing whatever comes into your head about your subject; it is spontaneous association with your material. It is like brainstorming on paper. This exercise helps you particularly to stop worrying about what or how to write and simply to begin writing. To be most effective, you should freewrite for 45 minutes about your subject and never lift your pen from the paper. At the end of the time, you should have some material to use, material you probably had not thought about before you began writing.

Another method of generating material for personal essays is through memory exercises in which you concentrate on remembering every possible detail about your subject. To perform the exercises effectively, you should sit in a quiet place with distracting sounds and sights at a minimum, and, in a spirit of meditation, attempt to pursue a line of thought about your subject that you can later develop into an essay.

Of course, if you keep a journal or diary, you have pages and pages of material just waiting to be shaped into a personal essay. You may never have considered your daily jottings as raw material for a finished product, but if you reread what you have written, looking for common threads running through it, you may find that one of these themes is worth developing.

For more formal essays, you might try asking yourself a series of questions about your subject, the answers to which will provide you with something to say. If you are writing a narration, for example, ask yourself the journalist's questions: Who was involved? Where did it happen? What happened? How did it happen? When did it happen? Why did it happen? Each of these questions will in turn generate many sub-questions as well, such as How many people were involved? What did they look like? What kind of people were they? All these answers will be grist for your mill.

Questioning is a method of finding something to say about most subjects. A descriptive essay answers the question "What does it look like?" Sharpen your powers of observation, and you will become involved in answering this question about the place about which you are writing.

A causal essay responds to such questions as "What caused it?" "Were there several causes?" "Which were more important?" "Were all apparent causes actual causes?" Or the reverse question: "What did it cause?" or "What will it cause?"

Other useful questions are "What is it like?" "What is it unlike?" for comparison and contrast subjects, "What does it mean?" for definitions, and such general questions appropriate to most subjects as "What examples are there of it?" "What details are important?" and "What analogies can be made with it?"

Another method of generating ideas is research. Research can involve observation, interviewing, or reading. If the subject is one that you simply are too unfamiliar with to create material for, then the research techniques of observing a situation, interviewing people, or reading up on a subject will surely fill in the gap.

How have the writers in this chapter generated ideas? While it is difficult to guess a writer's process after the fact, it is very likely that Anderson, like Angelou, wrote from memory and perhaps from diaries or journals as well. Ralbovsky no doubt wrote from memory also and from asking the questions "What caused it?" and "What did it cause?" to stimulate his interpretations of his memories. Goldstein, on the other hand, is writing about a type of adolescent, and his essay appears to be the result of research into adolescence through observation, interview perhaps, and possibly even reading.

Procedures to follow in generating ideas for an essay.

A. Consider whether the subject is personal or impersonal (that is objective or expository). If personal, search through diaries or journals if you have kept them, or try freewriting or memory exercises to shake the memories loose.

B. If the essay is not personal and yet is on a subject that you have thought about, then phrase appropriate questions about the subject that will evoke material-generating answers.

C. If the essay is not personal and is not on a subject about which you have any knowledge, then use research as your technique. Try direct observation, interviewing knowledgeable people, or reading about it.

 MARTIN RALBOVSKY

A Little Foul Play, the Coach's Way

By the turn of the 1950s, thousands of veterans from World War II had used their GI loans to transform the forests and the farmlands of rural America into what is now known, somewhat derisively, as Middle America. They left their rented cold-water flats in the decaying cities, and they moved their families out to suburbia. They bought their own homes. In 1952, my family moved from the ethnic ghetto that was called Flockie Boulevard in Schenectady, New York, to a suburb of that city called Rotterdam. (People in upstate New York were very big on naming their cities after current or ancient European capitals; besides Rotterdam, there are now, in upstate New York, an Amsterdam, a Berlin, a Rome, a Naples, a Troy, a Carthage, an Athens, a Warsaw, a Hamburg, a Dunkirk, and, of course, an Attica.)

It was in Rotterdam, in the middle of the 1950s, as I entered a junior high school named after some fellow named John Bigsbee, that I encountered my first real, live coach. Everybody said he was a nice guy. Everybody said that Sunday followed Saturday. His name, let's say, was Benchley Steele. In gym classes, Benchley Steele made fun of kids who happened to be lacking in coordination; he had derogatory nicknames for kids he didn't particularly like; he swore regularly at kids who happened to be rowdy, and every once in a while he would punch one. Benchley Steele was a fanatic about the game of soccer; most of the time, at the beginning of gym classes Benchley Steele would throw out a brown soccer ball, blow his silver whistle, and instruct us to go at each other with maniacal fervor. Benchley Steele would stand off to the side, chain-smoking cigarettes, and watch the mayhem that ensued, with, I always suspected, a certain amount of sadistic pleasure. Whenever a kid got kicked in the shins and started to cry, Benchley Steele would berate him for acting like a sissy. Nice guy, my first coach.

But it wasn't until my sophomore year in a spanking new high school, in the late 1950s, that I experienced rather genuine problems with Benchley Steele. (The spanking new high school was christened "Mohonosen"; they held a contest, and a kid named Vincent Bowers thought up the name, splicing together the first three letters of three decimated Indian nations that had once occupied the very same land, the Mohawks, the Onondagas, and the Senecas. He won five dollars.) The coach, Benchley Steele, followed us from the old junior high school to the spanking new high school, and he became the head coach of basketball there. Now, since I was a kid who had roots that traced back to the obliterated inner city, I already was something of a fanatic about the game of basketball. I was totally obsessed with it. By the time I got to the tenth grade, I already had five or six years of shooting jump shots under my belt; the jump shots were not merely shot in the stifling heat of summer, or in the gentle warmth of spring, or in the rustic coziness of autumn. They were also shot in the dead of winter, in temperatures that were twenty-three degrees below zero, with my hands wrapped in gloves, a skiing cap pulled over my head and ears, two sweaters and two jackets covering my chest, black, buckled galoshes over dirty black sneakers on my feet. I shot jump shots on large patches of ice, dribbling the ball deftly, bouncing the ball off cracks in the ice and using the ricochets as lead passes; if you knew how to use the ice to your advantage, and you bounced the ball at the right speed and the right angle off the cracks and the crevices, the richochets would come back to you in the form of perfectly thrown lead passes from imaginary teammates. My nose would run, the mucus would freeze in a straight line between my nostrils and my lips. My face looked like Niagara Falls, frozen over. People did not know whether my nose had suddenly begun to grow stalactites or my upper lip had suddenly begun to grow stalagmites. But I loved it. The neighbors, of course, recommended to my parents that I be whisked off to undergo psychiatric examination; surely, normal kids were not to be found outside during roaring blizzards, shooting a basketball, while dressed to resemble a refugee from Outer Mongolia. I got even with my neighbors during the summers. They mowed their own lawns.

After a while, I could shoot jump shots quite well in such things as freezing rain, sleet, high winds, and snowstorms. Wearing sneakers and shorts, and being inside a warm gymnasium, and shooting at a basket that happened to have a net dangling off the end of it were luxuries. I used to shoot two hundred jump shots a day, every day; I used to run off streaks of thirty-five or forty-five in a row. I kept score on myself. I never went into the house to eat supper (or because of darkness) without first popping a parting jumper. *Swish.* Even though there was never a net on the basket in my backyard, the imagined sound of rippling cords brought about by a soft-touch jump shot set the tuning forks in my brain to gyrating, and *that sound* made all the more palatable the waiting bowls of hot chicken soup. To this day, I can go over to the schoolyard in my neighborhood, bounce a basketball a few times, and start popping jump shots, stringing together seven, eight, and nine in a row. A boyhood spent in a blighted industrial city shooting jump shots is a boyhood not altogether wasted; little kids in my neighborhood are impressed today. My coach back then wasn't.

He cut me from the basketball team.

I remember the tryouts as if they occurred yesterday. It was a three-on-one drill that did me in. There I was, in my brand-new white, high-topped P. F. Keds, wearing red satin shorts with white stripes down the sides and a sparkling white sweatshirt, dribbling up the court in the image of Mr. Jump Shot himself, Paul Arizin. There was a kid on my right, streaking down the right side of the court; there was a kid on my left, running down the left side of the court. In front of me was the defensive player, tall and strong and experienced, with airplane wings for arms, stretched out wide like a middle linebacker waiting to devour his prey. I dribbled to the top of the key; the defensive player approached me, stalking, and trying to look intimidating. The other two kids were free, waving their arms in each corner of the court. I ignored them both. I opted for the jump shot; the ball left my fingertips softly, and it was perfectly arched and perfectly aimed. Impeccable trajectory. *Swish.* The cords rippled sensuously. The kids on the sidelines began cheering wildly. They appreciated artistry, no doubt.

Benchley Steele blew his whistle. He ordered me off the floor.

"Drive, goddammit, drive," he yelled at me.

The next day, I got a second chance. Three-on-one drills again. I was placed in the middle again, and I started dribbling up court as soon as the coach yelled, "Go!" I didn't want to drive smack into the defensive player. I didn't want to challenge him and run the risk of his getting his hand on the ball and cramming it straight back down my throat, which happened to be the insult of all insults. No sir. The jump shot was my equalizer. I had such confidence in the accuracy of my jump shot that I was convinced it was the most accurate thing inside that gymnasium; I was convinced that its chances of going into the basket were just as good as any other kid's layup was. But coaches such as Benchley Steele, I discovered, preferred layups to jump shots; percentages, the cliché goes. So I came up the floor, and somewhere around mid-court I decided to prove my point. Dribbling to my right, to my favorite spot on the floor, three feet beyond the perimeter of the keyhold, I went up. The ball sailed toward the basket with the lightness of a floating feather; the cords of the net danced ever so slightly — that soft *swish* was the result of a shooting touch that every kid in the gymnasium envied, which is why every kid in the gymnasium broke into spontaneous applause as soon as the ball had dropped through.

Benchley Steele blew his whistle again.

"Out!" he said, bristling. "Get out!"

I showered and got dressed, and I cried all the way home. The tears froze to my cheeks. I could not understand what had befallen me. The coach, this Benchley Steele, had just rejected the best damn jump shot in the whole school, and he was settling instead for a bunch of tall, strong, unpolished goons who had spent their summers husking corn instead of shooting baskets. He was picking the plumbers over the artist, damn him. I was convinced that there wasn't a kid in the school who could have beaten me in a game of one-on-one; I knew — and all the other kids knew, too — that I could string together seven, eight jump shots in a row and totally demoralize them, which is the secret to winning in one-on-one. (I already held the school record for winning the greatest number of unfinished one-on-one matches; with the scores at 9–2 or 8–1, my favor, my opponents would quit, rather than suffer the embarrassment of consummated defeat.) Size is not necessarily a factor in being successful in one-on-one; talent most definitely is. But size certainly was a factor in making the junior varsity basketball team; talent, I concluded that night, wasn't. I pretended I was sick when I got home. I took the next two days off from school, and I sulked. I could not bear to face the humiliation that I knew was waiting for me at school, at the hands of my own peer group. I knew that dozens of kids were salivating at the very prospect of my showing up at school, so that they could ease up beside me in the hall, between classes, and say, "Best jump shot, my ass."

A couple of weeks later, one of the kids who had made the junior varsity team stopped me in the hall and said, "Coach wants to see you."

I immediately presumed that Benchley Steele had finally reacquired his senses; surely nobody, not even Benchley Steele, could pass over such a jump shot — he was just teaching me a lesson, Mr. Steele was, for not following orders. I ran down the hall to the gym. I stopped abruptly at the door. I took a deep breath. Then I walked through the swinging doors, with all of the correctness and the composure of a British butler. The coach was sitting on the bottom row of the bleachers; the rest of the bleachers were folded up into the wall. I calmly walked over to him.

"You want to see me, Coach?" I asked, faking nonchalance.

"Sit down," he said.

I suspected that Benchley Steele was going to give me that old have-you-learned-your-lesson? routine. (I had been through that once already, in Little League, swinging at a 3-and-0 pitch instead of taking.) I wanted to spare him the embarrassment of elaborating on the merits of humility and conformity; I was quite willing to say, "Yes, Coach, I have learned my lesson. Layups from now on." But he surprised me; Benchley Steele did not say what I was expecting him to say.

He said, "I need a manager."

A manager? *Manager!* I was simultaneously mortified and outraged. Who in hell wanted to be a manager? Gathering up all of the dirty, sweaty, stinking towels after practice; sweeping off the court; pumping air into lifeless basketballs; keeping score at games. How could he do this to me? I felt that he was insulting me with his offer. *Manager.* Managers were gawky kids who had trouble with their eyesight, or else they were selfish kids who had no talent whatsoever but wanted to be a part of the team anyway. Jocksniffers. Kids who had the best jump shot in their schools definitely were not managers. No sir. It was clearly a matter of pride with me.

I did not answer him.

Then he said, "Look, I already got kids who are going to collect towels and sweep and all of that. I need somebody to be a scorekeeper at games. You're the only kid in school who seems to know what a box score is." He was pretty close to being right; most of the kids in that school didn't read newspapers. "I'll let you practice with the varsity every day. Then, next year, you'll have the inside track at tryouts. What more can you ask for? You go to all the games, home and away, free, and you practice every day with the varsity. All you have to do is keep score at games. What do you expect me to do? Make a scorekeeper out of Nicky Bernardino? He can't add four and six."

The coach had thrown me a curve. He had offered me a spot on the periphery: part of the team, but not really part of the team. I immediately envisioned myself working out with the varsity, tossing in endless strings of jump shots over the distorted and frustrated faces of first-stringers, looking so impressive and so confident and so suave that Benchley Steele would finally take me aside some afternoon after practice and tell me to suit up for the game on Friday night. Then, of course, there was the prospect of all those one-on-one games before practices began; whoever heard of a manager beating the varsity star in one-on-one, in front of the rest of the team? *I'll show them.* I said to myself, *I'll show him. Head manager . . .*

"Yes, I'll do it," I said to him.

The coach smiled at me, and he tapped me on the knee.

"Good," he said.

The first game that season was against Heatly High School in Green Island, New York. Now, if you happen to know where the city of

Cohoes, New York, is located, or where the city of Lansingburgh, New York, is located, or where the cities of Watervliet, Menands and Mechanicville, New York, are located, then you certainly will know where the village of Green Island is located. If not, suffice to say that the village of Green Island is located on the northernmost banks of the Hudson river. Green Island is not green; it is burned-charcoal gray, courtesy of the belching smokestacks of the Ford Motor Company plant there.

Before the game, Benchley Steele gave me my instructions: He said that he wanted to personally inspect the scorebook at half time of every game; he said that he wanted to see exactly who was doing what. Now, keeping score in basketball is not a difficult assignment. When a player makes a basket, you make an entry that looks like this: X. When a player attempts a free throw, you make an entry that looks like this: O. If the player makes the free throw, then you fill in the O with an X. So, if a player named Kelly, say, scores four baskets and converts three out of five free throws, for 11 points, his line in the scorebook would consist of the following:

	G. (Goals)	F. (Free Throws)	P. (Points)
Kelly	4	3-5	11

Heatly High School had a tremendous player on its team; his name was Dick Kendall. He scored 22 points in the first half. I dutifully brought the scorebook to the coach at half time; smoking a cigarette in the hallway, adjacent to the locker room, he scanned the X's and the O's. He also scanned the column that was reserved for each player's personal fouls; when a player committed a foul, the entry was: p-1. The second foul was p-2. And so on. Five fouls and he was out of the game. I quickly learned that Benchley Steele liked the personal-foul column best of all. He liked to see a lot of p-5's in the personal-foul column. Of the other team.

As he scanned the personal-foul column, the coach abruptly stopped, and he began screaming at me. Benchley Steele bellowed:

"What is this, two fouls on Kendall? *What is this?* Are you daydreaming or something? The kid's been fouling all night long; he must have four on him by now. Whose side are you on, anyway? Goddammit!"

I gulped.

I was sure that Dick Kendall had committed only two fouls. He had been too busy scoring points to commit fouls. Then I realized what my coach was up to: He was intimidating me. Benchley Steele was intimidating me for a reason. He wanted me to think that I had incurred his displeasure; he wanted me to go out there in the second half and eliminate Dick Kendall from the game with my mathematics. Then he would be happy, and I would be vindicated in his eyes. he wanted me to go out there in the second half and sneak in a quick p-3 and a quick p-4 on Dick Kendall when the other scorekeeper wasn't looking. That way, Dick Kendall would foul out of the game quicker. When Dick Kendall fouled out of the game, he would have to sit on the bench. He couldn't score any points while sitting on the bench. Then, my team could win the game.

Benchley Steele wanted me to cheat.

In the second half, he kept leaving the bench and coming over to the scorer's table. He kept asking me the same question:

"How many fouls on Kendall?"

"Two."

"Two? *Two?* Can you count past two? It's three."

After a while, I was afraid to answer him. Dick Kendall wasn't fouling anybody. He was just scoring points. He had 34 points after three quarters. My team was being obliterated by one player. Nobody could have stopped him but me. I could have penciled him out of the game. I didn't have the guts to do it. We lost. Dick Kendall wound up with 44 points in the game. I wound up with a tongue-lashing from Benchley Steele after the game. He was not very happy with me. He said:

"I got a moron for a scorekeeper. I not only get beat badly, but I got a moron for a scorekeeper. A *moron!"*

I had to make a decision that weekend. It was a pretty big decision for a fourteen-year-old boy to make: Either I was going to give the coach what he wanted, and I was going to cheat and doctor up the scorebook to foul out the teams' best players, or else I was going to have to turn in my pencil. I wrestled with the decision all weekend. Integrity was not the only thing at stake. My future as a basketball player was on the line as well. If I quit, and if I told the coach to shove his pencil into a dark and creviced spot, my chances of making the team the following year would be nil. I could swish fifteen jump shots in a row, I could bank layups, play defense, and throw perfect lead passes, but I still would be cut. The coach had placed me in one hell of a spot.

There was no one with whom to discuss the situation, either. My father, a reasonably honest man, would have advised me to quit immediately. He always told me that man could not live by basketball alone. If I had gone to the school principal — which I considered doing for a moment or two — he would have called the coach into his office and confronted him with my verbal evidence. Then the scenario would have gone like this: The coach would have said, "The kid's lying. He's just trying to get back at me for cutting him from the team. He thinks he's got a great jump shot, you know. You don't really think I would tell him to cheat, do you?" Then the principal would have agreed with him. I would have been out as the scorekeeper, too.

So, I did the only thing that any other fourteen-year-old kid with a great jump shot would have done under the circumstances. I decided to cheat.

The first time I did it was in the game against the Pebble Hill School in Syracuse. How a private, affluent, elite, Anglo-Saxon preparatory school ever wound up on our basketball schedule mystified me anyway. It was an all-male school; on the day we played them, a Saturday afternoon, the school had imported some cheerleaders from a private, affluent, elite, Anglo-Saxon girls' prep school nearby. The kid who was the scorekeeper for Pebble Hill was paying a lot of attention to the girls; it looked as if he had never seen any before. Every time there was a timeout, he would ogle the cheerleaders. While he was ogling, I was finagling.

I got the two best Pebble Hill players out of the game early in the third period. They never knew what hit them. As they left the floor and headed for the bench, they had bewildered looks on their faces. They said, "I've only got three, Coach; I've only got three." The scorebook said five. Out. The Pebble Hill coach, however, was a gentleman. He never came over to the scorer's table to demand a detailed accounting. It was obvious to me that he was so much of a gentleman that it never dawned upon him that a fourteen-year-old scorekeeper that he had never seen before was actually cheating him out of the game right before his very eyes. My school won that game.

After the game, my coach winked at me; it was one of those "nice job" winks. I got the message.

The second time I did it was in a game at Waterford, New York. Waterford is near Green Island; it is landlocked. Waterford High School had a superb basketball player named John Anderson. He had 12 points in the first period. I knew he had to go. Now, Waterford High School apparently didn't have enough boys in its student body to spare one as its scorekeeper; either that, or the male students were very poor in math. The Waterford scorekeeper was a girl. It was like taking candy from a baby. During a timeout in the second period, I slipped in a p-3 on John Anderson. Early in the third period, while the coaches and the referees were discussing a slippery spot on the court, I slipped in a p-4 on John Anderson. Just before the third period ended, damned if John Anderson didn't go ahead and commit p-5 himself.

I pressed the button that sounded the buzzer. The referee came over to the scorer's table. He asked what was wrong.

"That's five on Anderson," I said.

The girl scorekeeper next to me was mortified.

"Five?" she gasped. "I've, uh, only got him down for three."

She stuttered and became nervous; she just did not have the necessary steadfastness to back up her statistics. She panicked. Besides she was only a girl. What did she know about keeping score?

"How long you been keepin' score, son?" the referee asked me.

"Two years," I said, lying.

"How long you been keepin' score, miss?" he said.

"I, uh, just started," she said.

The referee called the Waterford coach over to the scorer's table.

"That's five on Anderson," he announced.

The Waterford coach went into a fit of apoplexy. He began screaming at his scorekeeper. She began to cry. Benchley Steele came over to the table, and he told the Waterford coach to stop screaming at that poor little innocent girl.

"What kind of man are you?" my coach asked the Waterford coach.

Sufficiently embarrassed, the Waterford coach apologized to his scorekeeper. He sent in a substitute for John Anderson. We won that game, too.

That summer, while playing basketball at all the local playgrounds, I carried around in the pit of my stomach this horrible feeling. I felt as if I were a criminal. Some days I rationalized my actions by telling myself that what I had done was done in the best interests of my basketball career. Surely, after winning three games for him from the scorer's table, the coach wouldn't cut me again. Surely, I had ingratiated myself with him; there would be a spot for me. I had earned it. I had showed him that I could follow orders correctly; I had showed him that I could be daring and yet discreet; I had showed him what a good scorekeeper could do, and that he could pattern all his future scorekeepers after me. But meanwhile, it was time I got mine. My reward was going to be a place on the varsity team.

I was wrong, of course.

He cut me from the team again, after a spectacular showing in tryouts. I drove to the basket and feinted, sending defensive stalwarts flying in all directions; I banked layups, dropped in jump shots from the far corners of the floor, and, on defense, stole basketballs from players' grasps or else slapped them loose and scooped them up myself. On the last day, when I was coming off the floor for the last time, all the other players applauded me. The coach then put up three pieces of paper on the bulletin board outside the gym.

The first list was headed by the words: "The following players have been selected to the freshman team . . ."

My name was not on that list.

The second list was headed by the words: "The following players have made the junior varsity team . . ."

My name was not on that list.

The third list was headed by the words: "The following players have made the varsity team . . ."

Nope. Cut again.

I didn't cry this time. I silently thought about cutting the coach's heart out with a pair of scissors and feeding it to the neighborhood stray cat. After having showered and gotten dressed, I walked slowly out of the locker room, hoping to bump into some smallish player so that I could start a fight with him and beat him up. The coach was waiting for me in the hall.

He motioned for me to follow him into the dark gymnasium. He sat on the first row of the bleachers again. He said to me:

"I need you again. Just like last year. You're more valuable to me as a scorekeeper than you are as a player. No way you're gonna win three games for me as a player. As a scorekeeper, you could win six, or eight."

I nodded, not saying a word.

"Now, look," he said, "I know you feel bad. But we'll have the same arrangement we had last year. You work out with the varsity all week. You keep scores at games, I'll get you a letter. I'll get you into the varsity club. I'll get you the sports column in the school paper. Put yourself in my shoes. You got a kid like you, what're you gonna do with him? Sit him on the bench as a player? Or let him win games for you as a scorekeeper?"

He put his arm around me, and he said: "I like you. You're one of my favorite kids. I've got a soft spot right here for you."

He pointed to somewhere below his left nipple. I was hooked.

"Okay," I said. "I'll do it."

We were in a new league that year, a league called the Suburban Council. It consisted of schools exactly like mine: new, glass fishbowls of schools that were pancaked over vast acres of rolling grassland. I was in the vanguard of the suburban-high-school explosion in America. The Suburban Council was supposed to be the model organization for upstate New York schools; it was going to be the prestige league. The sophisticated suburban kids were supposed to be more intelligent, more aware, than all of these rowdies left behind in the medieval city high schools. We wouldn't be playing in Green Island or Waterford any more; now we were going to be playing on real farmland, in schools that were called "Niskayuna," and "Shaker," and "Guilderland" and "Schalmont." Even the team nicknames were exotic: One school selected "Sabres," another "The Dutchmen," a third "The Blue Bison."

The gymnasiums were lavish, well-lighted, large, and acoustically correct.

When the basketball season started, I quickly realized that the scorekeepers in the Suburban Council were, indeed, a lot more sophisticated and a lot more aware than the scorekeepers I had bilked the year before.

Everybody cheated in the Suburban Council.

A kid from Schalmont, a tall Italian who said his name was Danny, actually had the audacity to attempt to sneak in a p-3 on me. Niskayuna had two scorekeepers, one to keep score and one to watch the other scorer so that he didn't pull any funny stuff. I realized right away that my work was going to be cut out for me. The other kids apparently had coaches just like mine. Their coaches apparently told them the same things that mine told me.

I ran out the string that season. The next year, my senior year in high school, I took a part-time job as a sports stringer for the evening newspaper in town, the *Union-Star*. Sports stringers are people who cover high-school basketball games on Friday and Saturday nights during the winter. They are paid five dollars a game. The job got me off the hook with Benchley Steele. He got himself a new cheater. I didn't see Benchley Steele much that season. In fact, the last time I saw him and spoke to him at any length was one Monday afternoon in the gym office. I had covered one of my own school's games the Friday night before. I had written the story that appeared in the Saturday paper. My school had lost. When I walked into the gym office, I could tell that Ol' Benchie Steele was mad.

"What the hell kind of headline was that?" he growled at me.

"What headline?" I asked.

"The one in Saturday's paper," he said.

The headline in the Saturday paper, I remembered, read: NIS KAS ROUT MOHONS, 72–58.

"What was wrong with it?" I asked.

He said, "What is this 'rout' business? We were only ten down with two minutes left. Tell me, is that a rout? Now, is it?"

I tried to explain to him that in newspaper offices the people who write the stories do not write the headlines. People who are called "Deskmen" do. Benchley Steele did not believe my explanation. He said, "You're selling me out, right down the river."

Then he walked away.

But I'm not really mad at my first coach today. In fact, every time I think about him I smile. When he retired, I heard that the people gave him a testimonial banquet. Beautiful. But he taught me one of the first real hard lessons that all young men must learn before they succeed in America: He taught me the art of cheating within the system. There is a big difference between cheating within the system and cheating outside the system. When you cheat within the system, you are praised for being smart, alert, and mature. When you cheat outside the system, you go to jail. Doctoring scorebooks in basketball games is cheating within the system. Doctoring blank checks that belong to somebody else is cheating outside the system. Cheating within the system is very big in America, even today.

Grown men cheat companies with fake expense accounts and by calling in sick when they feel chipper but feel like playing a round of golf instead of working. I knew old ladies who cheated at bingo games; they doctored up their transparent, round tokens with half-numbers. If they needed a 4 for bingo and there was a 1 on the card, they slipped their half-4 button over the 1. Then the 1 would look like a 4. Bingo.

In America today, it is entirely possible that millions of young males acquire their first lessons in cheating in the playgrounds of the neighborhood schools. The coaches do the honors. What do you think players practice everynight? How to be nice, and legal, and gentlemanly? No sir. They practice deceptive plays until they get them down pat. Deception in sports, for the ultimate good of the team, is revered. Parents and educators do not question the pick in basketball, or the curve ball in baseball, on moral grounds. But they become outraged when there is a little teamwork in the classroom, in the form of sharing test answers. Sports are separate entities; they have their own moral criteria.

Coaches rule these little empires. The only thing standing between coaches and moral anarchy is the referee. And sometimes even he doesn't help. Benchley Steele used to chew out referees at games very often. He chewed them out so often, and so loudly, that the referees became intimidated. They started worrying if they were going to be invited back to earn their fifteen dollars the following week. Then they started ignoring fouls, or else they started making judgment calls in my coach's favor. When that happened, they were always invited back. Someday Ol' Benchie Steele is going to make a deal with Lucifer — I just know it.

| PROBING FOR MEANING | 1. How is Benchley Steele described? Which of his characteristics does Ralbovsky emphasize? |

1. How is Benchley Steele described? Which of his characteristics does Ralbovsky emphasize?

2. Is the author typical of high-school students? After he is cut from the team and is offered the job of manager, what prompts him to accept?

3. How does the author feel about cheating while in high school? Why does he decide to cheat? Why doesn't he simply quit the team? How does Benchley Steele coerce him to doctor the scorebook?

4. What does the experience of the author say about the American sports system? How are sports a reflection of the morality of American society? Explain.

PROBING FOR METHOD

1. What was Ralbovsky's purpose in writing this essay? How has his purpose shaped his content?

2. The opening paragraph of the essay describes the postwar migration to the suburbs. How is the introduction connected to what follows? How effective is it as an opening paragraph?

3. What is the purpose of the description of the author's solitary winter practices? Is this description exaggerated? Why?

4. What is the cental idea (thesis) of the essay? Where is this central idea expressed?

 GEORGE ORWELL

Paddy the Tramp

Paddy was my mate for about the next fortnight, and, as he was the first tramp I had known at all well, I want to give an account of him. I believe that he was a typical tramp and there are tens of thousands in England like him.

He was a tallish man, aged about thirty-five, with fair hair going grizzled and watery blue eyes. His features were good, but his cheeks had lanked and had that greyish, dirty in the grain look that comes of a bread and margarine diet. He was dressed, rather better than most tramps, in a tweed shooting-jacket and a pair of old evening trousers with the braid still on them. Evidently the braid figured in his mind as a lingering scrap of respectability, and he took care to sew it on again when it came loose. He was careful of his appearance altogether, and carried a razor and bootbrush that he would not sell, though he had sold his "papers" and even his pocket-knife long since. Nevertheless, one would have known him for a tramp a hundred yards away. There was something in his drifting style of walk, and the way he had of hunching his shoulders forward, essentially abject. Seeing him walk, you felt instinctively that he would sooner take a blow than give one.

He had been brought up in Ireland, served two years in the war, and then worked in a metal polish factory, where he had lost his job two years earlier. He was horribly ashamed of being a tramp, but he had picked up all a tramp's ways. He browsed the pavements unceasingly, never missing a cigarette end, or even an empty cigarette packet, as he used the tissue paper for rolling cigarettes. On our way into Edbury he saw a newspaper parcel on the pavement, pounced on it, and found that it contained two mutton sandwiches, rather frayed at the edges; these he insisted on my sharing. He never passed an automatic machine without giving a tug at the handle, for he said that sometimes they are out of order and will eject pennies if you tug at them. He had no stomach for crime, however. When we were in the outskirts of Romton, Paddy noticed a bottle of milk on a doorstep, evidently left there by mistake. He stopped, eyeing the bottle hungrily.

"Christ!" he said, "dere's good food goin' to waste. Somebody could knock dat bottle off, eh? Knock it off easy."

I saw that he was thinking of "knocking it off" himself. He looked up and down the street; it was a quiet residential street and there was nobody in sight. Paddy's sickly, chap-fallen face yearned over the milk. Then he turned away, saying gloomily:

"Best leave it. It don't do a man no good to steal. T'ank God, I ain't never stolen nothin' yet."

It was funk, bred of hunger, that kept him virtuous. With only two or three sound meals in his belly, he would have found courage to steal the milk.

He had two subjects of conversation, the shame and comedown of being a tramp, and the best way of getting a free meal. As we drifted through the streets he would keep up a monologue in this style, in a whimpering, self-pitying Irish voice:

"It's hell bein' on de road, eh? It breaks yer heart goin' into dem bloody spikes. But what's a man to do else, eh? I ain't had a good meat meal for about two months, an' me boots is getting bad, an' — Christ! How'd it be if we was to try for a cup o' tay at one o' dem convents on de way to Edbury? Most times dey're good for a cup o' tay. Ah, what'd a man do widout religion, eh? I've took cups o' tay from de convents, an' de Baptists, an' de Church of England, an' all sorts. I'm a Catholic meself. Dat's to say, I ain't been to confession for about seventeen year, but still I got me religious feelin's, y'understand. An' dem convents is always good for a cup o' tay . . ." etc. etc. He would keep this up all day, almost without stopping.

His ignorance was limitless and appalling. He once asked me, for instance, whether Napoleon lived before Jesus Christ or after. Another time, when I was looking into a bookshop window, he grew very perturbed because one of the books was called *Of the Imitation of Christ*. He took this for blasphemy. "What de hell do dey want to go imitatin' of *Him* for?" he demanded angrily. He could read, but he had a kind of loathing for books. On our way from Romton to Edbury I went into a public library, and, though Paddy did not want to read, I suggested that he should come in and rest his legs. But he preferred to wait on the pavement. "No," he said, "de sight of all dat bloody print makes me sick."

Like most tramps, he was passionately mean about matches. He had a box of matches when I met him, but I never saw him strike one, and he used to lecture me for extravagance when I struck mine. His method was to cadge a light from strangers, sometimes going without a smoke for half an hour rather than strike a match.

Self-pity was the clue to his character. The thought of his bad

luck never seemed to leave him for an instant. He would break long silences to exclaim, apropos of nothing, "It's hell when yer clo'es begin to
go up de spout, eh?" or "Dat tay in de spike ain't tay, it's piss," as
though there was nothing else in the world to think about. And he had
a low, worm-like envy of anyone who was better off — not to the rich,
for they were beyond his social horizon, but of men in work. He pined
for work as an artist pines to be famous. If he saw an old man working
he would say bitterly, "Look at dat old ———— keepin' able-bodied men
out o' work"; or if it was a boy, "It's dem young devils what's takin' de
bread out of our mouths." And all foreigners to him were "dem bloody
dagoes" — for, according to his theory, foreigners were responsible for
unemployment.

He looked at women with a mixture of longing and hatred.
Young, pretty women were too much above him to enter into his ideas,
but his mouth watered at prostitutes. A couple of scarlet-lipped old
creatures would go past; Paddy's face would flush pale pink, and he
would turn and stare hungrily after the women. "Tarts!" he would
murmur, like a boy at a sweetshop window. He told me once that he
had not had to do with a woman for two years — since he had lost his
job, that is — and he had forgotten that one could aim higher than
prostitutes. He had the regular character of a tramp — abject, envious,
a jackal's character.

Nevertheless, he was a good fellow, generous by nature and capable of sharing his last crust with a friend; indeed he did literally share
his last crust with me more than once. He was probably capable of
work too, if he had been well fed for a few months. But two years of
bread and margarine had lowered his standards hopelessly. He had
lived on this filthy imitation of food till his own mind and body were
compounded of inferior stuff. It was malnutrition and not any native
vice that had destroyed his manhood.

PROBING FOR   1. Orwell says that Paddy was a "typical" tramp. What traits mark
MEANING   Paddy as typical of tramps in general?

2. What is it that keeps Paddy from stealing?

3. Orwell says that the clue to Paddy's character is self-pity. What
does Orwell mean?

4. Why does Orwell assert that Paddy was "a good fellow," despite
his faults? Why doesn't Orwell blame Paddy for his faults?

PROBING FOR   1. What does the detailed description of Paddy's appearance in the
METHOD   second paragraph help us to understand about the tramp's character?

2. What do the examples of Paddy's conversation illustrate about
him?

3. How would you sum up Orwell's attitude toward his subject? Is
there any one point in the essay where his overall attitude is most clearly
brought into focus? What was his purpose in writing about Paddy?

RICHARD GOLDSTEIN

Gear

Too early to get up, especially on Saturday. The sun peeks over his windowsill. Isolated footsteps from the street. Guys who have to work on Saturday. Boy! That's what they'll call you all your life if you don't stay in school. Forty-five definitions, two chapters in *Silas Marner*, and three chem labs. On Sunday night, he will sit in his room with the radio on, bobbing back and forth on his bed, opening the window wide and then closing it, taking a break to eat, to comb his hair, to dance, to hear the Stones — anything. Finally, cursing wildly and making ugly faces at himself in the mirror, he will throw *Silas Marner* under the bed and spend an hour watching his tortoise eat lettuce.

In the bathroom he breaks three screaming pimples. With a toothpick he removes four specks of food from his braces, skirting barbed wires and week-old rubber bands. Brooklyn Bridge, railroad tracks, they call him. Metal mouth. They said he smiled like someone was forcing him to. Bent fingers with filthy nails. Caved-in chest with eight dangling hairs. A face that looks like the end of a watermelon, and curly hair — not like the Stones, not at all like Brian Jones — but muddy curls running down his forehead and over his ears. A bump. Smashed by a bat thrown wildly. When he was eight. Hunchback Quasimodo — Igor — Rodan on his head. A bump. Nobody hip has a bump or braces. Or hair like a fucking Frankenstein movie. He licks his braces clean and practices smiling.

Hair straight and heavy. Nose full. Lips bulging like boiling frankfurters. Hung. Bell bottoms and boss black boots. He practices his Brian Jones expressions. Fist held close to the jaw. Ready to spring, ready to spit. Evil. His upper brace catches on a lip.

He walks past his parents' room, where his mother sleeps in a gauzy hairnet, the covers pulled over her chin, her baby feet swathed in yellow calluses. Her hand reaches over to the night table where her eyedrops and glasses lie. He mutters silently at her. The night before there had been a fight — the usual fight, with Mommy shouting "I'll give you money! Sure, you rotten kid! I'll give you clothing so you can throw it all over the floor — that's blood money in those pants of yours!" And him answering the usual "geh-awf-mah-bak" and her: "Don't you yell at me, don't you — you did hear that (to no one). Did you hear how that kid...?" and him slamming the door — the gray barrier — and above the muffled "... disrespects his mother ... He

treats me like dirt under his feet! . . . and he wants me to buy him . . .
he'll spit on my grave" . . . and finally dad's groaning shuffle and a
murmured "Ronnie, you better shut your mouth to your mother," and
him whispering silently, the climactic, the utter: "Fucking bitch. Cunt.
Cunt."

Now she smiles. So do crocodiles. He loves her. He doesn't
know why he cursed, except that she hates it. It was easy to make her
cry and though he shivers at the thought of her lying across the bed
sobbing into a pillow, her housedress pulled slightly over a varicose
thigh, he has to admit doing it was easy.

On the table he sees the pants she bought him yesterday. Her
money lining his pocket, he had taken the bus to Fordham Road and in
Alexander's he had cased out the Mod rack. Hands shaking, dying for a
cigarette, he found the pants — a size small but still a fit. He bought
them, carried them home clutched in his armpit, and desposited them
before her during prime "Star Trek" TV time.

"Get away. I can't see. Whatsamaddah, your father a glazier or
something?" and when he unveiled the pants and asked for the usual
cuff-making ritual (when he would stand on the ladder and she, holding a barrage of pins in her mouth, would run the tailor's chalk along
his shoe line and make him drag out the old black sewing machine), the
fight began — and ended within the hour. The pants, hemmed during
"The Merv Griffin Show" as the last labor of the night, now lay exposed
and sunlit on the table. $8.95 pants.

They shimmer. The houndstooth design glows against the for-
mica. Brown and green squares are suddenly visible within the gray
design. He brushes the fabric carefully so the wool bristles. He tries
them on, zipping up the two-inch fly, thinking at first that he has broken the zipper until he realizes that hip-huggers have no fly to speak of.
They buckle tightly around his hips, hug his thighs, and flare suddenly
at his knees. He races to the mirror and grins.

His hips are suddenly tight and muscular. His waist is sleek
and his ass round and bulging. Most important, the pants make him
look hung. Like the kids in the park. The odor of stale cigarettes over
their clothing, medallions dangling out of their shirts. Their belt buck-
les ajar. They are hip. They say "Check out that bike." Get bent on
Gypsy. Write the numbers of cruising police cars all over the walls.
ROT, they call themselves. Reign of Terror. In the park they buzz out
on glue, filling paper bags and breathing deeply, then sitting on the
grass slopes, watching the cars. Giggling. Grooving. High.

Sometimes they let him keep the models that come with the
glue. Or he grubs around their spot until, among the torn bags and
oozing tubes, he finds a Messerschmitt or Convair spread across the
grass ruins as though it had crashed there.

He unzips his pants and lets them hang on the door where he

can watch them from the living room. He takes a box of Oreos from the kitchen, stacking the cookies in loose columns on the rug. He pours a cup of milk and turns on the TV. Farmer Gray runs nervously up and down the screen while a pig squats at ease by his side. His pants are filled with hornets. He runs in a cloud of dust toward a pond which appears and disappears teasingly, leaving Farmer Gray grubbing in the sand. Outasight!

He fills his mouth with three Oreos and wraps his feet around the screen so he can watch Farmer Gray between his legs. Baby habit. Eating cookies on the floor and watching cartoons on Saturday morning. Like thumbsucking. They teased him about it until he threw imaginary furniture into their faces. A soft bulge on his left thumb from years of sucking — cost them a fortune in braces. Always busting his hump.

He kills the TV picture and puts the radio on softly, because he doesn't want to wake Daddy who is asleep on his cot in the middle of the living room, bunched up around the blanket, his face creased in a dream, hands gripping his stomach in mock tension. Daddy snores in soft growls.

He brushes a flock of Oreo crumbs under the TV and rubs a milk stain into the rug. Thrown out of your own bed for snoring. You feel cheap, like Little Bo Peep; beep beep beep beep.

There is nothing to stop him from going downstairs. The guys are out already, slung over cars and around lampposts. The girls are trickling out of the project. It's cloudy, but until it actually rains he knows they will be around the lamppost, spitting out into the street, horsing around, grubbing for hooks, singing. He finishes four more cookies and stuffs half an apple onto his chocolate-lined tongue.

Marie Giovanni put him down bad for his braces. When she laughs her tits shake. Her face is pink; her hair rises in a billowing bouffant. In the hallway, she let Tony get his fingers wet. Yesterday she cut on him; called him metal mouth.

He flicks the radio off, grabs the pants from the hanger, and slides into them. He digs out a brown turtleneck from under a rubble of twisted clothing (they dress him like a ragpicker) and shines his boots with spit. They are chipping and the heels are worn on one side, but they make him look an inch taller, so he wears them whenever he can.

He combs his hair in the mirror. Back on the sides, over the ears, so the curl doesn't show. Over the eyes in the front to cover up his bump. Straight down the back of his neck, so it rests on his collar. He checks his bald spot for progress and counts the hairs that come out in his brush. In two years he knows he will be bald in front and his bump will look like a boulder on his forehead.

He sits on his bed and turns the radio on. From under the phonograph he lifts a worn fan magazine — *Pop* in bright fuchsia letter-

ing — with Zal Yanovsky hunched over one P, Paul McCartney con-
torted over the other, and Nancy Sinatra touching her toes around the
O. He turns to the spread on the Stones and flips the pages until he sees
The Picture. Mick Jagger and Marianne Faithfull. Mick scowling, waving his fingers in the air. Marianne watching the camera. Marianne,
waiting for the photographer to shoot. Marianne. Marianne, eyes fading brown circles, lips slightly parted in flashbulb surprise, miniskirt
spread apart, tits like two perfect cones under her sweater. He had to
stop looking at Marianne Faithfull a week ago.

He turns the page and glances at the shots of Brian Jones and
then his eyes open wide because a picture in the corner shows Brian in
Ronnie's pants. The same check. The same rise and flare. Brian leaning
against a wall, his hands on the top of his magic hiphuggers. Wick-ked!

He flips the magazine away and stands in a curved profile
against the mirror. He watches the pants move as he does. From a
nearby flowerpot he gathers a fingerful of dirt and rubs it over his
upper lip. He checks hair, nose, braces, nails, and pants. He likes the
pants. They make him look hung. He reaches into his top drawer and
pulls out a white handkerchief. He opens his fly and inserts the rolled
cloth, patting it in place, and closing the zipper over it. He looks boss.
Unfuckinbelievable.

In the elevator Ronnie takes a cigarette from his three-day-old
pack and keeps it unlit in his mouth. Marie Giovanni will look at his
pants and giggle. Tony will bellow "Check out them pants," and everyone will groove on them. In the afternoon, they will take him down to
the park and turn him on, and he will feel the buzz they are always
talking about and the cars will speed by like sparks.

Brian Jones thoughts in his head. Tuff thoughts. He will slouch
low over the car and smoke with his thumb over the cigarette — the hip
way. And when he comes back upstairs they will finally get off his
back. Even on Fordham Road, where the Irish kids crack up when he
walks by, even in chemistry and gym, they will know who he is and
nod a soft "hey" when he comes by. He'll get laid.

Because clothing IS important. Especially if you've got braces
and bony fingers and a bump the size of a goddam coconut on your
head.

And especially if you're fourteen. Because — ask anyone.
Fourteen is shit.

PROBING FOR   1. In what ways is Ronnie a typical fourteen-year-old? Is there any-
MEANING   thing unique or unusual about him?

2. How would you characterize Ronnie's parents? Why does Ronnie
fight with his mother?

3. What kind of relationship does Ronnie have with his peers? How
would he like his peers to feel about him?

4. Why is Ronnie so sensitive about his appearance?

1. What effect does Goldstein achieve by imitating Ronnie's jargon? What does the use of such expressions as "outasight" and "wick-ked" and "unfuckinbelievable" indicate about Ronnie?

2. Why does Goldstein describe how Ronnie watches cartoons?

3. To what extent is Goldstein making fun of Ronnie? Where in the essay does the author most obviously satirize or mock his subject? What is Goldstein's attitude toward his subject overall?

4. Why does Goldstein make Ronnie's new pants the focus of the essay? What is Goldstein's thematic focus? Who is he writing for?

 RICHARD H. ROVERE

Wallace

As a schoolboy, my relations with teachers were almost always tense and hostile. I disliked my studies and did very badly in them. There are, I have heard, inept students who bring out the best in teachers, who challenge their skill and move them to sympathy and affection. I seemed to bring out the worst in them. I think my personality had more to do with this than my poor classroom work. Anyway, something about me was deeply offensive to the pedagogic temperament.

Often, it took a teacher no more than a few minutes to conceive a raging dislike for me. I recall an instructor in elementary French who shied a textbook at my head the very first day I attended his class. We had never laid eyes on each other until fifteen or twenty minutes before he assaulted me. I no longer remember what, if anything, provoked him to violence. It is possible that I said something that was either insolent or intolerably stupid. I guess I often did. It is also possible that I said nothing at all. Even my silence, my humility, my acquiescence, could annoy my teachers. The very sight of me, the mere awareness of my existence on earth, could be unendurably irritating to them.

This was the case with my fourth-grade teacher, Miss Purdy. In order to make the acquaintance of her new students on the opening day of school, she had each one rise and give his name and address as she called the roll. Her voice was soft and gentle, her manner sympathetic, until she came to me. Indeed, up to then I had been dreamily entertaining the hope that I was at last about to enjoy a happy association with a teacher. When Miss Purdy's eye fell on me, however, her face suddenly twisted and darkened with revulsion. She hesitated for a few moments while she looked me up and down and thought of a suitable comment on what she saw. "Aha!" she finally said, addressing not me but my new classmates, in a voice that was now coarse and cruel. "I don't have to ask *his* name. There, boys and girls, is Mr. J. Pierpont Morgan, lounging back in his mahogany-lined office."* She held each syllable of the financier's name on her lips as long as she was able to, so that my fellow-students could savor the full irony of it. I imagine my posture was a bit relaxed for the occasion, but I know well that she would not have resented anyone else's sprawl as much as she did mine. I can even hear her making some friendly, schoolmarmish quip about too much summer vacation to any other pupil. Friendly quips were never for me. In some unfortunate and mysterious fashion, my entire being rubbed Miss Purdy and all her breed the wrong way. Throughout the fourth grade, she persisted in tormenting me with her idiotic Morgan joke. "And perhaps Mr. J. P. Revere can tell us all about Vasco da Gama† this morning," she would say, throwing in a little added insult by mispronouncing my surname.

The aversion I inspired in teachers might under certain circumstances have been turned to good account. It might have stimulated me to industry; it might have made me get high marks, just so I could prove to the world that my persecutors were motivated by prejudice and perhaps by a touch of envy; or it might have bred a monumental rebelliousness in me, a contempt for all authority, that could have become the foundation of a career as the leader of some great movement against all tyranny and oppression.

It did none of these things. Instead, I became, so far as my school life was concerned, a thoroughly browbeaten boy, and I accepted the hostility of my teachers as an inescapable condition of life. In fact, I took the absolutely disastrous view that my teachers were unquestionably right in their estimate of me as a dense and altogether noxious creature who deserved, if anything, worse than he got. These teachers were, after all, men and women who had mastered the parts of speech, the multiplication tables, and a simply staggering number of imports and exports in a staggering number of countries. They could add up columns of figures the very sight of which made me dizzy and sick to the stomach. They could read "As You Like it"‡ with pleasure — so they said, anyway, and I believed everything they said. I felt that if such knowledgeable people told me that I was stupid, they certainly must know what they were talking about. In consequence, my grades sank lower and lower, my face became more noticeably blank,

* John Pierpont Morgan (1867–1943) was an enormously wealthy financier.
† Vasco da Gama was a fifteenth-century Portuguese explorer.
‡ *As You Like It* is a comedy by William Shakespeare (1564–1616).

my manner more mulish, and my presence in the classroom more ag-
gravating to whoever presided over it. To be sure, I hated my teachers
for their hatred of me, and I missed no chance to abuse them behind
their backs, but fundamentally I shared with them the view that I was a
worthless and despicable boy, as undeserving of an education as I was
incapable of absorbing one. Often, on school days, I wished that I were
dead.

This was my attitude, at least, until my second year in preparatory school, when, at fourteen, I fell under the exhilarating, regenera-
tive influence of my friend Wallace Duckworth. Wallace changed my
whole outlook on life. It was he who freed me from my terrible awe of
teachers; it was he who showed me that they could be brought to book
and made fools of as easily as I could be; it was he who showed me that
the gap between their knowledge and mine was not unbridgeable.
Sometimes I think that I should like to become a famous man, a United
States senator or something of that sort, just to be able to repay my debt
to Wallace. I should like to be so important that people would inquire
into the early influences on my life and I would be able to tell them
about Wallace.

I was freshly reminded of my debt to Wallace not long ago
when my mother happened to come across a packet of letters I had
written to her and my father during my first two years in a boarding
school on Long Island. In one of these, I reported that "There's a new
kid in school who's supposed to be a scientifical genius." Wallace was
this genius. In a series of intelligence and aptitude tests we all took in
the opening week, he achieved some incredible score, a mark that, according to the people who made up the tests, certified him as a genius
and absolutely guaranteed that in later life he would join the company
of Einstein, Steinmetz, and Edison. Naturally, his teachers were
thrilled — but not for long.

Within a matter of weeks, it became clear that although Wallace was unquestionably a genius, or at least an exceptionally bright
boy, he was disposed to use his considerable gifts not to equip himself
for a career in the service of mankind but for purely anti-social under-
takings. Far from making the distinguished scholastic record everyone
expected of him, he made an altogether deplorable one. He never did a
lick of schoolwork. He had picked up his scientific knowledge somewhere but evidently not from teachers. I am not sure about this, but I
think Wallace's record, as long as he was in school, was even worse
than mine. In my mind's eye there is a picture of the sheet of monthly
averages thumbtacked to the bulletin board across the hall from the
school post office; my name is one from the bottom, the bottom name
being Wallace's.

As a matter of fact, one look at Wallace should have been

enough to tell the teachers what sort of genius he was. At fourteen, he was somwhat shorter than he should have been and a good deal stouter. His face was round, owlish, and dirty. He had big, dark eyes, and his black hair, which hardly ever got cut, was arranged on his head as the four winds wanted it. He had been outfitted with attractive and fairly expensive clothes, but he changed from one suit to another only when his parents came to call on him and ordered him to get out of what he had on.

The two most expressive things about him were his mouth and the pocket of his jacket. By looking at his mouth, one could tell whether he was plotting evil or had recently accomplished it. If he was bent upon malevolence, his lips were all puckered up, like those of a billiard player about to make a difficult shot. After the deed was done, the pucker was replaced by a delicate, unearthly smile. How a teacher who knew anything about boys could miss the fact that both expressions were masks of Satan I'm sure I don't know. Wallace's pockets were less interesting than his mouth, perhaps, but more spectacular in a way. The side pockets of his jacket bulged out over his pudgy haunches like burro hampers. They were filled with tools — screwdrivers, pliers, files, wrenches, wire cutters, nail sets, and I don't know what else. In addition to all this, one pocket always contained a rolled-up copy of *Popular Mechanics*, while from the top of the other protruded *Scientific American* or some other such magazine. His breast pocket contained, besides a large collection of fountain pens and mechanical pencils, a picket fence of drill bits, gimlets, kitchen knives, and other pointed instruments. When he walked, he clinked and jangled and pealed.

Wallace lived just down the hall from me, and I got to know him one afternoon, a week or so after school started, when I was wrestling with an algebra lesson. I was really trying to get good marks at the time, for my father had threatened me with unpleasant reprisals if my grades did not show early improvement. I could make no sense of the algebra, though, and I thought that the scientific genius, who had not as yet been unmasked, might be generous enough to lend me a hand.

It was a study period, but I found Wallace stretched out on the floor working away at something he was learning to make from *Popular Mechanics*. He received me with courtesy, but after hearing my request he went immediately back to his tinkering. "I could do that algebra, all right," he said, "but I can't be bothered with it. Got to get this dingbat going this afternoon. Anyway, I don't care about algebra. It's too twitchy. Real engineers never do any of that stuff. It's too twitchy for them." I soon learned that "twitch" was an all-purpose word of Wallace's. It turned up, in one form or another, in about every third sentence he spoke. It did duty as a noun, an adjective, a verb, and an adverb.

I was disappointed by his refusal of help but fascinated by what he was doing. I stayed on and watched him as he deftly cut and spliced wires, removed and replaced screws, referring, every so often, to his magazine for further instruction. He worked silently, lips fiendishly puckered, for some time, then looked up at me and said, "Say, you know anything about that organ in the chapel?"

"What about it?" I asked.

"I mean do you know anything about how it works?"

"No," I said. "I don't know anything about that."

"Too bad," Wallace said, reaching for a pair of pliers. "I had a really twitchy idea." He worked at his wires and screws for quite a while. After perhaps ten minutes, he looked up again. "Well, anyhow," he said, "maybe you know how to get in the chapel and have a look at the organ?"

"Sure, that's easy," I said. "Just walk in. The chapel's always open. They keep it open so you can go in and pray if you want to, and things like that."

"Oh" was Wallace's only comment.

I didn't at all grasp what he had in mind until church time the following Sunday. At about six o'clock that morning, several hours before the service, he tiptoed into my room and shook me from sleep. "Hey, get dressed," he said. "Let's you and I twitch over to the chapel and have a look at the organ."

Game for any form of amusement, I got up and went along. In the bright, not quite frosty October morning, we scurried over the lawns to the handsome Georgian chapel. It was an hour before the rising bell.

Wallace had brought along a flashlight as well as his usual collection of hardware. We went to the rear of the chancel, where the organ was, and he poked the light underneath the thing and inside it for a few minutes. Then he got out his pliers and screwdrivers and performed some operations that I could neither see nor understand. We were in the chapel for only a few minutes. "There," Wallace said as he came up from under the keyboard. "I guess I got her twitched up just about right. Let's go." Back in my room, we talked softly until the rest of the school began to stir. I asked Wallace what, precisely, he had done to the organ. "You'll see," he said with that faint, faraway smile where the pucker had been. Using my commonplace imagination, I guessed that he had fixed the organ so it would give out peculiar noises or something like that. I didn't realize then that Wallace's tricks were seldom commonplace.

Church began as usual that Sunday morning. The headmaster delivered the invocation and then announced the number and title of the first hymn. He held up his hymnal and gave the genteel, throat-clearing cough that was his customary signal to the organist to get going. The organist came down on the keys but not a peep sounded from the pipes. He tried again. Nothing but a click.

When the headmaster realized that the organ wasn't working,

he walked quickly to the rear and consulted in whispers with the organist. Together they made a hurried inspection of the instrument, peering inside it, snapping the electric switch back and forth, and reaching to the base plug to make certain the juice was on. Everything seemed all right, yet the organ wouldn't sound a note.

"Something appears to be wrong with our organ," the headmaster said when he returned to the lectern. "I regret to say that for this morning's service we shall have to — "

At the first word of the announcement, Wallace, who was next to me in one of the rear pews, slid out of his seat and bustled noisily down the middle aisle. It was highly unusual conduct, and every eye was on him. His gaudy magazines flapped from his pockets, his portable workshop clattered and clanked as he strode importantly to the chancel and rose on tiptoe to reach the ear of the astonished headmaster. He spoke in a stage whisper that could be heard everywhere in the chapel. "Worked around organs quite a bit, sir," he said. "Think I can get this one going in a jiffy."

Given the chance, the headmaster would undoubtedly have declined Wallace's kind offer. Wallace didn't give him the chance. He scooted for the organ. For perhaps a minute, he worked on it, hands flying, tools tinkling.

Then, stuffing the tools back into his pockets, he returned to the headmaster. "There you are, sir," he said, smiling up at him. "Think she'll go all right now." The headmaster, with great doubt in his heart, I am sure, nodded to the organist to try again. Wallace stood by, looking rather like the inventor of a new kind of airplane waiting to see his brain child take flight. He faked a look of deep anxiety, which, when a fine, clear swell came from the pipes, was replaced by a faint smile of relief, also faked. On the second or third chord, he bustled back down the aisle, looking very solemn and businesslike and ready for serious worship.

It was a fine performance, particularly brilliant in its timing. If Wallace had had to stay at the organ even a few seconds longer — that is, if he had done a slightly more elaborate job of twitching it in the first place — he would have been ordered back to his pew before he had got done with the repairs. Moreover, someone would probably have guessed that it was he who had put it on the fritz in the first place. But no one did guess it. Not then, anyway. For weeks after that, Wallace's prestige in the school was enormous. Everyone had had from the beginning a sense of honor and pride at having a genius around, but no one up to then had realized how useful a genius could be. Wallace let on after church that Sunday that he was well up on the workings not merely of organs but also of heating and plumbing systems, automobiles, radios, washing machines, and just about everything else. He said he would be pleased to help out in any emergency. Everyone thought he was wonderful.

"That was a real good twitch, wasn't it?" he said to me when we were by ourselves. I said that it certainly was.

From that time on, I was proud and happy to be Wallace's cup-bearer. I find it hard now to explain exactly what his victory with the organ, and all his later victories over authority, meant to me, but I do know that they meant a very great deal. Partly, I guess, it was just the knowledge that he enjoyed my company. I was an authentic, certified dunce and he was an acknowledged genius, yet he liked being with me. Better yet was my discovery that this superbrain disliked schoolwork every bit as much as I did. He was bored silly, as I was, by "Il Penseroso" and completely unable to stir up any enthusiasm for "Silas Marner"* and all the foolish goings on over Eppie. Finally, and this perhaps was what made me love him most, he had it in his power to humiliate and bring low the very people who had so often humiliated me and brought me low.

As I spent the long fall and winter afternoons with Wallace, being introduced by him to the early novels of H. G. Wells,† which he admired extravagantly, and watching him make crystal sets, window-cleaning machines, automatic chair-rockers, and miniature steam turbines from plans in *Popular Mechanics*, I gradually absorbed bits of his liberating philosophy. "If I were you," he used to say, "I wouldn't be scared by those teachers. They don't know anything. They're twitches, those teachers, real twerpy, twitchy twitches." "Twerpy" was an adjective often used by Wallace to modify "twitch." It added several degrees of twitchiness to anything twitchy.

Although Wallace had refused at first to help me with my lessons, he later gave freely of his assistance. I explained to him that my father was greatly distressed about my work and that I really wanted to make him happier. Wallace was moved by this. He would read along in my Latin grammar, study out algebra problems with me, and explain things in language that seemed a lot more lucid than that of my teachers. Before long, I began to understand that half my trouble lay in my fear of my studies, my teachers, and myself. "Don't know why you get so twitched up over this stuff," Wallace would say a trifle impatiently as he helped me get the gist of a speech in "As You Like It." "There isn't anything hard about this. Fact, it's pretty good right in here. It's just those teachers who twitch it all up. I wish they'd all go soak their heads."

Wallace rode along for quite a while on the strength of his intelligence tests and his organ-fixing, but in time it became obvious that his disappointing classroom performance was not so much the result of

---

* "Il Penseroso" is a poem by John Milton (1608–1674), and *Silas Marner* (1861) is a novel by George Eliot.

† Herbert George Wells (1866–1946) was an English novelist and science-fiction writer.

failure to adjust to a new environment (as a genius, he received more tolerance in this respect than non-geniuses) as of out-and-out refusal to cooperate with the efforts being made to educate him. Even when he had learned a lesson in the course of helping me with it, he wouldn't give the teachers the satisfaction of thinking he had learned anything in their classes. Then, too, his pranks began to catch up with him. Some of them, he made no effort to conceal.

He was easily the greatest teacher-baiter I have ever known. His masterpiece, I think, was one he thought up for our algebra class. "Hey, you twitch," he called to me one day as I was passing his room on my way to the daily ordeal of "x"s and "y"s. "I got a good one for old twitch Potter." I went into his room, and he took down from his closet shelf a spool of shiny copper wire. "Now, watch this," he said. He took the free end of the wire and drew it up through the left sleeve of his shirt. Then he brought it across his chest, underneath the shirt, and ran it down the right sleeve. He closed his left fist over the spool and held the free end of the wire between right thumb and forefinger. "Let's get over to that dopey class," he said, and we went.

When the lesson was well started, Wallace leaned back in his seat and began to play in a languorous but ostentatious manner with the wire. It glistened brightly in the strong classroom light, and it took Mr. Potter, the teacher, only a few seconds to notice that Wallace was paying no mind to the blackboard equations but was, instead, completely absorbed in the business of fingering the wire.

"Wallace Duckworth, what's that you're fiddling with?" Mr. Potter said.

"Piece of wire, sir."

"Give it to me this instant."

"Yes, sir," Wallace said, extending his hand.

Mr. Potter had, no doubt, bargained on getting a stray piece of wire that he could unceremoniously pitch into the wastebasket. Wallace handed him about eighteen inches of it. As Mr. Potter took it, Wallace released several inches more.

"I want all that wire, Wallace," Mr. Potter said.

"I'm giving it to you, sir," Wallace answered. He let go of about two feet more. Mr. Potter kept pulling. His rage so far overcame his reason that he couldn't figure out what Wallace was doing. As he pulled, Wallace fed him more and more wire, and the stuff began to coil up on the floor around his feet. Guiding the wire with the fingers of his right hand, Wallace created quite a bit of tension, so that eventually Mr. Potter was pulling hand over hand, like a sailor tightening lines in a high sea. When he thought the tension was great enough, Wallace let two or three feet slip quickly through his hands, and Mr. Potter toppled to the floor, landing in a terrible tangle of wire.

I no longer remember all of Wallace's inventions in detail. Once, I recall, he made, in the chemistry laboratory, some kind of invisible paint — a sort of shellac, I suppose — and covered every blackboard in the school with it. The next day, chalk skidded along the slate and left about as much impression as it would have made on a cake of ice. The dormitory he and I lived in was an old one of frame construction, and when we had fire drills, we had to climb down outside fire escapes. One night, Wallace tied a piece of flypaper securely around each rung of each ladder in the building, then rang the fire alarm. Still another time, he went back to his first love, the organ, and put several pounds of flour in the pipes, so that when the organist turned on the pumps, a cloud of flour filled the chapel. One of his favorite tricks was to take the dust jacket from a novel and wrap it around a textbook. In a Latin class, then, he would appear to be reading "Black April"* when he should have been reading about the campaigns in Gaul. After several of his teachers had discovered that he had the right book in the wrong cover (he piously explained that he put the covers on to keep his books clean), he felt free to remove the textbook and really read a novel in class.

Wallace was expelled shortly before the Easter vacation. As the winter had drawn on, life had become duller and duller for him, and to brighten things up he had resorted to pranks of larger conception and of an increasingly anti-social character. He poured five pounds of sugar into the gasoline tank of the basketball coach's car just before the coach was to start out, with two or three of the team's best players in his car, for a game with a school about twenty-five miles away. The engine functioned adequately until the car hit an isolated spot on the highway, miles from any service place. Then it gummed up completely. The coach and the players riding with him came close to frostbite, and the game had to be called off. The adventure cost Wallace's parents a couple of hundred dollars for automobile repairs. Accused of the prank, which clearly bore his trademark, Wallace had freely admitted his guilt. It was explained to his parents that he would be given one more chance in school; another trick of any sort and he would be packed off on the first train.

Later, trying to justify himself to me, he said, "You don't like that coach either, do you? He's the twerpiest twitch here. All teachers are twitchy, but coaches are the worst ones of all."

I don't recall what I said. Wallace had not consulted me about several of his recent escapades, and although I was still loyal to him, I was beginning to have misgivings about some of them.

As I recall it, the affair that led directly to his expulsion was a relatively trifling one, something to do with blown fuses or short circuits. At any rate, Wallace's parents had to come and fetch him home. It was a sad occasion for me, for Wallace had built in me the founda-

* *Black April* is a novel by Julia Peterkin (1880–1961).

tions for a sense of security. My marks were improving, my father was happier, and I no longer cringed at the sight of a teacher. I feared, though, that without Wallace standing behind me and giving me courage, I might slip back into the old ways. I was very near to tears as I helped him pack up his turbines, his tools, and his stacks of magazines. He, however, was quite cheerful. "I suppose my Pop will put me in another one of these places, and I'll have to twitch my way out of it all over again," he said.

"Just remember how dumb all those teachers are," he said to me a few moments before he got into his parents' car. "They're so twitchy dumb they can't even tell if anyone else is dumb." It was rather a sweeping generalization, I later learned, but it served me well for a number of years. Whenever I was belabored by a teacher, I remembered my grimy genius friend and his reassurances. I got through school somehow or other. I still cower a bit when I find that someone I've met is a schoolteacher, but things aren't too bad and I am on reasonably civil terms with a number of teachers, and even a few professors.

PROBING FOR
MEANING

1. The author says that Wallace changed his whole outlook on life. What was his outlook before he met Wallace? What kind of boy was the author?

2. How did the author become friends with Wallace? Why did Wallace befriend him?

3. What did Wallace's pranks mean to the author?

4. Why did Wallace eventually help him with his homework?

5. What was it that motivated Wallace to play pranks? Why did Wallace refuse to "cooperate with the efforts being made to educate him"?

6. How did the author feel about the fact that Wallace's pranks became "increasingly anti-social" in character?

7. After describing Wallace's first prank with the organ, the author writes: "I was an authentic, certified dunce and he was an acknowledged genius." Were the two boys really as different as the author suggests? In what ways were the author and Wallace similar kinds of characters?

PROBING FOR
METHOD

1. Why does Rovere focus exclusively on the author in the first five paragraphs? Why doesn't he introduce Wallace right at the start?

2. Rovere describes a number of Wallace's pranks in detail. Do the details of each prank teach us different things about Wallace? For example, does the prank in Mr. Potter's class illustrate anything about Wallace that we might not have understood clearly if we had known only about the first prank with the organ?

3. Define "twitch."

4. At the end of the story, the author says, "I still cower a bit when I find that someone I've met is a schoolteacher." How seriously does he intend

this remark about himself to be taken? What is his attitude toward himself throughout the story?

 JAMES THURBER

The Secret Life of Walter Mitty

"We're going through!" The Commander's voice was like thin ice breaking. He wore his full-dress uniform, with the heavily braided white cap pulled down rakishly over one cold gray eye. "We can't make it, sir. It's spoiling for a hurricane, if you ask me." "I'm not asking you, Lieutenant Berg," said the Commander. "Throw on the power lights! Rev her up to 8,500! We're going through!" The pounding of the cylinders increased: ta-pocketa-pocketa-pocketa-*pocketa-pocketa*. The Commander stared at the ice forming on the pilot window. He walked over and twisted a row of complicated dials. "Switch on No. 8 auxiliary!" he shouted. "Switch on No. 8 auxiliary!" repeated Lieutenant Berg. "Full strength in No. 3 turret!" shouted the Commander. "Full strength in No. 3 turret!" The crew bending to their various tasks in the huge, hurtling eight-engined Navy hydroplane looked at each other and grinned. "The Old Man'll get us through," they said to one another. "The Old Man ain't afraid of Hell!" . . .

"Not so fast! You're driving too fast!" said Mrs. Mitty. "What are you driving so fast for?"

"Hmm?" said Walter Mitty. He looked at his wife, in the seat beside him, with shocked astonishment. She seemed grossly unfamiliar, like a strange woman who had yelled at him in a crowd. "You were up to fifty-five," she said. "You know I don't like to go more than forty. You were up to fifty-five." Walter Mitty drove on toward Waterbury in silence, the roaring of the SN202 through the worst storm in twenty years of Navy flying fading in the remote, intimate airways of his mind. "You're tensed up again," said Mrs. Mitty. "It's one of your days. I wish you'd let Dr. Renshaw look you over."

Walter Mitty stopped the car in front of the building where his wife went to have her hair done. "Remember to get those overshoes while I'm having my hair done," she said. "I don't need overshoes," said Mitty. She put her mirror back into her bag. "We've been all through that," she said, getting out of the car. "You're not a young man any longer." He raced the engine a little. "Why don't you wear your gloves? Have you lost your gloves?" Walter Mitty reached in a pocket and brought out the gloves. He put them on, but after she had turned and gone into the building and he had driven on to a red light, he took them off again. "Pick it up, brother!" snapped a cop as the light changed, and Mitty hastily pulled on his gloves and lurched ahead. He drove around the streets aimlessly for a time, and then he drove past the hospital on his way to the parking lot.

. . . "It's the millionaire banker, Wellington McMillan," said the pretty nurse. "Yes?" said Walter Mitty, removing his gloves slowly. "Who has the case?" "Dr. Renshaw and Dr. Benbow, but there are two specialists here, Dr. Remington from New York and Mr. Pritchard-Mitford from London. He flew over." A door opened down a long, cool corridor and Dr. Renshaw came out. He looked distraught and haggard. "Hello, Mitty," he said. "We're having the devil's own time with McMillan, the millionaire banker and close personal friend of Roosevelt. Obstreosis of the ductal tract. Tertiary. Wish you'd take a look at him." "Glad to," said Mitty.

In the operating room there were whispered introductions: "Dr. Remington, Dr. Mitty, Mr. Pritchard-Mitford, Dr. Mitty." "I've read your book on streptothricosis," said Pritchard-Mitford, shaking hands. "A brilliant performance, sir." "Thank you," said Walter Mitty. "Didn't know you were in the States, Mitty," grumbled Remington. "Coals to Newcastle, bringing Mitford and me up here for a tertiary." "You are very kind," said Mitty. A huge, complicated machine, connected to the operating table, with many tubes and wires, began at this moment to go pocketa-pocketa-pocketa. "The new anesthetizer is giving way!" shouted an interne. "There is no one in the East who knows how to fix it!" "Quiet, man!" said Mitty, in a low, cool voice. He sprang to the machine, which was now going pocketa-pocketa-queep-pocketa-queep. He began fingering delicately a row of glistening dials. "Give me a fountain pen!" he snapped. Someone handed him a fountain pen. He pulled a faulty piston out of the machine and inserted the pen in its place. "That will hold for ten minutes," he said. "Get on with the operation." A nurse hurried over and whispered to Renshaw, and Mitty saw the man turn pale. "Coreopsis has set in," said Renshaw nervously. "If you would take over, Mitty?" Mitty looked at him and at the craven figure of Benbow, who drank, and at the grave, uncertain faces of the two great specialists. "If you wish," he said. They slipped a white gown on him; he adjusted a mask and drew on thin gloves; nurses handed him shining . . .

"Back it up, Mac! Look out for that Buick!" Walter Mitty jammed on the brakes. "Wrong lane, Mac," said the parking-lot attendant, looking at Mitty closely. "Gee. Yeh," muttered Mitty. He began cautiously to back out of the lane marked "Exit Only." "Leave her sit there," said the attendant. "I'll put her away." Mitty got out of the car.

"Hey, better leave the key." "Oh," said Mitty, handing the man the ignition key. The attendant vaulted into the car, backed it up with insolent skill, and put it where it belonged.

They're so damn cocky, thought Walter Mitty, walking along Main Street; they think they know everything. Once he had tried to take his chains off, outside New Milford, and he had got them wound around the axles. A man had had to come out in a wrecking car and unwind them, a young, grinning garageman. Since then Mrs. Mitty always made him drive to a garage to have the chains taken off. The next time, he thought, I'll wear my right arm in a sling; they won't grin at me then. I'll have my right arm in a sling and they'll see I couldn't possibly take the chains off myself. He kicked at the slush on the sidewalk. "Overshoes," he said to himself, and he began looking for a shoe store.

When he came out into the street again, with the overshoes in a box under his arm, Walter Mitty began to wonder what the other thing was his wife had told him to get. She had told him twice, before they set out from their house for Waterbury. In a way he hated these weekly trips to town — he was always getting something wrong. Kleenex, he thought, Squibb's, razor blades? No. Toothpaste, toothbrush, bicarbonate, carborundum, initiative and referendum? He gave it up. But she would remember it. "Where's the what's-its-name?" she would ask. "Don't tell me you forgot the what's-its-name." A newsboy went up shouting something about the Waterbury trial.

. . . "Perhaps this will refresh your memory." The District Attorney suddenly thrust a heavy automatic at the quiet figure on the witness stand. "Have you ever seen this before?" Walter Mitty took the gun and examined it expertly. "This is my Webley-Vickers 50.80," he said calmly. An excited buzz ran around the courtroom. The judge rapped for order. "You are a crack shot with any sort of firearms, I believe?" said the District Attorney, insinuatingly. "Objection!" shouted Mitty's attorney. "We have shown that the defendant could not have fired the shot. We have shown that he wore his right arm in a sling on the night of the fourteenth of July." Walter Mitty raised his hand briefly and the bickering attorneys were stilled. "With any known make of gun," he said evenly, "I could have killed Gregory Fitzhurst at three hundred feet *with my left hand*." Pandemonium broke loose in the courtroom. A woman's scream rose about the bedlam and suddenly a lovely, dark-haired girl was in Walter Mitty's arms. The District Attorney struck at her savagely. Without rising from his chair, Mitty let the man have it on the point of the chin. "You miserable cur!" . . .

"Puppy biscuit," said Walter Mitty. He stopped walking and the buildings of Waterbury rose up out of the misty courtroom and surrounded him again. A woman who was passing laughed. "He said 'Puppy biscuit,'" she said to her companion. "That man said 'Puppy biscuit' to himself." Walter Mitty hurried on. He went into an A. & P., not the first one he came to but a smaller one farther up the street. "I want some biscuit for small, young dogs," he said to the clerk. "Any special brand, sir?" The greatest pistol shot in the world thought a moment. "It says 'Puppies Bark for It' on the box," said Walter Mitty.

His wife would be through at the hairdresser's in fifteen minutes, Mitty saw in looking at his watch, unless they had trouble drying it; sometimes they had trouble drying it. She didn't like to get to the hotel first; she would want him to be there waiting for her as usual. He found a big leather chair in the lobby, facing a window, and he put the overshoes and the puppy biscuit on the floor beside it. He picked up an old copy of *Liberty* and sank down into the chair. "Can Germany Conquer the World Through the Air?" Walter Mitty looked at the pictures of bombing planes and of ruined streets.

. . . "The cannonading has got the wind up in young Raleigh, sir," said the sergeant. Captain Mitty looked up at him through tousled hair. "Get him to bed," he said wearily. "With the others. I'll fly alone." "But you can't, sir," said the sergeant anxiously. "It takes two men to handle that bomber and the Archies are pounding hell out of the air. Von Richtman's circus is between here and Saulier." "Somebody's got to get that ammunition dump," said Mitty. "I'm going over. Spot of brandy?" He poured a drink for the sergeant and one for himself. War thundered and whined around the dugout and battered at the door. There was a rending of wood and splinters flew through the room. "A bit of a near thing," said Captain Mitty carelessly. "The box barrage is closing in," said the sergeant. "We only live once, Sergeant," said Mitty, with his faint, fleeting smile. "Or do we?" He poured another brandy and tossed it off. "I never see a man could hold his brandy like you, sir," said the sergeant. "Begging your pardon, sir." Captain Mitty stood up and strapped on his huge Webley-Vickers automatic. "It's forty kilometers through hell, sir," said the sergeant. Mitty finished one last brandy. "After all," he said softly, "what isn't?" The pounding of the cannon increased; there was the rat-tat-tatting of machine guns, and from somewhere came the menacing pocketa-pocketa-pocketa of the new flamethrowers. Walter Mitty walked to the door of the dugout humming "Auprès de Ma Blonde." He turned and waved to the sergeant. "Cheerio!" he said. . . .

Something struck his shoulder. "I've been looking all over this hotel for you," said Mrs. Mitty. "Why do you have to hide in this old chair? How did you expect me to find you?" "Things close in," said Walter Mitty vaguely. "What?" Mrs. Mitty said. "Did you get the what's-its-name? The puppy biscuit? What's in that box?" "Overshoes," said Mitty. "Couldn't you have put them on in the store?" "I was thinking," said Walter Mitty. "Does it ever occur to you that I am sometimes thinking?" She looked at him. "I'm going to take your temperature when I get you home," she said.

They went out through the revolving doors that made a faintly

derisive whistling sound when you pushed them. It was two blocks to
the parking lot. At the drugstore on the corner she said, "Wait here for
me. I forgot something. I won't be a minute." She was more than a minute. Walter Mitty lighted a cigarette. It began to rain, rain with sleet in
it. He stood up against the wall of the drugstore, smoking. . . . He put
his shoulders back and his heels together. "To hell with the handkerchief," said Walter Mitty scornfully. He took one last drag on his cigarette and snapped it away. Then, with that faint, fleeting smile playing
about his lips, he faced the firing squad; erect and motionless, proud
and disdainful. Walter Mitty the Undefeated, inscrutable to the last.

PROBING FOR
MEANING

1. What circumstances in reality occasion each of Walter Mitty's fantasies?

2. What single aspect do his fantasies have in common? How do people react to him in reality?

3. What evidence do we have as to why Walter Mitty fantasizes? Do
all people daydream as he does?

4. How does the last daydream differ from the previous ones? How
significant is this?

5. How dangerous are his fantasies? Is the story to be interpreted
seriously? Humorously? Explain.

PROBING FOR
METHOD

What is the author's attitude toward Mitty? Toward Mrs. Mitty? How
do the details of the overshoes and the puppy biscuits contribute to your understanding of the two characters?

 ADRIENNE RICH

Hattie Rice Rich

Your sweetness of soul was a mystery to me,
you who slip-covered chairs, glued broken china,
lived out of a wardrobe trunk in our guestroom
summer and fall, then took the Pullman train
in your darkblue dress and straw hat, to Alabama,
shuttling half-yearly between your son and daughter.
Your sweetness of soul was a convenience for everyone,
how you rose with the birds and children, boiled your own egg,

fished for hours on a pier, your umbrella spread,
took the street-car downtown shopping
endlessly for your son's whims, the whims of genius,
kept your accounts in ledgers, wrote letters daily.
All through World War Two the forbidden word
Jewish was barely uttered in your son's house;
your anger flared over inscrutable things.
Once I saw you crouched on the guestroom bed,
knuckles blue-white around the bedpost, sobbing
your one brief memorable scene of rebellion:
you didn't want to go back South that year.
You were never "Grandmother Rich" but "Anana";
you had money of your own but you were homeless,
Hattie, widow of Samuel, and no matriach,
dispersed among the children and grandchildren.

PROBING FOR   1. In what ways did Hattie exhibit what the poet calls her "sweetness
MEANING   of soul"? How did Hattie's family feel about her sweetness? Why did the poet
find it "a mystery"?
　　　　　2.　What kind of a life did Hattie lead? What did she have to rebel
against? What did she have to feel anger about?

PROBING FOR   1. Why does Rich tell us that the word "Jewish" was hardly ever spo-
METHOD   ken in Hattie's son's house during World War II? What does this help us to
understand about the son and his family? What insight does it give us into
Hattie's life?
　　　　　2. In what sense do the final lines of the poem constitute a thesis?
　　　　　3. What sort of mood does the poem convey? What, aside from a
sense of mystery, does the poet seem to feel about her subject?

TED HUGHES

Secretary

If I should touch her she would shriek and weeping
Crawl off to nurse the terrible wound: all
Day like a starling under the bellies of bulls
She hurries among men, ducking, peeping,

Off in a whirl at the first move of a horn.
At dusk she scuttles down the gauntlet of lust
Like a clockwork mouse. Safe home at last
She mends socks with holes, shirts that are torn,

For father and brother, and a delicate supper cooks;
Goes to bed early, shuts out with the light
Her thirty years, and lies with buttocks tight,
Hiding her lovely eyes until day break.

PROBING FOR
MEANING

1. In each of the three stanzas, the poet describes the secretary at a different period of each working day. What are these periods?

2. Why would a starling "duck and peep" under the belly of a bull? In what situations does his secretary act in the same way? How does this second image tie in with the first image in this stanza: "If I should touch her she would shriek and weeping/Crawl off to nurse the terrible wound . . ."?

3. What is a "gauntlet" as mentioned in the second verse? What is the "gauntlet of lust" that the secretary must "scuttle down"?

4. What do the facts in the third verse further reveal about the secretary? How does the poet know these details?

PROBING FOR
METHOD

1. What is the poet's attitude toward the secretary? Use evidence from the poem to substantiate your answer.

2. This poem contains many words not generally thought to be "poetic." Examples include *shriek, crawl, bellies,* and so on. What do some of these words contribute to the impact of the total poem?

 W. H. AUDEN

The Unknown Citizen

To JS/07/M/378
This Marble Monument
Is Erected by the State

He was found by the Bureau of Statistics to be
One against whom there was no official complaint,
And all the reports on his conduct agree
That, in the modern sense of an old-fashioned word, he was a
        saint,

For in everything he did he served the Greater Community.
Except for the War till the day he retired
He worked in a factory and never got fired,
But satisfied his employers, Fudge Motors Inc.
Yet he wasn't a scab or odd in his views,
For his Union reports that he paid his dues,
(Our report on his Union shows it was sound)
And our Social Psychology workers found
That he was popular with his mates and liked a drink.
The Press are convinced that he bought a paper every day
And that his reactions to advertisements were normal in every
        way.
Policies taken out in his name prove that he was fully insured,
And his Health-card shows he was once in hospital but left it
        cured.
Both Producers Research and High-Grade Living declare
He was fully sensible to the advantages of the Instalment Plan
And had everything necessary to the Modern Man,
A phonograph, a radio, a car and a frigidaire.
Our researchers into Public Opinion are content
That he held the proper opinions for the time of year;
When there was peace, he was for peace; when there was war
        he went.
He was married and added five children to the population,
Which our Eugenist says was the right number for a parent of
        his generation.
And our teachers report that he never interfered with their
        education.
Was he free? Was he happy? The question is absurd:
Had anything been wrong, we should certainly have heard.

PROBING FOR   1. According to the poem, what are the conditions for sainthood in the
MEANING   modern world?
                    2. What was the "Unknown Citizen" like? Did he have any distin-
guishing characteristics? What are the ways in which he conformed to his role
in society?
                    3. Given the logic of the poem, why are the questions "Was he free?"
and "Was He happy?" "absurd"?
                    4. Who is the "we" of the final line?

PROBING FOR   1. What deliberate irony is suggested by the title?
METHOD   2. What effect is achieved by having the poem rhyme? Does this contribute to the irony of the poem?
                    3. What words are used to emphasize the role of bureaucracy in con-
temporary life? The role of conformity?

Topics for Imitation

1. Who are the most important people in your life? Is there one person whom you understand as well as Anderson understood his father? If you can think of one person you would like to write about, choose one event, action, or conversation through which you can best reveal that person and write an essay in which you portray him or her through this specific moment.

2. Perhaps an important person in your experience is one you were acquainted with briefly or casually, as Orwell knew Paddy; Ralbovsky, his coach; Ted Hughes, his secretary. This relationship may be easier to describe than that with a person you know well, for if you do not have as many details from which to select, you can be less concerned with limiting the topic. Your emphasis will be creating a dominant mood about the person. Describe this individual, conveying through your choice of words your attitude toward him or her. Keep a specific audience in mind and write for that audience.

3. Compare the two short stories in this chapter. In what ways are the title characters comparable? In what ways is Thurber's attitude toward Mitty similar to Rovere's attitude toward Wallace? In what ways do the authors' attitudes differ?

4. Discuss the three poems in this chapter. Do differences exist in the writers' attitudes toward their subjects? Are there similarities? Explain, citing the language and selection of details to support your point of view.

5. Many of the selections make statements for or against conformity to accepted norms. In this connection, discuss the extent to which conformity or noncomformity has a part in the effectiveness of a person's development. Use evidence from the selections in your response.

6. Self-doubt is a theme of many of the selections in this chapter. Discuss how self-doubt affects the main characters in three selections. What effect does self-doubt have on a person's development?

7. Social class plays a role in several of the selections. Discuss the importance of class distinctions in the main character's lives in the Angelou, Goldstein, Orwell, and Auden selections.

8. People define winning and losing differently. Discuss the definitions of success and failure in the Anderson, Ralbovsky, Thurber, and Rovere selections.

TWO

 PLACES

". . . planet is dissimilar from planet"

"Although it wasn't wild, it was a fairly large and undisturbed lake and there were places in it which, to a child at least, seemed infinitely remote and primeval." In "Once More to the Lake" E. B. White succeeds in showing us that a place can have a considerable effect on our lives. Saul Bellow's senses and imagination are captivated by place — a very different kind of place, a kibbutz, which he describes as "a homeplace for body and soul." The effect of Las Vegas is more jarring: Joan Didion calls the city "bizarre and beautiful."

We react to places usually because of our emotional associations with them, as Eldridge Cleaver does in "A Day in Folsom Prison." In "Knoxville: Summer 1915" James Agee captures the complexity of our relationship to places, particularly to the place where we grew up. In the short stories, Sammy and Tommy Castelli find claustrophobic the stores they work in.

The poets also emphasize the effect of places. Arna Bontemps portrays years of slavery in the American South; Gary Snyder captures the crispness of a cold late summer afternoon in the American West; and Denise Levertov recreates "a night of misery" in a lonely urban center.

Analyze the places you have known — rooms, cities, countries. Think of the various ways in which they have affected you. Perhaps some have left a greater impression than others. What factors govern your reactions to place?

Describing a Place and Organizing the Essay

Writing that gives emphasis to place is usually developed through one of two methods: use of spatial movement and exact description, or use of dominant mood impression. In the former, the narrator assumes the role of movie cameraman and attempts to give the reader as much detail about the place as possible. The narrator's observations are structured in camera-movement sequences: near to far, left to right, bottom to top, and so on. In the latter, dominant mood impression, the narrator selects and comments upon aspects of the place that give it a dominant mood related to what he or she wishes to say. Which method does each of the writers in this chapter use?

Spatial description is just one of the many ways in which you can organize an essay. Organization of your points is usually a step in both the prewriting and writing stages of the writing process. We attempt to organize what we want to say before writing and then reorganize it as we write and perhaps again once we have finished a rough draft. As you read each essay in this chapter, attempt to trace the organization as a model for your own work. More discussion of description and organization follows the first two essays of the chapter: *Describing a Place* after "On a Kibbutz" on pp. 62–64 and *Organizing the Paper* after "Once More to the Lake" on pp. 70–73.

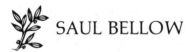

SAUL BELLOW

On a Kibbutz

On a kibbutz.

Lucky is Nola's dog. John's dog is Mississippi. But John loves Lucky too, and Nola dotes on Mississippi. And then there are the children — one daughter in the army, and a younger child who still sleeps in the kibbutz dormitory. Lucky is a woolly brown dog, old and nervous. His master was killed in the Golan. When there is a sonic boom over the kibbutz, the dog rushes out, growling. He seems to remember the falling bombs. He is too feeble to bark, too old to run, his teeth are bad, his eyes under the brown fringe are dull, and he is clotted under the tail. Mississippi is a big, long-legged, short-haired, brown-and-white, clever, lively, affectionate, and greedy animal. She is a "child dog" — sits in your lap, puts a paw on your arm when you reach for a tidbit to get it for herself. Since she weighs fifty pounds or more she is not welcome in my lap, but she sits on John and Nola and on the guests — those who permit it. She is winsome but also flatulent. She eats too many sweets but is good company, a wonderful listener and conversationalist; she growls and snuffles when you speak directly to her. She "sings" along with the record player. The Auerbachs are proud of this musical yelping.

In the morning we hear the news in Hebrew and then again on the BBC. We eat an Israeli breakfast of fried eggs, sliced cheese, cucumbers, olives, green onions, tomatoes, and little salt fish. Bread is toasted on the coal-oil heater. The dogs have learned the trick of the door and bang in and out. Between the rows of small kibbutz dwellings the lawns are ragged but very green. Light and warmth come from the sea. Under the kibbutz lie the ruins of Herod's Caesarea. There are Roman fragments everywhere. Marble columns in the grasses. Fallen capitals make garden seats. You have only to prod the ground to find fragments of pottery, bits of statuary, a pair of dancing satyr legs. John's tightly packed bookshelves are fringed with such relics. On the crowded desk stands a framed photograph of the dead son, with a small beard like John's, smiling with John's own warmth.

We walk in the citrus groves after breakfast, taking Mississippi with us (John is seldom without her); the soil is kept loose and soft among the trees, the leaves are glossy, the ground itself is fragrant. Many of the trees are still unharvested and bending, tangerines and lemons as dense as stars. "Oh that I were an orange tree/That busie plant!" wrote George Herbert. To put forth such leaves, to be hung with oranges, to be a blessing — one feels the temptation of this on such a morning and I even feel a fibrous woodiness entering my arms as I consider it. You want to take root and stay forever in the most temperate and blue of temperate places. John mourns his son, he always mourns his son, but he is also smiling in the sunlight.

In the exporting of oranges there is competition from the North African countries and from Spain. "We are very idealistic here, but when we read about frosts in Spain we're glad as hell," John says.

All this was once dune land. Soil had to be carted in and mixed with the sand. Many years of digging and tending made these orchards. Relaxing, breathing freely, you feel what a wonderful place has been created here, a homeplace for body and soul; then you remember that on the beaches there are armed patrols. It is always possible that terrorists may come in rubber dinghies that cannot be detected by radar. They entered Tel Aviv itself in March 1975 and seized a hotel at the seashore. People were murdered. John keeps an Uzi in his bedroom cupboard. Nola scoffs at this. "We'd both be dead before you could reach your gun," she says. Cheerful Nola laughs. An expressive woman — she uses her forearm to wave away John's preparations. "Sometimes he does the drill and I time him to see how long it takes to jump out of bed, open the cupboard, get the gun, put in the clip, and turn around. They'd mow us down before he could get a foot on the floor."

Mississippi is part of the alarm system. "She'd bark," says John.

Just now Mississippi is racing through the orchards, nose to the ground. The air is sweet, and the sun like a mild alcohol makes you yearn for good things. You rest under a tree and eat tangerines, only slightly heavyhearted.

From the oranges we go to the banana groves. The green bananas are tied up in plastic tunics. The great banana flower hangs groundward like the sexual organ of a stallion. The long leaves resemble manes. After two years the ground has to be plowed up and lie fallow. Groves are planted elsewhere — more hard labor. "You noticed before," says John, "that some of the orange trees were withered. Their roots get into Roman ruins and they die. Some years ago, while we were plowing, we turned up an entire Roman street."

He takes me to the Herodian Hippodrome. American archeologists have dug out some of the old walls. We look down into the diggings, where labels flutter from every stratum. There are more potsherds than soil in these bluffs — the broken jugs of the slaves who raised the walls two thousand years ago. At the center of the Hippodrome, a long, graceful ellipse, is a fallen monolith weighing many tons. We sit under fig trees on the slope while Mississippi runs through the high smooth grass. The wind is soft and works the grass gracefully. It makes white air courses in the green.

Whenever John ships out he takes the dog for company. He had enough of solitude when he sailed on German ships under forged papers. He does not like to be alone. Now and again he was under suspicion. A German officer who sensed that he was Jewish threatened to turn him in, but one night when the ship was only hours out of Danzig she struck a mine and went down, the officer with her. John himself was pulled from the sea by his mates. Once he waited in a line of nude men whom a German doctor, a woman, was examining for venereal disease. In that lineup he alone was circumcised. He came before the woman and was examined; she looked into his face and she let him live.

John and I go back through the orange groves. There are large weasels living in the bushy growth along the pipeline. We see a pair of them at a distance in the road. They could easily do for Mississippi. She is luckily far off. We sit under a pine on the hilltop and look out to sea where a freighter moves slowly toward Ashkelon. Nearer to shore, a trawler chuffs. The kibbutz does little fishing now. Off the Egyptian coast, John has been shot at, and not long ago several members of the kibbutz were thrown illegally into jail by the Turks, accused of fishing in Turkish waters. Twenty people gave false testimony. They could have had a thousand witnesses. It took three months to get these men released. A lawyer was found who knew the judge. His itemized bill came to ten thousand dollars — five for the judge, five for himself.

Enough of this sweet sun and the transparent blue-green. We turn our backs on it to have a drink before lunch. Kibbutzniks ride by on clumsy old bikes. They wear cloth caps and pedal slowly; their day starts at six. Plain-looking working people from the tile factory and from the barn steer toward the dining hall. The kibbutzniks are a mixed group. There is one lone Orthodox Jew, who has no congregation to pray with. There are several older gentiles, one a Spaniard, one a Scandinavian, who married Jewish women and settled here. The Spaniard, an anarchist, plans to return to Spain now that Franco has died. One member of the kibbutz is a financial wizard, another was a high-ranking army officer who for obscure reasons fell into disgrace. The dusty tarmac path we follow winds through the settlement. Beside the undistinguished houses stand red poinsettias. Here, too, lie Roman relics. Then we come upon a basketball court, and then the rusty tracks of a children's choo-choo, and then the separate quarters for young women of eighteen, and a museum of antiquities, and a recreation hall. A strong odor of cattle comes from the feeding lot. I tell John that Gurdjiev had Katherine Mansfield resting in the stable at Fontainebleau, claiming that the cows' breath would cure her tuberculosis. John loves to hear such bits of literary history. We go into his house and Mississippi climbs into his lap while we drink Russian vodka. "We could live with those bastards if they limited themselves to making this Stolichnaya."

These words put an end to the peaceful morning. At the north there swells up the Russian menace. With arms from Russia and Europe, the PLO and other Arab militants and the right-wing Christians are now destroying Lebanon. The Syrians have involved themselves; in the eyes of the Syrians, Israel is Syrian land. Suddenly this temperate Mediterranean day and the orange groves and the workers steering their bikes and the children's playground flutter like illustrated paper. What is there to keep them from blowing away?

PROBING FOR MEANING

1. What pleasures does life on the kibbutz offer according to Bellow? What does he mean when he calls the kibbutz "a homeplace for body and soul"?

2. How would you characterize John? What sort of a life has he had? How does he feel about his life on the kibbutz?

3. John says that the kibbutzniks are "idealistic." What does he mean?

4. How does what Bellow calls "the Russian menace" affect the quality of life on the kibbutz?

5. What overall impression does Bellow's description convey?

PROBING FOR   1. Bellow refers to the Roman ruins twice in the essay. Why are the
METHOD   ruins a significant detail in his description?

2. Why does Bellow tell us about the incident when the Turks jailed several members of the kibbutz illegally?

3. Why does Bellow begin the essay by describing Lucky and Mississippi? What do the dogs help us to understand about life on the kibbutz?

4. Bellow tells us that John mourns his son yet smiles in the sunlight. What is Bellow's attitude toward John? What is his attitude toward the kibbutz in general?

Describing a Place

How does Bellow describe his place?   Bellow has decided upon a circular spatial pattern for presenting the sensuous details of his day on an Israeli kibbutz. Beginning with breakfast in a kibbutz dwelling, he describes the various tastes of fish, tomatoes, cucumbers, and cheese and, briefly, the appearance of the house both from inside and from without. As he and his host move away from the kibbutz toward the citrus groves, he evokes a third sense, touch, as the warm breeze from the sea and rays of the sun reach him. He also comments that the air is sweet. As he and his host pass through the citrus to the banana groves and beyond them to the Roman ruins, and then continue the cycle until they end up back at the kibbutz, he constantly evokes other sensuous details — the sight of green grass waving white in the wind, the taste of tangerines, the strong odor of cattle.

Throughout this sensuous description of his day, Bellow weaves warnings that this peaceful, almost pagan atmosphere can suddenly be disrupted. He first warns us in the opening paragraph where he contrasts the two dogs: Lucky, who is old and nervous from his experiences of war, and Mississippi, who seems to be a dog of peacetime Israel. Bellow frequently mentions also John's son who was killed in the Golan. These dark details in the bright day prepare us for Bellow's concluding paragraph that cements our sense of the precariousness of the Israeli existence.

Describing a place.   Description involves both content and arrangement. You need to be concerned both with what you want to say about the place and the manner in which to present your subject to the reader.

Description of a place generally involves two aspects: how a place is experienced sensuously — by the senses — and how it is experienced emotionally. A good description may concentrate on either the sensuous or the emotional, or it may combine them. The sensuous description usually evokes primarily visual details, because sight is ordinarily our strongest sense and the one on which we depend the most, although smells, sounds, and even taste and touch may be brought to bear on what the writer wishes the reader to experience. A mood description, which seeks to implant a particular emotion about a place, may use sensuous details, or the writer may employ emotional scenes or encounters or additional, nonsensuous information in the description of the place.

In this chapter, for example, E. B. White's and James Agee's essays are largely mood pieces infused with sensuous detail. Visual details are present as are sounds, smells, taste, and touch, and they use them very skillfully in conveying their emotional reactions. Eldridge Cleaver employs sound and sight in evoking the mood of Folsom Prison, but the bulk of his essay concentrates on the interactions among the prisoners, and between the prisoners and the authorities, to convey what the prison is like.

Saul Bellow uses the senses in describing his place — the kibbutz — even more than do White, Agee, and Cleaver, as his purpose is to contrast the fruitful lushness of the land with the fear the people constantly experience. Sensuous and emotional details are here played off against each other. While Joan Didion uses some sensuous detail, her description of Las Vegas focuses on the ironies of a city where call girls and brides, casinos and bridal chapels coexist. Her description is largely intellectual, although mood and the senses contribute to the irony of her essay.

The object of description is to aid your reader in sharing your experience of the place. This sharing is done by supplying details that paint a picture or evoke a mood. The more vividly these details are presented, the more vividly the scene is shared by the reader.

The arrangement of description depends upon one's purpose in writing. If purely sensuous description is the aim, then the writer can choose one of several spatial or visual patterns or orientations for describing the place:

Left to right (for rooms, stages, or landscapes)
Top to bottom (for buildings, people, or objects)
Outer to inner (for buildings, or other places that permit several perspectives: the Grand Canyon, for example)
Main impression to detail (similar to the motion-film technique of "panning"; for places, objects, or people)

The other sense impressions can be described as one moves along visually, or the essay can be divided into sections for the different senses: sight, followed by sounds, smells. It is also possible, of course, to describe a place as though you were blind, and to let the senses other than sight dominate.

In writing a mood piece, any spatial pattern can be used to organize the description. However, main-impression-to-detail (or its reverse) is the most frequent pattern of arrangement. The writer states the main impression (mood) of the place and then proceeds to support that impression with details, or uses details to lead to a conclusion about the emotional atmosphere. The writer of a mood description may also work out two arrangements simultaneously: one for the mood of the piece, the other for the sensuous details.

Several of the writers in this chapter use a climactic arrangement in presenting the details of their places. White begins with relaxed moments shared with his son and gradually builds up to the terror of his final dual experience. Agee follows a similar arrangement of presenting casual details that swell imperceptibly to his final climactic sentence. Bellow, as we have seen above, spatially moves the reader in a circle from kibbutz dwelling to citrus and banana groves to Roman ruins and then back to groves and dwelling, while simultaneously he leads the reader emotionally from the family life of the kibbutz with its relative harmony to the terror facing Israel politically. Cleaver moves from his cell to the rest of the prison in an inner-to-outer spatial pattern, while moving the reader emotionally from his daily routines to the larger implications for our society of life in prison.

Didion, however, who describes Las Vegas on a more abstract plane, uses none of the four descriptive patterns, but instead employs a cause-and-effect organization more appropriate for her purpose.

Procedures to follow in describing a place.

    A. What is the purpose of your description? Is it sensuous or emotional or a combination?

    B. Observe what details must be included to convey the main impression. What details could be omitted without distortion or blurring?

    C. Determine how best to present your description. The following are two useful patterns of organization that work for both types of description:

        1. Begin with an overall impression and then add contributing details.
        2. Begin with details and conclude with an overall impression for a climactic effect.

    D. For purely sensuous description, choose a pattern that works from left to right, inner to outer, top to bottom, or the reverse of any of these. Follow your order carefully so as not to confuse your reader.

 E. B. WHITE

Once More to the Lake

One summer, along about 1904, my father rented a camp on a lake in Maine and took us all there for the month of August. We all got ringworm from some kittens and had to rub Pond's Extract on our arms and legs night and morning, and my father rolled over in a canoe with all his clothes on; but outside of that the vacation was a success and from then on none of us ever thought there was any place in the world like that lake in Maine. We returned summer after summer — always on August 1st for one month. I have since become a salt-water man, but sometimes in summer there are days when the restlessness of the tides and the fearful cold of the sea water and the incessant wind which blows across the afternoon and into the evening make me wish for the placidity of a lake in the woods. A few weeks ago this feeling got so strong I bought myself a couple of bass hooks and a spinner and returned to the lake where we used to go, for a week's fishing and to revisit old haunts.

I took along my son, who had never had any fresh water up his nose and who had seen lily pads only from train windows. On the journey to the lake I began to wonder what it would be like. I wondered how time would have marred this unique, this holy spot — the coves and streams, the hills that the sun set behind, the camps and the paths behind the camps. I was sure the tarred road would have found it out and I wondered in what other ways it would be desolated. It is strange how much you can remember about places like that once you allow your mind to return into the grooves which lead back. You remember one thing, and that suddenly reminds you of another thing. I guess I remembered clearest of all the early mornings, when the lake was cool and motionless, remembered how the bedroom smelled of the lumber it was made of and of the wet woods whose scent entered through the screen. The partitions in the camp were thin and did not extend clear to the top of the rooms, and as I was always the first up I would dress softly so as not to wake the others, and sneak out into the sweet outdoors and start out in the canoe, keeping close along the shore in the long shadows of the pines. I remembered being very careful never to rub my paddle against the gunwale for fear of disturbing the stillness of the cathedral.

The lake had never been what you would call a wild lake.

There were cottages sprinkled around the shores, and it was in farming country although the shores of the lake were quite heavily wooded. Some of the cottages were owned by nearby farmers, and you would live at the shore and eat your meals at the farmhouse. That's what our family did. But although it wasn't wild, it was a fairly large and undisturbed lake and there were places in it which, to a child at least, seemed infinitely remote and primeval.

I was right about the tar: it led to within half a mile of the shore. But when I got back there, with my boy, and we settled into a camp near a farmhouse and into the kind of summertime I had known, I could tell that it was going to be pretty much the same as it had been before — I knew it, lying in bed the first morning, smelling the bedroom, and hearing the boy sneak quietly out and go off along the shore in a boat. I began to sustain the illusion that he was I, and therefore, by simple transposition, that I was my father. This sensation persisted, kept cropping up all the time we were there. It was not an entirely new feeling, but in this setting it grew much stronger. I seemed to be living a dual existence. I would be in the middle of some simple act, I would be picking up a bait box or laying down a table fork, or I would be saying something, and suddenly it would be not I but my father who was saying the words or making the gesture. It gave me a creepy sensation.

We went fishing the first morning. I felt the same damp moss covering the worms in the bait can, and saw the dragonfly alight on the tip of my rod as it hovered a few inches from the surface of the water. It was the arrival of this fly that convinced me beyond any doubt that everything was as it always had been, that the years were a mirage and there had been no years. The small waves were the same, chucking the rowboat under the chin as we fished at anchor, and the boat was the same boat, the same color green and the ribs broken in the same places, and under the floor-boards the same freshwater leavings and debris — the dead helgramite,* the wisps of moss, the rusty discarded fishook, the dried blood from yesterday's catch. We stared silently at the tips of our rods, at the dragonflies that came and went. I lowered the tip of mine into the water, tentatively, pensively dislodging the fly, which darted two feet away, posed, darted two feet back, and came to rest again a little farther up the rod. There had been no years between the ducking of this dragonfly and the other one — the one that was part of memory. I looked at the boy, who was silently watching his fly, and it was my hands that held his rod, my eyes watching. I felt dizzy and didn't know which rod I was at the end of.

We caught two bass, hauling them in briskly as though they were mackerel, pulling them over the side of the boat in a businesslike manner without any landing net, and stunning them with a blow on the

---

* The nymph of the May-fly, used as bait.

back of the head. When we got back for a swim before lunch, the lake was exactly where we had left it, the same number of inches from the dock, and there was only the merest suggestion of a breeze. This seemed an utterly enchanted sea, this lake you could leave to its own devices for a few hours and come back to, and find that it had not stirred, this constant and trustworthy body of water. In the shallows, the dark, water-soaked sticks and twigs, smooth and old, were undulating in clusters on the bottom against the clean ribbed sand, and the track of the mussel was plain. A school of minnows swam by, each minnow with its small individual shadow, doubling the attendance, so clear and sharp in the sunlight. Some of the other campers were in swimming, along the shore, one of them with a cake of soap, and the water felt thin and clear and insubstantial. Over the years there had been this person with the cake of soap, this cultist, and here he was. There had been no years.

Up to the farmhouse to dinner through the teeming, dusty field, the road under our sneakers was only a two-track road. The middle track was missing, the one with the marks of the hooves and the splotches of dried, flaky manure. There had always been three tracks to choose from in choosing which track to walk in; now the choice was narrowed down to two. For a moment I missed terribly the middle alternative. But the way led past the tennis court, and something about the way it lay there in the sun reassured me; the tape had loosened along the backline, the alleys were green with plantains and other weeds, and the net (installed in June and removed in September) sagged in the dry noon, and the whole place steamed with midday heat and hunger and emptiness. There was a choice of pie for dessert, and one was blueberry and one was apple, and the waitresses were the same country girls, there having been no passage of time, only the illusion of it as in a dropped curtain — the waitresses were still fifteen; their hair had been washed, that was the only difference — they had been to the movies and seen the pretty girls with the clean hair.

Summertime, oh summertime, pattern of life indelible, the fade-proof lake, the woods unshatterable, the pasture with the sweet fern and the juniper forever and ever, summer without end; this was the background, and the life along the shore was the design, the cottages with their innocent and tranquil design, their tiny docks with the flagpole and the American flag floating against the white clouds in the blue sky, the little paths over the roots of the trees leading from camp to camp and the paths leading back to the outhouses and the can of lime for sprinkling, and at the souvenir counters at the store the miniature birch-bark canoes and the post cards that showed things looking a little better than they looked. This was the American family at play, escaping the city heat, wondering whether the newcomers in the camp at the head of the cove were "common" or "nice," wondering whether it was true that the people who drove up for Sunday dinner at the farmhouse were turned away because there wasn't enough chicken.

It seemed to me, as I kept remembering all this, that those times and those summers had been infinitely precious and worth saving. There had been jollity and peace and goodness. The arriving (at the beginning of August) had been so big a business in itself, at the railway station the farm wagon drawn up, the first smell of the pine-laden air, the first glimpse of the smiling farmer, and the great importance of the trunks and your father's enormous authority in such matters, and the feel of the wagon under you for the long ten-mile haul, and at the top of the last long hill catching the first view of the lake after eleven months of not seeing this cherished body of water. The shouts and cries of the other campers when they saw you, and the trunks to be unpacked, to give up their rich burden. (Arriving was less exciting nowadays, when you sneaked up in your car and parked it under a tree near the camp and took out the bags and in five minutes it was all over, no fuss, no loud wonderful fuss about trunks.)

Peace and goodness and jollity. The only thing that was wrong now, really, was the sound of the place, an unfamiliar nervous sound of the outboard motors. This was the note that jarred, the one thing that would sometimes break the illusion and set the years moving. In those other summertimes all motors were inboard; and when they were at a little distance, the noise they made was a sedative, an ingredient of summer sleep. They were one-cylinder and two-cylinder engines, and some were make-and-break and some were jump-spark,* but they all made a sleepy sound across the lake. The one-lungers throbbed and fluttered and the twin-cylinder ones purred and purred, and that was a quiet sound too. But now the campers all had outboards. In the daytime, in the hot mornings, these motors made a petulant, irritable sound; at night, in the still evening when the afterglow lit the water, they whined about one's ears like mosquitoes. My boy loved our rented outboard, and his great desire was to achieve singlehanded mastery over it, and authority, and he soon learned the trick of choking it a little (but not too much), and the adjustment of the needle valve. Watching him I would remember the things you could do with the old one-cylinder engine with the heavy flywheel, how you could have it eating out of your hand if you got really close to it spiritually. Motor boats in those days didn't have clutches, and you would make a landing by shutting off the motor at the proper time and coasting in with a dead rudder. But there was a way of reversing them, if you learned the trick, by cutting the switch and putting it on again exactly on the final dying revolution of the flywheel, so that it would kick back against compression and begin reversing. Approaching a dock in a strong following breeze, it

* Methods of ignition timing.

was difficult to slow up sufficiently by the ordinary coasting method, and if a boy felt he had complete mastery over his motor, he was tempted to keep it running beyond its time and then reverse it a few feet from the dock. It took a cool nerve, because if you threw the switch a twentieth of a second too soon you would catch the flywheel when it still had speed enough to go up past center, and the boat would leap ahead, charging bull-fashion at the dock.

We had a good week at the camp. The bass were biting well and the sun shone endlessly, day after day. We would be tired at night and lie down in the accumulated heat of the little bedrooms after the long hot day and the breeze would stir almost imperceptibly outside and the smell of the swamp drift in through the rusty screens. Sleep would come easily and in the morning the red squirrel would be on the roof, tapping out his gay routine. I kept remembering everything, lying in bed in the morning — the small steamboat that had a long rounded stern like the lip of a Ubangi, and how quietly she ran on the moonlight sails; when the older boys played their mandolins and the girls sang and we ate doughnuts dipped in sugar, and how sweet the music was on the water in the shining light, and what it had felt like to think about girls then. After breakfast we would go up to the store and the things were in the same place — the minnows in a bottle, the plugs and spinners disarranged and pawed over by the youngsters from the boys' camp, the fig newtons and the Beeman's gum. Outside, the road was tarred and cars stood in front of the store. Inside, all was just as it had always been, except there was more Coca-Cola and not so much Moxie and root beer and birch beer and sarsaparilla. We would walk out with a bottle of pop apiece and sometimes the pop would backfire up our noses and hurt. We explored the streams, quietly, where the turtles slid off the sunny logs and dug their way into the soft bottom; and we lay on the town wharf and fed worms to the tame bass. Everywhere we went I had trouble making out which was I, the one walking at my side, the one walking in my pants.

One afternoon while we were there at that lake a thunderstorm came up. It was like the revival of an old melodrama that I had seen long ago with childish awe. The second-act climax of the drama of the electrical disturbance over a lake in America had not changed in any important respect. This was the big scene, still the big scene. The whole thing was so familiar, the first feeling of oppression and heat and a general air around camp of not wanting to go very far away. In midafternoon (it was all the same) a curious darkening of the sky, and a lull in everything that had made life tick; and then the way the boats suddenly swung the other way at their moorings with the coming of a breeze out of the new quarter, and the premonitory rumble. Then the kettle drum, then the snare, then the bass drum and cymbals, then crackling light against the dark, and the gods grinning and licking their chops in the hills. Afterward the calm, the rain steadily rustling in the calm lake, the return of light and hope and spirits, and the campers running out in joy and relief to go swimming in the rain, their bright cries perpetuating the deathless joke about how they were getting simply drenched, and the children screaming with delight at the new sensation of bathing in the rain, and the joke about getting drenched linking the generations in a strong indestructible chain. And the comedian who waded in carrying an umbrella.

When the others went swimming my son said he was going in too. He pulled his dripping trunks from the line where they had hung all through the shower, and wrung them out. Languidly, and with no thought of going in, I watched him, his hard little body, skinny and bare, saw him wince slightly as he pulled up around his vitals the small, soggy, icy garment. As he buckled the swollen belt suddenly my groin felt the chill of death.

PROBING FOR   1. White describes the Maine lake as a "holy spot." What details
MEANING   from the essay defend this description?

2. What particular features distinguish this lake from others?

3. What does the author mean by "I seemed to be living a dual existence"? What importance does this statement have for the essay?

4. "Arriving was less exciting nowadays." What other differences does the author discover between his childhood and adult visits to the lake?

5. What does the last sentence mean? Does it have any connection with the rest of the essay?

PROBING FOR   1. White describes the reflection of the tall pines on the surface of the
METHOD   lake as a "cathedral." What other similes and metaphors does he use?

2. Did White have to limit his topic? What might his broader topic have been? What sentence might be his thesis sentence?

3. What was White's purpose in writing his essay? How would you categorize the audience he is writing for?

4. Does White at any point in the essay foreshadow the last sentence? Does he prepare us for it in any way?

Organizing the Paper

What framework is evident in White's essay?   White first gives the reader some background on his earlier visits to the lake, and also a general description of the lake, before developing the main idea of his essay: the "dual existence" experiences. His outline might have looked like the following:

I. Introduction (paragraphs 1 to 3)
   A. Background (paragraph 1)

White's essay is long, no doubt longer than any you will have to write, and he takes three paragraphs to supply background before introducing his thesis statement in paragraph 4. In these paragraphs he adopts a folksy tone about summer vacations, thus drawing his audience into his experience. He then presents his thesis statement: "I began to sustain the illusion that he was I, and therefore, by simple transposition, that I was my father." The order of the middle of the essay is climactic. He begins with relaxed experiences — fishing, dinner at the farmhouse, the arriving — and moves slowly to a climax through the unpleasant sound of the motorboats to the resounding conclusion about these experiences that no matter what he does he is living a "dual existence," and finally to the thunderstorm and his realization of the meaning of this strange experience. The essay ends, therefore, not with a simple summary, but with a resounding revelation of the significance of all that has gone before.

Organizing the paper.   Good writing results from much effort. One important step in writing the essay, which is time-consuming but necessary, is developing the outline. The outline helps you focus sharply on a subject by eliminating wandering from the subject, repeating earlier points, or neglecting major aspects of the subject. The outline also helps the writer focus on the order in which he presents his points.

There are at least two ways of approaching the organization of an essay through outlining. The traditional method is to list all aspects of a topic, arrange them in appropriate sequence, and proceed to write. Many writers find that a second method works better since they do not know what they want to say until they actually begin writing. These writers prefer to make their outlines after they have written a first draft. With all their ideas down on paper, they then sort them into a logical sequence. After changing, rearranging, eliminating, and/or adding, they proceed to the final draft.

There are various patterns of organization, and we will be exploring some of these in this and subsequent chapters: spatial order (pp. 62–64 above), chronological order (Chapter 3, pp. 111–113), cause-to-effect or effect-to-cause (Chapter 4, pp. 165–167), comparisons and contrasts (Chapter 5, pp. 221–223). Other patterns that may be adapted to an essay, often in combination, regardless of the subject matter, are familiar-to-unfamiliar (Anderson, Ralbovsky, Agee) whole-to-part (Didion) or part-to-whole (Bellow, White), climactic order (White, Bellow, Agee, Anderson), or particular-to-general (Orwell) or general-to-particular (Didion).

These patterns apply largely to the middle, or body, of the essay. The introduction has a dual function: to interest the reader in the essay and to give him or her some idea of its purpose (the thesis statement is usually located in this paragraph). The introduction should present the subject in such a way as to make the audience aware that the writer is interested in the reader's reactions to his subject matter.

The conclusion to a short essay should do more than simply summarize the paper; only in long essays, where the reader might forget earlier points is the summary conclusion effective. The conclusion instead should present to the reader aspects of the subject about which he or she might think further. It should also leave an impact on the reader's mind. Most important, it should have a note of finality that assures the reader that the essay has been concluded.

Procedures to follow in organizing your paper.

A. Write your thesis sentence at the top of the page, making sure it is phrased as clearly as possible.

B. Make an outline under the first method: (1) List all of the ideas that occur to you in thinking about your topic. (2) Once you have made an extensive list, rearrange the items into headings and subheadings. Your headings will form the major points that will later constitute the body of your paper. (3) Group all the other items under the major headings, eliminating those that, on second thought, obviously do not fit in. Your subheadings should develop your headings, just as your headings develop your paper topic. (4) Check to see that each division is distinct from the others to avoid overlapping. (5) Determine if any major points have been omitted. (6) Arrange your points in a logical order.

C. If you prefer the second method of outlining, begin with a first draft of your topic. Next, make an outline based on the draft, with each paragraph topic a heading and each example supporting the topic a subheading. Scrutinize your outline carefully. Does each heading belong? Are any repeated? Are the points arranged in a logical order? What other points can you now think of to include? Once you have answered these questions and made the necessary adjustments, you are ready to begin the final draft.

 JAMES AGEE

Knoxville: Summer 1915

We are talking now of summer evenings in Knoxville, Tennessee in the time that I lived there so successfully disguised to myself as a child. It was a little bit mixed sort of block, fairly solidly lower middle class, with one or two juts apiece on either side of that. The houses corresponded: middle-sized gracefully fretted wood houses built in the late nineties and early nineteen hundreds, with small front and side and more spacious back yards, and trees in the yards, and porches. These were softwooded trees, poplars, tulip trees, cottonwoods. There were fences around one or two of the houses, but mainly the yards ran into each other with only now and then a low hedge that wasn't doing very well. There were few good friends among the grown people, and they were not poor enough for the other sort of intimate acquaintance, but everyone nodded and spoke, and even might talk short times, trivially, and at the two extremes of the general or the particular, and ordinarily nextdoor neighbors talked quite a bit when they happened to run into each other, and never paid calls. The men were mostly small businessmen, one or two very modestly executives, one or two worked with their hands, most of them clerical, and most of them between thirty and forty-five.

But it is of these evenings, I speak.

Supper was at six and was over by half past. There was still daylight, shining softly and with a tarnish, like the lining of a shell; and the carbon lamps lifted at the corners were on in the light, and the locusts were started, and the fire flies were out, and a few frogs were flopping in the dewy grass, by the time the fathers and the children came out. The children ran out first hell bent and yelling those names by which they were known; then the fathers sank out leisurely in crossed suspenders, their collars removed and their necks looking tall and shy. The mothers stayed back in the kitchen washing and drying, putting things away, recrossing their traceless footsteps like the lifetime journeys of bees, measuring out the dry cocoa for breakfast. When they came out they had taken off their aprons and their skirts were dampened and they sat in rockers on their porches quietly.

It is not of the games children play in the evening that I want to speak now, it is of a contemporaneous atmosphere that has little to do with them: that of the fathers of families, each in his space of lawn, his shirt fishlike pale in the unnatural light and his face nearly anonymous, hosing their lawns. The hoses were attached at spigots that stood out of the brick foundations of the houses. The nozzles were variously set but usually so there was a long sweet stream of spray, the nozzle wet in the hand, the water trickling the right forearm and the peeled-back cuff, and the water whishing out a long loose and low-curved cone, and so gentle a sound. First an insane noise of violence in the nozzle, then the still irregular sound of adjustment, then the smoothing into steadiness and a pitch as accurately tuned to the size and style of stream as any violin. So many qualities of sound out of one hose: so many choral differences out of those several hoses that were in earshot. Out of any one hose, the almost dead silence of the release, and the short still arch of the separate big drops, silent as a held breath, and the only noise the flattering noise on leaves and the slapped grass at the fall of each big drop. That, and the intense hiss with the intense stream; that, and that same intensity not growing less but growing more quiet and delicate with the turn of the nozzle, up to that extreme tender whisper when the water was just a wide bell of film. Chiefly, though, the hoses were set much alike, in a compromise between distance and tenderness of spray (and quite surely a sense of art behind this compromise, and a quiet deep joy, too real to recognize itself), and the sounds therefore were pitched much alike; pointed by the snorting start of a new hose; decorated by some man playful with the nozzle; left empty, like God by the sparrow's fall, when any single one of them desists: and all, though near alike, of various pitch; and in this unison. These sweet pale streamings in the light lift out their pallors and their voices all together, mothers hushing their children, the hushing unnaturally prolonged, the men gentle and silent and each snail-like withdrawn into the quietude of what he singly is doing, the urination of huge children stood loosely military against an invisible wall, and gentle happy and peaceful, tasting the mean goodness of their living like the last of their suppers in their mouths; while the locusts carry on this noise of hoses on their much higher and sharper key. The noise of the locust is dry, and it seems not to be rasped or vibrated but urged from him as if through a small orifice by a breath that can never give out. Also there is never one locust but an illusion of at least a thousand. The noise of each locust is pitched in some classic locust range out of which none of them varies more than two full tones: and yet you seem to hear each locust discrete from all the rest, and there is a long, slow, pulse in their noise, like the scarcely defined arch of a long and high set bridge. They are all around in every tree, so that the noise seems to come from nowhere and every-where at once, from the whole shell heaven, shivering in your flesh and teasing your eardrums, the boldest of all the sounds of night. And yet it is habitual to summer nights, and is of the great order of noises, like the noises of the sea and of the blood her precocious grandchild, which you realize you are hearing only when you catch yourself listening. Mean-time from low in the dark, just outside the swaying horizons of the hoses, conveying always grass in the damp of dew and its strong green-black smear of smell, the regular yet spaced noises of the crickets, each a sweet cold silver noise threenoted, like the slipping each time of three matched links of a small chain.

But the men by now, one by one, have silenced their hoses and drained and coiled them. Now only two, and now only one, is left, and you see only ghostlike shirt with the sleeve garters, and sober mystery of his mild face like the lifted face of large cattle enquiring of your presence in a pitchdark pool of meadow; and now he too is gone; and it has become that time of evening when people sit on their porches, rocking gently and talking gently and watching the street and the standing up into their sphere of possession of the trees, of birds' hung havens, hangars. People go by; things go by. A horse, drawing a buggy, breaking his hollow iron music on the asphalt; a loud auto; a quiet auto; people in pairs, not in a hurry, scuffling, switching their weight of aestival body, talking casually, the taste hovering over them of vanilla, strawberry, pasteboard and starched milk, the image upon them of lovers and horsemen, squared with clowns in hueless amber. A street car raising its iron moan; stopping, belling and starting; stertorous; rousing and raising again its iron increasing moan and swimming its gold windows and straw seats on past and past and past, the bleak spark crackling and cursing above it like a small malignant spirit set to dog its tracks; the iron whine rises on rising speed; still risen, faints; halts; the faint stinging bell; rises again, still fainter; fainting, lifting, lifts, faints forgone: forgotten. Now is the night one blue dew.

Now is the night one blue dew, my father has drained, he has coiled the hose.
Low on the length of lawns, a frailing of fire who breathes.
Content, silver, like peeps of light, each cricket makes his comment over and over in the drowned grass.
A cold toad thumpily flounders.
Within the edges of damp shadows of side yards are hovering chil-dren nearly sick with joy of fear, who watch the unguarding of a telephone pole.
Around white carbon corner lamps bugs of all sizes are lifted elliptic,

solar systems. Big hardshells bruise themselves, assailant: he is
fallen on his back, legs squiggling.
Parents on porches: rock and rock: From damp strings morning
glories: hang their ancient faces.
The dry and exalted noise of the locusts from all the air at once en-
chants my eardrums.

On the rough wet grass of the back yard my father and mother
have spread quilts. We all lie there, my mother, my father, my uncle,
my aunt, and I too am lying there. First we were sitting up, then one of
us lay down, and then we all lay down, on our stomachs, or on our
sides, or on our backs, and they have kept on talking. They are not
talking much, and the talk is quiet, of nothing in particular, of nothing
at all in particular, of nothing at all. The stars are wide and alive, they
seem each like a smile of great sweetness, and they seem very near. All
my people are larger bodies than mine, quiet, with voices gentle and
meaningless like the voices of sleeping birds. One is an artist, he is living at home. One is a musician, she is living at home. One is my mother
who is good to me. One is my father who is good to me. By some
chance, here they are, all on this earth; and who shall ever tell the sorrow of being on this earth, lying, on quilts, on the grass, in a summer
evening, among the sounds of the night. May God bless my people, my
uncle, my aunt, my mother, my good father, oh, remember them kindly
in their time of trouble; and in the hour of their taking away.

After a little I am taken in and put to bed. Sleep, soft smiling,
draws me unto her: and those receive me, who quietly treat me, as one
familiar and well-beloved in that home: but will not, oh, will not, not
now, not ever; but will not ever tell me who I am.

PROBING FOR
MEANING

1. What does Agee mean when he describes his neighborhood as
"solidly lower middle class"?

2. What sounds does Agee describe in the essay? What kind of feelings does he seem to associate with the sounds of a summer evening in Knoxville in 1915?

3. Why is Agee concerned at the end with his identity? What meaning does the last paragraph of the essay convey?

4. What is the overall impression that Agee offers of Knoxville in the
summer of 1915?

PROBING FOR
METHOD

1. Why does Agee focus as much if not more on sound than on sight
in his description?

2. What significance does the image of the men who are watering
their lawns hold?

3. Why does Agee compare the sound of the locusts to "the noises of
the sea and of the blood her precocious grandchild"? What other similes does
Agee use?

4. The language of the first paragraph is fairly straightforward and declarative. How does the language change after that? What is the effect of the verses toward the end? Why does Agee end the essay with a prayer?

 ELDRIDGE CLEAVER

A Day in Folsom Prison

Folsom Prison, September 19, 1965

My day begins officially at 7:00, when all inmates are required to get out of bed and stand before their cell doors to be counted by guards who walk along the tier saying, "1, 2, 3 . . ." However, I never remain in bed until 7. I'm usually up by 5:30. The first thing I do is make up my bed. Then I pick up all my books, newspapers, etc., off the floor of my cell and spread them over my bed to clear the floor for calisthenics. In my cell, I have a little stool on which I lay a large plywood board, about 2½ by 3 feet, which I use as a typing and writing table. At night, I load this makeshift table down with books and papers, and when I read at night I spill things all over the floor. When I leave my cell, I set this board, loaded down, on my bed, so that if a guard comes into my cell to search it, he will not knock the board off the stool, as has happened before. Still in the nude, the way I sleep, I go through my routine: kneebends, butterflies, touching my toes, squats, windmills. I continue for about half an hour.

Sometimes, if I have something I want to write or type so that I can mail it that morning, I forgo my calisthenics. But this is unusual. (We are required, if we want our mail to go out on a certain day, to have it in the mailbox by about 8:00. When we leave our cells at 7:30 to go to breakfast, we pass right by the mailbox and drop in our mail on the way to mess hall.)

Usually, by the time I finish my calisthenics, the trustee (we call him tiertender, or keyman) comes by and fills my little bucket with hot water. We don't have hot running water ourselves. Each cell has a small sink with a cold-water tap, a bed, a locker, a shelf or two along the wall, and a commode. The trustee has a big bucket, with a long spout like the ones people use to water their flowers, only without the sprinkler. He pokes the spout through the bars and pours you about a gallon of hot water. My cell door doesn't have bars on it; it is a solid slab of steel with fifty-eight holes in it about the size of a half dollar, and a slot in the center, at eye level, about an inch wide and five inches long. The trustee sticks the spout through one of the little holes and pours my hot water, and in the evenings the guard slides my mail in to me through the slot. Through the same slot the convicts pass newspapers, books, candy, and cigarettes to one another.

When the guard has mail for me he stops at the cell door and calls my name, and I recite my number — A29498 — to verify that I am the right Cleaver. When I get mail I avert my eyes so I can't see who it's from. Then I sit down on my bed and peep at it real slowly, like a poker player peeping at his cards. I can feel when I've got a letter from you, and when I peep up on your name on the envelope I let out a big yell. It's like having four aces. But if the letter is not from you, it's like having two deuces, a three, a four, and a five, all in scrambled suits. A bum kick. Nothing. What is worse is when the guard passes my door without pausing. I can hear his keys jingling. If he stops at my door the keys sound like Christmas bells ringing, but if he keeps going they just sound like — keys.

I live in the honor block. In the other blocks, the fronts of the cells consist of nothing but bars. When I first moved into the honor block, I didn't like it at all. The cells seemed made for a dungeon. The heavy steel doors slammed shut with a clang of finality that chilled my soul. The first time that door closed on me I had the same wild, hysterical sensation I'd felt years ago at San Quentin when they first locked me in solitary. For the briefest moment I felt like yelling out for help, and it seemed that in no circumstances would I be able to endure that cell. All in that split second I felt like calling out to the guards, pleading with them to let me out of the cell, begging them to let me go, promising them that I would be a good boy in the future.

But just as quickly as the feeling came, it went, dissolved, and I felt at peace with myself. I felt that I could endure anything, everything, even the test of being broken on the rack. I've been in every type of cell they have in the prisons of California, and the door to my present cell seems the most cruel and ugly of all. However, I have grown to like this door. When I go out of my cell, I can hardly wait to get back in, to slam that cumbersome door, and hear the sharp click as the trustee snaps the lock behind me. The trustees keep the keys to the cells of the honor block all day, relinquishing them at night, and to get into your cell, all you have to do is round up the trustee in charge of your tier. Once inside my cell, I feel safe: I don't have to watch the other convicts any more or the guards in the gun towers. If you live in a cell with nothing but bars on the front, you cannot afford to relax; someone can walk along the tier and throw a Molotov cocktail in on you before you know it, something I've seen happen in San Quentin. Whenever I live in one of those barred cells, I keep a blanket within easy reach in case of emergency, to smother a fire if need be. Paranoia? Yes, but it's the least one can do for oneself. In my present cell, with its impregnable door, I don't worry about sabotage — although if someone wanted to badly enough, they could figure something out.

Well . . . after I've finished my calisthenics and the hot water has arrived, I take me a bird (jailbird) bath in the little sink. It's usually about 6:00 by then. From then until 7:30, when we are let out for breakfast, I clean up my cell and try to catch a little news over the radio. Radio? — each cell has a pair of earphones! — with only two channels on it. The programs are monitored from the radio room. The radio schedule is made up by the radio committee, of which I am a member.

At 7:30, breakfast. From the mess hall, every day except Saturday, my day off, I go straight to the bakery, change into my white working clothes, and that's me until about noon. From noon, I am "free" until 3:20, the evening mandatory lockup, when we are required, again, to stand before our cell doors and be counted. There is another count at 6:30 P.M. — three times every day without fail.

When I'm through working in the bakery, I have the choice of (1) going to my cell; (2) staying in the dining room to watch TV; (3) going down to the library; or (4) going out to the yard to walk around, sit in the sun, lift weights, play some funny game — like checkers, chess, marbles, horseshoes, handball, baseball, shuffleboard, beating on the punching bag, basketball, talk, TV, paddle-tennis, watching the other convicts who are watching other convicts. When I first came to Folsom, I was astonished to see the old grizzled cons playing marbles. The marble players of Folsom are legendary throughout the prison system: I first heard about them years ago. There is a sense of ultimate defeat about them. Some guy might boast about how he is going to get out next time and stay out, and someone will put him down by saying he'll soon be back, playing marbles like a hasbeen, a neverwas, blasted back into childhood by a crushing defeat to his final dream. The marble players have the game down to an art, and they play all day long, fanatically absorbed in what they are doing.

If I have a cell partner who knows the game, I play him chess now and then, maybe a game each night. I have a chess set of my own and sometimes when I feel like doing nothing else, I take out a little envelope in which I keep a collection of chess problems clipped from newspapers, and run off one or two. But I have never been able to give all my time to one of these games. I am seldom able to play a game of chess out on the yard. Whenever I go out on the yard these days, I'm usually on my way to the library.

On the yard there is a little shack off to one corner which is the office of the Inmates Advisory Council (IAC). Sometimes I visit the

shack to shoot the bull and get the latest drawings (news). And sometimes I go to the weight-lifting area, strip down to a pair of trunks, and
push a little iron for a while and soak up the sun.

At 3:20, lockup. Stand for count. After count, off to the evening
meal. Back to the cell. Stand for count at 6:30. After the 6:30 count, we
are all let out of our cells, one tier at a time, for showers, to exchange
dirty socks and towels for clean ones, a haircut, then back to the cell. I
duck this crush by taking my showers in the bakery. At night, I only go
to exchange my linen. In the honor block, we are allowed to come out
after 6:30 count every Saturday, Sunday, and Wednesday night to
watch TV until 10:00, before we are locked up for the night. The only
time I went out for TV was to dig the broads on Shindig and Holly-
wood-A-Go-Go, but those programs don't come on anymore. We recently got the rule changed so that, on TV nights, those in the honor
block can type until 10:00. It used to be that no typing was allowed after
8:00. I am very pleased to be able to get in that extra typing time: I can
write you more letters.

On Thursday I go out of my cell after the 6:30 count to attend
the weekly IAC meetings. These meetings adjourn promptly at 9:00.
On Saturday mornings, my day off, I usually attend the meeting of the
Gavel Club, but this past Saturday I was in the middle of my last letter
to you and I stole away to my cell. I enjoyed it so much that I am
tempted to put the Gavel Club down, but I hope that I don't because
that's where I'm gaining some valuable experience and technique in
public speaking.

On the average I spend approximately seventeen hours a day in
my cell. I enjoy the solitude. The only drawback is that I am unable to
get the type of reading material I want, and there is hardly anyone with
a level head to talk to.

There are quite a few guys here who write. Seems that every
convict wants to. Some of them have managed to sell a piece here and
there. They have a writers' workshop which meets in the library under
the wing of our librarian. I've never had a desire to belong to this
workshop, partly because of my dislike for the attitude of the librarian
and partly because of the phony, funny-style convicts. Mostly, I suppose, it's because the members of the workshop are all white and all
sick when it comes to color. They're not all sick, but they're not for real.
They're fair-weather types, not even as lukewarm as good white liber-
als, and they conform to the Mississippi atmosphere prevalent here in
Folsom. Blacks and whites do not fraternize together in comfort here.
Harry Golden's concept of vertical integration and horizontal segregation about covers it. The whites want to talk with you out on the yard or
at work, standing up, but they shun you when it comes to sitting down.
For instance, when we line up for chow, the lines leading into the mess
halls are integrated. But once inside the mess hall, blacks sit at tables by
themselves and whites sit with themselves or with the Mexicans.

There's this one Jewish stud out of New York who fell out of Frisco. He thinks he is another Lenny Bruce. In point of fact he is funny and very glib, and I dig rapping (talking) with him. He's a hype but he is very down with the current scene. Says that he lived in North Beach and all that, and that he has this chick who writes him who is a member of the DuBois Club in Frisco. Well, this cat is well read and we exchange reading material. He says that at home he has every copy of *The Realist* published up to the time of his fall. *The Evergreen Review* kills him. We communicate pretty well and I know that stud is not a racist, but he is a conformist — which in my book is worse, more dangerous, than an out-and-out foe. The other day we were talking about the Free Speech Movement. He was reading a book by Paul Goodman, *Growing Up Absurd,* which he had with him. We were very hung up talking and then it. was time for lunch. We got in line and continued our conversation. He was trying to convince me that the whole FSM was predicated on the writings of Paul Goodman, and that he had heard, with his own ears, Mario Savio say as much. Then all of a sudden I noticed this cat grow leery and start looking all around. He made me nervous. I thought maybe someone was trying to sneak up on us with a knife or something. When he kept doing this, I asked him what the f--- was the matter with him. He turned real red and said that he "just remembered" that he had to talk to another fellow. I dug right away what the kick was, so I said, "later," and he split. I'm used to such scenes, having a 400-year heritage of learning to roll with that type of punch. I saw him in the mess hall looking very pushed out of shape. I had to laugh at him. I felt that he was probably thinking that if the whites put the blacks in the gas chambers they might grab him too if he was with me. That thought tickled me a little as I watched him peeping around like a ferret. One of his points of indignation is that, he says, he will never forgive Israel for kidnaping and killing Eichmann, and he gets mad at me because I take Israel's side, just to keep the conversation alive. Too much agreement kills a chat. What really bugs him is when I say that there are many blacks who, if they were in the position, would do a little rounding up of the Eichmann types in America. A few days later he told me, "You saw through me the other day, didn't you?"

"I see through you every day," I told him. He looked as if he expected or wanted me to hit him or something. I told him that he was good for nothing but to be somebody's jailhouse wife and he laughed, then launched into a Lenny Bruce-type monologue.

My own reaction is to have as little as possible to do with whites. I have no respect for a duck who runs up to me on the yard all buddy-buddy, and then feels obliged not to sit down with me. It's not that I'm dying to sit with him either, but there is a principle involved which cuts me deeply.

Talk about hypocrisy: you should see the library. We are allowed to order, from the state library, only non-fiction and law books.

Of the law books, we can only order books containing court opinion. We can get any decision of the California District Court of Appeals, the California Supreme Court, the U.S. District Courts, the Circuit Courts, and the U.S. Supreme Court. But books of an explanatory nature are prohibited. Many convicts who do not have lawyers are forced to act *in propria persona*. They do all right. But it would be much easier if they could get books that showed them how properly to plead their cause, how to prepare their petitions and briefs. This is a perpetual sore point with the Folsom Prison Bar Association, as we call ourselves.

All of the novels one *needs* to read are unavailable, and the librarian won't let you send for them. I asked him once if he had read a certain book.

"Oh, yes!" he exclaimed.

"What did you think of it?" I asked.

"Absolutely marvelous!" he said.

"How about letting me send to the state library for it?" I asked.

"No."

Books that one wants to read — so bad that it is a taste in the mouth, like Calvin C. Hernton's *Sex and Racism in America* — he won't let you have.

"The warden says 'no sex,' " is his perpetual squelch.

There is a book written by a New York judge which give case histories of prostitutes. The authors explore why white prostitutes, some of them from the deepest South, had Negroes for pimps, and I wanted to reread it.

"No sex," said the librarian. He is indifferent to the fact that it is a matter of life and death to me! I don't know how he justifies this because you can go over to the inmate canteen and buy all the prurient pot-boiling anti-literature that has ever been written. But everything that "is happening" today is verboten. I've been dying to read Norman Mailer's *An American Dream*, but that too is prohibited. You can have *Reader's Digest*, but *Playboy?* — not a chance. I have long wanted to file suit in Federal Court for the right to receive *Playboy* magazine. Do you think Hugh Hefner would finance such an action? I think some very nice ideas would be liberated.

The library does have a selection of very solid material, things done from ten years ago all the way back to the Bible. But it is unsatisfactory to a stud who is trying to function in the last half of the twentieth century. Go down there and try to find Hemingway, Mailer, Camus, Sartre, Baldwin, Henry Miller, Terry Southern, Julian Mayfield, Bellow, William Burroughs, Allen Ginsberg, Herbert Gold, Robert Gover, J. O. Killens, etc. — no action. They also have this sick thing going when it comes to books by and about Negroes. Robert F. Williams' book, *Negroes with Guns*, is not allowed anymore. I ordered it from the state library before it was too popular around here. I devoured it and let a few friends read it, before the librarian dug it and put it on the blacklist. Once I ordered two books from the inmate canteen with my own money. When they arrived here from the company, the librarian impounded them, placing them on my "property" the same as they did my notebooks.

I want to devote my time to reading and writing, with everything else secondary, but I can't do that in prison. I have to keep my eyes open at all times or I won't make it. There is always some madness going on, and whether you like it or not you're involved. There is no choice in the matter: you cannot sit and wait for things to come to you. So I engage in all kinds of petty intrigue which I've found necessary to survival. It consumes a lot of time and energy. But it is necessary.

PROBING FOR
MEANING

1. Why does Cleaver choose to relate the chronology of his day in describing Folsom Prison to his lawyer (the "you" of the essay)?

2. Cleaver writes of prison life with great restraint and understatement. In which paragraphs can you read between the lines and imagine he must feel or think more than he says? Are there situations in which he expresses himself or his emotions fully? Why does he vary his degree of honesty?

3. How would you characterize Cleaver from this essay? How is he different from the other convicts?

4. What is his reaction to Folsom Prison? Why does he choose these particular details of prison life to describe?

5. To what does "Harry Golden's concept of vertical integration and horizontal segregation" refer? Some conditions of Folsom which Cleaver describes characterize prison society but not the world beyond the walls. For example, censorship of mails, radio programs, and reading material applies only to prison. Does the concept of "vertical integration and horizontal segregation" pertain to the outside society as well? Explain.

PROBING FOR
METHOD

1. This essay depicts the author's attitude toward place even though it gives very little exact detail about place. You actually know very little about what the prison looks like. Instead, Cleaver uses selection of details and choice of words to convey the feeling of being in prison. What examples of careful selection of language and detail can you cite?

2. At what point in the essay does Cleaver use spatial description? Why has he elected to describe these parts of Folsom Prison and not others?

3. Cleaver's writing is designed to give emphasis to the claustrophobic prison atmosphere. Notice, for example, his fifth paragraph. What specific aspects of his style underscore the closed-in feeling?

4. What word would you use to describe the tone of this essay? What elements of Cleaver's style give support to tone? How does his audience affect his tone? Who is his audience?

5. This essay begins with a chronological organization but moves to a detailed discussion of important problems. At what point does this shift occur?

Is it smooth? What would have happened to the essay had Cleaver continued to write in strict chronological order? Is there a thesis to unify the entire essay?

 JOAN DIDION

Marrying Absurd

To be married in Las Vegas, Clark County, Nevada, a bride must swear that she is eighteen or has parental permission and a bridegroom that he is twenty-one or has parental permission. Someone must put up five dollars for the license. (On Sundays and holidays, fifteen dollars. The Clark County Courthouse issues marriage licenses at any time of the day or night except between noon and one in the afternoon, between eight and nine in the evening, and between four and five in the morning.) Nothing else is required. The State of Nevada, alone among these United States, demands neither a premarital blood test nor a waiting period before or after the issuance of a marriage license. Driving in across the Mojave from Los Angeles, one sees the signs way out on the desert, looming up from that moonscape of rattlesnakes and mesquite, even before the Las Vegas lights appear like a mirage on the horizon: "GETTING MARRIED? Free License Information First Strip Exit." Perhaps the Las Vegas wedding industry achieved its peak operational efficiency between 9:00 P.M. and midnight of August 26, 1965, an otherwise unremarkable Thursday which happened to be, by Presidential order, the last day on which anyone could improve his draft status merely by getting married. One hundred and seventy-one couples were pronounced man and wife in the name of Clark County and the State of Nevada that night, sixty-seven of them by a single justice of the peace, Mr. James A. Brennan. Mr. Brennan did one wedding at the Dunes and the other sixty-six in his office, and charged each couple eight dollars. One bride lent her veil to six others. "I got it down from five to three minutes," Mr. Brennan said later of his feat. "I could've married them en masse, but they're people, not cattle. People expect more when they get married."

What people who get married in Las Vegas actually do expect — what, in the largest sense, their "expectations" are — strikes one as a curious and self-contradictory business. Las Vegas is the most extreme and allegorical of American settlements, bizarre and beautiful in its venality and in its devotion to immediate gratification, a place the tone of which is set by mobsters and call girls and ladies' room attendants with amyl nitrite poppers in their uniform pockets. Almost everyone notes that there is no "time" in Las Vegas, no night and no day and no past and no future (no Las Vegas casino, however, has taken the obliteration of the ordinary time sense quite so far as Harold's Club in Reno, which for a while issued, at odd intervals in the day and night, mimeographed "bulletins" carrying news from the world outside); neither is there any logical sense of where one is. One is standing on a highway in the middle of a vast hostile desert looking at an eighty-foot sign which blinks "STARDUST" or "CAESAR'S PALACE." Yes, but what does that explain? This geographical implausibility reinforces the sense that what happens there has no connection with "real" life; Nevada cities like Reno and Carson are ranch towns, Western towns, places behind which there is some historical imperative. But Las Vegas seems to exist only in the eye of the beholder. All of which makes it an extraordinarily stimulating and interesting place, but an odd one in which to want to wear a candlelight satin Priscilla of Boston wedding dress with Chantilly lace insets, tapered sleeves and a detachable modified train.

And yet the Las Vegas wedding business seems to appeal to precisely that impulse. "Sincere and Dignified Since 1954," one wedding chapel advertises. There are nineteen such wedding chapels in Las Vegas, intensely competitive, each offering better, faster, and, by implication, more sincere services than the next: Our Photos Best Anywhere, Your Wedding on A Phonograph Record, Candlelight with Your Ceremony, Honeymoon Accommodations, Free Transportation from Your Motel to Courthouse to Chapel and Return to Motel, Religious or Civil Ceremonies, Dressing Rooms, Flowers, Rings, Announcements, Witnesses Available, and Ample Parking. All of these services, like most others in Las Vegas (sauna baths, payroll-check cashing, chinchilla coats for sale or rent), are offered twenty-four hours a day, seven days a week, presumably on the premise that marriage, like craps, is a game to be played when the table seems hot.

But what strikes one most about the Strip chapels, with their wishing wells and stained-glass paper windows and their artificial bouvardia, is that so much of their business is by no means a matter of simple convenience, of late-night liaisons between show girls and baby Crosbys. Of course there is some of that. (One night about eleven o'clock in Las Vegas I watched a bride in an orange minidress and masses of flame-colored hair stumble from a Strip chapel on the arm of her bridegroom, who looked the part of the expendable nephew in movies like *Miami Syndicate*. "I gotta get the kids," the bride whimpered. "I gotta pick up the sitter, I gotta get to the midnight show."

"What you gotta get," the bridegroom said, opening the door of a Cadillac Coupe de Ville and watching her crumple on the seat, "is sober.") But Las Vegas seems to offer something other than "convenience"; it is merchandising "niceness," the facsimile of proper ritual, to children who do not know how else to find it, how to make the arrangements, how to do it "right." All day and evening long on the Strip, one sees actual wedding parties, waiting under the harsh lights at a crosswalk, standing uneasily in the parking lot of the Frontier while the photographer hired by The Little Church of the West ("Wedding Place of the Stars") certifies the occasion, takes the picture: the bride in a veil and white satin pumps, the bridegroom usually in a white dinner jacket, and even an attendant or two, a sister or a best friend in hot pink *peau de soie*, a flirtation veil, a carnation nosegay. "When I Fall in Love It Will Be Forever," the organist plays, and then a few bars of Lohengrin. The mother cries; the stepfather, awkward in his role, invites the chapel hostess to join them for a drink at the Sands. The hostess declines with a professional smile; she has already transferred her interest to the group waiting outside. One bride out, another in, and again the sign goes up on the chapel door: "One moment please — Wedding."

I sat next to one such wedding party in a Strip restaurant the last time I was in Las Vegas. The marriage had just taken place; the bride still wore her dress, the mother her corsage. A bored waiter poured out a few swallows of pink champagne ("on the house") for everyone but the bride, who was too young to be served. "You'll need something with more kick than that," the bride's father said with heavy jocularity to his new son-in-law; the ritual jokes about the wedding night had a certain Panglossian character, since the bride was clearly several months pregnant. Another round of pink champagne, this time not on the house, and the bride began to cry. "It was just as nice," she sobbed, "as I hoped and dreamed it would be."

PROBING FOR   1. What are the requirements for a marriage in Clark County? Why
MEANING   do couples want to be married in Las Vegas? What does Las Vegas offer besides "convenience"?

2. What is self-contradictory about the expectations of those who marry in Las Vegas?

3. What details do you find particularly apt in describing Las Vegas and its involvement with marriage? What does the parenthetical anecdote about the bride in the orange minidress say about marriage in Las Vegas?

PROBING FOR   1. What is the thesis of Didion's essay? Where is the thesis ex-
METHOD   pressed?

2. Point out any examples of irony employed by Didion.

3. What is demonstrated by the description of the wedding party in the final paragraph? Why has Didion chosen this particular scene to conclude her essay?

 JOHN UPDIKE

A & P

In walks these three girls in nothing but bathing suits. I'm in the third checkout slot, with my back to the door, so I don't see them until they're over by the bread. The one that caught my eye first was the one in the plaid green two-piece. She was a chunky kid, with a good tan and a sweet broad soft-looking can with those two crescents of white just under it, where the sun never seems to hit, at the top of the backs of her legs. I stood there with my hand on a box of HiHo crackers trying to remember if I rang it up or not. I ring it up again and the customer starts giving me hell. She's one of these cash-register-watchers, a witch about fifty with rouge on her cheekbones and no eyebrows, and I know it made her day to trip me up. She'd been watching cash registers for fifty years and probably never seen a mistake before.

By the time I got her feathers smoothed and her goodies into a bag — she gives me a little snort in passing, if she'd been born at the right time they would have burned her over in Salem — by the time I get her on her way the girls had circled around the bread and were coming back, without a pushcart, back my way along the counters, in the aisle between the checkouts and the Special bins. They didn't even have shoes on. There was this chunky one, with the two-piece — it was bright green and the seams on the bra were still sharp and her belly was still pretty pale so I guessed she just got it (the suit) — there was this one, with one of those chubby berryfaces, the lips all bunched together under her nose, this one, and a tall one, with black hair that hadn't quite frizzed right, and one of these sunburns right across under the eyes, and a chin that was too long — you know, the kind of girl other girls think is very "striking" and "attractive" but never quite makes it, as they very well know, which is why they like her so much — and then the third one, that wasn't quite so tall. She was the queen. She kind of led them, the other two peeking around and making their shoulders round. She didn't look around, not this queen, she just walked straight on slowly, on these long white prima-donna legs. She came down a little hard on her heels, as if she didn't walk in her bare feet that much, putting down her heels and then letting the weight move along to her toes as if she was testing the floor with every step, putting a little deliberate extra action into it. You never know for sure how girls' minds work (do you really think it's a mind in there or just a little buzz like a bee in a glass jar?) but you got the idea she had talked the other two into coming in here with her, and now she was showing them how to do it, walk slow and hold yourself straight.

She had on a kind of dirty-pink — beige maybe, I don't know — bathing suit with a little nubble all over it, and what got me, the straps were down. They were off her shoulders looped loose around the cool tops of her arms, and I guess as a result the suit had slipped a little on her, so all around the top of the cloth there was this shining rim. If it hadn't been there you wouldn't have known there could have been anything whiter than those shoulders. With the straps pushed off, there was nothing between the top of the suit and the top of her head except just *her*, this clean bare plane of the top of her chest down from the shoulder bones like a dented sheet of metal tilted in the light. I mean, it was more than pretty.

She had sort of oaky hair that the sun and salt had bleached, done up in a bun that was unravelling, and a kind of prim face. Walking into the A & P with your straps down, I suppose it's the only kind of face you *can* have. She held her head so high her neck, coming up out of those white shoulders, looked kind of stretched, but I didn't mind. The longer her neck was, the more of her there was.

She must have felt in the corner of her eye me and over my shoulder Stokesie in the second slot watching, but she didn't tip. Not this queen. She kept her eyes moving across the racks, and stopped, and turned so slow it made my stomach rub the inside of my apron, and buzzed to the other two, who kind of huddled against her for relief, and then they all three of them went up the cat-and-dog-food-breakfast-cereal-macaroni-rice-raisins-seasonings-spreads-spaghetti-soft-drinks-crackers-and-cookies aisle. From the third slot I look straight up this aisle to the meat counter, and I watched them all the way. The fat one with the tan sort of fumbled with the cookies, but on second thought she put the package back. The sheep pushing their carts down the aisle — the girls were walking against the usual traffic (not that we have one-way signs or anything) — were pretty hilarious. You could see them, when Queenie's white shoulders dawned on them, kind of jerk, or hop, or hiccup, but their eyes snapped back to their own baskets and on they pushed. I bet you could set off dynamite in an A & P and the people would by and large keep reaching and checking oatmeal off their lists and muttering "Let me see, there was a third thing, began with A, asparagus, no, ah, yes, applesauce!" or whatever it is they do mutter. But there was no doubt, this jiggled them. A few houseslaves in pin curlers even looked around after pushing their carts past to make sure what they had seen was correct.

You know, it's one thing to have a girl in a bathing suit down on the beach, where what with the glare nobody can look at each other much anyway, and another thing in the cool of the A & P, under the fluorescent lights, against all those stacked packages, with her feet paddling along naked over our checkerboard green-and-cream rubber-tile floor.

"Oh Daddy," Stokesie said beside me. "I feel so faint."

"Darling," I said. "Hold me tight." Stokesie's married, with two babies chalked up on his fuselage already, but as far as I can tell that's the only difference. He's twenty-two, and I was nineteen this April.

"Is it done?" he asks, the responsible married man finding his voice. I forgot to say he thinks he's going to be manager some sunny day, maybe in 1990 when it's called the Great Alexandrov and Petrooshki Tea Company or something.

What he meant was, our town is five miles from a beach, with a big summer colony out on the Point, but we're right in the middle of town, and the women generally put on a shirt or shorts or something before they get out of the car into the street. And anyway these are usually women with six children and varicose veins mapping their legs and nobody, including them, could care less. As I say, we're right in the middle of town, and if you stand at our front doors you can see two banks and the Congregational church and the newspaper store and three real-estate offices and about twenty-seven old freeloaders tearing up Central Street because the sewer broke again. It's not as if we're on the Cape; we're north of Boston and there's people in this town haven't seen the ocean for twenty years.

The girls had reached the meat counter and were asking McMahon something. He pointed, they pointed, and they shuffled out of sight behind a pyramid of Diet Delight peaches. All that was left for us to see was old McMahon patting his mouth and looking after them sizing up their joints. Poor kids, I began to feel sorry for them, they couldn't help it.

Now here comes the sad part of the story, at least my family says it's sad, but I don't think it's so sad myself. The store's pretty empty, it being Thursday afternoon, so there was nothing much to do except lean on the register and wait for the girls to show up again. The whole store was like a pinball machine and I didn't know which tunnel they'd come out of. After a while they come around out of the far aisle, around the light bulbs, records at discount of the Caribbean Six or Tony Martin Sings or some such gunk you wonder they waste wax on, sixpacks of candy bars, and plastic toys done up in cellophane that fall apart when a kid looks at them anyway. Around they come, Queenie still leading the way, and holding a little gray jar in her hand. Slots Three through Seven are unmanned and I could see her wondering between Stokes and me, but Stokesie with his usual luck draws an old party in baggy gray pants who stumbles up with four giant cans of pineapple juice (what do these bums *do* with all that pineapple juice? I've often asked myself) so the girls come to me. Queenie puts down the jar and I take it into my fingers icy cold. Kingfish Fancy Herring Snacks in Pure Sour Cream: 49¢. Now her hands are empty, not a ring or a bracelet, bare as God made them, and I wonder where the money's coming from. Still with that prim look she lifts a folded dollar bill out of the hollow at the center of her nubbled pink top. The jar went heavy in my hand. Really, I thought that was so cute.

Then everybody's luck begins to run out. Lengel comes in from haggling with a truck full of cabbages on the lot and is about to scuttle into that door marked MANAGER behind which he hides all day when the girls touch his eye. Lengel's pretty dreary, teaches Sunday school and the rest, but he doesn't miss much. He comes over and says, "Girls, this isn't the beach."

Queenie blushes, though maybe it's just a brush of sunburn I was noticing for the first time, now that she was so close. "My mother asked me to pick up a jar of herring snacks." Her voice kind of startled me, the way voices do when you see the people first, coming out so flat and dumb yet kind of tony, too, the way it ticked over "pick up" and "snacks." All of a sudden I slid right down her voice into her living room. Her father and the other men were standing around in ice-cream coats and bow ties and the women were in sandals picking up herring snacks on toothpicks off a big glass plate and they were all holding drinks the color of water with olives and sprigs of mint in them. When my parents have somebody over they get lemonade and if it's a real racy affair Schlitz in tall glasses with "They'll Do It Every Time" cartoons stencilled on.

"That's all right," Lengel said. "But this isn't the beach." His repeating this struck me as funny, as if it had just occurred to him, and he had been thinking all these years the A & P was a great big sand dune and he was the head lifeguard. He didn't like my smiling — as I say he doesn't miss much — but he concentrates on giving the girls that sad Sunday-school-superintendent stare.

Queenie's blush is no sunburn now, and the plump one in plaid, that I like better from the back — a really sweet can — pipes up, "We weren't doing any shopping. We just came in for the one thing."

"That makes no difference," Lengel tells her, and I could see from the way his eyes went that he hadn't noticed she was wearing a two-piece before. "We want you decently dressed when you come in here."

"We *are* decent," Queenie says suddenly, her lower lip pushing, getting sore now that she remembers her place, a place from which the crowd that runs the A & P must look pretty crummy. Fancy Herring Snacks flashed in her very blue eyes.

"Girls, I don't want to argue with you. After this come in here with your shoulders covered. It's our policy." He turns his back. That's policy for you. Policy is what the kingpins want. What the others want is juvenile delinquency.

All this while, the customers had been showing up with their carts but, you know, sheep, seeing a scene, they had all bunched up on Stokesie, who shook open a paper bag as gently as peeling a peach, not wanting to miss a word. I could feel in the silence everybody getting nervous, most of all Lengel, who asks me, "Sammy, have you rung up their purchase?"

I thought and said "No" but it wasn't about that I was thinking. I go through the punches, 4, 9, GROC, TOT — it's more complicated than you think, and after you do it often enough, it begins to make a little song, that you hear words to, in my case "Hello (*bing*) there, you (*gung*) happy *pee-pul* (*splat*)!" — the *splat* being the drawer flying out. I uncrease the bill, tenderly as you may imagine, it just having come from between the two smoothest scoops of vanilla I had ever known were there, and pass a half and a penny into her narrow pink palm, and nestle the herrings in a bag and twist its neck and hand it over, all the time thinking.

The girls, and who'd blame them, are in a hurry to get out, so I say "I quit" to Lengel quick enough for them to hear, hoping they'll stop and watch me, their unsuspected hero. They keep right on going, into the electric eye; the door flies open and they flicker across the lot to their car, Queenie and Plaid and Big Tall Goony-Goony (not that as raw material she was so bad), leaving me with Lengel and a kink in his eyebrow.

"Did you say something, Sammy?"

"I said I quit."

"I thought you did."

"You didn't have to embarrass them."

"It was they who were embarrassing us."

I started to say something that came out "Fiddle-de-doo." It's a saying of my grandmother's, and I know she would have been pleased.

"I don't think you know what you're saying," Lengel said.

"I know you don't," I said. "But I do." I pull the bow at the back of my apron and start shrugging it off my shoulders. A couple customers that had been heading for my slot begin to knock against each other, like scared pigs in a chute.

Lengel sighs and begins to look very patient and old and gray. He's been a friend of my parents for years. "Sammy, you don't want to do this to your Mom and Dad," he tells me. It's true. I don't. But it seems to me that once you begin a gesture it's fatal not to go through with it. I fold the apron, "Sammy" stitched in red on the pocket, and put it on the counter, and drop the bow tie on top of it. The bow tie is theirs, if you've ever wondered. "You'll feel this for the rest of your life," Lengel says, and I know that's true, too, but remembering how he made that pretty girl blush makes me so scrunchy inside I punch the No Sale tab and the machine whirs "pee-pul" and the drawer splats out. One advantage to this scene taking place in summer, I can follow this up with a clean exit, there's no fumbling around getting your coat and galoshes, I just saunter into the electric eye in my white shirt that my mother ironed the night before, and the door heaves open, and outside the sunshine is skating around on the asphalt.

I look around for my girls, but they're gone, of course. There wasn't anybody but some young married screaming with her children about some candy they didn't get by the door of a powder-blue Falcon station wagon. Looking back in the big windows, over the bags of peat moss and aluminum lawn furniture stacked on the pavement, I could see Lengel in my place in the slot, checking the sheep through. His face was dark gray and his back stiff, as if he'd just had an injection of iron, and my stomach kind of fell as I felt how hard the world was going to be to me hereafter.

PROBING FOR MEANING

1. Characterize Queenie. Sammy can tell that she's from a wealthy family. Does he admire her for her money or for some other reason?

2. Why does Sammy quit? Is it only to impress the girls? Why is his quitting going to make his life harder hereafter? Is his quitting a futile gesture?

3. The manager's awareness of place causes him to humiliate the girls. Is he justified in telling them that they aren't "decent"? Discuss.

PROBING FOR METHOD

1. How does Updike describe the supermarket? Does he include spatial description? What other methods does he use to develop his dominant mood?

2. At one point the narrator compares the whole store to a pinball machine. How effective is this metaphor? Exactly what are some similarities between what is happening in the store and what might happen on a pinball machine?

3. The story ends with the customers' being described as sheep. Why is this metaphor particular fitting to Updike's meaning?

 BERNARD MALAMUD

The Prison

Though he tried not to think of it, at twenty-nine Tommy Castelli's life was a screaming bore. It wasn't just Rosa or the store they tended for profits counted in pennies, or the unendurably slow hours and endless drivel that went with selling candy, cigarettes, and soda

water; it was this sick-in-the-stomach feeling of being trapped in old
mistakes, even some he had made before Rosa changed Tony into
Tommy. He had been as Tony a kid of many dreams and schemes,
especially getting out of this tenement-crowded, kid-squawking neighborhood, with its lousy poverty, but everything had fouled up against
him before he could. When he was sixteen he quit the vocational school
where they were making him into a shoemaker, and began to hang out
with the gray-hatted, thick-soled-shoe boys, who had the spare time
and the mazuma and showed it in fat wonderful rolls down in the cellar
clubs to all who would look, and everybody did, popeyed. They were
the ones who had brought the silver caffe espresso urn and later the
television, and they arranged the pizza parties and had the girls down;
but it was getting in with them and their cars, leading to the holdup of a
liquor store, that had started all the present trouble. Lucky for him the
coal-and-ice man who was their landlord knew the leader in the district, and they arranged something so nobody bothered him after that.
Then before he knew what was going on — he had been frightened sick
by the whole mess — there was his father cooking up a deal with Rosa
Agnello's old man that Tony would marry her and the father-in-law
would, out of his savings, open a candy store for him to make an honest
living. He wouldn't spit on a candy store, and Rosa was too plain and
lank a chick for his personal taste, so he beat it off to Texas and
bummed around in too much space, and when he came back everybody
said it was for Rosa and the candy store, and it was all arranged again
and he, without saying no, was in it.

That was how he landed on Prince Street in the Village, working from eight in the morning to almost midnight every day, except for
an hour off each afternoon when he went upstairs to sleep, and on
Tuesdays, when the store was closed and he slept some more and went
at night alone to the movies. He was too tired always for schemes now,
but once he tried to make a little cash on the side by secretly taking in
punchboards some syndicate was distributing in the neighborhood, on
which he collected a nice cut and in this way saved fifty-five bucks that
Rosa didn't know about; but then the syndicate was written up by a
newspaper, and the punchboards all disappeared. Another time, when
Rosa was at her mother's house, he took a chance and let them put in a
slot machine that could guarantee a nice piece of change if he kept it
long enough. He knew of course he couldn't hide it from her, so when
she came and screamed when she saw it, he was ready and patient, for
once not yelling back when she yelled, and he explained it was not the
same as gambling because anybody who played it got a roll of mints
every time he put in a nickel. Also the machine would supply them a
few extra dollars cash they could use to buy a television so he could see
the fights without going to a bar; but Rosa wouldn't let up screaming,
and later her father came in shouting that he was a criminal and
chopped the machine apart with a plumber's hammer. The next day the

cops raided for slot machines and gave out summonses wherever they found them, and though Tommy's place was practically the only candy store in the neighborhood that didn't have one, he felt bad about the machine for a long time.

Mornings had been his best time of day because Rosa stayed upstairs cleaning, and since few people came into the store till noon, he would sit around alone, a toothpick in his teeth, looking over the *News* and *Mirror* on the fountain counter, or maybe gab with one of the old cellar-club guys who had happened to come by for a pack of butts, about a horse that was running that day or how the numbers were paying lately; or just sit there, drinking coffee and thinking how far away he could get on the fifty-five he had stashed away in the cellar. Generally the mornings were this way, but after the slot machine, usually the whole day stank and he along with it. Time rotted in him, and all he could think of the whole morning, was going to sleep in the afternoon, and he would wake up with the sour remembrance of the long night in the store ahead of him, while everybody else was doing as he damn pleased. He cursed the candy store and Rosa, and cursed, from its beginning, his unhappy life.

It was on one of these bad mornings that a ten-year-old girl from around the block came in and asked for two rolls of colored tissue paper, one red and one yellow. He wanted to tell her to go to hell and stop bothering, but instead went with bad grace to the rear, where Rosa, whose bright idea it was to keep the stuff, had put it. He went from force of habit, for the girl had been coming in every Monday since the summer for the same thing, because her rock-faced mother, who looked as if she arranged her own widowhood, took care of some small kids after school and gave them the paper to cut out dolls and such things. The girl, whose name he didn't know, resembled her mother, except her features were not quite so sharp and she had very light skin with dark eyes; but she was a plain kid and would be more so at twenty. He had noticed, when he went to get the paper, that she always hung back as if afraid to go where it was dark, though he kept the comics there and most of the other kids had to be slapped away from them; and that when he brought her the tissue paper her skin seemed to grow whiter and her eyes shone. She always handed him two hot dimes and went out without glancing back.

It happened that Rosa, who trusted nobody, had just hung a mirror on the back wall, and as Tommy opened the drawer to get the girl her paper this Monday morning that he felt so bad, he looked up and saw in the glass something that made it seem as if he were dreaming. The girl had disappeared, but he saw a white hand reach into the candy case for a chocolate bar and for another, then she came forth from behind the counter and stood there, innocently waiting for him. He felt at first like grabbing her by the neck and socking till she threw up, but he had been caught, as he sometimes was, by his thought of how his Uncle Dom, years ago before he went away, used to take with him Tony alone of all the kids, when he went crabbing to Sheepshead Bay. Once they went at night and threw the baited wire traps into the water and after a while pulled them up and they had this green lobster in one, and just then this fat-faced cop came along and said they had to throw it back unless it was nine iches. Dom said it was nine inches, but the cop said not to be a wise guy so Dom measured it and it was ten, and they laughed about the lobster all night. Then he remembered how he had felt after Dom was gone, and tears filled his eyes. He found himself thinking about the way his life had turned out, and then about this girl, moved that she was so young and a thief. He felt he ought to do something for her, warn her to cut it out before she got trapped and fouled up her life before it got started. His urge to do this was strong, but when he went forward she looked up frightened because he had taken so long. The fear in her eyes bothered him and he didn't say anything. She thrust out the dimes, grabbed at the tissue rolls and ran out of the store.

He had to sit down. He kept trying to make the desire to speak to her go away, but it came back stronger than ever. He asked himself what difference does it make if she swipes candy — so she swipes it; and the role of reformer was strange and distasteful to him, yet he could not convince himself that what he felt he must do was unimportant. But he worried he would not know what to say to her. Always he had trouble speaking right, stumbled over words, especially in new situations. He was afraid he would sound like a jerk and she would not take him seriously. He had to tell her in a sure way so that even if it scared her, she would understand he had done it to set her straight. He mentioned her to no one but often thought about her, always looking around whenever he went outside to raise the awning or wash the window, to see if any of the girls playing in the street was her, but they never were. The following Monday, an hour after opening the store he had smoked a full pack of butts. He thought he had found what he wanted to say but was afraid for some reason she wouldn't come in, or if she did, this time she would be afraid to take the candy. He wasn't sure he wanted that to happen until he had said what he had to say. But at about eleven, while he was reading the *News,* she appeared, asking for the tissue paper, her eyes shining so he had to look away. He knew she meant to steal. Going to the rear he slowly opened the drawer, keeping his head lowered as he sneaked a look into the glass and saw her slide behind the counter. His heart beat hard and his feet felt nailed to the floor. He tried to remember what he had intended to do, but his mind was like a dark, empty room so he let her, in the end, slip away and stood tongue-tied, the dimes burning his palm.

Afterwards, he told himself that he hadn't spoken to her because it was while she still had the candy on her, and she would have been scared worse than he wanted. When he went upstairs, instead of sleeping, he sat at the kitchen window, looking out into the back yard. He blamed himself for being too soft, too chicken, but then he thought, no there was a better way to do it. He would do it indirectly, slip her a hint he knew, and he was pretty sure that would stop her. Sometime after, he would explain to her why it was good she had stopped. So next time he cleaned out this candy platter she helped herself from, thinking she might get wise he was on to her, but she seemed not to, only hesitated with her hand before she took two candy bars from the next plate and dropped them into the black patent leather purse she always had with her. The time after that he cleaned out the whole top shelf, and still she was not suspicious, and reached down to the next and took something different. One Monday he put some loose change, nickels and dimes, on the candy plate, but she left them there, only taking the candy, which bothered him a little. Rosa asked him what he was mooning about so much and why was he eating chocolate lately. He didn't answer her, and she began to look suspiciously at the women who came in, not excluding the little girls; and he would have been glad to rap her in the teeth, but it didn't matter as long as she didn't know what he had on his mind. At the same time he figured he would have to do something sure soon, or it would get harder for the girl to stop her stealing. He had to be strong about it. Then he thought of a plan that satisfied him. He would leave two bars on the plate and put in the wrapper of one a note she could read when she was alone. He tried out on paper many messages to her, and the one that seemed best he cleanly printed on a strip of cardboard and slipped it under the wrapper of one chocolate bar. It said, "Don't do this any more or you will suffer your whole life." He puzzled whether to sign it A Friend or Your Friend and finally chose Your Friend.

This was Friday, and he could not hold his impatience for Monday. But on Monday she did not appear. He waited for a long time until Rosa came down, then he had to go up and the girl still hadn't come. He was greatly disappointed because she had never failed to come before. He lay on the bed, his shoes on, staring at the ceiling. He felt hurt, the sucker she had played him for and was now finished with because she probably had another on her hook. The more he thought about it the worse he felt. He worked up a splitting headache that kept him from sleeping, then he suddenly slept and woke without it. But he had awaked depressed, saddened. He thought about Dom getting out of jail and going away God knows where. He wondered whether he would ever meet up with him somewhere, if he took the fifty-five bucks and left. Then he remembered Dom was a pretty old guy now, and he might not know him if they did meet. He thought about life. You never really got what you wanted. No matter how hard you tried you made mistakes and couldn't get past them. You could never see the sky outside or the ocean because you were in a prison, except nobody called it a prison, and if you did they didn't know what you were talking about, or they said they didn't. A pall settled on him. He lay motionless, without thought or sympathy for himself or anybody.

But when he finally went downstairs, ironically amused that Rosa had allowed him so long a time without bitching, there were people in the store and he could hear her screeching. Shoving his way through the crowd he saw in one sickening look that she had caught the girl with the candy bars and was shaking her so hard that the kid's head bounced back and forth like a balloon on a stick. With a curse he tore her away from the girl, whose sickly face showed the depth of her fright.

"Whatsamatter," he shouted at Rosa, "you want her blood?"

"She's a thief," cried Rosa.

"Shut your face."

To stop her yowling he slapped her across her mouth, but it was a harder crack than he had intended. Rosa fell back with a gasp. She did not cry but looked around dazedly at everybody, and tried to smile, and everybody there could see her teeth were flecked with blood.

"Go home," Tommy ordered the girl, but then there was a movement near the door and her mother came into the store.

"What happened?"she said.

"She stole my candy," Rosa cried.

"I let her take it," said Tommy

Rosa stared at him as if she had been hit again, then with mouth distorted began to sob.

"One was for you, Mother," said the girl.

Her mother socked her hard across the face. "You little thief, this time you'll get your hands burned good."

She pawed at the girl, grabbed her arm and yanked it. The girl, like a grotesque dancer, half ran, half fell forward, but at the door she managed to turn her white face and thrust out at him her red tongue.

PROBING FOR
MEANING

1. Malamud portrays two different stages in the life of the central character. What were the characteristics of Tony's life as opposed to Tommy's? Why does Tommy keep thinking of his Uncle Dom?

2. Why did Tommy return from Texas? What does this point out about him?

3. What is your reaction to Rosa? To what extent is she to blame for Tommy's conception of life as a prison?

4. What function does the little girl have in the story? Why is Tommy so upset about her? Why doesn't he confront her? Is Tommy naive in thinking that he could influence her? Why does she react to him as she does at the end?

5. What is Malamud's attitude toward Tommy? Compare Malamud's attitude to your own.

1. From whose point of view is the story told—the author's or Tony's? What effect does this narrative point of view achieve?

2. Describe the introduction to the story. How does the opening set the tone for the entire story?

3. What details does Malamud include to create a claustrophobic atmosphere for the reader as well as for Tommy?

 ARNA BONTEMPS

Southern Mansion

Poplars are standing there still as death
And ghosts of dead men
Meet their ladies walking
Two by two beneath the shade
And standing on the marble steps.

There is a sound of music echoing
Through the open door
And in the field there is
Another sound tinkling in the cotton:
Chains of bondmen dragging on the ground.

The years go back with an iron clank,
A hand is on the gate,
A dry leaf trembles on the wall.
Ghosts are walking.
They have broken roses down
And poplars stand there still as death.

1. Who are the ghosts referred to in the first stanza? What sort of event might they be attending? When might they have lived?

2. What does the poet mean when he writes that the years "go back with an iron clank"? In what sense does this line focus on a central theme of the poem?

3. What kind of a place is the mansion? What overall impression of it does the poet convey?

PROBING FOR
METHOD

1. Why doesn't the poet describe the physical appearance of the mansion in more detail? What elements of the place does he focus our attention on?

2. Why does the poet alter the first line when he uses it to end the poem?

3. How does the poet feel about the mansion? What significance does it hold for him?

 GARY SNYDER

Mid-August at Sourdough Mountain Lookout

Down valley a smoke haze
Three days heat, after five days rain
Pitch glows on the fir-cones
Across rocks and meadows
Swarms of new flies.

I cannot remember things I once read
A few friends, but they are in cities.
Drinking cold snow-water from a tin cup
Looking down for miles
Through high still air.

PROBING FOR
MEANING

1. What does the speaker see from his lookout on Sourdough Mountain? What impression does he give of the valley?

2. What is the atmosphere like on the mountain? In what ways is it different from the atmosphere of the valley?

3. How has being on Sourdough Mountain affected the speaker? Why is it significant that he cannot remember things he once read?

PROBING FOR
METHOD

1. What images does the speaker focus on in order to emphasize the difference between the valley and the mountain? In what sense do the images of the second stanza represent the speaker's mood? What is his mood?

2. How ambiguous is the pronoun reference "they" in line 7? Of what significance is this ambiguity?

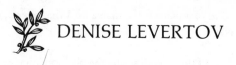

DENISE LEVERTOV

From the Roof

This wild night, gathering the washing as if it were flowers
    animal vines twisting over the line and
    slapping my face lightly, soundless merriment
    in the gesticulation of the shirtsleeves,
I recall out of my joy a night of misery

walking in the dark and the wind over broken earth,
    halfmade foundations and unfinished
    drainage trenches and the spaced-out
        circles of glaring light
    marking streets that were to be,
walking with you but so far from you,

and now alone in October's
first decision towards winter, so close to you—
    my arms full of playful rebellious linen, a freighter
    going down-river two blocks away, outward bound,
    the green wolf-eyes of the Harborside Terminal
        glittering on the Jersey shore,
and a train somewhere under ground bringing you towards me
to our new living-place from which we can see

a river and its traffic (the Hudson and the
hidden river, who can say which it is we see, we see
something of both. Or who can say
the crippled broom-vendor yesterday, who passed
just as we needed a new broom, was not
one of the Hidden Ones?)
    Crates of fruit are unloading
    across the street on the cobbles,
    and a brazier flaring
    to warm the men and burn trash. He wished us
luck when we bought the broom. But not luck
brought us here. By design

clear air and cold wind polish
the river lights, by design
we are to live now in a new place.

PROBING FOR
MEANING

1. Where is the speaker? What is she doing? What is it that makes her recall "a night of misery"?

2. What is the place she recalls in the second stanza? How is it different from the place where she is now, as she describes the latter in the third and fourth stanzas?

3. What is the "hidden river" to which the speaker refers to in the third stanza?

4. What does the speaker mean when she says at the end that it was not luck but "design" that brought them to a new place?

PROBING FOR
METHOD

1. Why does the speaker describe the laundry as if it were alive? Compare her description of the crates of fruit in the fourth stanza.

2. What role does the broom-vendor play in the poem? What do you make of the fact that he is crippled?

3. To whom is the poem addressed?

4. To what degree does the poem's title describe not only the speaker's situation but her mood? Describe the feelings that her description seems to symbolize. How important are the contrasts in her imagery to an understanding of her mood?

Topics for Imitation

1. Has any place affected you as the lake did White, as Knoxville did Agee, or as Folsom Prison did Cleaver? Describe this place, trying also to convey your response to it.

2. Write a visual description of a place that you know well. Use spatial order to help your reader see it as you do or once did. Decide the spacial pattern that you wish to use before beginning. Use comparison if appropriate.

3. Discuss the various descriptions of city life found in the selections of this chapter. How does the attitude toward the city differ from author to author?

4. Places often affect people's behavior. Discuss the influence of the lake, Folsom Prison, Las Vegas, and the kibbutz on the characters in the various selections. How might these or similar places affect people in general?

5. People's behavior also affects the atmosphere of a place. To what extent have the supermarket in "A&P" and the candy store in "The Prison" been shaped by personal or cultural behavior or attitudes?

6. Discuss the responses to nature of White, Bellow, and Snyder. Account as much as possible for the differences in their attitudes.

7. In "Once More to the Lake," "Knoxville: Summer 1915," and "On a Kibbutz," place evokes an important insight for the author or a character. Discuss the interaction between person and place that made the insight possible.

THREE

EVENTS AND EXPERIENCES

*". . . first snow
and kiss and fight"*

In late April 1944, on the eve of his deportation to the concentration camp in Auschwitz, Eli Wiesel buried his most priceless possession, the gold watch he had received three years previously for his bar mitzvah. Twenty years later he returns to the tiny Hungarian village of Sighet to reclaim it.

> Covered with dirt and rust, crawling with worms, it is unrecognizable, revolting. Unable to move, wondering what to do . . . I am angry with myself for having yielded to curiosity. But disappointment gives way to profound pity: the watch too lived through war and holocaust. . . . In its way, it too is a survivor, a ghost infested with humiliating sores and obsolete memories.

His initial impulses are to touch, repossess, and to try to restore his watch. He leaves the garden and is halfway down the street when he realizes he has committed his first theft. He rushes back to rebury the only concrete symbol of his past and concludes his essay with these words: "Since that day, the town of my childhood has ceased being just another town. It has become the face of a watch."

Wiesel's return to Sighet was an intensely moving experience which he felt he must record not only for his own people but for future generations. The role of the survivor is to testify, and you will share another survivor's experience in

103

Hana Wehle's account of her ambivalence as she returns from the concentration camps to her native city of Prague.

Like Wiesel and Wehle, the other writers in this chapter recall experiences and narrate events, some pleasant, some unpleasant. Richard Selzer recounts an experience he had as a surgeon, E. B. White relates his encounter with a family of geese, and Joyce Maynard evaluates her elementary school years.

In the short stories, one protagonist, a foreign correspondent, confronts his past; another amuses us with his first encounter with the clergy when he was a child. The poems capture life's vicissitudes: "Disabled" depicts the aftermath of war, "I Taste a Liquor Never Brewed" dramatizes a transcendent moment, and "A Blessing" offers an epiphany.

Narrating an Event and Developing the Paragraph

When organizing an essay about an event one might best narrate the sequence of happenings. Narration can take many forms such as straight chronological order, a simple flashback approach, or a complex presentation of events using flashbacks on many time levels. What narrative patterns have the writers in this chapter followed? For an in-depth discussion of *Narrating an Event,* turn to pp. 111–113 following E. B. White's essay "The Geese."

Developing the paragraph is part of the writing process and is intricately interwoven with the organization of the essay, as paragraph structure both reflects and determines the pattern of thought. The spotlight in this chapter will be on paragraph structure, and a further discussion of it can be found in *Developing the Paragraph* at the conclusion of Joyce Maynard's essay "The Lion Tamers" on pp. 117–121. The paragraphs in this chapter's essays are of varying length and purpose. What guidelines about paragraph division can be drawn from these essays?

E. B. WHITE

The Geese

Allen Cove, July 9, 1971

To give a clear account of what took place in the barnyard early in the morning on that last Sunday in June, I will have to go back more than a year in time, but a year is nothing to me these days. Besides, I intend to be quick about it, and not dawdle.

I have had a pair of elderly gray geese — a goose and a gander — living on this place for a number of years, and they have been my friends. "Companions" would be a better word; geese are friends with no one, they badmouth everybody and everything. But they are companionable once you get used to their ingratitude and their false accusations. Early in the spring, a year ago, as soon as the ice went out of the pond, my goose started to lay. She laid three eggs in about a week's time and then died. I found her halfway down the lane that connects the barnyard with the pasture. There were no marks on her — she lay with wings partly outspread, and with her neck forward in the grass, pointing downhill. Geese are rarely sick, and I think this goose's time had come and she had simply died of old age. I had noticed that her step had slowed on her trips back from the pond to the barn where her nest was. I had never known her age, and so had nothing else to go on. We buried her in our private graveyard, and I felt sad at losing an acquaintance of such long standing — long standing and loud shouting.

Her legacy, of course, was the three eggs. I knew they were good eggs and did not like to pitch them out. It seemed to me that the least I could do for my departed companion was to see that the eggs she had left in my care were hatched. I checked my hen pen to find out whether we had a broody, but there was none. During the next few days, I scoured the neighborhood for a broody hen, with no success. Years ago, if you needed a broody hen, almost any barn or henhouse would yield one. But today broodiness is considered unacceptable in a hen; the modern hen is an egg-laying machine, and her natural tendency to sit on eggs in springtime has been bred out of her. Besides, not many people keep hens anymore — when they want a dozen eggs, they don't go to the barn, they go to the First National.

Days went by. My gander, the widower, lived a solitary life —

nobody to swap gossip with, nobody to protect. He seemed dazed. The three eggs were not getting any younger, and I myself felt dazed — restless and unfulfilled. I had stored the eggs down cellar in the arch where it is cool, and every time I went down there for something they seemed silently to reproach me. My plight had become known around town, and one day a friend phoned and said he would lend me an incubator designed for hatching the eggs of waterfowl. I brought the thing home, cleaned it up, plugged it in, and sat down to read the directions. After studying them, I realized that if I were to tend eggs in that incubator, I would have to withdraw from the world for thirty days — give up everything, just as a broody goose does. Obsessed though I was with the notion of bringing life into three eggs, I wasn't quite prepared to pay the price.

Instead, I abandoned the idea of incubation and decided to settle the matter by acquiring three ready-made goslings, as a memorial to the goose and a gift for the lonely gander. I drove up the road about five miles and dropped in on Irving Closson. I knew Irving had geese; he has everything — even a sawmill. I found him shoeing a very old horse in the doorway of his barn, and I stood and watched for a while. Hens and geese wandered about the yard, and a turkey tom circled me, wings adroop, strutting. The horse, with one forefoot between the man's knees, seemed to have difficulty balancing himself on three legs but was quiet and sober, almost asleep. When I asked Irving if he planned to put shoes on the horse's hind feet, too, he said, "No, it's hard work for me, and he doesn't use those hind legs much anyway." Then I brought up the question of goslings, and he took me into the barn and showed me a sitting goose. He said he thought she was covering more than twenty eggs and should bring off her goslings in a couple of weeks and I could buy a few if I wanted. I said I would like three.

I took to calling at Irving's every few days — it is about the pleasantest place to visit anywhere around. At last, I was rewarded: I pulled into the driveway one morning and saw a goose surrounded by green goslings. She had been staked out, like a cow. Irving had simply tied a piece of string to one leg and fastened the other end to a peg in the ground. She was a pretty goose — not as large as my old one had been, and with a more slender neck. She appeared to be a cross-bred bird, two-toned gray, with white markings — a sort of particolored goose. The goslings had the cheerful, bright, innocent look that all baby geese have. We scooped up three and tossed them into a box, and I paid Irving and carried them home.

My next concern was how to introduce these small creatures to their foster father, my old gander. I thought about this all the way home. I've had just enough experience with domesticated animals and birds to know that they are a bundle of eccentricities and crotchets, and I was not at all sure what sort of reception three strange youngsters would get from a gander who was full of sorrows and suspicions. (I once saw a gander, taken by surprise, seize a newly hatched gosling and hurl it the length of the barn floor.) I had an uneasy feeling that my three little charges might be dead within the hour, victims of a grief-crazed old fool. I decided to go slow. I fixed a makeshift pen for the goslings in the barn, arranged so that they would be separated from the gander but visible to him, and he would be visible to them. The old fellow, when he heard youthful voices, hustled right in to find out what was going on. He studied the scene in silence and with the greatest attention. I could not tell whether the look in his eye was one of malice or affection — a goose's eye is a small round enigma. After observing this introductory scene for a while, I left and went into the house.

Half an hour later, I heard a commotion in the barnyard: the gander was in full cry. I hustled out. The goslings, impatient with life indoors, had escaped from their hastily constructed enclosure in the barn and had joined their foster father in the barnyard. The cries I had heard were his screams of welcome — the old bird was delighted with the turn that events had taken. His period of mourning was over, he now had interesting and useful work to do, and he threw himself into the role of father with immense satisfaction and zeal, hissing at me with renewed malevolence, shepherding the three children here and there, and running interference against real and imaginary enemies. My fears were laid to rest. In the rush of emotion that seized him at finding himself the head of a family, his thoughts turned immediately to the pond, and I watched admiringly as he guided the goslings down the long, tortuous course through the weedy lane and on down across the rough pasture between blueberry knolls and granite boulders. It was a sight to see him hold the heifers at bay so the procession could pass safely. Summer was upon us, the pond was alive again. I brought the three eggs up from the cellar and dispatched them to the town dump.

At first, I did not know the sex of my three goslings. But nothing on two legs grows any faster than a young goose, and by early fall it was obvious that I had drawn one male and two females. You tell the sex of a goose by its demeanor and its stance — the way it holds itself, its general approach to life. A gander carries his head high and affects a threatening attitude. Females go about with necks in a graceful arch and are less aggressive. My two young females looked like their mother, particolored. The young male was quite different. He feathered out white all over except for his wings, which were a very light, pearly gray. Afloat on the pond, he looked almost like a swan, with his tall, thin white neck and his cocked-up white tail — a real dandy, full of pompous thoughts and surly gestures.

Winter is a time of waiting, for man and goose. Last winter was a long wait, the pasture deep in drifts, the lane barricaded, the pond inaccessible and frozen. Life centered in the barn and the barnyard.

When the time for mating came, conditions were unfavorable, and this was upsetting to the old gander. Geese like a body of water for their coupling; it doesn't have to be a large body of water — just any wet place in which a goose can become partly submerged. My old gander, studying the calendar, inflamed by passion, unable to get to the pond, showed signs of desperation. On several occasions, he tried to manage with a ten-quart pail of water that stood in the barnyard. He would chivvy one of his young foster daughters over to the pail, seize her by the nape, and hold her head under water while he made his attempt. It was never a success and usually ended up looking more like a comedy tumbling act than like coitus. One got the feeling during the water-pail routine that the gander had been consulting one of the modern sex manuals describing peculiar positions. Anyway, I noticed two things: the old fellow confined his attentions to one of the two young geese and let the other alone, and he never allowed his foster son to approach either of the girls — he was very strict about that, and the handsome young male lived all spring in a state of ostracism.

Eventually, the pond opened up, the happy band wended its way down across the melting snows, and the breeding season was officially opened. My pond is visible from the house, but it is at quite a distance. I am not a voyeur and do not spend my time watching the sex antics of geese or anything else. But I try to keep reasonably well posted on all the creatures around the place, and it was apparent that the young gander was not allowed by his foster father to enjoy the privileges of the pond and that the old gander's attentions continued to be directed to just one of the young geese. I shall call her Liz to make this tale easier to tell.

Both geese were soon laying. Liz made her nest in the barn cellar; her sister, Apathy, made hers in the tie-ups on the main floor of the barn. It was the end of April or the beginning of May. Still awfully cold — a reluctant spring.

Apathy laid three eggs, then quit. I marked them with a pencil and left them for the time being in the nest she had constructed. I made a mental note that they were infertile. Liz, unlike her sister, went right on laying, and became a laying fool. She dallied each morning at the pond with her foster father, and she laid and laid and laid, like a commercial hen. I dutifully marked the eggs as they arrived — 1, 2, 3, and so on. When she had accumulated a clutch of fifteen, I decided she had all she could cover. From then on, I took to removing the oldest egg from the nest each time a new egg was deposited. I also removed Apathy's three eggs from *her* nest, discarded them, and began substituting the purloined eggs from the barn cellar — the ones that rightfully belonged to Liz. Thus I gradually contrived to assemble a nest of fertile eggs for each bird, all of them laid by the fanatical Liz.

During the last week in May, Apathy, having produced only

three eggs of her own but having acquired ten through the kind offices of her sister and me, became broody and began to sit. Liz, with a tally of twenty-five eggs, ten of them stolen, showed not the slightest desire to sit. Laying was her thing. She laid and laid, while the other goose sat and sat. The old gander, marveling at what he had wrought, showed a great deal of interest in both nests. The young gander was impressed but subdued. I continued to remove the early eggs from Liz's nest, holding her to a clutch of fifteen and discarding the extras. In late June, having produced forty-one eggs, ten of which were under Apathy, she at last sat down.

I had marked Apathy's hatching date on my desk calendar. On the night before the goslings were due to arrive, when I made my rounds before going to bed, I looked in on her. She hissed, as usual, and ran her neck out. When I shone my light at her, two tiny green heads were visible, thrusting their way through her feathers. The goslings were here — a few hours ahead of schedule. My heart leapt up. Outside, in the barnyard, both ganders stood vigil. They knew very well what was up: ganders take an enormous interest in family affairs and are deeply impressed by the miracle of the egg-that-becomes-goose. I shut the door against them and went to bed.

Next morning, Sunday, I rose early and went straight to the barn to see what the night had brought. Apathy was sitting quietly while five goslings teetered about on the slopes of the nest. One of them, as I watched, strayed from the others, and, not being able to find his way back, began sending out cries for help. They were the kind of distress signal any anxious father would instantly respond to. Suddenly, I heard sounds of a rumble outside in the barnyard where the ganders were — loud sounds of scuffling. I ran out. A fierce fight was in progress — it was no mere skirmish, it was the real thing. The young gander had grabbed the old one by the stern, his white head buried in feathers right where it would hurt the most, and was running him around the yard, punishing him at every turn — thrusting him on ahead and beating him unmercifully with his wings. It as an awesome sight, these two great male birds locked in combat, slugging it out — not for the favors of a female but for the dubious privilege of assuming the responsibilities of parenthood. The young male had suffered all spring the indignities of a restricted life at the pond; now he had turned, at last, against the old one, as though to get even. Round and round, over rocks and through weeds, they raced, struggling and tripping, the old one in full retreat and in apparent pain. It was a beautiful late-June morning, with fair-weather clouds and a light wind going, the grasses long in the orchard — the kind of morning that always carries for me overtones of summer sadness, I don't know why. Overhead, three swallows circled at low altitude, pursuing one white feather, the coveted trophy of nesting time. They were like three tiny fighter planes giving air support to the battle that raged below. For a moment, I thought of climbing the fence and trying to separate the combatants, but instead I just watched. The engagement was soon over. Plunging desperately down the lane, the old gander sank to the ground. The young one let go, turned, and walked back, screaming in triumph, to the door behind which his newly won family were waiting: a strange family indeed — the sister who was not even the mother of the babies, and the babies who were not even his own get.

When I was sure the fight was over, I climbed the fence and closed the barnyard gate, effectively separating victor from vanquished. The old gander had risen to his feet. He was in almost the same spot in the lane where his first wife had died mysteriously more than a year ago. I watched as he threaded his way slowly down the narrow path between clumps of thistles and daisies. His head was barely visible above the grasses, but his broken spirit was plain to any eye. When he reached the pasture bars, he hesitated, then painfully squatted and eased himself under the bottom bar and into the pasture, where he sat down on the cropped sward in the bright sun. I felt very deeply his sorrow and his defeat. As things go in the animal kingdom, he is about my age, and when he lowered himself to creep under the bar, I could feel in my own bones his pain at bending down so far. Two hours later, he was still sitting there, the sun by this time quite hot. I had seen his likes often enough on the benches of the treeless main street of a Florida city — spent old males, motionless in the glare of the day.

Toward the end of the morning, he walked back up the lane as far as the gate, and there he stood all afternoon, his head and orange bill looking like the head of a great snake. The goose and her goslings had emerged into the barnyard. Through the space between the boards of the gate, the old fellow watched the enchanting scene: the goslings taking their frequent drinks of water, climbing in and out of the shallow pan for their first swim, closely guarded by the handsome young gander, shepherded by the pretty young goose.

After supper, I went into the tie-ups and pulled the five remaining, unhatched eggs from the nest and thought about the five lifeless chicks inside the eggs — the unlucky ones, the ones that lacked what it takes to break out of an egg into the light of a fine June morning. I put the eggs in a basket and set the basket with some other miscellany consigned to the dump. I don't know anything sadder than a summer's day.

PROBING FOR
MEANING

1. Why is White concerned about getting the old goose's three eggs hatched? What prevents him from doing so?

2. How would you characterize the old gander? What sort of relationship does White have with him?

3. White says that the two ganders fight "for the dubious privilege of

assuming the responsibilities of parenthood." Why does he call this a "dubious" privilege?

4. What do you make of the sadness White expresses at the end of the essay? In what sense is White's sadness a critical theme of the essay?

PROBING FOR METHOD

1. White begins the essay with a flashback, then proceeds to offer a straightforward chronological account of the events following the death of the old goose. What theme does the introduction focus upon? How well does White keep to his intention of narrating his story quickly? How do his intention and the chronological account that results from it reflect the thematic focus in the introduction?

2. White personifies the old gander, writing about him as if his emotions were human. What is White's purpose in doing this?

3. Of what significance is the contrast that White draws between Liz and Apathy? What other contrasts does White emphasize in the essay? How important a role do these contrasts play in the development of White's paragraphs? To what degree is the essay as a whole structured out of a series of contrasts?

4. Explain the irony of the last line of the essay. Why does White conclude the essay on an ironic note?

5. How thoroughly does White evaluate the significance of the event that he narrates?

Narrating an Event

How does White narrate the events of "The Geese"?   White begins by referring to the outcome of his narrative and then goes back to the beginning a year before. He then proceeds sequentially to the conclusion once again. In adopting this flashback technique of beginning at the end (Z) and then reverting to the beginning and following the action through chronologically (A to Z), White adds the elements of suspense to his essay. By using flashback, he also is able to suggest a meaning to "what took place in the barnyard" that we do not ordinarily associate with the life cycles of geese.

He subtly reminds us throughout his narrative of this deeper level of meaning: through his indication in the introduction that he himself is old, through his sadness at the death of the old goose, through his identification with the defeated old gander, and finally by the last sentence of the essay. His narrative therefore has a strong sense of unity.

As narrator, he is both a participant in the action and an observer of it. While he might have chosen to be simply an observer, his involvement strengthens our belief in his identification with and sorrow for the defeated old gander.

What makes "The Geese" enjoyable to read are the details that White gives us. He quickly bestows personalities on the geese; they "badmouth everybody and everything." The old gander, when faced with a new family, "was delighted with the turn that events had taken. His period of mourning was over, he now had interesting and useful work to do, and he thew himself into the role of father with immense satisfaction and zeal, hissing at me with renewed malevolence, shepherding the three children here and there, and running interference against real and imaginary enemies." The young male was "a real dandy, full of pompous thoughts and surly gestures." He supplies no unnecessary details, however; as the males alone are to be the center of the drama, he does not describe the females in similar detail.

Narrating an event.   A good narration includes a meaningful event, thoughtful organization, a clear point of view, and telling details that evoke interest and contribute to meaning.

Many events seem to happen at random, either because they are unexpected or because the participants do not invest them with meaning. In narrating an event, however, you, as narrator, should decide beforehand what meaning you wish to convey to the reader. This meaning will give unity to your essay if you select your organization, point of view, and details with your theme in mind. This meaning does not have to be earth-shattering, just as the event you write about need not be cataclysmic.

How you organize the essay often helps to convey the meaning of an event. Just as White's flashback technique allowed him to announce that the event had significance at the very outset, so Hana Wehle's flashbacks immeasurably enrich her narrative of her train ride home. Whereas White's Z–A–Z pattern is fairly simple, Wehle's is much more complex as her mind darts back and forth across her life in a W-X-V-Y-U-A-Z pattern. Selzer and Wiesel use a straight chronological approach (A to Z) perhaps because the events they recount are dramatic enough by themselves to suggest meaning, as the interaction among White's geese and Wehle's train ride cannot.

All of the narrators are involved in the action, as indeed are most narrators of personal experience. However, the degree of their involvement differs. Wehle and Wiesel are the foci of their narratives, whereas Selzer shares the stage with the ailing mailman. White is not actually part of the action of which he writes although he does not completely remove himself from it as a purely objective narrator would. For an example of objective narration, examine the narrative sections of Alexander Petrunkevitch's "The Spider and the Wasp." The narrator recounts and explains the action, but his presence and his reactions are not accounted for, and the meaning of the narrative rests on an intellectual plane alone.

Telling details flesh out the framework provided by meaning, organization, and point of view. Without them, the narrative is a spindly skeleton indeed. Telling a good story is an ancient art, and people still love to hear one. They love the suspense and appreciate the meaning, but above all they remember the details. Having finished Selzer's essay, one remembers the vivid descriptions of the patient's cavernous stomach; once finished with "The Geese" one remembers the old defeated gander painfully easing himself under the fence, just as one is most impressed with Wehle's grandmother's dumplings and Wiesel's aching fingers. Through details, the narrative springs to life.

Procedures to follow in narrating an event.

     A. Choose an event that you have witnessed or an experience you have had that you wish to convey to a reader. Impart the meaning of the event to the reader as you narrate the experience.

     B. Organize your essay to establish a narrative pattern — either straight chronology (A to Z) or a flashback arrangement (Z–A–Z or a more complicated sequence).

     C. Decide on your point of view as narrator. Will you be an actor in the event or a spectator on the sidelines — or somewhere in between?

     D. Select telling details that will grasp the imagination of the reader.

 JOYCE MAYNARD

The Lion Tamers

     I watch them every year, the six-year-olds, buying lunch boxes and snap-on bow ties and jeweled barrettes, swinging on their mothers' arms as they approach the school on registration day or walking ahead a little, stiff in new clothes. Putting their feet on the shoe salesman's metal foot measure, eying the patent leather and ending up with sturdy brown tie oxfords, sitting rigid in the barber's chair, heads balanced on white-sheeted bodies like cherries on cupcakes, as the barber snips away the kindergarten hair for the new grown-up cut, striding past the five-year-olds with looks of knowing pity (ah, youth) they enter elementary school, feigning reluctance — with scuffing heels and dying TV cowboy groans shared in the cloakroom, but filled with hope and anticipation of all the mysteries waiting in the cafeteria and the water fountain and the paper closet, and in the pages of the textbooks on the teachers' desks. With pink erasers and a sheath of sharpened pencils, they file in so really bravely, as if to tame lions, or at least subdue the alphabet. And instead, I long to warn them, watching this green young crop pass by each year, seeing them enter a red-brick, smelly-staircase world of bathroom passes and penmanship drills, gongs and red x's, and an unexpected snap to the teacher's slingshot voice (so slack and giving, when she met the mothers). I want to tell them about the back pages in the teacher's record book, of going to the principal's office or staying behind an extra year. Quickly they learn how little use they'll have for lion-taming apparatus. They are, themselves, about to meet the tamer.

I can barely remember it now, but I know that I once felt that first-day eagerness too. Something happened, though, between that one pony-tail-tossing, skirt-flouncing, hand-waving ("*I* know the answer — call on *me*") day and the first day of all the other years I spent in public school. It wasn't just homework and the struggle to get up at seven every morning, it was the *kind* of homework assignments we were given and the prospect of just what it was that we were rousing ourselves for — the systematic breaking down, workbook page by workbook page, drill after drill, of all the joy we started out with. I don't think I'm exaggerating when I say that, with very few exceptions, what they did to (not *for*) us in elementary school was not unlike what I would sometimes do to my cats: dress them up in doll clothes because they looked cute that way.

We were forever being organized into activities that, I suspect, looked good on paper and in school board reports. New programs took over and disappeared as approaches to child education changed. One year we would go without marks, on the theory that marks were a "poor motivating factor," "an unnatural pressure," and my laboriously researched science and social studies reports would come back with a check mark or a check plus inside the margin. Another year every activity became a competition, with posters tacked up on the walls showing who was ahead that week, our failures and our glories bared to all the class. Our days were filled with electrical gimmicks, film strips and movies and overhead projectors and tapes and supplementary TV shows, and in junior high, when we went audio-visual, a power failure would have been reason enough to close down the school.

But though the educational jargon changed, the school's basic attitude remained constant. Anything too different (too bad or too exceptional), anything that meant making another column in the record book, was frowned upon. A lone recorder, in a field of squeaking flutophones, a reader of Dickens, while the class was laboring page by page (out loud, pace set by the slowest oral readers) with the adventures of the Marshall family and their dog Ranger, a ten-page story when the teacher had asked for a two-pager — they all met with suspicion. Getting straight A's was fine with the school as long as one pursued the steady, earnest, unspectacular course. But to complete a piece of work well, without having followed the prescribed steps — that seemed a threat to the school, proof that we could progress without it.

Vanity rears its head everywhere, even in the classroom, but surely extra guards against it should be put up there. I remember an English teacher who wouldn't grant me an A until second term, an indication, for whoever cared about that sort of thing, that under her tutelage I had *improved*. Every composition was supposed to have evolved from three progressively refined rough drafts. I moved in just the opposite direction for the school's benefit: I wrote my "final drafts" the first time around, then deliberately aged them a bit with earnest-looking smudges and erasures.

Kids who have gone through elementary school at the bottom of their class might argue here that it *was* the smart ones who got special attention — independent study groups, free time to spend acting in plays and writing novels (we were always starting autobiographies) and researching "Special Reports" — all the things that kept our groups self-perpetuating, with the children lucky enough to start out on top forever in the teachers' good graces, and those who didn't start there always drilling on decimals and workbook extra-work pages. But Oyster River was an exemplary democratic school and showed exemplary concern for slow students — the under-achievers — and virtuously left the quick and bright to swim for themselves, or tread water endlessly.

It always seemed to me as a Group One member, that there was little individual chance to shine. It was as if school had just discovered the division of labor concept, and oh, how we divided it. Book reports, math problems, maps for history and even art projects — we did them all in committee. Once we were supposed to write a short story that way, pooling our resources of Descriptive Adjectives and Figures of Speech to come up with an adventure that read like one of those typing-book sentences ("A quick brown fox . . ."), where every letter of the alphabet is represented. Our group drawings had the look of movie magazine composites that show the ideal star, with Paul Newman's eyes, Brando's lips, Steve McQueen's hair. Most people loved group work — the kids because working together meant not working very hard, tossing your penny in the till and leaving it for someone else to count, the teachers because committee projects prepared us for community work (getting along with the group, leadership abilities . . .) and, more important, I think, to some of them, they required a lot less marking time than individual projects did. The finished product didn't matter so much — in fact, anything too unusual seemed only to rock our jointly rowed canoe.

The school day was for me, and for most of us, I think, a mixture of humiliation and boredom. Teachers would use their students for the entertainment of the class. Within the first few days of the new term, someone quickly becomes the class jester, someone is the class genius, the "brain" who, the teacher, with doubtful modesty, reminds us often, probably has a much higher IQ than she. Some student is the troublemaker black sheep (the one who always makes her sigh), the one who will be singled out as the culprit when the whole class seems like a stock exchange of note passing, while all the others stare at him, looking shocked.

Although their existence is denied now, in this modern, psychologically enlightened age, teachers' pets are still very much around, sometimes in the form of the girl with super-neat penmanship and Breck-clean hair, sometimes in the person of the dependable Brain, who always gets called on when the superintendent is visiting the class. Teachers, I came to see, could be intimidated by a class, coerced or conned into liking the students who were popular among the kids, and it was hard not to miss, too, that many teachers were not above using unpopular students to gain acceptance with the majority. They had an instinct, teachers did, for who was well-liked and who wasn't; they learned all the right nicknames and turned away, when they could, if one of their favorites was doing the kind of thing that brought a 3 in conduct. We saw it all, like underlings watching the graft operations of ambitious politicians, powerless to do anything about it.

That was what made us most vulnerable: our powerlessness. Kids don't generally speak up or argue their case. No one is a child long enough, I suppose, or articulate enough, while he is one, to become a spokesman for his very real, and often oppressed, minority group. And then when we outgrow childhood, we no longer care, and feel, in fact, that if *we* went through it all, so should the next generation. Children are *expected* to be adversaries of school and teachers, so often, in the choosing up of sides, parents will side with the school. Nobody expects children to like school; therefore it's no surprise when they don't. What should be a surprise is that they dislike it for many good reasons.

It would be inaccurate to say I hated school. I had a good time sometimes, usually when I was liked, and therefore on top. And with all the other clean-haired girls who had neat penmanship and did their homework, I took advantage of my situation. When I was on the other side of the teacher's favor though, I realized that my sun-basking days had always depended on there being someone in the shade. That was the system — climbing up on one another's heads, putting someone down so one's own stature could be elevated. Elementary school was a club that not only reinforced the class system but created it — a system in which the stutterer and the boy who can't hit a baseball start out, and remain, right at the bottom, a system where being in the middle — not too high or low — is best of all.

I had imagined, innocently, on my first day at school, that once the kids saw how smart I was, they'd all be my friends. I see similar hopes on the faces I watch heading to the front every September — all the loved children, tops in their parents' eyes, off to be "reevaluated" in a world where only one of thirty can be favorite, each child unaware, still, that he is not the only person in the universe, and about to discover that the best means of survival is to blend in (adapting to the group, it's called), to go from being one to being one in a crowd of many, many others.

PROBING FOR
MEANING

1. With what "lion-taming apparatus" do children begin first grade? How do they instead become "the tamed"?

2. What fault does Maynard find with the innovative programs attempted in her own elementary school?

3. She accuses teachers and students of playing games with each other. How effectively does she analyze the dynamics of the classroom?

4. Maynard speaks of the powerlessness of children throughout the essay. Why do teachers and administration enforce this powerlessness?

5. "Elementary school was a club that not only reinforced the class system but created it." In how many instances does the author prove this to be true?

6. What suggestions does she give of what an ideal school would be like?

PROBING FOR
METHOD

1. Discuss the author's use of comparisons — similes and metaphors. How effective are they in each context?

2. How in her conclusion does Maynard allude to her introduction? Why would a writer build such a "frame" around her essay?

3. Has Maynard effectively limited her topic? Why or why not? What is the major thrust of her argument?

4. What is Maynard's purpose in writing the essay? To what audience is she appealing? How effectively does she convey her purpose to her audience?

5. To what extent does she use chronological development in recounting this experience?

Developing the Paragraph

How does Maynard structure her paragraphs in "The Lion Tamers"? Each paragraph of her essay develops one major aspect of her thesis, so that the essay proceeds in an orderly way from main contention to supporting examples and elaboration of the thesis, to a conclusion that hints at the wider implications of the issue. An outline of the piece might look as follows:

I. Introduction (paragraphs 1 and 2)
II. Schools enforce . . .
   A. Ill-considered experimentation (paragraph 3)
   B. Mediocrity
      1. Teacher's misplaced vanity (paragraph 4)
      2. "Democracy" (paragraph 5)
   C. Group work (paragraph 6)

D. Teacher's humiliation of student for . . .
   1. Entertainment (paragraph 7)
   2. Acceptance by other students (paragraph 8)
E. Students' powerlessness (paragraph 9)
F. The class system (paragraph 10)
     III. Conclusion (paragraph 11)

In each paragraph Maynard employs a technique used by many good writers, which is to express the main idea concretely in one sentence somewhere in the paragraph, usually in the beginning or concluding sentence. Notice, for example, that the last two sentences of paragraph 1 summarize the idea of that paragraph as well as state the thesis of the essay. And in paragraph 2, the second sentence is a topic sentence. The first sentence of paragraph 3 introduces the topic of the paragraph, just as the second sentence does in the following paragraph. Which sentences in the remaining paragraphs summarize the topics of those units?

Maynard has developed the main idea of each paragraph in various ways throughout the essay. The sentences in paragraph 1, for example, contrast details of kids' expectations with reality. In paragraph 2, subsequent sentences analyze her topic sentence; that is, they expand on the process of disillusionment and the "taming" that schoolchildren undergo.

Paragraphs 3 and 4 use examples to support the main idea, as do paragraphs 6 and 8. Paragraphs 5 and 11 again use contrast, while listing reasons is the technique for development of paragraphs 6 and 9. Other techniques are classification (paragraph 7) and cause-and-effect reasoning (paragraph 10).

Paragraphs 1 and 11 fulfill special functions. The author's first paragraph introduces the essay by (1) interesting the reader in the material through an entertaining description of six-year-olds preparing for school and (2) indicating by the end of the paragraph what the essay is to be about. Maynard's last paragraph contains a note of finality. By referring to the ideas of the introduction, she erects a frame around the essay, thus underlining its unity while at the same time concluding it.

Developing the paragraph. The basic structure of the paragraph is similar to that of the essay as a whole. Like the essay, the paragraph is limited to one topic that can be expanded within a limited space. Also, just as the essay outline follows a certain method of development, so the sentences in the paragraph must develop the topic logically. The first paragraph of the essay usually introduces the thesis, and correspondingly, the first sentence of the paragraph often is an introduction or topic sentence. Finally, in long paragraphs, the last sentences may act as a conclusion.

A simplified method of forming good paragraphs with effective topic sentences involves the use of the essay outline. Each of the major headings when stated in sentence form can serve as the topic sentence of a paragraph. The development of each paragraph requires the development of the point in the topic sentence.

A method of paragraph development that writers frequently use is to give examples that illustrate the topic sentence. Paragraphs may also be expanded by adapting those methods that apply to the essay as a whole: spatial order, chronological order, contrast-and-comparison, cause-and-effect, definition, process analysis, and so forth.

Paragraphs, regardless of the method of their development, follow variations on one of two possible patterns: ideas are either coordinate (equal in value) or subordinate (unequal). The introduction to Maynard's essay, for example, proceeds coordinately with each idea parallel to every other as she lists the ways in which six-year-olds are excited about school. Her second and third paragraphs, on the other hand, combine subordination with coordination. The first two sentences in each paragraph are coordinate, but the subsequent sentences explain those that precede them. Paragraph 2, outlined, looks like this:

Sentence 1: I can barely remember it now, but I know that I once felt that first-day eagerness too.

Sentence 2: Something happened, though, between that one pony-tail-tossing, skirt-flouncing, hand-waving (*"I* know the answer — call on *me"*) day and the first day of all the other years I spent in public school.

> *Sentence 3:* It wasn't just homework and the struggle to get up at seven every morning, it was the *kind* of homework assignments we were given and the prospect of just what it was that we were rousing ourselves for — the systematic breaking down, workbook page by workbook page, drill after drill, of all the joy we started out with.
>
> *Sentence 4:* I don't think I'm exaggerating when I say that, with very few exceptions, what they did to (not *for*) us in elementary school was not unlike what I would sometimes do to my cats: dress them up in doll clothes because they looked cute that way.

Paragraph 3, outlined, follows a similar pattern:

Sentence 1
Sentence 2
> Sentence 3
> Sentence 4
> Sentence 5

In writing your paragraphs, therefore, determine the needs of your readers: do they require you to enumerate or list points about your subjects or do they need an explanation of it? Would they benefit from both coordination and subordination? This method of inquiry should help you develop any topic into a paragraph once you have determined your readers' needs.

In writing your essay, you may have difficulty with two paragraphs, the introduction and the conclusion. The former has a dual function: to interest the reader in the essay and to give him or her some idea of its purpose. The first sentence is important in capturing the reader's attention. If it is framed as a question, it may arouse curiosity. If it is composed as a startling statement, it may intrigue the reader. Your first paragraph is a come-on and should give just enough information on your topic to compel the reader's interest.

The conclusion to a short essay should do more than simply summarize the paper; only in long essays, where the reader might forget earlier points, is the summary conclusion effective. The conclusion should suggest to the reader aspects of your subject about which he or she might think further. It should, like the introduction, make a dramatic and effective impact. Most important, it should leave no doubt in the reader's mind that the thoughts on the paper have been brought together with some degree of finality.

The paragraph structures of the essays in this chapter vary considerably. White's paragraphs, like Maynard's, are of uniform length for the most part, but, for emphasis, his climactic one on the fight between the two ganders is longer than the rest. Wiesel, on the other hand, uses a one-line paragraph to emphasize the major point of his essay — that this return to his birthplace took place just after World War II. Emphasis is achieved in an unusually long paragraph through sustaining the reader's involvement, while it is achieved in a short one by bringing the reader up short. The writer's purpose determines which effect to create.

Selzer's explanatory paragraphs are introduced by topic sentences, but his narrative paragraphs are not. Since narration seeks to capture the drama of time, it cannot be summarized in an initial sentence and still retain its sense of forward movement; for this reason, narrative paragraphs seldom have topic sentences.

Selzer's paragraphs also reflect another rule of paragraphing: in writing dialogue, form a new paragraph each time the conversation switches from one person to another.

White's introduction and conclusion both emphasize the sadness of his experience with the geese, just as Selzer's introduction and conclusion come together on his theme of the absence of God in windowless operating rooms. In each selection, the introduction and conclusion "frame" the essay.

Procedures to follow in developing paragraphs. Method 1: Write each major heading in your outline in sentence form. Use each sentence as the topic sentence of a paragraph in your paper. Once you have formulated the topic sentence for each paragraph, use the subheadings in your outline to develop the rest of the paragraph.

Method 2: If you prefer to outline your essay after writing the first draft, then once you have determined the major points of your draft, make sure each one forms a separate paragraph.

A. Develop each paragraph logically; that is, arrange the sentences in an effective pattern.

    1. If the paragraph describes a place, follow the spatial pattern described in Chapter 2.

    2. If it narrates an event, develop a chronological arrangement.

    3. For the more complex methods of paragraph development, see

Chapter 4 for cause-and-effect organization and Chapter 5 for contrast and comparison. Paragraphs developed by these methods will also follow a coordinate or subordinate pattern: if you wish to explain your causes or comparisons to your reader, arrange your details in a subordinate pattern. If you wish simply to list them, follow a coordinate pattern.

B. No rules have been formulated for the length of paragraphs, but some guidelines are useful:

1. A heading from your outline that can be explained in a sentence or two is not usually worth a separate paragraph. Unless you want a short paragraph for emphasis, you should, if possible, join it to either the preceding or the following heading or simply delete it.

2. Some headings may need to be divided into two or more paragraphs if the subject requires more than five or six well-developed sentences. In this case, each subheading should be written in sentence form and serve as a topic sentence for a second (or third) paragraph.

3. Short paragraphs create dramatic emphasis if used at the right point in an essay and if used sparingly.

4. Longer paragraphs can be used to develop major points but should at most be half a page in length so as not to engulf the reader.

C. Use your thesis sentence in developing your introduction. Your introduction should fulfill two purposes: it should state the topic and it should engage the reader.

D. The conclusion should not simply summarize the essay; it should stress a particular aspect of the topic for the reader to think about on his or her own. Its tone of finality should clearly indicate that the essay is concluded.

 RICHARD SELZER

An Absence of Windows

Not long ago, operating rooms had windows. It was a boon and a blessing in spite of the occasional fly that managed to strain through the screens and threaten our very sterility. For the adventurous insect drawn to such a ravishing spectacle, a quick swat and, Presto! The door to the next world sprang open. But for us who battled on, there was the benediction of the sky, the applause and reproach of thunder. A Divine consultation crackled in on the lightning! And at night, in Emergency, there was the pomp, the longevity of the stars to deflate a surgeon's ego. It did no patient a disservice to have Heaven looking over his doctor's shoulder. I very much fear that, having bricked up our windows, we have lost more than the breeze; we have severed a celestial connection.

Part of my surgical training was spent in a rural hospital in eastern Connecticut. The building was situated on the slope of a modest hill. Behind it, cows grazed in a pasture. The operating theater occupied the fourth, the ultimate floor, wherefrom huge windows looked down upon the scene. To glance up from our work and see the lovely cattle about theirs, calmed the frenzy of the most temperamental of prima donnas. Intuition tells me that our patients had fewer wound infections and made speedier recoveries than those operated upon in the airless sealed boxes where now we strive. Certainly the surgeons were of a gentler stripe.

I have spent too much time in these windowless rooms. Some part of me would avoid them if I could. Still, even here, in these bloody closets, sparks fly up from the dry husks of the human body. Most go unnoticed, burn out in an instant. But now and then, they coalesce into a fire which is an inflammation of the mind of him who watches.

Not in large cities is it likely to happen, but in towns the size of ours, that an undertaker will come to preside over the funeral of a close friend; a policeman will capture a burglar only to find that the miscreant is the uncle of his brother's wife. Say that a fire breaks out. The fire truck rushes to the scene; it proves to be the very house where one of the firemen was born, and the luckless man is now called on to complete, axe and hose, the destruction of his natal place. Hardly a civic landmark, you say, but for him who gulped first air within those walls, it is a hard destiny. So it is with a hospital, which is itself a community. Its citizens — orderlies, maids, nurses, x-ray technicians, doctors, a hundred others.

A man whom I knew has died. He was the hospital mailman. It was I that presided over his death. A week ago I performed an exploratory operation upon him for acute surgical abdomen. That is the name given to an illness that is unknown, and for which there is no time to make a diagnosis with tests of the blood and urine, x-rays. I saw him writhing in pain, rolling from side to side, his knees drawn up, his breaths coming in short little draughts. The belly I lay the flat of my hand upon was hot to the touch. The slightest pressure of my fingers caused him to cry out — a great primitive howl of vowel and diphthong. This kind of pain owns no consonants. Only later, when the pain settles in, long and solid, only then does it grow a spine to sharpen the glottals and dentals a man can grip with his teeth, his throat. Fiercely then, to hide it from his wife, his children, for the pain shames him.

In the emergency room, fluid is given into the mailman's veins. Bags of blood are sent for, and poured in. Oxygen is piped into his nostrils, and a plastic tube is let down into his stomach. This, for suction. A dark tarry yield slides into a jar on the wall. In another moment, a second tube has sprouted from his penis, carrying away his urine. Such is the costume of acute surgical abdomen. In an hour, I know that nothing has helped him. At his wrist, a mouse skitters, stops, then darts away. His slaty lips insist upon still more oxygen. His blood pressure, they say, is falling. I place the earpieces of my stethoscope, this ever-asking Y, in my ears. Always, I am comforted a bit by this ungainly little hose. It is my oldest, my dearest friend. More, it is my lucky charm. I place the disc upon the tense mounding blue-tinted belly, gently, so as not to shock the viscera into commotion (those vowels!), and I listen for a long time. I hear nothing. The bowel sleeps. It plays possum in the presence of the catastrophe that engulfs it. We must go to the operating room. There must be an exploration. I tell this to the mailman. Narcotized, he nods and takes my fingers in his own, pressing. Thus has he given me all of his trust.

A woman speaks to me.

"Do your best for him, Doctor. Please."

My best? An anger rises toward her for the charge she has given. Still, I cover her hand with mine.

"Yes," I say, "my best."

An underground tunnel separates the buildings of our hospital. I accompany the stretcher that carries the mailman through that tunnel, cursing for the thousandth time the demonic architect that placed the emergency room in one building, and the operating room in the other.

Each tiny ridge in the cement floor is a rut from which rise and echo still more vowels of pain, new sounds that I have never heard before. Pain invents its own language. With this tongue, we others are not conversant. Never mind, we shall know it in our time.

We lift the mailman from the stretcher to the operating table. The anesthetist is ready with still another tube.

"Go to sleep, Pete," I say into his ear, my lips so close it is almost a kiss. "When you wake up, it will all be over, all behind you."

I should not have spoken his name aloud! No good will come of it. The syllable has peeled from me something, a skin that I need. In a minute, the chest of the mailman is studded with electrodes. From his mouth a snorkel leads to tanks of gas. Each of these tanks is painted a different color. One is bright green. That is for oxygen. They group behind the anesthetist, hissing. I have never come to this place without seeing that dreadful headless choir of gas tanks.

Now red paint tracks across the bulging flanks of the mailman. It is a harbinger of the blood to come.

"May we go ahead?" I ask the anesthetist.

"Yes," he says. And I pull the scalpel across the framed skin, skirting the navel. There are arteries and veins to be clamped, cut, tied, and cauterized, fat and fascia to divide. The details of work engage a man, hold his terror at bay. Beneath us now, the peritoneum. A slit, and we are in. Hot fluid spouts through the small opening I have made. It is gray, with flecks of black. Pancreatitis! We all speak the word at once. We have seen it many times before. It is an old enemy. I open the peritoneum its full length. My fingers swim into the purse of the belly, against the tide of the issuing fluid. The pancreas is swollen, necrotic; a dead fish that has gotten tossed in, and now lies spoiling across the upper abdomen. I withdraw my hand.

"Feel," I invite the others. They do, and murmur against the disease. But they do not say anything that I have not heard many times. Unlike the mailman, who was rendered eloquent in its presence, we others are reduced to the commonplace at the touch of such stuff.

We suction away the fluid that has escaped from the sick pancreas. It is rich in enzymes. If these enzymes remain free in the abdomen, they will digest the tissues there, the other organs. It is the pancreas alone that can contain them safely. This mailman and his pancreas — careful neighbors for fifty-two years until the night the one turned rampant and set fire to the house of the other. The digestion of tissues has already begun. Soap has formed here and there, from the compounding of the liberated calcium and the fat. It would be good to place a tube (still another tube) into the common bile duct, to siphon away the bile that is a stimulant to the pancreas. At least that. We try, but we cannot even see the approach to that duct, so swollen is the pancreas about it. And so we mop and suck and scour the floors and walls of this ruined place. Even as we do, the gutters run with new streams of the fluid. We lay in rubber drains and lead them to the outside. It is all that is left to us to do.

"Zero chromic on a Lukens," I say, and the nurse hands me the suture for closure.

I must not say too much at the operating table. There are new medical students here. I must take care what sparks I let fly toward such inflammable matter.

The mailman awakens in the recovery room. I speak his magic name once more.

"Pete." Again, "Pete," I call.

He sees me, gropes for my hand.

"What happens now?" he asks me.

"In a day or two, the pain will let up," I say. "You will get better."

"Was there any . . . ?"

"No," I say, knowing. "There was no cancer. You are clean as a whistle."

"Thank God," he whispers, and then, "Thank *you*, Doctor."

It took him a week to die in fever and pallor and pain.

It is the morning of the autopsy. It has been scheduled for eleven o'clock. Together, the students and I return from our coffee. I walk slowly. I do not want to arrive until the postmortem examination is well under way. It is twenty minutes past eleven when we enter the morgue. I pick the mailman out at once from the others. Damn! They have not even started. Anger swells in me, at being forced to face the *whole* patient again.

It isn't fair! Dismantled, he would at least be at some remove . . . a tube of flesh. But look! There is an aftertaste of life in him. In his fallen mouth a single canine tooth, perfectly embedded, gleams, a badge of better days.

The pathologist is a young resident who was once a student of mine. A tall lanky fellow with a bushy red beard. He wears the green pajamas of his trade. He pulls on rubber gloves, and turns to greet me.

"I've been waiting for you," he smiles. "Now we can start."

He steps to the table and picks up the large knife with which he will lay open the body from neck to pubis. All at once, he pauses, and, reaching with his left hand, he closes the lids of the mailman's eyes. When he removes his hand, one lid comes unstuck and slowly rises. Once more, he reaches up to press it down. This time it stays. The gesture stuns me. My heart is pounding, my head trembling. I think that the students are watching me. Perhaps my own heart has become visible, beating beneath this white laboratory coat.

The pathologist raises his knife.

"Wait," I say. "Do you always do that? Close the eyes?"

He is embarrassed. He smiles faintly. His face is beautiful, soft.

"No," he says, and shakes his head. "But just then, I remembered that he brought the mail each morning . . . how his blue eyes used to twinkle."

Now he lifts the knife, and, like a vandal looting a gallery, carves open the body.

To work in windowless rooms is to live in a jungle where you cannot see the sky. Because there is no sky to see, there is no grand vision of God. Instead, there are the numberless fragmented spirits that lurk behind leaves, beneath streams. The one is no better than the other, no worse. Still, a man is entitled to the temple of his preference. Mine lies out on a prairie, wondering up at Heaven. Or in a many-windowed operating room where, just outside the panes of glass, cows graze, and the stars shine down upon my carpentry.

PROBING FOR   1. Why does Selzer feel that windows in an operating room were "a
MEANING   boon and a blessing"?

2. What was wrong with the mailman? What did he fear was wrong with him?

3. What does Selzer mean when he writes that "pain invents its own language"?

4. Why does Selzer regret having spoken the mailman's name? How does the fact that he knows the mailman personally affect him?

5. What is it that embarrasses the pathologist?

6. At the end of the essay, Selzer writes that windowless rooms are really no better or worse than rooms with windows. What prompts him to write this? Why, despite this, would he prefer to avoid windowless rooms?

PROBING FOR METHOD

1. How does the introductory description of the operating room in the rural hospital in Connecticut help to illustrate the essay's thematic focus?

2. At times, Selzer states directly what he is feeling, as when he becomes angry at finding that the autopsy has not started. What does his narrative help us to understand about the cause of his feelings toward himself and his profession? What is his attitude toward himself and his profession overall?

3. Selzer compares the mailman's pancreas to a dead fish. What does this comparison capture about Selzer's feelings? What other analogies does he draw? What effect do they have on the reader?

4. Selzer does not stop to define the medical terms that he uses. Does this make his narrative more difficult to understand? Does it help us better understand a theme of the essay in any way?

5. During the operation, Selzer warns himself against saying too much in front of the new medical students. "I must take care," he says, "what sparks I let fly toward such inflammable matter." Where else do images of sparks and inflammation appear in the essay? What might these images symbolize?

 HANA WEHLE

Return

The air raid sirens are quiet, the bombers are grounded, the bowels of the crematoria furnaces are covered with human ashes — the war is over.

My face presses against the cool windowpane of the train carrying repatriates from various parts of Europe. My destination: Prague, Czechoslovakia. As the black engine hisses through the German countryside, the cities of the Reich stare at me from under the ashes and ruins. I plunge again into the nightmare of the recent past, to be awakened occasionally by the penetrating sound of the engine whistle.

"QUARANTINE" — the big letters obstruct my view. I am lying among the many half-corpses on the wooden planks. My body is tossing restlessly with typhoid fever. My lips are parched, my eyes are searching for water. Unconsciously, my head is turning toward the slowly opening door of the barracks. I see my mother's pale, frightened face. She forces a smile as she nods. She has come to say goodbye before I die. Or — is it she who is parting from me? With glassy eyes I am trying desperately to send her a smile. The monotonous sound of the clattering wheels overshadows the mirage of my mother's face. The wheels are turning on the shiny rails as the train crawls around a bend. My hollowed-out soul struggles to separate my thoughts of the bottomless pit of death from the sounds of whistle and clatter. . . .

The engine puffs out the last cloud of steam and the train comes to a stop. Clutching my shabby bundle of belongings, I uncertainly descend the steps of the train. Soon I am swallowed up by the once so familiar noise and smell of the railroad station. My legs march with the crowds. Once I belonged to them as they belonged to me. There was a balance and harmony in which everyone was both himself and a part of others. Today, a strange, invisible wall of loneliness and fear separates me from them. I never knew that the arrival would be as hard as the departure. In the camps, freedom had seemed so unattainable, glorious and beautiful!

Now I am not marching as I dreamed I would. My body is filling up mercilessly with pain. I see the Square of Saint Wenceslas, the beautiful center of the city of Prague, as it unfolds in front of me. Its pavement, it seems, still reverberates with the sound of marching boots; the frozen eyes, half hidden under the caps of the SS uniforms, form a net of hatred. They pierce the Star of David, no longer fastened on my coat but still scorching my heart.

The sky is gray. The fine drizzle is wetting the roofs of the city. I stand in front of the National Museum, waiting for a trolley car. I feel the moisture mixing with the tears rolling down my cheeks. Twenty-two years ago, I stood here with my mother and my sister, Helen. Then also we waited for a trolley car to come. We were on our way to visit our grandmother. Holding onto our mother's hands, we laughed as I mischievously pulled on Helen's blond braids. The brightly painted cars announced their coming and going with chimelike bells. It was Eastertime. The air was full of holiday mood and the smell of spring. The aroma of the golden chicken soup, lovingly prepared by our grandmother, filled my imagination. The little dumplings moved playfully around the floating rings of fat in the hot liquid which steamed from the fine china designed with a blue onion pattern.

From the bend of a side street, a rattling sound draws my attention. I am forced to emerge from the state of elation, in which everything in me has melted with happiness. In front of me a faded trolley car stops with a squeak. I board the half-empty car mechanically. I feel alone, so alone! As through a veil, my eyes slide from one passenger to another, my body sways from side to side with the music of the wheels. Did my sister survive? Will I find her under the same address? When I left her, three years ago, she was protected by her non-Jewish husband. Did he divorce her? And what about their children? What do I tell them all? How can it be told! Who will believe that I survived my own death? Why me, while our mother, father, and brother had to die? Can they understand? I survived and I have a message from the dead. But what words will I choose to tell it all?

The downpour of thoughts cuts through the silence around me. Yes, I have arrived at my destination. A sudden jerk of the trolley car brings me to my feet. As if in a daze, I walk the familiar street — tracing the gray building in front of me. Here is my sister's house! I need to loosen the stranglehold around my heart as I slowly mount the twisting staircase in the dark hallway. I inhale the collective aromas of the dinners, slipping through and around the many apartment doors in the hall. A small rectangular label shines on a door. This is unmistakably Helen's place! My shaky hand timidly presses the little doorbell. A click of the lock; a slow movement of the opening door lets a wedge of light into the dark hall. . . . Two happy shouts echo through the building. My sister and I look at each other in amazement. We both sense a miracle — we both survived! The invisible wall thrust between us through the Nuremberg Laws* can no longer separate us.

Helen's and my faces are drenched with tears of happiness and sorrow as we cling together in the open doorway. This mixture, streaming down our cheeks, suddenly forms the unspoken words I have been so anxiously searching for. There is one kind of knowledge: we both are together again, we each have a different story to tell. . . .

PROBING FOR
MEANING

1. Hana Wehle tells us near the end of her essay that her mother died in the concentration camp. Where does the author give the first evidence of her possible death? Explain.

2. The memories of the author constantly overwhelm her. At how many points in the essay does she succumb to them? What scenes in the past do these thoughts revive?

3. Why does the author feel the arrival is "as hard as the departure"?

---

* In 1939, the Reichs Protector of Bohemia and Moravia placed the Jews under German jurisdiction in accordance with the so-called Nuremberg Laws, adopted by the German parliament (Reichstag) in 1935. These comprehensive decrees defined the status of the Jews and limited their rights, thus establishing anti-Semitism in law.

Why is her present freedom not as "glorious and beautiful" as she had thought it would be while she was in the concentration camp?

4. Why does the author believe that the Nazis might not have sent her sister to a camp? Why is she nevertheless not sure that her sister survived?

5. Why does the author fear that she will not know how to tell her sister about her experience in the concentration camp? Why do their tears at the end form "the unspoken words" she has been "so anxiously searching for"?

PROBING FOR METHOD

1. The author uses the past tense ("I belonged to them") in relating some of her memories, but she uses the progressive tense ("I am lying") in relating others. Why doesn't she use the past tense throughout? What function does the progressive tense fulfill?

2. Why is it significant that the sky is gray and that it is drizzling out? What other details take on symbolic overtones?

3. What is the function of flashbacks in this particular narrative?

 ELIE WIESEL

The Watch

For my bar mitzvah, I remember, I had received a magnificent gold watch. It was the customary gift for the occasion, and was meant to remind each boy that henceforth he would be held responsible for his acts before the Torah and its timeless laws.

But I could not keep my gift. I had to part with it the very day my native town became the pride of the Hungarian nation by chasing from its confines every single one of its Jews. The glorious masters of our municipality were jubilant: they were rid of us, there would be no more kaftans on the streets. The local newspaper was brief and to the point: from now on, it would be possible to state one's place of residence without feeling shame.

The time was late April, 1944.

In the early morning hours of that particular day, after a sleepless night, the ghetto was changed into a cemetery and its residents into gravediggers. We were digging feverishly in the courtyard, the garden, the cellar, consigning to the earth, temporarily we thought, whatever remained of the belongings accumulated by several generations, the sorrow and reward of long years of toil.

My father took charge of the jewelry and valuable papers. His head bowed, he was silently digging near the barn. Not far away, my mother, crouched on the damp ground, was burying the silver candelabra she used only on Shabbat eve; she was moaning softly, and I avoided her eyes. My sisters burrowed near the cellar. The youngest, Tziporah, had chosen the garden, like myself. Solemnly shoveling, she declined my help. What did she have to hide? Her toys? Her school notebooks? As for me, my only possession was my watch. It meant a lot to me. And so I decided to bury it in a dark, deep hole, three paces away from the fence, under a poplar tree whose thick, strong foliage seemed to provide a reasonably secure shelter.

All of us expected to recover our treasures. On our return, the earth would give them back to us. Until then, until the end of the storm, they would be safe.

Yes, we were naïve. We could not foresee that the very same evening, before the last train had time to leave the station, an excited mob of well-informed friendly neighbors would be rushing through the ghetto's wide-open houses and courtyards, leaving not a stone or beam unturned, throwing themselves upon the loot.

Twenty years later, standing in our garden, in the middle of the night, I remember the first gift, also the last, I ever received from my parents. I am seized by an irrational, irresistible desire to see it, to see if it is still there in the same spot, and if defying all laws of probability, it has survived — like me — by accident, not knowing how or why. My curiosity becomes obsession. I think neither of my father's money nor of my mother's candlesticks. All that matters in this town is my gold watch and the sound of its ticking.

Despite the darkness, I easily find my way in the garden. Once more I am the bar mitzvah child; here is the barn, the fence, the tree. Nothing has changed. To my left, the path leading to the Slotvino Rebbe's house. The Rebbe, though, had changed: the burning bush burned itself out and there is nothing left, not even smoke. What could he possibly have hidden the day we went away? His phylacteries? His prayer shawl? The holy scrolls inherited from his famous ancestor Rebbe Meirl of Premishlan? No, probably not even that kind of treasure. He had taken everything along, convinced that he was thus protecting not only himself but his disciples as well. He was proved wrong, the wonder rabbi.

But I mustn't think of him, not now. The watch, I must think of the watch. Maybe it was spared. Let's see, three steps to the right. Stop. Two forward. I recognize the place. Instinctively, I get ready to re-enact the scene my memory recalls. I fall on my knees. What can I use to dig? There is a shovel in the barn; its door is never locked. But by groping around in the dark I risk stumbling and waking the people sleeping in the house. They would take me for a marauder, a thief, and hand me over to the police. They might even kill me. Never mind, I'll have to manage without a shovel. Or any other tool. I'll use my hands, my nails. But it is difficult; the soil is hard, frozen, it resists as if determined to keep its secret. Too bad, I'll punish it by being the stronger.

Feverishly, furiously, my hands claw the earth, impervious to cold, fatigue and pain. One scratch, then another. No matter. Continue. My nails inch ahead, my fingers dig in. I bear down, my every fiber participates in the task. Little by little the hole deepens. I must hurry. My forehead touches the ground. Almost. I break out in a cold sweat, I am drenched, delirious. Faster, faster. I shall rip the earth from end to end, but I must know. Nothing can stop or frighten me. I'll go to the bottom of my fear, to the bottom of night, but I will know.

What time is it? How long have I been here? Five minutes, five hours? Twenty years. This night was defying time. I was laboring to exhume not an object but time itself, the soul and memory of that time. Nothing could be more urgent, more vital.

Suddenly a shiver goes through me. A sharp sensation, like a bite. My fingers touch something hard, metallic, rectangular. So I have not been digging in vain. The garden is spinning around me, over me. I stand up to catch my breath. A moment later, I'm on my knees again. Cautiously, gently I take the box from its tomb. Here it is, in the palm of my hand: the last relic, the only remaining symbol of everything I had loved, of everything I had been. A voice inside me warns: Don't open it, it contains nothing but emptiness, throw it away and run. I cannot heed the warning; it is too late to turn back. I need to know, either way. A slight pressure of my thumb and the box opens. I stifle the cry rising in my throat: the watch is there. Quick, a match. And another. Fleetingly, I catch a glimpse of it. The pain is blinding: could this thing, this object, be my gift, my pride? My past? Covered with dirt and rust, crawling with worms, it is unrecognizable, revolting. Unable to move, wondering what to do, I remain staring at it with the disgust one feels for love betrayed or a body debased. I am angry with myself for having yielded to curiosity. But disappointment gives way to profound pity: the watch too lived through war and holocaust, the kind reserved for watches perhaps. In its way, it too is a survivor, a ghost infested with humiliating sores and obsolete memories. Suddenly I feel the urge to carry it to my lips, dirty as it is, to kiss and console it with my tears, as one might console a living being, a sick friend returning from far away and requiring much kindness and rest, especially rest.

I touch it, I caress it. What I feel, besides compassion, is a strange kind of gratitude. You see, the men I had believed to be immortal had vanished into fiery clouds. My teachers, my friends, my guides had all deserted me. While this thing, this nameless, lifeless thing had survived for the sole purpose of welcoming me on my return and providing an epilogue to my childhood. And there awakens in me a desire to confide in it, to tell it my adventures, and in exchange, listen to its own. What had happened in my absence: who had first taken possession of my house, my bed? Or rather, no; our confidences could wait for another time, another place: Paris, New York, Jerusalem. But first I would entrust it to the best jeweler in the world, so that the watch might recover its luster, its memory of the past.

It is growing late. The horizon is turning a deep red. I must go. The tenants will soon be waking, they will come down to the well for water. No time to lose. I stuff the watch into my pocket and cross the garden. I enter the courtyard. From under the porch a dog barks. And stops at once: he knows I am not a thief, anything but a thief. I open the gate. Halfway down the street I am overcome by violent remorse: I have just committed my first theft.

I turn around, retrace my steps through courtyard and garden. Again I find myself kneeling, as at Yom Kippur* services, beneath the poplar. Holding my breath, my eyes refusing to cry, I place the watch back into its box, close the cover, and my first gift once more takes refuge deep inside the hole. Using both hands, I smoothly fill in the earth to remove all traces.

Breathless and with pounding heart, I reach the still deserted street. I stop and question the meaning of what I have just done. And find it inexplicable.

In retrospect, I tell myself that probably I simply wanted to leave behind me, underneath the silent soil, a reflection of my presence. Or that somehow I wanted to transform my watch into an instrument of delayed vengeance: one day, a child would play in the garden, dig near the tree and stumble upon a metal box. He would thus learn that his parents were usurpers, and that among the inhabitants of his town, once upon a time, there had been Jews and Jewish children, children robbed of their future.

The sun was rising and I was still walking through the empty streets and alleys. For a moment I thought I heard the chanting of schoolboys studying Talmud; I also thought I heard the invocations of Hasidim reciting morning prayers in thirty-three places at once. Yet above all these incantations, I heard distinctly, but as though coming from far away, the tick-tock of the watch I had just buried in accordance with Jewish custom. It was, after all, the very first gift that a Jewish child had once been given for his very first celebration.

* The Day of Atonement — the most solemn day of the Jewish year.

Since that day, the town of my childhood has ceased being just another town. It has become the face of a watch.

PROBING FOR
MEANING
1. What did the watch represent to Wiesel when he was a boy? Why did he bury it?

2. What prompts him to dig up the watch twenty years later? What does he mean when he says that he was laboring to exhume "time itself, the soul and memory of that time"?

3. How does he feel when he first sees the dirty, rusted condition of the watch? What thoughts lead his feelings to change?

4. What reasons does he give for going back and reburying the watch? Can you suggest other possible reasons why he doesn't keep it?

5. What does the watch represent to Wiesel after he has reburied it? What answer to this question do the last two paragraphs provide?

PROBING FOR
METHOD
1. Wiesel says that as a boy he, like his family, was naïve. Just how might you define what he means by the term "naïve"? In what ways does he indicate that his attitude is less naïve twenty years later?

2. Except for the opening section of the essay, most of the narrative is written in the present tense. Where in the account of his return to his native town after twenty years does Wiesel revert to the past tense? Why does he do so? What effect does he achieve?

 CARSON McCULLERS

The Sojourner

The twilight border between sleep and waking was a Roman one this morning: splashing fountains and arched, narrow streets, the golden lavish city of blossoms and age-soft stone. Sometimes in this semiconsciousness he sojourned again in Paris, or German war rubble, or a Swiss skiing and a snow hotel. Sometimes, also, in a fallow Georgia field at hunting dawn. Rome it was this morning in the yearless region of dreams.

John Ferris awoke in a room in a New York hotel. He had the feeling that something unpleasant was awaiting him — what it was, he did not know. The feeling, submerged by matinal necessities, lingered even after he had dressed and gone downstairs. It was a cloudless autumn day and the pale sunlight sliced between the pastel skyscrapers. Ferris went into the next-door drugstore and sat at the end booth next to the window glass that overlooked the sidewalk. He ordered an American breakfast with scrambled eggs and sausage.

Ferris had come from Paris to his father's funeral which had taken place the week before in his home town in Georgia. The shock of death had made him aware of youth already passed. His hair was receding and the veins in his now naked temples were pulsing and prominent and his body was spare except for an incipient belly bulge. Ferris had loved his father and the bond between them had once been extraordinarily close — but the years had somehow unraveled this filial devotion; the death, expected for a long time, had left him with an unforeseen dismay. He had stayed as long as possible to be near his mother and brothers at home. His plane for Paris was to leave the next morning.

Ferris pulled out his address book to verify a number. He turned the pages with growing attentiveness. Names and addresses from New York, the capitals of Europe, a few faint ones from his home state in the South. Faded, printed names, sprawled drunken ones. Betty Wills: a random love, married now. Charlie Williams: wounded in the Hürtgen Forest, unheard of since. Grand old Williams — did he live or die? Don Walker: a B.T.O. in television, getting rich. Henry Green: hit the skids after the war, in a sanitarium now, they say. Cozie Hall: he had heard that she was dead. Heedless, laughing Cozie — it was strange to think that she too, silly girl, could die. As Ferris closed the address book, he suffered a sense of hazard, transience, almost of fear.

It was then that his body jerked suddenly. He was staring out of the window when there, on the sidewalk, passing by, was his ex-wife. Elizabeth passed quite close to him, walking slowly. He could not understand the wild quiver of his heart, nor the following sense of recklessness and grace that lingered after she was gone.

Quickly Ferris paid his check and rushed out to the sidewalk. Elizabeth stood on the corner waiting to cross Fifth Avenue. He hurried toward her meaning to speak, but the lights changed and she crossed the street before he reached her. Ferris followed. On the other side he could easily have overtaken her, but he found himself lagging unaccountably. Her fair hair was plainly rolled, and as he watched her Ferris recalled that once his father had remarked that Elizabeth had a "beautiful carriage." She turned at the next corner and Ferris followed, although by now his intention to overtake her had disappeared. Ferris questioned the bodily disturbance that the sight of Elizabeth aroused in him, the dampness of his hands, the hard heartstrokes.

It was eight years since Ferris had last seen his ex-wife. He knew that long ago she had married again. And there were children.

During recent years he had seldom thought of her. But at first, after the divorce, the loss had almost destroyed him. Then after the anodyne of time, he had loved again, and then again. Jeannine, she was now. Certainly his love for his ex-wife was long since past. So why the unhinged body, the shaken mind? He knew only that his clouded heart was oddly dissonant with the sunny, candid autumn day. Ferris wheeled suddenly and, walking with long strides, almost running, hurried back to the hotel.

Ferris poured himself a drink, although it was not yet eleven o'clock. He sprawled out in an armchair like a man exhausted, nursing his glass of bourbon and water. He had a full day ahead of him as he was leaving by plane the next morning for Paris. He checked over his obligations: take luggage to Air France, lunch with his boss, buy shoes and an overcoat. And something — wasn't there something else? Ferris finished his drink and opened the telephone directory.

His decision to call his ex-wife was impulsive. The number was under Bailey, the husband's name, and he called before he had much time for self-debate. He and Elizabeth had exchanged cards at Christmastime, and Ferris had sent a carving set when he received the announcement of her wedding. There was no reason *not* to call. But as he waited, listening to the ring at the other end, misgiving fretted him.

Elizabeth answered; her familiar voice was a fresh shock to him. Twice he had to repeat his name, but when he was identified, she sounded glad. He explained he was only in town for that day. They had a theater engagement, she said — but she wondered if he would come by for an early dinner. Ferris said he would be delighted.

As he went from one engagement to another, he was still bothered at odd moments by the feeling that something necessary was forgotten. Ferris bathed and changed in the late afternoon, often thinking about Jeannine: he would be with her the following night. "Jeannine," he would say, "I happened to run into my ex-wife when I was in New York. Had dinner with her. And her husband, of course. It was strange seeing her after all these years."

Elizabeth lived in the East Fifties, and as Ferris taxied uptown he glimpsed at intersections the lingering sunset, but by the time he reached his destination it was already autumn dark. The place was a building with a marquee and a doorman, and the apartment was on the seventh floor.

"Come in, Mr. Ferris."

Braced for Elizabeth or even the unimagined husband, Ferris was astonished by the freckled red-haired child; he had known of the children, but his mind had failed somehow to acknowledge them. Surprise made him step back awkwardly.

"This is our apartment," the child said politely. "Aren't you Mr. Ferris? I'm Billy. Come in."

In the living room beyond the hall, the husband provided another surprise; he too had not been acknowledged emotionally. Bailey was a lumbering red-haired man with a deliberate manner. He rose and extended a welcoming hand.

"I'm Bill Bailey. Glad to see you. Elizabeth will be in, in a minute. She's finishing dressing."

The last words struck a gliding series of vibrations, memories of the other years. Fair Elizabeth, rosy and naked before her bath. Half-dressed before the mirror of her dressing table, brushing her fine, chestnut hair. Sweet, casual intimacy, the soft-fleshed loveliness indisputably possessed. Ferris shrank from the unbidden memories and compelled himself to meet Bill Bailey's gaze.

"Billy, will you please bring that tray of drinks from the kitchen table?"

The child obeyed promptly, and when he was gone Ferris remarked conversationally, "Fine boy you have there."

"We think so."

Flat silence until the child returned with a tray of glasses and a cocktail shaker of Martinis. With the priming drinks they pumped up conversation: Russia, they spoke of, and the New York rain-making, and the apartment situation in Manhattan and Paris.

"Mr. Ferris is flying all the way across the ocean tomorrow," Bailey said to the little boy who was perched on the arm of his chair, quiet and well behaved. "I bet you would like to be a stowaway in his suitcase."

Billy pushed back his limp bangs. "I want to fly in an airplane and be a newspaperman like Mr. Ferris." He added with sudden assurance, "That's what I would like to do when I am big."

Bailey said, "I thought you wanted to be a doctor."

"I do!" said Billy. "I would like to be both. I want to be a atom-bomb scientist too."

Elizabeth came in carrying in her arms a baby girl.

"Oh, John!" she said. She settled the baby in the father's lap. "It's grand to see you. I'm awfully glad you could come."

The little girl sat demurely on Bailey's knees. She wore a pale pink crepe de Chine frock, smocked around the yoke with rose, and a matching silk hair ribbon tying back her pale soft curls. Her skin was summer tanned and her brown eyes flecked with gold and laughing. When she reached up and fingered her father's horn-rimmed glasses, he took them off and let her look through them a moment. "How's my old Candy?"

Elizabeth was very beautiful, more beautiful perhaps than he had ever realized. Her straight clean hair was shining. Her face was softer, glowing and serene. It was a madonna loveliness, dependent on the family ambiance.

"You've hardly changed at all," Elizabeth said, "but it has been a long time."

"Eight years." His hand touched his thinning hair self-consciously while further amenities were exchanged.

Ferris felt himself suddenly a spectator — an interloper among these Baileys. Why had he come? He suffered. His own life seemed so solitary, a fragile column supporting nothing amidst the wreckage of the years. He felt he could not bear much longer to stay in the family room.

He glanced at his watch. "You're going to the theater?"

"It's a shame," Elizabeth said, "but we've had this engagement for more than a month. But surely, John, you'll be staying home one of these days before long. You're not going to be an expatriate, are you?"

"Expatriate," Ferris repeated. "I don't much like the word."

"What's a better word?" she asked.

He thought for a moment. "Sojourner might do."

Ferris glanced again at his watch, and again Elizabeth apologized. "If only we had known ahead of time — "

"I just had this day in town. I came home unexpectedly. You see, Papa died last week."

"Papa Ferris is dead?"

"Yes, at Johns Hopkins. He had been sick there nearly a year. The funeral was down home in Georgia."

"Oh, I'm so sorry, John. Papa Ferris was always one of my favorite people."

The little boy moved from behind the chair so that he could look into his mother's face. He asked, "Who is dead?"

Ferris was oblivious to apprehension; he was thinking of his father's death. He saw again the outstretched body on the quilted silk within the coffin. The corpse flesh was bizarrely rouged and the familiar hands lay massive and joined above a spread of funeral roses. The memory closed and Ferris awakened to Elizabeth's calm voice.

"Mr. Ferris's father, Billy. A really grand person. Somebody you didn't know."

"But why did you call him *Papa* Ferris?"

Bailey and Elizabeth exchanged a trapped look. It was Bailey who answered the questioning child. "A long time ago," he said, "your mother and Mr. Ferris were once married. Before you were born — a long time ago."

"Mr. Ferris?"

The little boy stared at Ferris, amazed and unbelieving. And Ferris's eyes, as he returned the gaze, were somehow unbelieving too. Was it indeed true that at one time he had called this stranger, Elizabeth, Little Butterduck during nights of love, that they had

lived together, shared perhaps a thousand days and nights and —
finally — endured in the misery of sudden solitude the fiber by fiber
(jealousy, alcohol and money quarrels) destruction of the fabric of
married love?

Bailey said to the children, "It's somebody's suppertime. Come
on now."

"But Daddy! Mama and Mr. Ferris — I — "

Billy's everlasting eyes — perplexed and with a glimmer of
hostility — reminded Ferris of the gaze of another child. It was the
young son of Jeannine — a boy of seven with a shadowed little face and
knobby knees whom Ferris avoided and usually forgot.

"Quick march!" Bailey gently turned Billy toward the door.
"Say good night now, son."

"Good night, Mr. Ferris." He added resentfully, "I thought I
was staying up for the cake."

"You can come in afterward for the cake," Elizabeth said. "Run
along now with Daddy for your supper."

Ferris and Elizabeth were alone. The weight of the situation
descended on those first moments of silence. Ferris asked permission to
pour himself another drink and Elizabeth set the cocktail shaker on the
table at his side. He looked at the grand piano and noticed the music on
the rack.

"Do you still play as beautifully as you used to?"

"I still enjoy it."

"Please play, Elizabeth."

Elizabeth rose immediately. Her readiness to perform when
asked had always been one of her amiabilities; she never hung back,
apologized. Now as she approached the piano there was the added
readiness of relief.

She began with a Bach prelude and fugue. The prelude was as
gaily iridescent as a prism in a morning room. The first voice of the
fugue, an announcement pure and solitary, was repeated intermingling
with a second voice, and again repeated within an elaborated frame, the
multiple music, horizontal and serene, flowed with unhurried majesty.
The principal melody was woven with two other voices, embellished
with countless ingenuities — now dominant, again submerged, it had
the sublimity of a single thing that does not fear surrender to the whole.
Toward the end, the density of the material gathered for the last
enriched insistence on the dominant first motif and with a chorded final
statement the fugue ended. Ferris rested his head on the chair back and
closed his eyes. In the following silence a clear, high voice came from
the room down the hall.

"Daddy, how *could* Mama and Mr. Ferris — " A door was
closed.

The piano began again — what was this music? Unplaced, familiar, the limpid melody had lain a long while dormant in his heart. Now it spoke to him of another time, another place — it was the music Elizabeth used to play. The delicate air summoned a wilderness of memory. Ferris was lost in the riot of past longings, conflicts, ambivalent desires. Strange that the music, catalyst for this tumultuous anarchy, was so serene and clear. The singing melody was broken off by the appearance of the maid.

"Miz Bailey, dinner is out on the table now."

Even after Ferris was seated at the table between his host and hostess, the unfinished music still overcast his mood. He was a little drunk.

"*L'improvisation de la vie humaine,*" he said. "There's nothing that makes you so aware of the improvisation of human existence as a song unfinished. Or an old address book."

"Address book?" repeated Bailey. Then he stopped, noncommittal and polite.

"You're still the same old boy, Johnny," Elizabeth said with a trace of the old tenderness.

It was a Southern dinner that evening, and the dishes were his old favorites. They had fried chicken and corn pudding and rich, glazed candied sweet potatoes. During the meal Elizabeth kept alive a conversation when the silences were overlong. And it came about that Ferris was led to speak of Jeannine.

"I first knew Jeannine last autumn — about this time of the year — in Italy. She's a singer and she had an engagement in Rome. I expect we will be married soon."

The words seemed so true, inevitable, that Ferris did not at first acknowledge to himself the lie. He and Jeannine had never in that year spoken of marriage. And indeed, she was still married — to a White Russian money-changer in Paris from whom she had been separated for five years. But it was too late to correct the lie. Already Elizabeth was saying: "This really makes me glad to know. Congratulations, Johnny."

He tried to make amends with truth. "The Roman autumn is so beautiful. Balmy and blossoming." He added, "Jeannine has a little boy of six. A curious trilingual little fellow. We go to the Tuileries sometimes."

A lie again. He had taken the boy once to the gardens. The sallow foreign child in shorts that bared his spindly legs had sailed his boat in the concrete pond and ridden the pony. The child had wanted to go in to the puppet show. But there was not time, for Ferris had an engagement at the Scribe Hotel. He had promised they would go to the guignol another afternoon. Only once had he taken Valentin to the Tuileries.

There was a stir. The maid brought in a white-frosted cake

with pink candles. The children entered in their night clothes. Ferris still did not understand.

"Happy birthday, John," Elizabeth said. "Blow out the candles."

Ferris recognized his birthday date. The candles blew out lingeringly and there was the smell of burning wax. Ferris was thirty-eight years old. The veins in his temples darkened and pulsed visibly.

"It's time you started for the theater."

Ferris thanked Elizabeth for the birthday dinner and said the appropriate good-byes. The whole family saw him to the door.

A high, thin moon shone above the jagged, dark skyscrapers. The streets were windy, cold. Ferris hurried to Third Avenue and hailed a cab. He gazed at the nocturnal city with the deliberate attentiveness of departure and perhaps farewell. He was alone. He longed for flight-time and the coming journey.

The next day he looked down on the city from the air, burnished in sunlight, toylike, precise. Then America was left behind and there was only the Atlantic and the distant European shore. The ocean was milky pale and placid beneath the clouds. Ferris dozed most of the day. Toward dark he was thinking of Elizabeth and the visit of the previous evening. He thought of Elizabeth among her family with longing, gentle envy and inexplicable regret. He sought the melody, the unfinished air, that had so moved him. The cadence, some unrelated tones, were all that remained; the melody itself evaded him. He had found instead the first voice of the fugue that Elizabeth had played — it came to him, inverted mockingly and in a minor key. Suspended above the ocean the anxieties of transience and solitude no longer troubled him and he thought of his father's death with equanimity. During the dinner hour the plane reached the shore of France.

At midnight Ferris was in a taxi crossing Paris. It was a clouded night and mist wreathed the lights of the Place de la Concorde. The midnight bistros gleamed on the wet pavements. As always after a transocean flight the change of continents was too sudden. New York at morning, this midnight Paris. Ferris glimpsed the disorder of his life: the succession of cities, of transitory loves; and time, the sinister glissando of the years, time always.

"Vite! Vite!" he called in terror. "Dépêchez-vous."

Valentin opened the door to him. The little boy wore pajamas and an outgrown red robe. His grey eyes were shadowed and, as Ferris passed into the flat, they flickered momentarily.

"J'attends Maman."

Jeannine was singing in a night club. She would not be home before another hour. Valentin returned to a drawing, squatting with his crayons over the paper on the floor. Ferris looked down at the drawing — it was a banjo player with notes and wavy lines inside a comic-strip balloon.

"We will go again to the Tuileries."

The child looked up and Ferris drew him closer to his knees. The melody, the unfinished music that Elizabeth had played, came to him suddenly. Unsought, the load of memory jettisoned — this time bringing only recognition and sudden joy.

"Monsieur Jean," the child said, "did you see him?"

Confused, Ferris thought only of another child — the freckled, family-loved boy. "See who, Valentin?"

"Your dead papa in Georgia." The child added, "Was he okay?"

Ferris spoke with rapid urgency: "We will go often to the Tuileries. Ride the pony and we will go into the guignol. We will see the puppet show and never be in a hurry any more."

"Monsieur Jean," Valentin said. "The guignol is now closed."

Again, the terror, the acknowledgment of wasted years and death. Valentin, responsive and confident, still nestled in his arms. His cheek touched the soft cheek and felt the brush of the delicate eyelashes. With inner desperation he pressed the child close — as though an emotion as protean as his love could dominate the pulse of time.

PROBING FOR MEANING

1. His father's death has caused Ferris to evaluate his own life. What is your impression of the way he is living? What reaction does he have to the names and addresses in his address book?

2. Elizabeth is described in considerable detail. What is she like? Whose fault does it seem to be that they divorced?

3. What is the difference in connotation between the words *sojourner* and *expatriate?*

4. What reaction does Ferris have to his visit with the Baileys? What prompts him to lie to Elizabeth? Do you think that the visit will change his relationship with Jeannine and Valentin?

5. What insight does Ferris have while in the taxi crossing Paris? What is the connection between this insight and Ferris's behavior with Valentin? Explain the meaning of the last sentence of the story.

PROBING FOR METHOD

1. What effect does the author create through the descriptions of the first paragraph? How would you characterize the style of sentences such as "Rome it was this morning in the yearless region of dreams," and "It was a cloudless autumn day and the pale sunlight sliced between the pastel skyscrapers"?

2. How is the narration handled? Does the reader learn the inner thoughts of anyone besides Ferris? What effect is created by this narrative point of view?

3. Why does the author describe the musical interlude in so much depth? Why is it important that Elizabeth plays a fugue (a musical composition in which two opposite themes are interwoven)? What symbolism is involved in

the fact that Ferris can recall the fugue but that the second piece that Elizabeth played evades his memory?

4. Many of the difficult words in the story are central to the writer's themes. Determine the meanings of the following words. Organize them into groups reflecting different themes in the story.

ambiance	guignol
amiabilities	incipient
anodyne	limpid
bistros	matinal
cadence	motif
dissonant	protean
equanimity	sojourner
expatriate	sublimity
filial	transience
fugue	transitory
glissando	

FRANK O'CONNOR

First Confession

All the trouble began when my grandfather died and my grandmother — my father's mother — came to live with us. Relations in the one house are a strain at the best of times, but, to make matters worse, my grandmother was a real old countrywoman and quite un-suited to the life in town. She had a fat, wrinkled old face, and, to Mother's great indignation, went round the house in bare feet — the boots had her crippled, she said. For dinner she had a jug of porter and a pot of potatoes with — sometimes — a bit of salt fish, and she poured out the potatoes on the table and ate them slowly, with great relish, using her fingers by way of a fork.

Now, girls are supposed to be fastidious, but I was the one who suffered most from this. Nora, my sister, just sucked up to the old woman for the penny she got every Friday out of the old-age pension, a thing I could not do. I was too honest, that was my trouble; and when I was playing with Bill Connell, the sergeant-major's son, and saw my grandmother steering up the path with the jug of porter sticking out from beneath her shawl I was mortified. I made excuses not to let him come into the house, because I could never be sure what she would be up to when we went in.

When Mother was at work and my grandmother made the dinner I wouldn't touch it. Nora once tried to make me, but I hid under the table from her and took the bread-knife with me for protection. Nora let on to be very indignant (she wasn't, of course, but she knew Mother saw through her, so she sided with Gran) and came after me. I lashed out at her with the bread-knife, and after that she left me alone. I stayed there till Mother came in from work and made my dinner, but when Father came in later Nora said in a shocked voice: "Oh, Dadda, do you know what Jackie did at dinnertime?" Then, of course, it all came out; Father gave me a flaking; Mother interfered, and for days after that he didn't speak to me and Mother barely spoke to Nora. And all because of that old woman! God knows, I was heart-scalded.

Then, to crown my misfortunes, I had to make my first confession and communion. It was an old woman called Ryan who prepared us for these. She was about the one age with Gran; she was well-to-do, lived in a big house on Montenotte, wore a black cloak and bonnet, and came every day to school at three o'clock when we should have been going home, and talked to us of hell. She may have mentioned the other place as well, but that could only have been by accident, for hell had the first place in her heart.

She lit a candle, took out a new half-crown, and offered it to the first boy who would hold one finger — only one finger! — in the flame for five minutes by the school clock. Being always very ambitious I was tempted to volunteer, but I thought it might look greedy. Then she asked were we afraid of holding one finger — only one finger! — in a little candle flame for five minutes and not afraid of burning all over in roasting hot furnaces for all eternity. "All eternity! Just think of that! A whole lifetime goes by and it's nothing, not even a drop in the ocean of your sufferings." The woman was really interesting about hell, but my attention was all fixed on the half-crown. At the end of the lesson she put it back in her purse. It was a great disappointment; a religious woman like that, you wouldn't think she'd bother about a thing like a half-crown.

Another day she said she knew a priest who woke one night to find a fellow he didn't recognize leaning over the end of his bed. The priest was a bit frightened — naturally enough — but he asked the fellow what he wanted, and the fellow said in a deep, husky voice that he wanted to go to confession. The priest said it was an awkward time and wouldn't it do in the morning, but the fellow said that last time he went to confession, there was one sin he kept back, being ashamed to mention it, and now it was always on his mind. Then the priest knew it was a bad case, because the fellow was after making a bad confession and committing a mortal sin. He got up to dress, and just then the cock crew in the yard outside, and — lo and behold! — when the priest looked round there was no sign of the fellow, only a smell of burning timber, and when the priest looked at his bed didn't he see the print of two hands burned in it? That was because the fellow had made a bad confession. This story made a shocking impression on me.

But the worst of all was when she showed us how to examine our conscience. Did we take the name of the Lord, our God, in vain? Did we honor our father and our mother? (I asked her did this include grandmothers and she said it did.) Did we love our neighbors as ourselves? Did we covet our neighbor's goods? (I thought of the way I felt about the penny that Nora got every Friday.) I decided that, between one thing and another, I must have broken the whole ten commandments, all on account of that old woman, and so far as I could see, so long as she remained in the house I had no hope of ever doing anything else.

I was scared to death of confession. The day the whole class went I let on to have a toothache, hoping my absence wouldn't be noticed; but at three o'clock, just as I was feeling safe, along comes a chap with a message from Mrs. Ryan that I was to go to confession myself on Saturday and be at the chapel for communion with the rest. To make it worse, Mother couldn't come with me and sent Nora instead.

Now, that girl had ways of tormenting me that Mother never knew of. She held my hand as we went down the hill, smiling sadly and saying how sorry she was for me, as if she were bringing me to the hospital for an operation.

"Oh, God help us!" she moaned. "Isn't it a terrible pity you weren't a good boy? Oh, Jackie, my heart bleeds for you! How will you ever think of all your sins? Don't forget you have to tell him about the time you kicked Gran on the shin."

"Lemme go!" I said, trying to drag myself free of her. "I don't want to go to confession at all."

"But sure, you'll have to go to confession, Jackie," she replied in the same regretful tone. "Sure, if you didn't, the parish priest would be up to the house, looking for you. 'Tisn't, God knows, that I'm not sorry for you. Do you remember the time you tried to kill me with the bread-knife under the table? And the language you used to me? I don't know what he'll do with you at all, Jackie. He might have to send you up to the bishop."

I remember thinking bitterly that she didn't know the half of what I had to tell — if I told it. I knew I couldn't tell it, and understood perfectly why the fellow in Mrs. Ryan's story made a bad confession; it seemed to me a great shame that people wouldn't stop criticizing him. I remember that steep hill down to the church, and the sunlit hillsides beyond the valley of the river, which I saw in the gaps between the houses like Adam's last glimpse of Paradise.

Then, when she had maneuvered me down the long flight of steps to the chapel yard, Nora suddenly changed her tone. She became the raging malicious devil she really was.

"There you are!" she said with a yelp of triumph, hurling me through the church door. "And I hope he'll give you the penitential psalms, you dirty little caffler."

I knew then I was lost, given up to eternal justice. The door with the colored-glass panels swung shut behind me, the sunlight went out and gave place to deep shadow, and the wind whistled outside so that the silence within seemed to crackle like ice under my feet. Nora sat in front of me by the confession box. There were a couple of old women ahead of her, and then a miserable-looking poor devil came and wedged me in at the other side, so that I couldn't escape even if I had the courage. He joined his hands and rolled his eyes in the direction of the roof, muttering aspirations in an anguished tone, and I wondered had he a grandmother too. Only a grandmother could account for a fellow behaving in that heartbroken way, but he was better off than I, for he at least could go and confess his sins; while I would make a bad confession and then die in the night and be continually coming back and burning people's furniture.

Nora's turn came, and I heard the sound of something slamming, and then her voice as if butter wouldn't melt in her mouth, and then another slam, and out she came. God, the hypocrisy of women! Her eyes were lowered, her head was bowed, and her hands were joined very low down on her stomach, and she walked up the aisle to the side altar looking like a saint. You never saw such an exhibition of devotion; and I remembered the devilish malice with which she had tormented me all the way from our door, and wondered were all religious people like that, really. It was my turn now. With the fear of damnation in my soul I went in, and the confessional door closed of itself behind me.

It was pitch-dark and I couldn't see priest or anything else. Then I really began to be frightened. In the darkness it was a matter between God and me, and He had all the odds. He knew what my intentions were before I ever started; I had no chance. All I had ever been told about confession got mixed up in my mind, and I knelt to one wall and said: "Bless me, father, for I have sinned; this is my first confession." I waited for a few minutes, but nothing happened, so I tried it on the other wall. Nothing happened there either. He had me spotted all right.

It must have been then that I noticed the shelf at about one height with my head. It was really a place for grown-up people to rest their elbows, but in my distracted state I thought it was probably the place you were supposed to kneel. Of course, it was on the high side and not very deep, but I was always good at climbing and managed to get up all right. Staying up was the trouble. There was room only for my knees, and nothing you could get a grip on but a sort of wooden moulding a bit above it. I held on to the moulding and repeated the words a little louder, and this time something happened all right. A slide was slammed back; a little light entered the box, and a man's voice said: "Who's there?"

" 'Tis me, father," I said for fear he mightn't see me and go away again. I couldn't see him at all. The place the voice came from was under the moulding, about level with my knees, so I took a good grip of the moulding and swung myself down till I saw the astonished face of a young priest looking up at me. He had to put his head on one side to see me, and I had to put mine on one side to see him, so we were more or less talking to one another upside-down. It struck me as a queer way of hearing confessions, but I didn't feel it my place to criticize.

"Bless me, father, for I have sinned; this is my first confession," I rattled off all in one breath, and swung myself down the least shade more to make it easier for him.

"What are you doing up there?" he shouted in an angry voice, and the strain the politeness was putting on my hold of the moulding, and the shock of being addressed in such an uncivil tone, were too much for me. I lost my grip, tumbled, and hit the door an unmerciful wallop before I found myself flat on my back in the middle of the aisle. The people who had been waiting stood up with their mouths open. The priest opened the door of the middle box and came out, pushing his biretta back from his forehead; he looked something terrible. Then Nora came scampering down the aisle.

"Oh, you dirty little caffler!" she cried. "I might have known you'd do it. I might have known you'd disgrace me. I can't leave you out of my sight for one minute."

Before I could even get to my feet to defend myself she bent down and gave me a clip across the ear. This reminded me that I was so stunned I had even forgotten to cry, so that people might think I wasn't hurt at all, when in fact I was probably maimed for life. I gave a roar out of me.

"What's all this about?" the priest hissed, getting angrier than ever and pushing Nora off me. "How dare you hit the child like that, you little vixen?"

"But I can't do my penance with him, father," Nora cried, cocking an outraged eye up at him.

"Well, go and do it, or I'll give you some more to do," he said, giving me a hand up. "Was it coming to confession you were, my poor man?" he asked me.

" 'Twas, father," said I with a sob.

"Oh," he said respectfully, "a big hefty fellow like you must have terrible sins. Is this your first?"

" 'Tis, father," said I.

"Worse and worse," he said gloomily. "The crimes of a lifetime. I don't know will I get rid of you at all today. You'd better wait now till I'm finished with these old ones. You can see by the looks of them they haven't much to tell."

"I will, father," I said with something approaching joy.

The relief of it was really enormous. Nora stuck out her tongue at me from behind his back, but I couldn't even be bothered retorting. I knew from the very moment that man opened his mouth that he was intelligent above the ordinary. When I had time to think, I saw how right I was. It only stood to reason that a fellow confessing after seven years would have more to tell than people that went every week. The crimes of a lifetime, exactly as he said. It was only what he expected, and the rest was the cackle of old women and girls with their talk of hell, the bishop, and the penitential psalms. That was all they knew. I started to make my examination of conscience, and barring the one bad business of my grandmother it didn't seem so bad.

The next time, the priest steered me into the confession box himself and left the shutter back the way I could see him get in and sit down at the further side of the grille from me.

"Well, now," he said, "what do they call you?"

"Jackie, father," said I.

"And what's a-trouble to you, Jackie?"

"Father," I said, feeling I might as well get it over while I had him in good humor, "I had it all arranged to kill my grandmother."

He seemed a bit shaken by that, all right, because he said nothing for quite a while.

"My goodness," he said at last, "that'd be a shocking thing to do. What put that into your head?"

"Father," I said, feeling very sorry for myself, "she's an awful woman."

"Is she?" he asked. "What way is she awful?"

"She takes porter, father," I said, knowing well from the way Mother talked of it that this was a mortal sin, and hoping it would make the priest take a more favorable view of my case.

"Oh, my!" he said, and I could see he was impressed.

"And snuff, father," said I.

"That's a bad case, sure enough, Jackie," he said.

"And she goes round in her bare feet, father," I went on in a rush of self-pity, "and she knows I don't like her, and she gives pennies to Nora and none to me, and my da sides with her and flakes me, and one night I was so heart-scalded I made up my mind I'd have to kill her."

"And what would you do with the body?" he asked with great interest.

"I was thinking I could chop that up and carry it away in a barrow I have," I said.

"Begor, Jackie," he said, "do you know you're a terrible child?"

"I know, father," I said, for I was just thinking the same thing myself. "I tried to kill Nora too with a bread-knife under the table, only I missed her."

"Is that the little girl that was beating you just now?" he asked.

" 'Tis, father."

"Someone will go for her with a bread-knife one day, and he won't miss her," he said rather cryptically. "You must have great courage. Between ourselves, there's a lot of people I'd like to do the same to but I'd never have the nerve. Hanging is an awful death."

"Is it, father?" I said with the deepest interest — I was always very keen on hanging. "Did you ever see a fellow hanged?"

"Dozens of them," he said solemnly. "And they all died roaring."

"Jay!" I said.

"Oh, a horrible death!" he said with great satisfaction. "Lots of the fellows I saw killed their grandmothers too, but they all said 'twas never worth it."

He had me there for a full ten minutes talking, and then walked out the chapel yard with me. I was genuinely sorry to part with him, because he was the most entertaining character I'd ever met in the religious line. Outside, after the shadow of the church, the sunlight was like the roaring of waves on a beach; it dazzled me; and when the frozen silence melted and I heard the screech of trams on the road my heart soared. I knew now I wouldn't die in the night and come back, leaving marks on my mother's furniture. It would be a great worry to her, and the poor soul had enough.

Nora was sitting on the railing, waiting for me, and she put on a very sour puss when she saw the priest with me. She was mad jealous because a priest had never come out of the church with her.

"Well," she asked coldly, after he left me, "what did he give you?"

"Three Hail Marys," I said.

"Three Hail Marys," she repeated incredulously. "You mustn't have told him anything."

"I told him everything," I said confidently.

"About Gran and all?"

"About Gran and all."

(All she wanted was to be able to go home and say I'd made a bad confession.)

"Did you tell him you went for me with the bread-knife?" she asked with a frown.

"I did to be sure."

"And he only gave you three Hail Marys?"

"That's all."

She slowly got down from the railing with a baffled air. Clearly, this was beyond her. As we mounted the steps back to the main road she looked at me suspiciously.

"What are you sucking?" she asked.

"Bullseyes."

"Was it the priest gave them to you?"

" 'Twas."

"Lord God," she wailed bitterly, "some people have all the luck! 'Tis no advantage to anybody trying to be good. I might just as well be a sinner like you."

PROBING FOR MEANING

1. Characterize Jackie. How typical a child is he? Why is he so obsessed with making a bad confession?

2. Compare and contrast the reactions of Nora and Jackie to their grandmother. What does the difference in reactions reveal? Does Jackie's reaction reflect his mother's indignation over the grandmother's arrival? Explain.

3. Characterize the priest. How does he react to Jackie's sins? To Nora's behavior? Why does he give Jackie such light penance and the bullseyes?

4. Does the story make a serious statement about religious belief? Sibling rivalry? Family relationships? Growing up? Explain fully.

PROBING FOR METHOD

1. This story, a recollection of a childhood experience, is told in the past tense. What are the advantages of this narrative style? Would the story differ if Nora were to tell it? The priest? Explain.

2. Do you find the story humorous? Point out two humorous passages and attempt to explain how the humor is achieved.

 WILFRED OWEN

Disabled

He sat in a wheeled chair, waiting for dark,
And shivered in his ghastly suit of grey,
Legless, sewn short at elbow. Through the park
Voices of boys rang saddening like a hymn,
Voices of play and pleasures after day,
Till gathering sleep had mothered them from him.

About this time Town used to swing so gay
When glow-lamps budded in the light blue trees,
And girls glanced lovelier as the air grew dim, —
In the old times, before he threw away his knees.
Now he will never feel again how slim
Girl's waists are, or how warm their subtle hands;
All of them touch him like some queer disease.

There was an artist silly for his face,
For it was younger than his youth, last year.
Now, he is old; his back will never brace;
He's lost his colour very far from here,
Poured it down shell-holes till the veins ran dry,
And half his lifetime lapsed in the hot race,
And leap of purple spurted from his thigh.

One time he liked a blood-smear down his leg,
After the matches, carried shoulder-high.
It was after football, when he'd drunk a peg,
He thought he'd better join. — He wonders why.
Someone had said he'd look a god in kilts,
That's why; and may be, too, to please his Meg;
Aye, that was it, to please the giddy jilts
He asked to join. He didn't have to beg;
Smiling they wrote his lie; aged nineteen years.
Germans he scarcely thought of; all their guilt,
And Austria's, did not move him. And no fears
Of Fear came yet. He thought of jewelled hilts
For daggers in plaid socks; of smart salutes;
And care of arms; and leave; and pay arrears;
Esprit de corps; and hints for young recruits.
And soon he was drafted out with drums and cheers.

Some cheered him home, but not as crowds cheer Goal.
Only a solemn man who brought him fruits
Thanked him; and then inquired about his soul.

Now, he will spend a few sick years in Institutes,
And do what things the rules consider wise,
And take whatever pity they may dole.
To-night he noticed how the woman's eyes
Passed from him to the strong men that were whole.
How cold and late it is! Why don't they come
And put him into bed? Why don't they come?

PROBING FOR   1. How was the young man disabled?
    MEANING   2. What was his attitude toward life before he was hurt? How has his
attitude changed?
                   3. Why did he go off to war?
                   4. How does his society treat him, now that he is disabled?

PROBING FOR   1. To what degree does the poet employ chronological narration?
     METHOD   What effects does he gain by interrupting the narrative to focus on the present?
                   2. What is the poet's attitude toward the soldier? How does he feel
about the treatment the soldier receives?
                   3. Why does the poet describe the voices of the boys at play in the
first stanza? What theme does this image introduce?

 EMILY DICKINSON

I Taste a Liquor Never Brewed

I taste a liquor never brewed —
From Tankards scooped in Pearl —
Not all the Frankfort Berries
Yield such an Alcohol!

Inebriate of Air — am I —
And Debauchee of Dew —
Reeling — thro endless summer days —
From inns of Molten Blue —

When "Landlords" turn the drunken Bee
Out of the Foxglove's door —
When Butterflies — renounce their "dram" —
I shall but drink the more!

Till Seraphs swing their snowy Hats —
And Saints — to windows run —
To see the little Tippler
From Manzanilla come!

PROBING FOR   1. What sort of "liquor" does the speaker drink? Where does she do
MEANING   her drinking?

      2. How long will she continue to drink?

      3. What kind of experience is she actually describing?

PROBING FOR   1. How does the poet extend the metaphor of the first stanza
METHOD   throughout the poem? How does the first stanza prepare us to understand such
images as the "inns of Molten Blue" and the "Landlords of Foxglove"?

      2. What kind of exaggeration does the poet employ in the last two
stanzas? How does this exaggeration help us to understand her mood?

 JAMES WRIGHT

A Blessing

Just off the highway to Rochester, Minnesota,
Twilight bounds softly forth on the grass.
And the eyes of those two Indian ponies
Darken with kindness.
They have come gladly out of the willows
To welcome my friend and me.
We step over the barbed wire into the pasture
Where they have been grazing all day, alone.
They ripple tensely, they can hardly contain their happiness
That we have come.
They bow shyly as wet swans. They love each other.
There is no loneliness like theirs.
At home once more,
They begin munching the young tufts of spring in the dark-
      ness.
I would like to hold the slenderer one in my arms,
For she has walked over to me
And nuzzled my left hand.
She is black and white,
Her mane falls wild on her forehead,
And the light breeze moves me to caress her long ear
That is delicate as the skin over a girl's wrist.
Suddenly I realize
That if I stepped out of my body I would break
Into blossom.

PROBING FOR
MEANING

1. What are the ponies like? How do they respond to the speaker and his friend? What does the speaker mean when he says, "There is no loneliness like theirs"?

2. When does the speaker visit the ponies? In what way is the time of the visit significant?

3. Describe the nature of the experience that the speaker has. Why does he call his experience "a blessing"?

PROBING FOR
METHOD

1. The speaker employs simile twice to describe the ponies. What impression does he create by comparing the ponies to "wet swans"? Why does he use the modifier "wet"? What is the effect of his comparing the ear of the black and white pony to the skin of a girl's wrist? Does the speaker use metaphor in the poem?

2. Just how realistic is the poet's description of the ponies' emotions? Do animals have emotions similar to ours?

3. Although the speaker's experience must actually be over by the time he writes the poem, he chooses to narrate the experience in the simple present tense. Why? Would the poem affect us differently if it were written in the past tense?

Topics for Imitation

1. Most writers of narratives choose events and experiences that are of value to their readers. If you have witnessed an event or had an experience that other people can learn from, relate that event in chronological order, including the wisdom you obtained from that experience that you want to share.

2. Choose an experience you have had — dating, school, camping, traveling — and form a conclusion about that experience that can be of value to other people. For example, you might conclude that dating many different types of people is an education itself. Using your conclusion as a thesis statement, organize your outline and form topic sentences for your paragraphs. Use your own experience to supply details and examples in developing your paragraphs. Use Joyce Maynard's essay as a model; in other words, use analysis rather than chronological order.

3. Both E. B. White and Elie Wiesel concern themselves with the passage of time and the changes that this brings. Write an essay in which you compare the attitudes the authors take toward time's passage.

4. Both Wehle and Wiesel were victims of racism. Compare the effects such victimization had on the authors.

5. Discuss Hana Wehle's essay in the light of James Wright's poem.

6. In many of this chapter's selections the meaning of the narrative is rendered symbolically. Discuss how symbolic images convey significant information about an event or experience in selections by White, Selzer, Wiesel, and/or Dickinson.

7. The major characters in both "First Confession" and "The Sojourner" endure an agonizing experience in order to learn an important truth. Analyze their experiences and the truths they learned.

FOUR

EMOTIONS

"To each his world is private"

While we experience our emotions individually, as members of society we often have feelings that others share. Social forces influence us just as do individual people, places, and events. For example, the writers in this chapter believe that factors in our society cause Americans at times to feel revengeful, exploited, prejudiced, violent, and afraid. They attempt to explain the causes of these emotions which we share with one another, hoping thereby to ease our isolation and help us search for solutions.

Loren Eiseley examines the elusiveness of our emotional need for belonging; George Orwell discusses the futility of revenge; and Marya Mannes explains that television commercials project hurtful images of Americans, and American women in particular. Herbert Gold tries "to work out an explanation for the upsurge in violence in contemporary America," and Lewis Thomas encourages us "to give up the notion that death is catastrophe, or detestable, or avoidable or even strange."

The short stories dramatize the effects of these communal emotions on individuals. Ann Petry depicts the devastating effect of racial prejudice on individual relationships, and Ralph Ellison dramatizes the indignities of poverty.

"First Practice" exposes how society perpetuates violence in the young, "Disillusionment of Ten O'Clock" depicts conformity, and "Colours," the precariousness of human emotions.

Analyzing Causes and Effects and Achieving Coherence

Another approach to organizing an essay is through a presentation of the causes and/or effects of the subject. If, in your prewriting stage of generating ideas, you sought to analyze the causes and effects of your subject, then a causal pattern should emerge as you write. Also, as you are writing, you should make your presentation of your subject and your organization of your essay as clear to your reader as possible through techniques that establish the coherence or unity of your work. To learn more about this causal pattern, turn to pp. 165–167 at the end of Loren Eiseley's essay "The Brown Wasps." Techniques for establishing coherence are discussed on pp. 170–172 following George Orwell's "Revenge is Sour." Analyze these two essays and the others in the chapter for the causal patterns that emerge and the techniques used by the writers to establish the coherence of those patterns.

 LOREN EISELEY

The Brown Wasps

There is a corner in the waiting room of one of the great Eastern stations where women never sit. It is always in the shadow and overhung by rows of lockers. It is, however, always frequented — not so much by genuine travelers as by the dying. It is here that a certain element of the abandoned poor seeks a refuge out of the weather, clinging for a few hours longer to the city that has fathered them. In a precisely similar manner I have seen, on a sunny day in midwinter, a few old brown wasps creep slowly over an abandoned wasp nest in a thicket. Numbed and forgetful and frost-blackened, the hum of the spring hive still resounded faintly in their sodden tissues. Then the temperature would fall and they would drop away into the white oblivion of the snow. Here in the station it is in no way different save that the city is busy in its snows. But the old ones cling to their seats as though these were symbolic and could not be given up. Now and then they sleep, their gray old heads resting with painful awkwardness on the backs of the benches.

Also they are not at rest. For an hour they may sleep in the gasping exhaustion of the ill-nourished and aged who have to walk in the night. Then a policeman comes by on his round and nudges them upright.

"You can't sleep here," he growls.

A strange ritual then begins. An old man is difficult to waken. After a muttered conversation the policeman presses a coin into his hand and passes fiercely along the benches prodding and gesturing toward the door. In his wake, like birds rising and settling behind the passage of a farmer through a cornfield, the men totter up, move a few paces, and subside once more upon the benches.

One man, after a slight, apologetic lurch, does not move at all. Tubercularly thin, he sleeps on steadily. The policeman does not look back. To him, too, this has become a ritual. He will not have to notice it again officially for another hour.

Once in a while one of the sleepers will not awake. Like the brown wasps, he will have had his wish to die in the great droning center of the hive rather than in some lonely room. It is not so bad here with the shuffle of footsteps and the knowledge that there are others who share the bad luck of the world. There are also the whistles and the sounds of everyone, everyone in the world, starting on journeys. Amidst too many journeys somebody is bound to come out all right. Somebody.

Maybe it was on a like thought that the brown wasps fell away from the old paper nest in the thicket. You hold till the last, even if it is only to a public seat in a railroad station. You want your place in the hive more than you want a room or a place where the aged can be eased gently out of the way. It is the place that matters, the place at the heart of things. It is life that you want, that bruises your gray old head with the hard chairs; a man has a right to his place.

But sometimes the place is lost in the years behind us. Or sometimes it is a thing of air, a kind of vaporous distortion above a heap of rubble. We cling to a time and a place because without them man is lost, not only man but life. This is why the voices, real or unreal, which speak from the floating trumpets at spiritualist seances are so unnerving. They are voices out of nowhere whose only reality lies in their ability to stir the memory of a living person with some fragment of the past. Before the medium's cabinet both the dead and the living revolve endlessly about an episode, a place, an event that has already been engulfed by time.

This feeling runs deep in life; it brings stray cats running over endless miles, and birds homing from the ends of the earth. It is as though all living creatures, and particularly the more intelligent, can survive only by fixing or transforming a bit of time into space or by securing a bit of space with its objects immortalized and made permanent in time. For example, I once saw, on a flower pot in my own living room, the efforts of a field mouse to build a remembered field. I have lived to see this episode repeated in a thousand guises, and since I have spent a large portion of my life in the shade of a nonexistent tree I think I am entitled to speak for the field mouse.

One day as I cut across the field which at that time extended on one side of our suburban shopping center, I found a giant slug feeding from a runnel of pink ice cream in an abandoned Dixie cup. I could see his eyes telescope and protrude in a kind of dim uncertain ecstasy as his dark body bunched and elongated in the curve of the cup. Then, as I stood there at the edge of the concrete, contemplating the slug, I began to realize it was like standing on a shore where a different type of life creeps up and fumbles tentatively among the rocks and sea wrack. It knows its place and will only creep so far until something changes. Little by little as I stood there I began to see more of this shore that surrounds the place of man. I looked with sudden care and attention at things I had been running over thoughtlessly for years. I even waded out a short way into the grass and the wild-rose thickets to see more. A huge blackbelted bee went droning by and there were some indistinct scurryings in the underbrush.

Then I came to a sign which informed me that this field was to be the site of a new Wanamaker suburban store. Thousands of obscure lives were about to perish, the spores of puffballs would go smoking off to new fields, and the bodies of little white-footed mice would be crunched under the inexorable wheels of the bulldozers. Life disappears or modifies its appearances so fast that everything takes on an aspect of illusion — a momentary fizzing and boiling with smoke rings, like pouring dissident chemicals into a retort. Here a man was advancing, but in a few years his plaster and bricks would be disappearing once more into the insatiable maw of the clover. Being of an archaeological cast of mind, I thought of this fact with an obscure sense of satisfaction and waded back through the rose thickets to the concrete parking lot. As I did so, a mouse scurried ahead of me, frightened of my steps if not of that ominous Wanamaker sign. I saw him vanish in the general direction of my apartment house, his little body quivering with fear in the great open sun on the blazing concrete. Blinded and confused, he was running straight away from his field. In another week scores would follow him.

I forgot the episode then and went home to the quiet of my living room. It was not until a week later, letting myself into the apartment, that I realized I had a visitor. I am fond of plants and had several ferns standing on the floor in pots to avoid the noon glare by the south window.

As I snapped on the light and glanced carelessly around the room, I saw a little heap of earth on the carpet and a scrabble of pebbles that had been kicked merrily over the edge of one of the flower pots. To my astonishment I discovered a full-fledged burrow delving downward among the fern roots. I waited silently. The creature who had made the burrow did not appear. I remembered the wild field then, and the flight of the mice. No house mouse, no *Mus domesticus*, had kicked up this little heap of earth or sought refuge under a fern root in a flower pot. I thought of the desperate little creature I had seen fleeing from the wild-rose thicket. Through intricacies of pipes and attics, he, or one of his fellows, had climbed to this high green solitary room. I could visualize what had occurred. He had an image in his head, a world of seed pods and quiet, of green sheltering leaves in the dim light among the weed stems. It was the only world he knew and it was gone.

Somehow in his flight he had found his way to this room with drawn shades where no one would come till nightfall. And here he had smelled green leaves and run quickly up the flower pot to dabble his paws in common earth. He had even struggled half the afternoon to carry his burrow deeper and had failed. I examined the hole, but no whiskered twitching face appeared. He was gone. I gathered up the earth and refilled the burrow. I did not expect to find traces of him again.

Yet for three nights thereafter I came home to the darkened room and my ferns to find the dirt kicked gaily about the rug and the burrow reopened, though I was never able to catch the field mouse within it. I dropped a little food about the mouth of the burrow, but it was never touched. I looked under beds or sat reading with one ear cocked for rustlings in the ferns. It was all in vain; I never saw him. Probably he ended in a trap in some other tenant's room.

But before he disappeared I had come to look hopefully for his evening burrow. About my ferns there had begun to linger the insubstantial vapor of an autumn field, the distilled essence, as it were, of a mouse brain in exile from its home. It was a small dream, like our dreams, carried a long and weary journey along pipes and through spider webs, past holes over which loomed the shadows of waiting cats, and finally, desperately, into this room where he had played in the shuttered daylight for an hour among the green ferns on the floor. Every day these invisible dreams pass us on the street, or rise from beneath our feet, or look upon us from beneath a bush.

Some years ago the old elevated railway in Philadelphia was torn down and replaced by a subway system. This ancient El with its barnlike stations containing nut-vending machines and scattered food scraps had, for generations, been the favorite feeding ground of flocks of pigeons, generally one flock to a station along the route of the El. Hundreds of pigeons were dependent upon the system. They flapped in and out of its stanchions and steel work or gathered in watchful little audiences about the feet of anyone who rattled the peanut-vending machines. They even watched people who jingled change in their hands, and prospected for food under the feet of the crowds, who gathered between trains. Probably very few among the waiting people who tossed a crumb to an eager pigeon realized that this El was like a food-bearing river, and that the life which haunted its banks was dependent upon the running of the trains with their human freight.

I saw the river stop.

The time came when the underground tubes were ready; the traffic was transferred to a realm unreachable by pigeons. It was like a great river subsiding suddenly into desert sands. For a day, for two days, pigeons continued to circle over the El or stand close to the red vending machines. They were patient birds, and surely this great river which had flowed through the lives of unnumbered generations was merely suffering from some momentary drought.

They listened for the familiar vibrations that had always heralded an approaching train; they flapped hopefully about the head of an occasional workman walking along the steel runways. They passed from one empty station to another, all the while growing hungrier. Finally they flew away.

I thought I had seen the last of them about the El, but there was a revival and it provided a curious instance of the memory of living things for a way of life or a locality that has long been cherished. Some weeks after the El was abandoned workmen began to tear it down. I went to work every morning by one particular station, and the time came when the demolition crews reached this spot. Acetylene torches showered passers-by with sparks, pneumatic drills hammered at the base of the structure, and a blind man who, like the pigeons, had clung with his cup to a stairway leading to the change booth, was forced to give up his place.

It was then, strangely, momentarily, one morning that I witnessed the return of a little band of the familiar pigeons. I even recognized one or two members of the flock that had lived around this particular station before they were dispersed into the streets. They flew bravely in and out among the sparks and the hammers and the shouting workmen. They had returned — and they had returned because the hubbub of the wreckers had convinced them that the river was about to flow once more. For several hours they flapped in and out through the empty windows, nodding their heads and watching the fall of girders with attentive little eyes. By the following morning the station was reduced to some burned-off stanchions in the street. My bird friends had gone. It was plain, however, that they retained a memory for an insubstantial structure now compounded of air and time. Even the blind man clung to it. Someone had provided him with a chair, and he sat at the same corner staring sightlessly at an invisible stairway where, so far as he was concerned, the crowds were still ascending to the trains.

I have said my life has been passed in the shade of a nonexistent tree, so that such sights do not offend me. Prematurely I am one of the brown wasps and I often sit with them in the great droning hive of the station, dreaming sometimes of a certain tree. It was planted sixty years ago by a boy with a bucket and a toy spade in a little Nebraska town. That boy was myself. It was a cottonwood sapling and the boy remembered it because of some words spoken by his father and because everyone died or moved away who was supposed to wait and grow old under its shade. The boy was passed from hand to hand, but the tree for some intangible reason had taken root in his mind. It was under its branches that he sheltered; it was from this tree that his memories, which are my memories, led away into the world.

After sixty years the mood of the brown wasps grows heavier upon one. During a long inward struggle I thought it would do me good to go and look upon that actual tree. I found a rational excuse in which to clothe this madness. I purchased a ticket and at the end of two thousand miles I walked another mile to an address that was still the same. The house had not been altered.

I came close to the white picket fence and reluctantly, with great effort, looked down the long vista of the yard. There was nothing there to see. For sixty years that cottonwood had been growing in my mind. Season by season its seeds had been floating farther on the hot prairie winds. We had planted it lovingly there, my father and I, because he had a great hunger for soil and live things growing, and because none of these things had long been ours to protect. We had planted the little sapling and watered it faithfully, and I remembered that I had run out with my small bucket to drench its roots the day we moved away. And all the years since it had been growing in my mind, a huge tree that somehow stood for my father and the love I bore him. I took a grasp on the picket fence and forced myself to look again.

A boy with the hard bird eye of youth pedaled a tricycle slowly up beside me.

"What'cha lookin' at?" he asked curiously.

"A tree," I said.

"What for?" he said.

"It isn't there," I said, to myself mostly, and began to walk away at a pace just slow enough not to seem to be running.

"What isn't there?" the boy asked. I didn't answer. It was obvious I was attached by a thread to a thing that had never been there, or certainly not for long. Something that had to be held in the air, or sustained in the mind, because it was part of my orientation in the universe and I could not survive without it. There was more than an animal's attachment to a place. There was something else, the attachment of the spirit to a grouping of events in time; it was part of our mortality.

So I had come home at last, driven by a memory in the brain as surely as the field mouse who had delved long ago into my flower pot or the pigeons flying forever amidst the rattle of nut-vending machines. These, the burrow under the greenery in my living room and the red-bellied bowls of peanuts now hovering in midair in the minds of pigeons, were all part of an elusive world that existed nowhere and yet everywhere. I looked once at the real world about me while the persistent boy pedaled at my heels.

It was without meaning, though my feet took a remembered path. In sixty years the house and street had rotted out of my mind. But the tree, the tree that no longer was, that had perished in its first season, bloomed on in my individual mind, unblemished as my father's words. "We'll plant a tree here, son, and we're not going to move any more. And when you're an old, old man you can sit under it and think how we planted it here, you and me, together."

I began to outpace the boy on the tricycle.

"Do you live here, Mister?" he shouted after me suspiciously. I took a firm grasp on airy nothing — to be precise, on the bole of a great tree. "I do," I said. I spoke for myself, one field mouse, and several pigeons. We were all out of touch but somehow permanent. It was the world that had changed.

PROBING FOR MEANING

1. What is it that Eiseley finds the old brown wasps have in common with the old men in the station? What feeling do both seem to share?

2. What did Eiseley feel when he discovered that a Wanamaker store was to be built on the field next to the shopping center? What did he feel about the mouse who burrowed in the flower pot in his apartment?

3. Why does he think that the pigeons returned to the El station after it had been abandoned?

4. What was it that prompted Eiseley to return to Nebraska? Why did he feel that he needed "a rational excuse in which to clothe this madness"? Was his desire to return to the shade of a "nonexistent tree" irrational? What did the tree represent to him?

5. What does Eiseley mean when, at the end of the essay, he says of himself, the mouse, and the pigeons, "We were all out of touch but somehow permanent"?

PROBING FOR METHOD

1. Eiseley alternates narrative and descriptive passages with explanatory passages. How fully does he explain the causes and the effects of what he calls "the mood of the brown wasps" in the latter passages? What information do his narratives and descriptions provide about these causes and effects?

2. Occasionally, Eiseley does not depend upon such surface transitional devices as conjunctions and adverbs or repetition of key phrases, instead choosing to link passages by means of a shared image. What image serves as a primary transition between the narrative of the field mouse and the description of the pigeons? What image links the latter description with Eiseley's memory of his return to Nebraska?

3. How often does Eiseley rely upon metaphor or simile, as when he describes the El as a "food-bearing river"? Select one such metaphor, simile, or symbol from the essay and discuss the attitude it implies toward the person or thing it describes.

4. Eiseley says that he is of "an archaeological cast of mind." How well does this define his attitude toward his subject in general? What is the overall tone of the essay? To what degree is Eiseley's tone a reflection of the mood of the brown wasps? To what degree does he convey a sense of objective distance from the emotion he describes?

Analyzing Causes and Effects

How does Eiseley analyze the causes of the behavior in "The Brown Wasps"?   Eiseley cites several phenomena in human and animal life as the effect of the need of all creatures for "a place at the heart of things. . . . without them man is lost, not only man but life."

He asks first why the old and poor congregate in stations to die. He connects this human behavior with the tendency of old brown wasps to cling to their nests. He concludes that both wasps and people need to belong, and will associate a particular place with their need. He then discusses other effects of this same feeling: the field mouse who disappeared from the construction site and burrowed in his flower pot, the pigeons who returned to the old elevated railway even as it was being dismantled, and he himself who one day visited the cottonwood tree his father had planted for the family to live and die under.

Analyzing causes and effects.   As indicated in previous chapters, the subject about which you are writing usually suggests a particular method of organization. For example, when describing a place, spatial cohesion is the logical method of development; when relating events, chronological order is followed.

A third common method of development is useful when you analyze the causes of a particular situation or, conversely, its effects. This cause-and-effect technique either presents an effect and then proceeds to analyze the causes, or predicts effects that could result from existing forces.

In analyzing the causes of an effect, you must be careful to establish that the causes you suggest actually did create the effect. In other words, determine that without A, B, would not have come about. For example, would it be correct to say that without women's liberation, the divorce rate would not have increased?

In predicting the effects of a situation, you must also determine that the effect will necessarily follow. Whenever there is A, in other words, there will be B. For example, would it be correct to say that the easing of divorce laws leads necessarily to the disintegration of marriage?

Also, you must be sure to include all major causes of an effect. If women's liberation is only one cause of the disintegration of marriage, then there must be others. While B might exist without A_1, it would surely exist with a combination of A_1, A_2, and A_3. It might be fair to say that women's liberation, the easing of divorce laws, and the peculiar demands placed upon marriage in our time lead to the disintegration of marriage.

Just as you must carefully determine all causes, you must also analyze all effects: whenever there is A, there will be B_1 and B_2. The easing of divorce laws may contribute to the disintegration of marriage, but it will also allow people who cannot live together to find happiness apart.

The writers of the essays in this chapter illustrate all of these four cause-and-effect assertions. Eiseley, Gold, Thomas, and Orwell illustrate the first one: Without A, B would not have come about. Eiseley, as we have seen, analyzes several isolated patterns of human and animal behavior as the effect of the need to belong. Gold claims that the causes of random violence are modern man's feelings of helplessness and powerlessness as well as parental and societal permissiveness. Thomas believes that death will not be in the open until we can no longer hide it. Orwell knows that revenge is sour only when the enemy has been rendered helpless. But Mannes does not argue that television advertising is the only cause of psychic disintegration; "multiple forces" have caused it, she admits.

Mannes, Eiseley, and Thomas argue that "whenever there is A, there will be B." Mannes asserts that whenever there is television advertising, there is psychic disintegration. Eiseley would agree that as all life needs to belong, there will always be such patterns of behavior as those he cites. Thomas affirms that when our population doubles and we can no longer avoid the thought of death, then death will finally be in the open. Gold, however, does not claim that helpless victims of a permissive society are always violent.

Gold would uphold the third assertion, that B is the result of several causes: neither permissiveness alone nor helplessness by itself leads necessarily to random acts of violence. He believes that both causes must be present for violence to occur. As we have seen, Mannes admits that "multiple forces" have created the psychic disintegration of American society.

And the fourth assertion, that A leads to several, even contradictory, effects, is claimed by Mannes who believes that while television advertising may be witty, helpful at times, and the sole support of the networks, it also contributes to "the diminution of human worth, the infusion and hardening of social attitudes no longer valid or desirable, pervasive discontent, and psychic fragmentation."

Procedures to follow in developing a cause-and-effect essay.

A. Analyze your topic. Does it suggest a cause-and-effect organization? In other words, are you interested in determining why a situation has come about or, on the other hand, what effect an existing situation might cause?

B. Check your analysis of the causes of your effect to make sure that you have not been illogical, either by assigning as causes factors that did not contribute to the effect, or by omitting other important causes.

C. Check your analysis of effects to ascertain that your cause will necessarily lead to this effect and that you have included all effects of your cause.

 GEORGE ORWELL

Revenge Is Sour

Whenever I read phrases like "war guilt trials," "punishment of war criminals," and so forth, there comes back into my mind the memory of something I saw in a prisoner-of-war camp in South Germany, earlier this year.

Another correspondent and myself were being shown round the camp by a little Viennese Jew who had been enlisted in the branch of the American army which deals with the interrogation of prisoners. He was an alert, fair-haired, rather good-looking youth of about twenty-five, and politically so much more knowledgeable than the average American officer that it was a pleasure to be with him. The camp was on an airfield, and, after we had been round the cages, our guided led us to a hangar where various prisoners who were in a different category from the others were being "screened."

Up at one end of the hangar about a dozen men were lying in a row on the concrete floor. These, it was explained, were SS officers who had been segregated from the other prisoners. Among them was a man in dingy civilian clothes who was lying with his arm across his face and apparently asleep. He had strangely and horribly deformed feet. The two of them were quite symmetrical, but they were clubbed out into an extraordinary globular shape which made them more like a horse's hoof than anything human. As we approached the group the little Jew seemed to be working himself up into a state of excitement.

"That's the real swine!" he said, and suddenly he lashed out with his heavy army boot and caught the prostrate man a fearful kick right on the bulge of one of his deformed feet.

"Get up, you swine!" he shouted as the man started out of sleep, and then repeated something of the kind in German. The prisoner scrambled to his feet and stood clumsily to attention. With the same air of working himself up into a fury — indeed he was almost dancing up and down as he spoke — the Jew told us the prisoner's history. He was a "real" Nazi: his party number indicated that he had been a member since the very early days, and he had held a post corresponding to a General in the political branch of the SS. It could be taken as quite certain that he had had charge of concentration camps and had presided over tortures and hangings. In short, he represented everything that we had been fighting against during the past five years.

Meanwhile, I was studying his appearance. Quite apart from the scrubby, unfed, unshaven look that a newly captured man generally has, he was a disgusting specimen. But he did not look brutal or in any way frightening: merely neurotic and, in a low way, intellectual. His pale, shifty eyes were deformed by powerful spectacles. He could have been an unfrocked clergyman, an actor ruined by drink, or a spiritualist medium. I have seen very similar people in London common lodging houses, and also in the Reading Room of the British Museum. Quite obviously he was mentally unbalanced — indeed, only doubtfully sane, though at this moment sufficiently in his right mind to be frightened of getting another kick. And yet everything that the Jew was telling me of his history could have been true, and probably was true! So the Nazi torturer of one's imagination, the monstrous figure against whom one had struggled for so many years, dwindled to this pitiful wretch, whose obvious need was not for punishment, but for some kind of psychological treatment.

Later, there were further humiliations. Another SS officer, a large, brawny man, was ordered to strip to the waist and show the blood-group number tattooed on his under-arm; another was forced to explain to us how he had lied about being a member of the SS and attempted to pass himself off as an ordinary soldier of the Wehrmacht. I wondered whether the Jew was getting any real kick out of this new-found power that he was exercising. I concluded that he wasn't really enjoying it, and that he was merely — like a man in a brothel, or a boy smoking his first cigar, or a tourist traipsing round a picture gallery — *telling* himself that he was enjoying it, and behaving as he had planned to behave in the days when he was helpless.

It is absurd to blame any German or Austrian Jew for getting his own back on the Nazis. Heaven knows what scores this particular man may have had to wipe out; very likely his whole family had been murdered; and, after all, even a wanton kick to a prisoner is a very tiny thing compared with the outrages committed by the Hitler régime. But what this scene, and much else that I saw in Germany, brought home to me was that the whole idea of revenge and punishment is a childish day-dream. Properly speaking, there is no such thing as revenge. Revenge is an act which you want to commit when you are powerless and because you are powerless: as soon as the sense of impotence is removed, the desire evaporates also.

Who would not have jumped for joy, in 1940, at the thought of seeing SS officers kicked and humiliated? But when the thing becomes possible, it is merely pathetic and disgusting. It is said that when Mussolini's corpse was exhibited in public, an old woman drew a revolver and fired five shots into it, exclaiming, "Those are for my five sons!" It is the kind of story that the newspapers make up, but it might be true. I wonder how much satisfaction she got out of those five shots, which, doubtless, she had dreamed years earlier of firing. The condition of her being able to get near enough to Mussolini to shoot at him was that he should be a corpse.

In so far as the big public in this country is responsible for the monstrous peace settlement now being forced on Germany, it is because of a failure to see in advance that punishing an enemy brings no satisfaction. We acquiesced in crimes like the expulsion of all Germans from East Prussia — crimes which in some cases we could not prevent but might at least have protested against — because the Germans had angered and frightened us, and therefore we were certain that when they were down we should feel no pity for them. We persist in these policies, or let others persist in them on our behalf, because of a vague feeling that, having set out to punish Germany, we ought to go ahead and do it. Actually there is little acute hatred of Germany left in this country, and even less, I should expect to find, in the army of occupation. Only the minority of sadists, who must have their "atrocities" from one source or another, take a keen interest in the hunting-down of war criminals and quislings. If you ask the average man what crime Goering, Ribbentrop and the rest are to be charged with at their trial, he cannot tell you. Somehow the punishment of these monsters ceases to seem attractive when it becomes possible: indeed, once under lock and key, they almost cease to be monsters.

Unfortunately, there is often need of some concrete incident before one can discover the real state of one's feelings. Here is another memory from Germany. A few hours after Stuttgart was captured by the French army, a Belgian journalist and myself entered the town, which was still in some disorder. The Belgian had been broadcasting throughout the war for the European Service of the BBC, and, like nearly all Frenchmen or Belgians, he had a very much tougher attitude towards "the Boche" than an Englishman or an American would have. All the main bridges into the town had been blown up, and we had to enter by a small footbridge which the Germans had evidently made efforts to defend. A dead German soldier was lying supine at the foot of the steps. His face was a waxy yellow. On his breast someone had laid a bunch of the lilac which was blossoming everywhere.

The Belgian averted his face as we went past. When we were well over the bridge he confided to me that this was the first time he had seen a dead man. I suppose he was thirty-five years old, and for four years he had been doing war propaganda over the radio. For several days after this, his attitude was quite different from what it had been earlier. He looked with disgust at the bomb-wrecked town and the humiliations the Germans were undergoing, and even on one occasion intervened to prevent a particularly bad bit of looting. When he left, he gave the residue of the coffee we had brought with us to the Germans on whom we were billeted. A week earlier he would probably have been scandalised at the idea of giving coffee to a "Boche." But his feelings, he told me, had undergone a change at the sight of "ce pauvre mort" beside the bridge: it had suddenly brought home to him the meaning of war. And yet, if we had happened to enter the town by another route, he might have been spared the experience of seeing even one corpse out of the — perhaps — twenty million that the war has produced.

PROBING FOR MEANING

1. Why does the Viennese Jew react with such fury to the prisoner that he calls "the real swine"? What effect does the prisoner's appearance have on Orwell?

2. What does Orwell mean when he writes, "Properly speaking, there is no such thing as revenge"?

3. What is it, according to Orwell, that causes the English to persist in carrying out policies of revenge against Germany? Do you agree with his argument that the punishment of Nazi criminals "ceases to seem attractive when it becomes possible"?

4. What does the incident in Stuttgart help the Belgian journalist to discover about his feelings? How does this incident clarify Orwell's feelings?

PROBING FOR METHOD

1. What does the story of the woman who shot Mussolini's corpse add to our understanding of the effects of revenge? Why did Orwell include this story?

2. Orwell writes that "there is often need of some concrete incident before one can discover the state of one's true feelings." In what sense does this statement underscore the organizational principle of the essay? In what sense does it represent a central theme?

3. What is Orwell's tone? How objectively does he analyze his own feelings? What purpose motivates him to write this essay?

Achieving Coherence

How does Orwell achieve coherence?   The various sentences and paragraphs connect to each other and to the thesis of the essay largely through Orwell's repetition of key words and phrases. Since the actors in Orwell's drama are few, and since he refers to them in stark terms such as the Jew, the prisoner, the Germans, the Americans, and the Belgian, the reader is always clear as to who is being referred to and as to the connection of that person to the thesis of the essay.

The actions are fewer than the actors, and again, Orwell uses key terms in referring to these actions so that we constantly are aware of the unity of the essay. He begins by describing the kick that the Jew delivers to the deformed foot of the prisoner. He refers several times throughout the essay to the kick, but also, in order to avoid boring repetition, he varies his expression with "humiliations," "punishments," and, finally, his key word "revenge." These four words are interspersed throughout, linking the various parts into a coherent essay.

Sentences are linked with sentences and paragraphs with paragraphs as well. Paragraphs 6 and 7, for example, begin with words ("meanwhile" and "later") that connect them in time to the sequence of events. The sentences within paragraph 2 are linked to each other by various devices. The pronoun "he" in the second sentence refers to the "little Viennese Jew" of sentence 1. The "average American officer" of sentence 2 connects with "branch of the American army" in sentence 1. "The camp" and "various prisoners" in sentence 3 refers to the prisoner-of-war camp mentioned in the first paragraph. The conjunction "and" in sentence 3 gives the two parts of the sentence equal status, and the conjunction "after" expresses a chronological connection between two other parts of the sentence.

In paragraph 3, "up at one end of the hanger" makes a connection between paragraphs and establishes a spatial pattern, just as "meanwhile" and "later" establish narrative patterns. The demonstrative adjective "these" in the next sentence connects the first two sentences of paragraph 3. "Among them" at the beginning of sentence 3 connects that sentence with the previous one. The pronoun "them" in sentence 5 connects sentences 4 and 5. The conjunction "but" connects the two parts of sentence five by pointing out an apparent contradiction. "As we approached the group" in the last sentence of paragraph 3 shows a movement in time.

Achieving coherence.   Transitions are words and phrases that establish connections between words, sentences, and paragraphs. Through the use of transitions, the writer gives the essay the coherence necessary if the reader is to understand the progression of ideas. The most common form of transition is the conjunction. Conjunctions establish such logical relations between thoughts as addition (*and*), contrast (*but*), comparison (*as*), causation (*for*), choice (*or*), and chronology (*before* and *after*). Transitional phrases can also be used to make similar connections: *in addition, on the other hand, as well as, as a result, after a while.*

A second means of creating connections between thoughts is by repeating key words that refer to the organizing idea (or synonyms or pronouns clearly referring to it). The repetition of key words assures the reader of the unity of the paper, of its development of one organizing idea.

Principles for achieving coherence.

A. Indicate very clearly to your reader that the various parts of your essay — paragraphs, sentences, and clauses — are connected to each other by repeating the key words of your essay throughout. (Avoid boring repetition by occasionally substituting synonyms and demonstrative adjectives or pronouns.)

B. Connect paragraphs by means of introductory words and phrases to establish chronological order, spatial order, cause-and-effect logic, or whatever principle your organization is built upon.

C. Connect sentences by these same transitional phrases and words. Between clauses and phrases, use conjunctions that clearly establish their relationship.

 MARYA MANNES

Television Advertising: The Splitting Image

A bride who looks scarcely fourteen whispers, "Oh, Mom, I'm so *happy!*" while a doting family adjust her gown and veil and a male voice croons softly, "A woman is a harder thing to be than a man. She has more feelings to feel." The mitigation of these excesses, it appears, is a feminine deodorant called Secret, which allows our bride to approach the altar with security as well as emotion.

Eddie Albert, a successful actor turned pitchman, bestows his attention on a lady with two suitcases, which prompt him to ask her whether she has been on a journey. "No," she says, or words to that effect, as she opens the suitcases. "My two boys bring back their soiled clothes every weekend from college for me to wash." And she goes into the familiar litany of grease, chocolate, mud, coffee, and fruit-juice stains, which presumably record the life of the average American male from two to fifty. Mr. Albert compliments her on this happy device to bring her boys home every week and hands her a box of Biz, because "Biz *is* better."

Two women with stony faces meet cart to cart in a supermarket as one takes a jar of peanut butter off a shelf. When the other asks her in a voice of nitric acid why she takes that brand, the first snaps, "Because I'm choosy for my family!" The two then break into delighted smiles as Number Two makes Number One taste Jiffy for "mothers who are choosy."

If you have not come across these dramatic interludes, it is because you are not home during the day and do not watch daytime television. It also means that your intestinal tract is spared from severe assaults, your credibility unstrained. Or, for that matter, you may look at commercials like these every day and manage either to ignore them or find nothing — given the fact of advertising — wrong with them. In that case, you are either so brainwashed or so innocent that you remain unaware of what this daily infusion may have done and is doing to an entire people as the long-accepted adjunct of free enterprise and support of "free" television.

"Given the fact" and "long-accepted" are the key words here. Only socialists, communists, idealists (or the BBC) fail to realize that a mass television system cannot exist without the support of sponsors, that the massive cost of maintaining it as a free service cannot be met without the massive income from selling products. You have only to read of the unending struggle to provide financial support for public, noncommercial television for further evidence.

Besides, aren't commercials in the public interest? Don't they help you choose what to buy? Don't they provide needed breaks from programming? Aren't many of them brilliantly done, and some of them funny? And now, with the new sexual freedom, all those gorgeous chicks with their shining hair and gleaming smiles? And if you didn't have commercials taking up a good part of each hour, how on earth would you find enough program material to fill the endless space/time void?

Tick off the yesses and what have you left? You have, I venture to submit, these intangible but possibly high costs: the diminution of human worth, the infusion and hardening of social attitudes no longer valid or desirable, pervasive discontent, and psychic fragmentation.

Should anyone wonder why deception is not an included detriment, I suggest that our public is so conditioned to promotion as a way of life, whether in art or politics or products, that elements of exaggeration or distortion are taken for granted. Nobody really believes that a certain shampoo will get a certain swain, or that an unclogged sinus can make a man a swinger. People are merely prepared to hope it will.

But the diminution of human worth is much more subtle and just as pervasive. In the guise of what they consider comedy, the producers of television commercials have created a loathsome gallery of men and women patterned, presumably, on Mr. and Mrs. America. Women liberationists have a major target in the commercial image of woman flashed hourly and daily to the vast majority. There are, indeed, only four kinds of females in this relentless sales procession: the gorgeous teen-age swinger with bouncing locks; the young mother teaching her baby girl the right soap for skin care; the middle-aged housewife with a voice like a power saw; and the old lady with dentures and irregularity. All these women, to be sure, exist. But between the swinging sex object and the constipated granny there are millions of females never shown in commercials. These are — married or single — intelligent, sensitive women who bring charm to their homes, who work at jobs as well as lend grace to their marriages, who support themselves, who have talents or hobbies or commitments, or who are skilled at their professions.

To my knowledge, as a frequent if reluctant observer, I know of only one woman on a commercial who has a job: a comic plumber pushing Comet. Funny, heh? Think of a dame with a plunger.

With this one representative of our labor force, which is well over thirty million women, we are left with nothing but the full-time housewife in all her whining glory: obsessed with whiter wash, moister cakes, shinier floors, cleaner children, softer diapers, and greaseless fried chicken. In the rare instances when these ladies are not in the kitchen, at the washing machine, or waiting on hubby, they are buying beauty shops (fantasy, see?) to take home so that their hair will have more body. Or out at the supermarket being choosy.

If they were attractive in their obsessions, they might be bearable. But they are not. They are pushy, loud-mouthed, stupid, and — of all things now — bereft of sexuality. Presumably, the argument of the tenets of advertising is that once a woman marries she changes overnight from plaything to floor-waxer.

To be fair, men make an equivalent transition in commercials. The swinging male with the mod hair and the beautiful chick turns inevitably into the paunchy slob who chokes on his wife's cake. You will notice, however, that the voice urging the viewer to buy the product is nearly always male: gentle, wise, helpful, seductive. And the visible presence telling the housewife how to get shinier floors and whiter wash and lovelier hair is almost invariably a man: the Svengali* in modern dress, the Trilby (if only she were!) his willing object.

Woman, in short, is consumer first and human being fourth. A wife and mother who stays home all day buys a lot more than a woman who lives alone or who — married or single — has a job. The young girl hell-bent on marriage is the next most susceptible consumer. It is entirely understandable, then, that the potential buyers of detergents, foods, polishes, toothpastes, pills, and housewares are the housewives, and that the sex object spends most of *her* money on cosmetics, hair lotions, soaps, mouthwashes, and soft drinks.

Here we come, of course, to the youngest class of consumers, the swinging teen-agers so beloved by advertisers keen on telling them (and us) that they've "got a lot to live, and Pepsi's got a lot to give." This affords a chance to show a squirming, leaping, jiggling group of beautiful kids having a very loud high on rock and — of all things — soda pop. One of commercial TV's most dubious achievements, in fact, is

---

* Svengali: a Hungarian musician in George du Maurier's novel *Trilby.* He controls Trilby's stage singing through hypnosis. Hence, a Svengali is capable of exercising a sinister influence over another person.

the reinforcement of the self-adulation characteristic of the young as a group.

As for the aging female citizen, the less shown of her the better. She is useful for ailments, but since she buys very little of anything, not having a husband or any children to feed or house to keep, nor — of course — sex appeal to burnish, society and commercials have little place for her. The same is true, to be sure, of older men, who are handy for Bosses with Bad Breath or Doctors with Remedies. Yet, on the whole, men hold up better than women at any age — in life or on television. Lines on their faces are marks of distinction, while on women they are signatures of decay.

There is no question, in any case, that television commercials (and many of the entertainment programs, notably the soap serials that are part of the selling package) reinforce, like an insistent drill, the assumption that a woman's only valid function is that of wife, mother, and servant of men: the inevitable sequel to her earlier function as sex object and swinger.

At a time when more and more women are at long last learning to reject these assumptions as archaic and demeaning, and to grow into individual human beings with a wide option of lives to live, the sellers of the nation are bent upon reinforcing the ancient pattern. They know only too well that by beaming their message to the Consumer Queen they can justify her existence as the housebound Mrs. America: dumber than dumb, whiter than white.

The conditioning starts very early: with the girl child who wants the skin Ivory soap has reputedly given her mother, with the nine-year-old who brings back a cake of Camay instead of the male deodorant her father wanted. (When she confesses that she bought it so she could be "feminine," her father hugs her, and, with the voice of a child-molester, whispers, "My little girl is growing up on me, huh.") And then, before long, comes the teen-aged bride who "has feelings to feel."

It is the little boys who dream of wings, in an airplane commercial; who grow up (with fewer cavities) into the doers. Their little sisters turn into *Cosmopolitan* girls, who in turn become housewives furious that their neighbors' wash is cleaner than theirs.

There is good reason to suspect that this maniac obsession with cleanliness, fostered, quite naturally, by the giant soap and detergent interests, may bear some responsibility for the cultivated sloppiness of so many of the young in their clothing as well as in their chosen hideouts. The compulsive housewife who spends more time washing and vacuuming and polishing her possessions than communicating to or stimulating her children creates a kind of sterility that the young would instinctively reject. The impeccably tidy home, the impeccably tidy lawn are — in a very real sense — unnatural and confining.

Yet the commercials confront us with broods of happy children, some of whom — believe it or not — notice the new fresh smell their clean, white sweatshirts exhale thanks to Mom's new "softener."

Some major advertisers, for that matter, can even cast a benign eye on the population explosion. In another Biz commercial, the genial Eddie Albert surveys with surprise a long row of dirty clothes heaped before him by a young matron. She answers his natural query by telling him gaily they are the products of her brood of eleven "with one more to come!" she adds as the twelfth turns up. "That's great!" says Mr. Albert, curdling the soul of Planned Parenthood and the future of this planet.

Who are, one cannot help but ask, the writers who manage to combine the sales of products with the selling-out of human dreams and dignity? Who people this cosmos of commercials with dolts and fools and shrews and narcissists? Who know so much about quirks and mannerisms and ailments and so little about life? So much about presumed wants and so little about crying needs?

Can women advertisers so demean their own sex? Or are there no women in positions of decision high enough to see that their real selves stand up?

Do they not know, these extremely clever creators of commercials, what they could do for their audience even while they exploit and entertain them? How they could raise the levels of manners and attitudes while they sell their wares? Or do they really share the worm's-eye view of mass communication that sees, and addresses, only the lowest common denominator?

It can be argued that commercials are taken too seriously, that their function is merely to amuse, engage, and sell, and that they do this brilliantly. If that were all to this wheedling of millions, well and good. But it is not. There are two more fallouts from this chronic sales explosion that cannot be measured but that at least can be expected. One has to do with the continual celebration of youth at the expense of maturity. In commercials only the young have access to beauty, sex, and joy in life. What do older women feel, day after day, when love is the exclusive possession of a teen-age girl with a bobbing mantle of hair? What older man would not covet her in restless impotence?

The constant reminder of what is inaccessible must inevitably produce a subterranean but real discontent, just as the continual sight of things and places beyond reach has eaten deeply into the ghetto soul. If we are constantly presented with what we are not or cannot have, the dislocation deepens, contentment vanishes, and frustration reigns. Even for the substantially secure, there is always a better thing, a better way, to buy. That none of these things makes a better life may be consciously acknowledged, but still the desire lodges in the spirit, nagging and pulling.

This kind of fragmentation works in potent ways above and

beyond the mere fact of program interruption, which is much of the time more of a blessing than a curse, especially in those rare instances when the commercial is deft and funny: the soft and subtle sell. Its overall curse, due to the large number of commercials in each hour, is that it reduces the attention span of a people already so conditioned to constant change and distraction that they cannot tolerate continuity in print or on the air.

Specifically, commercial interruption is most damaging during that 10 per cent of programming (a charitable estimate) most important to the mind and spirit of a people: news and public affairs, and drama.

To many (and among these are network news producers), commercials have no place or business during the vital process of informing the public. There is something obscene about a newscaster pausing to introduce a deodorant or shampoo commercial between an airplane crash and a body count. It is more than an interruption; it tends to reduce news to a form of running entertainment, to smudge the edges of reality by treating death or disaster or diplomacy on the same level as household appliances or a new gasoline.

The answer to this would presumably be to lump the commercials before and after the news or public affairs broadcasts — an answer unpalatable, needless to say, to the sponsors who support them.

The same is doubly true of that most unprofitable sector of television, the original play. Essential to any creative composition, whether drama, music or dance, are mood and continuity, both inseparable from form and meaning. They are shattered by the periodic intrusion of commercials, which have become intolerable to the serious artists who have deserted commercial television in droves because the system allows them no real freedom or autonomy. The selling comes first, the creation must accommodate itself. It is the rare and admirable sponsor who restricts or fashions his commercials so as to provide a minimum of intrusion or damaging inappropriateness.

If all these assumptions and imponderables are true, as many suspect, what is the answer or alleviation?

One is in the course of difficult emergence: the establishment of a public television system sufficiently funded so that it can give a maximum number of people an alternate diet of pleasure, enlightenment, and stimulation free from commercial fragmentation. So far, for lack of funds to buy talent and equipment, this effort has been in terms of public attention a distinctly minor operation.

Even if public television should, hopefully, greatly increase its scope and impact, it cannot in the nature of things and through long public conditioning equal the impact and reach the size of audience now tuned to commercial television.

Enormous amounts of time, money, and talent go into commercials. Technically they are often brilliant and innovative, the product not only of the new skills and devices but of imaginative minds. A few of them are both funny and endearing. Who, for instance, will forget the miserable young man with the appalling cold, or the kids taught to use — as an initiation into manhood — a fork instead of a spoon with a certain spaghetti? Among the enlightened sponsors, moreover, are some who manage to combine an image of their corporation and their products with accuracy and restraint.

What has to happen to mass medium advertisers as a whole, and especially on TV, is a totally new approach to their function not only as sellers but as social influencers. They have the same obligation as the broadcast medium itself: not only to entertain but to reflect, not only to reflect but to enlarge public consciousness and human stature.

This may be a tall order, but it is a vital one at a time when Americans have ceased to know who they are and where they are going, and when all the multiple forces acting upon them are daily diminishing their sense of their own value and purpose in life, when social upheaval and social fragmentation have destroyed old patterns, and when survival depends on new ones.

If we continue to see ourselves as the advertisers see us, we have no place to go. Nor, I might add, has commercial broadcasting itself.

PROBING FOR
MEANING

1. How does television, according to Mannes, influence social attitudes and create standards of how people should look and act? For example, what is the influence of the four stereotypes of women presented by television advertising?

2. What does Mannes suggest is the reason for the success of those commercials founded on deception?

3. What does the author believe to be television advertising's most damaging effects?

4. What does she feel are the beneficial possibilities of television commercials? What does she feel is necessary to bring about positive change?

PROBING FOR
METHOD

1. Mannes begins her essay with examples to intrigue the reader. Are her specific references to brand names and actual ads effective?

2. What is the thesis of the essay, and where is it stated? How does the thesis help to organize the entire essay?

3. Notice how Mannes includes transitional sentences and paragraphs to provide connections between ideas. Point out one such transition and explain how it works.

HERBERT GOLD

"Let's Kill the First
Red-haired Man We See . . ."

1

A group of amiable artists and rock musicians came together a
summer ago to plan a grand free outdoor festival of their joyful crafts in
San Francisco, but a man who called himself Mother John appeared at
their meetings and said he'd tear them apart, he'd burn them down: "I
ain't rational and I'll wipe you out."

"What's your last name, sir?"

"Motherf —— John from Out-of-Town."

The insurance went up and the folks got scared. There were ten
or twenty or thirty of these mothers, or maybe the same one with ten,
twenty, or thirty faces, but they were all talking about burning, ripping,
exploding, and such. The festival in the park was canceled.

Why did the mothers threaten? They wanted to hurt. *Why?*
Well, maybe they were fascist right-wing third-world meth-freak
Maoist hippie deviationist paranoids, or maybe they were just out-
people wanting in, fearing that someone might find fun and profit in the
festival. They really don't know or can't say. They are rebels without a
pause.

The man who commits random violence always thinks his attack is justified, of course. "He gave me a lotta lip" — the true-life explanation, folks, for shooting a fellow shopper. Or: "I just don't like
guys who smile to themselves." But we know that the gesture is in excess of the provocation. Maybe logically we can't explain it, but a lotta
lip isn't reason enough to kill in a busy department store during the
January White Sale.

In my novel *The Great American Jackpot,* a young man named Al
Dooley robs a bank because he's lonely and seeks meaning. Well, there
are other reasons, even good ones. But *he* doesn't really know them, and
to the world, too, his action seems eccentric, unpredictable, irrational.
He is strung out and strange to himself, and a menace to others. He
wants to greet reality with an answering blow. I think him a frequent
American.

Traditional violence usually had a clear aim. The man with the
stick hit the other man to grab his goods, land, or woman. Contempo-

rary random violence has murky origins — killing without hatred, rape without lust, war against phantom enemies. It hits first because otherwise someone might hit back. Causeless violence? No, but action far in excess of cause, similar to methedrine speed in excess of organic velocity.

On the Lower East Side of New York, for example, a fertile plantation area for the Mother Johns of this world, speed freaks, motorcyclists, disaffected workers, chafing neighborhood nationality groups, blacks, cops and mimeograph Maoists, all are battling each other in some weird parody of the troubadour games of murder. "Okay, world," they seem to be saying, toeing the earth shyly, "here we go with a free outdoor X-rated movie. And bring the kiddies to the slaughter."

This is a violent country.

Everyone who walks the streets of America knows it. If you can't walk, you read the newspapers. If you can't read, you see it on television. The subtle mining of violence under the surface control of America goes beyond anything a law-and-order manipulation of police authority can resolve.

For a time I accepted a wry, half-paranoid suspicion that my own person (horn-rimmed novelist, nosy face) invited attack. I've gradually come to realize that I'm no worse than others, but just being alive invites attack. For example:

I was walking in a heavy rain. The street was deserted. A man came toward me in black-militant drag, boots, leather, beret, and his lips moving, discussing with invisible enemies. But I was visible. Our eyes met. I stopped for a moment to let him by and he glared at me. "Hi," I said weakly.

"Man, I don't see it like that," he said. "I'm gonna *kill* you."

But there was no action. There was only the wish to murder.

And there is also, oddly enough — this is often ignored — the reciprocal wish to have violence done. I know a girl, a very pretty actress, who has been raped twice. Does she invite it? Well, she undresses at night, with shades up, and when she hears a sound at the window, she goes to open the door to see what's happening. And I was standing on the street near the San Francisco Art Museum where I saw an old acquaintance, the girl friend of a friend, and I jokingly went up to her and said, "Hey, chick, you want to do something really filthy?"

She paused and looked up into my face with a welcoming smile: "What?" Then her face darkened with disappointment. "Oh," she said, "it's Herb. I didn't recognize you at first." She later explained that she was kind of upset that day and bored and — oh, you know, looking for something to do. I realized an odd fact about rapists and molesters. They are offering a product which not many women want to buy — *but some do.*

There is no lack, of course, of the traditional kinds of violence — between colors, races, generations, classes.

My wife and I were strolling in Berkeley after a party. A group of cops was hassling a couple in an old station wagon decorated with hippie, love and peace insignia. The five policemen were teasing the kids, looking for drugs, it seemed, or maybe just *looking*. A boy of high school age, long hair, blue jeans, called out, "They don't have a search warrant! You don't have to let them!"

It was careless of him to incite the police.

One huge cop went lazily moving toward the kid. The kid started to run, very fast — ahah, he'll get away. The cop thumped after him. We kept walking in response to the other cops' jerking thumbs: *Keep moving.* But in the direction of the kid. He slipped and fell, bounced to his feet and kept running, but the cop was close now. Suddenly, to our amazement, we heard a thud of feet. *All* the five cops had abandoned the car and were chasing this boy who had yelled at them. They passed us, grinning, clutching clubs, with their hands on their pistols. They rounded the corner and I heard the boy scream, "I surrender!" He stood with hands up, trembling. The first cop to reach him cracked him on the head with his club and sent him staggering and bleeding. The others gathered around as a small Saturday-night crowd appeared. He gave them his papers. He was okay. He was even white. A couple of Berkeley ladies, spinsters or schoolteachers or grandmothers, were standing nearby. The cop who had hit him said, "Okay, kid, go home now."

They didn't arrest him. They had made their investigation, administered justice, and dismissed the case, all in one swift comment of billy club on skull. He was bleeding from the nose. He was vomiting. He needed to see a doctor. The ladies soothed him and led him away.

The cops were pleased that they had made another request for polite attention to one's elders. But they had created another cop-hating radical, ready to kill. And not just the boy, of course, but the ladies and me, too.

2

While trying to work out an explanation for the upsurge in violence in contemporary America, random violence beyond the traditional violences, I happened to be in my bank in New York City, formerly Fun City, during the months when it is supposed to be a Summer Festival. New York offers a natural environment for thinking about random violence. I was waiting to have a check certified (speeding ticket, speedometer defective, H. Gold the Mild-Mannered Novelist feeling morose). A mousy young man came up to the desk, wrote his name and account number on a slip of paper, and said to the bank bureaucrat, "Excuse me, sir, I'd like to know how much money I have."

"How should I know?"

"I mean, in my account."

"What do you mean, don't you get a statement?"

"Yes, but there's a discrepancy —"

"Can't you add?"

"I think so, but it doesn't come out the same —"

"It'll cost you a dollar. There'll be a charge of a dollar."

Timidly the supplicant said, "Won't you tell me what I have in my account?"

It was like the tide rushing through a weak place in the wall. The put-upon, underpaid, not overbright bank clerk saw weakness and found pleasure in crushing it. "We can't just stand here all day and answer stupid questions from stupid people who can't add. I said it'll cost you a dollar. You want me to call downstairs?"

The dejected supplicant took his slip of paper with his name and number on it and walked away, gray and defeated. No matter that the bank probably wouldn't and couldn't legally charge him for the service. No matter: he believed in the authority of the Man Behind the Desk, a man exasperated and rubbed raw in the great city, a loser himself. The teller turned to me and said, "Stupid idiots, asking stupid questions, they think all I got to do here is answer them?"

I said that the supplicant walked away gray and defeated, but I'm sure there was also murder in his heart. Not against the bank or the teller, not a cop, not some authority. But against someone weaker than himself — a black man, a hippie, a kid. Isolation from power makes men look for a mob in which they can be strong.

Random violence is not really random or accidental, of course, and the man or mob, kid or gang, deciding to kill the first red-haired man in sight is not unconnected with the rest of the fate of America and the world. There are fifty or sixty million more people in America than there were when I was a child. The rat-sink theory holds that animals go crazy — perverse, violent, self-destructive — when the density of population increases beyond a certain needed living space. No reason to think that the anxiety of rats is sharper than that of overcrowded human beings. Every study of ambulatory psychosis and neurosis comes up with a large store of ticking time bombs walking the streets — and driving, waiting on people, directing traffic. They are damaged, we are told, by broken families and crippled families, by historical examples of cruelty, by rage and resentment, by boredom and anxiety, by jealousy and frustration. Now we also hear of chromosome damage and genetic defects leading men toward senseless attack. Prison systems all have isolation chambers for enraged men who snarl like beasts and want only to destroy, who must be kept apart, unreachable by therapy; and some of these seem to burn out and are released, and some have not yet committed acts which get them in prison. Repressed, suppressed, tormented, unconscious, the desire to kill is a part of the risk of city life, like postnasal drip. High school basketball games turn into rampages. A community in Washington protects itself from the world with fences, towers, electric eyes, dogs, guards, patrols — an armed concentration camp for suburban luxury living. The statistics about senseless crime, child beating, sniping at strangers, arson and assault, and gang sadism should make Jean Jacques Rousseau spin in his quiet Swiss grave. If man is naturally good, he is sure going against his nature more and more of the time. It sounds like a bad joke: the paranoids are after us.

Violence pours out of city men like water out of broken fire hydrants. And it's not just the city, of course. The small-town jukebox roars out Johnny Cash songs or "Happiness Is a Warm Gun," and the bouncers hit and the cops flail and the shards of plate glass decorate the pavements.

Nietzsche said: "It is only the powerful who know how to honor, it is their art, their domain for invention." In other words, power is the opposite of violence. The powerful man can respect the stranger, not fear him. The sense of being cut off makes men want to find reality through the ancient pride in bloodletting. Powerlessness corrupts; absolute powerlessness corrupts absolutely. Stabbing strange women or setting drunks on fire does not seem to be the moral equivalent of war, which William James said America needed. But if the tax man and your parents and your employer give you trouble, and you can't strike at them openly, why not declare war on their surrogates, on the weak or the strange, on humanity itself?

3

The psychiatrist Bruno Bettelheim argues that a misunderstood Freudianism has led to a hypocritical pseudo-permissiveness on the part of frightened parents, and this in turn leads to guilt and weak control in children. The kids know their parents want them to be decent human beings, but also that the parents are afraid to assert authority. The child needs authority to provide examples for learning. The childish temper tantrum is a common means of testing. It needs to be mastered, but often isn't by the time the child has an adult's body. The character-disordered or psychopathic personality may seem to be intelligent, controlled and in touch; but, in fact, all it knows is one lesson: I want, I want at once, I want only what *I* want — and I'll take it.

When a man respects no one, and not himself either, but wants wants *wants*, there is no reason to defer his hatreds and revenges; and when he doesn't really know why he hates and needs revenge, he may express his childish storm of temper with a high-powered rifle from a rooftop or a knife in a crowd. How quickly the "love generation" turns to hating yippies under pressure about Vietnam and cynicism about American virtue. The kids can throw flowers, turn on, and make lovely rock music, but if they are goal-less amid affluence, they grow impatient with a doctrinaire forever springtime designed like a record jacket. The tender communal living arrangements seem to work out fine, as they did for a sweet flower child I knew a few years ago: "We love each other, we live at peace, we share everything."

"How long has this been going on?"

"Five days,"she said.

But the grooviness ended with thievery, fights, jealous rage, and a contagion of breakdowns. A Panglossian reaction might be: Okay, let's work out the violence, it's the price we pay for superorganization. The trouble with this is that violence *expresses* other feelings, but only *communicates* itself — the desire to hurt. It does no good to the victim, unlike the victim of a poem or a song, who may benefit from the composer's expressed rage. And it does no good to the perpetrator, who comes to understand nothing, but may develop a taste for blood.

A businessman in Detroit hopes that holdup men are rational and want his money; he can offer money — it's the ones who just want to kill him that are a bother. A childhood friend, a funny red-haired man from Cleveland, carries a teargas gun in his pocket. Why?" I asked him.

"Some people don't like red hair," he said.

Mace, karate, judo, personal weapons — HELP! Stop! The police say that the worst criminals are the amateurs, out for kicks, not purses; pleasure, not gain. A presidential report on violence, released on the first anniversary of the assassination of Robert Kennedy, says that Americans are a "rather bloody-minded people." In the past, it notes, violence was generally initiated by white Anglo-Saxons against Catholics, black men, labor organizers, and pacifists. Now black violence, campus violence, antiwar violence, political assassinations, and spooky random violence are added to our turbulent past. Eric Hoffer, who hollered on television that we are not a violent people, wrote in his column in the San Francisco *Examiner* (June 9, 1969): "A day of wrath is waiting around the corner, when the saturated resentment of the long-suffering majority crystallizes in retaliation." He bemoaned an "incredible submissiveness in an age of violence," and seemed to be urging the public to rush the "foul-mouthed, bushy-faced punks." People shouldn't put limitations on the police; do-gooders are the enemy. His solution to the problem is on a similar level to the one reported in the *New York Times*, where Associate Justice Paul C. Reardon of the Massachusetts Supreme Court urged that a campaign should be mounted in the nation's schools to search "for a brief synonym for police officer and policeman to supplant that unfortunate word all Americans currently employ." The headline reads: NEW WORD FOR "COP" SOUGHT. Obviously the word "pig" won't do, but if we call the cops "angels," it won't be long until the word "angel" means what "cop" means. If there is violence and hatred in America, new words won't make them sweeter.

How can we live with random violence? Well, one way which is seldom mentioned is just to go on going on, as we do with automobiles, smog, cigarettes, airplane failures, brush-fire wars — making irritated little gestures toward improving our chances but essentially enduring what malfunction or destiny bring. In the rat-sink city we may have to think of berserk paranoids as another health hazard, like leaking stoves. Recently I visited a prisoner in California who was convicted of kidnapping and tormenting a child. He is intelligent, gentle, thoughtful, and says he doesn't mind prison so much because it gives him a chance to catch up on his reading. (It has also dried out the drugs in his blood.) But when he is caught up on his reading and ready for the world once again, and maybe ready to try speeding through his mind with the help of methedrine sulfate, are we to think of him as just another hazard, like the defective automobile or the mysterious disturbances in our lungs which come from breathing city air?

Suppose we're not content with this new hazard of sudden death by twitch and impulse?

The police, either kindly or repressive, must always be fallible solutions. Either they are there when you need them or they are too much there. Massed police tend to riot; police power means police brutality. What about personal armament, going about with little private jets of mace, which can be bought in grocery stores and "at fine cosmetic counters everywhere." There are too many quick tempers abroad. When everyone is armed to protect himself, who will protect us from the protectors? What about that walled suburb of Washington? This sort of panic is a reversion to the life envisaged during the great fallout-shelter craze, a retreat to something fetal and subhuman in human nature. Then what?

Other styles of child rearing, deeper and truer education, meaningful work, creative interchanges among people — everyone talks about the ways that might make it possible for masses of men to live together on a limited planet. Improved medicine calms the distraught, tranquilizes the defective. The reform of cities, and a public life which is less hypocritical about suffering, war and injustice, can influence people to meet each other without rage. Drugs, cops, institutions and karate — well, these stopgap controls may be with us forever and we will use them when we must. Humankind requires deep solutions to the demand for animal and spiritual joy. Rage, violence, ulcers, twitches, crying jags, and melancholia reflect an imbalance of personal expression and opportunity in the world. A song of a few years ago claimed morosely, "I ain't got no sat-is-fac-tion," and I've heard that song danced and sung in Los Angeles, New York, Paris, and Biafra. It's a universal anthem. The dream of love and joy seems further away than ever. Doctrinaire injunctions to love one another — love! love goddammit! — clearly don't work. Nor does anarchic self-expression when *my* freedom binds *you* to pay the price. The others out there will find their pleasure in revenge.

The billions are here, and billions more coming fast, and we must learn to live with them. There will be more of everything, including red-haired men. Is the red-haired man coming toward you your brother? No, in fact, he's not. He may be your friend or your enemy. He takes up your space, he eats your food, he jostles you. He covets what you covet.

A few days ago, waiting at the post office, a sallow, irritable, self-absorbed young man tried to slip in line between a couple of women ahead of me. I reached out to put my hands on his shoulder. I smiled sweetly. I said, "Okay, fella, tell you what. You take that place in line and I'll take you, okay? agreed? fine?"

He looked at me and saw a menace to society. I wanted to kill. The ladies in line shrank away from me. I was Mother Herb from Out-of-Town. I was not rational. And worse of all, I was proud of it.

PROBING FOR MEANING

1. What are "fascist right-wing third-world meth-freak Maoist hippie deviationist paranoids"? How do they differ from "out-people wanting in"?

2. Gold puns on the title of the movie *Rebel Without a Cause* in describing the "mothers" as "rebels without a pause." How does his pun describe these violence-prone people? What examples of this type of rebelliousness does Gold cite throughout the essay?

3. How does "traditional" violence differ from "random" violence? What examples of traditional violence substantiate the author's distinction between these two types?

4. Gold claims one cause of random violence is powerlessness. Does his discussion of the "mousy young man" at the bank justify the conclusion that the young man will go out and be violent? What examples can you give to support or attack Gold's point?

5. How does the "rat-sink theory" explain random violence? What effects of overcrowding does Gold mention? Do you agree that "violence pours out of city men like water out of broken fire hydrants"? Does Gold exclude small towns from his violent world? Explain.

6. Another cause Gold mentions is parental permissiveness. What argument does he give that parents have been too permissive? Why does permissiveness lead to violence? Is the hippie movement a good example of the bad aspects of permissiveness? What others can you think of?

7. Gold asks, "How can we live with random violence?" What an-

swers does he reject as unworkable? What answers does he think might work?

8. For what reasons does Gold divide the essay into three sections?'

PROBING FOR
METHOD

1. What method of introduction does Gold use? To what extent does it fulfill the requirements of a good introduction?

2. Gold employs an unusual number of examples in making his points. How effective is this abundance of anecdote?

3. Gold also uses humor at several points in the essay. What are some specific instances? What overall effect is created by his sometimes humorous approach to a very serious subject?

4. The author mentions several causes of random violence. To what extent does he also develop the effects of it?

5. Analyze Gold's audience. Defend your choice of reader.

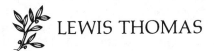 LEWIS THOMAS

Death in the Open

Most of the dead animals you see on highways near the cities are dogs, a few cats. Out in the countryside, the forms and coloring of the dead are strange; these are the wild creatures. Seen from a car window they appear as fragments, evoking memories of woodchucks, badgers, skunks, voles, snakes, sometimes the mysterious wreckage of a deer.

It is always a queer shock, part a sudden upwelling of grief, part unaccountable amazement. It is simply astounding to see an animal dead on a highway. The outrage is more than just the location; it is the impropriety of such visible death, anywhere. You do not expect to see dead animals in the open. It is the nature of animals to die alone, off somewhere, hidden. It is wrong to see them lying out on the highway; it is wrong to see them anywhere.

Everything in the world dies, but we only know about it as a kind of abstraction. If you stand in a meadow, at the edge of a hillside, and look around carefully, almost everything you can catch sight of is in the process of dying, and most things will be dead long before you are. If it were not for the constant renewal and replacement going on before your eyes, the whole place would turn to stone and sand under your feet.

There are some creatures that do not seem to die at all; they simply vanish totally into their own progeny. Single cells do this. The cell becomes two, then four, and so on, and after a while the last trace is gone. It cannot be seen as death; barring mutation, the descendants are simply the first cell, living all over again. The cycles of the slime mold have episodes that seem as conclusive as death, but the withered slug, with its stalk and fruiting body, is plainly the transient tissue of a developing animal; the free-swimming amebocytes use this organ collectively in order to produce more of themselves.

There are said to be a billion billion insects on the earth at any moment, most of them with very short life expectancies by our standards. Someone has estimated that there are 25 million assorted insects hanging in the air over every temperate square mile, in a column extending upward for thousands of feet, drifting through the layers of the atmosphere like plankton. They are dying steadily, some by being eaten, some just dropping in their tracks, tons of them around the earth, disintegrating as they die, invisibly.

Who ever sees dead birds, in anything like the huge numbers stipulated by the certainty of the death of all birds? A dead bird is an incongruity, more startling than an unexpected live bird, sure evidence to the human mind that something has gone wrong. Birds do their dying off somewhere, behind things, under things, never on the wing.

Animals seem to have an instinct for performing death alone, hidden. Even the largest, most conspicuous ones find ways to conceal themselves in time. If an elephant missteps and dies in an open place, the herd will not leave him there; the others will pick him up and carry the body from place to place, finally putting it down in some inexplicably suitable location. When elephants encounter the skeleton of an elephant out in the open, they methodically take up each of the bones and distribute them, in a ponderous ceremony, over neighboring acres.

It is a natural marvel. All of the life of the earth dies, all of the time, in the same volume as the new life that dazzles us each morning, each spring. All we see of this is the odd stump, the fly struggling on the porch floor of the summer house in October, the fragment on the highway. I have lived all my life with an embarrassment of squirrels in my backyard, they are all over the place, all year long, and I have never seen, anywhere, a dead squirrel.

I suppose it is just as well. If the earth were otherwise, and all the dying were done in the open, with the dead there to be looked at, we would never have it out of our minds. We can forget about it much of the time, or think of it as an accident to be avoided, somehow. But it does make the process of dying seem more exceptional than it really is, and harder to engage in at the times when we must ourselves engage.

In our way, we conform as best we can to the rest of nature. The obituary pages tell us of the news that we are dying away, while the birth announcements in finer print, off at the side of the page, inform us of our replacements, but we get no grasp from this of the enormity of scale. There are 3 billion of us on the earth, and all 3 billion must be dead, on a schedule, within this lifetime. The vast mortality, involving something over 50 million of us each year, takes place in relative secrecy. We can only really know of the deaths in our households, or among our friends. These, detached in our minds from all the rest, we take to be unnatural events, anomalies, outrages. We speak of our own dead in low voices; struck down, we say, as though visible death can only occur for cause, by disease or violence, avoidably. We send off for flowers, grieve, make ceremonies, scatter bones, unaware of the rest of the 3 billion on the same schedule. All of that immense mass of flesh and bone and consciousness will disappear by absorption into the earth, without recognition by the transient survivors.

Less than a half century from now, our replacements will have more than doubled the numbers. It is hard to see how we can continue to keep the secret, with such multitudes doing the dying. We will have to give up the notion that death is catastrophe, or detestable, or avoidable, or even strange. We will need to learn more about the cycling of life in the rest of the system, and about our connection to the process. Everything that comes alive seems to be in trade for something that dies, cell for cell. There might be some comfort in the recognition of synchrony, in the formation that we all go down together, in the best of company.

PROBING FOR MEANING

1. Why, according to Thomas, do we feel shocked by the body of a dead animal on a highway?

2. What effects does the animal world's "instinct for performing death alone" have upon human beings? How do humans express this instinct?

3. Why does Thomas feel that we will have to give up the notion that death is "catastrophe, or detestable, or avoidable, or even strange"? What effect might giving up this notion have on us?

PROBING FOR METHOD

1. Is there a logic to the order in which Thomas offers examples of how animals perform death alone? What effect does he achieve by pointing to insects, then birds, then elephants? Why does he mention squirrels last?

2. How scientific is the cause-and-effect analysis offered by Thomas? To what degree would you describe his tone as argumentative?

3. For what sort of audience is Thomas writing?

 RALPH ELLISON

King of the Bingo Game

The woman in front of him was eating roasted peanuts that smelled so good that he could barely contain his hunger. He could not even sleep and wished they'd hurry and begin the bingo game. There, on his right, two fellows were drinking wine out of a bottle wrapped in a paper bag, and he could hear soft gurgling in the dark. His stomach gave a low, gnawing growl. "If this was down South," he thought, "all I'd have to do is lean over and say, 'Lady, gimme a few of those peanuts, please ma'am,' and she'd pass me the bag and never think nothing of it." Or he could ask the fellows for a drink in the same way. Folks down South stuck together that way; they didn't even have to know you. But up here it was different. Ask somebody for something, and they'd think you were crazy. Well, I ain't crazy. I'm just broke, 'cause I got no birth certificate to get a job, and Laura 'bout to die 'cause we got no money for a doctor. But I ain't crazy. And yet a pinpoint of doubt was focused in his mind as he glanced toward the screen and saw the hero stealthily entering a dark room and sending the beam of a flashlight along a wall of bookcases. This is where he finds the trapdoor, he remembered. The man would pass abruptly through the wall and find the girl tied to a bed, her legs and arms spread wide, and her clothing torn to rags. He laughed softly to himself. He had seen the picture three times, and this was one of the best scenes.

On his right the fellow whispered wide-eyed to his companion, "Man, look ayonder!"

"Damn!"

"Wouldn't I like to have her tied up like that . . ."

"Hey! That fool's letting her loose!"

"Aw, man, he loves her."

"Love or no love!"

The man moved impatiently beside him, and he tried to involve himself in the scene. But Laura was on his mind. Tiring quickly of watching the picture he looked back to where the white beam filtered from the projection room above the balcony. It started small and grew large, specks of dust dancing in its whiteness as it reached the screen. It was strange how the beam always landed right on the screen and didn't mess up and fall somewhere else. But they had it all fixed. Everything was fixed. Now suppose when they showed that girl with her dress torn the girl started taking off the rest of her clothes, and when the guy came in he didn't untie her but kept her there and went to taking off his own clothes? *That* would be something to see. If a picture got out of hand like that those guys up there would go nuts. Yeah, and there'd be so many folks in here you couldn't find a seat for nine months! A strange sensation played over his skin. He shuddered. Yesterday he'd seen a bedbug on a woman's neck as they walked out into the bright street. But exploring his thigh through a hole in his pocket he found only goose pimples and old scars.

The bottle gurgled again. He closed his eyes. Now a dreamy music was accompanying the film and train whistles were sounding in the distance, and he was a boy again walking along a railroad trestle down South, and seeing the train coming, and running back as fast as he could go, and hearing the whistle blowing, and getting off the trestle to solid ground just in time, with the earth trembling beneath his feet, and feeling relieved as he ran down the cinder-strewn embankment onto the highway, and looking back and seeing with terror that the train had left the track and was following him right down the middle of the street, and all the white people laughing as he ran screaming . . .

"Wake up there, buddy! What the hell do you mean hollering like that? Can't you see we trying to enjoy this here picture?"

He stared at the man with gratitude.

"I'm sorry, old man," he said. "I musta been dreaming."

"Well, here, have a drink. And don't be making no noise like that, damn!"

His hands trembled as he tilted his head. It was not wine, but whiskey. Cold rye whiskey. He took a deep swoller, decided it was better not to take another, and handed the bottle back to its owner.

"Thanks, old man," he said.

Now he felt the cold whiskey breaking a warm path straight through the middle of him, growing hotter and sharper as it moved. He had not eaten all day, and it made him light-headed. The smell of the peanuts stabbed him like a knife, and he got up and found a seat in the middle aisle. But no sooner did he sit than he saw a row of intense-faced young girls, and got up again, thinking, "You chicks musta been Lindy-hopping* somewhere." He found a seat several rows ahead as the lights came on, and he saw the screen disappear behind a heavy red and gold curtain; then the curtain rising, and the man with the microphone and a uniformed attendant coming on stage.

He felt for his bingo cards, smiling. The guy at the door wouldn't like it if he knew about his having *five* cards. Well, not everyone played the bingo game; and even with five cards he didn't have much of a chance. For Laura, though, he had to have faith. He studied

* Dancing.

the cards, each with its different numerals, punching the free center hole in each and spreading them neatly across his lap; and when the lights faded he sat slouched in his seat so that he could look from his cards to the bingo wheel with but a quick shifting of his eyes.

Ahead, at the end of the darkness, the man with the microphone was pressing a button attached to a long cord and spinning the bingo wheel and calling out the number each time the wheel came to rest. And each time the voice rang out his finger raced over the cards for the number. With five cards he had to move fast. He became nervous; there were too many cards, and the man went too fast with his grating voice. Perhaps he should just select one and throw the others away. But he was afraid. He became warm. Wonder how much Laura's doctor would cost? Damn that, watch the cards! And with despair he heard the man call three in a row which he missed on all five cards. This way he'd never win . . .

When he saw the row of holes punched across the third card, he sat paralyzed and heard the man call three more numbers before he stumbled forward, screaming.

"Bingo! Bingo!"

"Let that fool up there," someone called.

"Get up there, man!"

He stumbled down the aisle and up the steps to the stage into a light so sharp and bright that for a moment it blinded him, and he felt that he had moved into the spell of some strange, mysterious power. Yet it was as familiar as the sun, and he knew it was the perfectly familiar bingo.

The man with the microphone was saying something to the audience as he held out his card. A cold light flashed from the man's finger as the card left his hand. His knees trembled. The man stepped closer, checking the card against the numbers chalked on the board. Suppose he had made a mistake? The pomade on the man's hair made him feel faint, and he backed away. But the man was checking the card over the microphone now, and he had to stay. He stood tense, listening.

"Under the O, forty-four," the man chanted. "Under the I, seven. Under the G, three. Under the B, ninety-six. Under the N, thirteen!"

His breath came easier as the man smiled at the audience.

"Yes sir, ladies and gentlemen, he's one of the chosen people!"

The audience rippled with laughter and applause.

"Step right up to the front of the stage."

He moved slowly forward, wishing that the light was not so bright.

"To win tonight's jackpot of $36.90 the wheel must stop between the double zero, understand?"

He nodded, knowing the ritual from the many days and nights

he had watched the winners march across the stage to press the button that controlled the spinning wheel and receive the prizes. And now he followed the instructions as though he'd crossed the slippery stage a million prize-winning times.

The man was making some kind of joke, and he nodded vacantly. So tense had he become that he felt a sudden desire to cry and shook it away. He felt vaguely that his whole life was determined by the bingo wheel; not only that which would happen now that he was at last before it, but all that had gone before, since his birth, and his mother's birth and the birth of his father. It had always been there, even though he had not been aware of it, handing out the unlucky cards and numbers of his days. The feeling persisted, and he started quickly away. I better get down from here before I make a fool of myself, he thought.

"Here, boy," the man called. "You haven't started yet."

Someone laughed as he went hesitantly back.

"Are you all reet?"

He grinned at the man's jive talk, but no words would come, and he knew it was not a convincing grin. For suddenly he knew that he stood on the slippery brink of some terrible embarassment.

"Where are you from, boy?" the man asked.

"Down South."

"He's from down South, ladies and gentlemen," the man said. "Where from? Speak right into the mike."

"Rocky Mont," he said, "Rock' Mont, North Car'lina."

"So you decided to come down off that mountain to the U.S.," the man laughed. He felt that the man was making a fool of him, but then something cold was placed in his hand, and the lights were no longer behind him.

Standing before the wheel he felt alone, but that was somehow right, and he remembered his plan. He would give the wheel a short quick twirl. Just a touch of the button. He had watched it many times, and always it came close to double zero when it was short and quick. He steeled himself; the fear had left, and he felt a profound sense of promise, as though he were about to be repaid for all the things he'd suffered all his life. Trembling, he pressed the button. There was a whirl of lights, and in a second he realized with finality that though he wanted to, he could not stop. It was as though he held a high-powered line in his naked hand. His nerves tightened. As the wheel increased its speed it seemed to draw him more and more into its power, as though it held his fate; and with it came a deep need to submit, to whirl, to lose himself in its swirl of color. He could not stop it now. So let it be.

The button rested snugly in his palm where the man had placed it. And now he became aware of the man beside him, advising him through the microphone, while behind the shadowy audience hummed with noisy voices. He shifted his feet. There was still that feeling of helplessness within him, making part of him desire to turn back, even now that the jackpot was right in his hand. He squeezed the button until his fist ached. Then, like the sudden shriek of a subway whistle, a doubt tore through his head. Suppose he did not spin the wheel long enough? What could he do, and how could he tell? And then he knew, even as he wondered, that as long as he pressed the button, he could control the jackpot. He and only he could determine whether or not it was to be his. Not even the man with the microphone could do anything about it now. He felt drunk. Then, as though he had come down from a high hill into a valley of people, he heard the audience yelling.

"Come down from there, you jerk!"

"Let somebody else have a chance . . ."

"Ole Jack thinks he done found the end of the rainbow . . ."

The last voice was not unfriendly, and he turned and smiled dreamily into the yelling mouths. Then he turned his back squarely on them.

"Don't take too long, boy," a voice said.

He nodded. They were yelling behind him. Those folks did not understand what had happened to him. They had been playing the bingo game day in and night out for years, trying to win rent money or hamburger change. But not one of those wise guys had discovered this wonderful thing. He watched the wheel whirling past the numbers and experienced a burst of exaltation: This is God! This is the really truly God! He said it aloud. "This is God!"

He said it with such absolute conviction that he feared he would fall fainting into the footlights. But the crowd yelled so loud that they could not hear. Those fools, he thought. I'm here trying to tell them the most wonderful secret in the world, and they're yelling like they gone crazy. A hand fell upon his shoulder.

"You'll have to make a choice now, boy. You've taken too long."

He brushed the hand violently away.

"Leave me alone, man. I know what I'm doing!"

The man looked surprised and held on to the microphone for support. And because he did not wish to hurt the man's feelings he smiled, realizing with a sudden pang that there was no way of explaining to the man just why he had to stand there pressing the button forever.

"Come here," he called tiredly.

The man approached, rolling the heavy microphone across the stage.

"Anybody can play this bingo game, right?" he said.

"Sure, but . . ."

He smiled, feeling inclined to be patient with this slick looking white man with his blue shirt and his sharp gabardine suit.

"That's what I thought," he said. "Anybody can win the jack-pot as long as they get the lucky number, right?"

"That's the rule, but after all . . ."

"That's what I thought," he said. "And the big prize goes to the man who knows how to win it?"

The man nodded speechlessly.

"Well then, go on over there and watch me win like I want to. I ain't going to hurt nobody," he said, "and I'll show you how to win. I mean to show the whole world how it's got to be done."

And because he understood, he smiled again to let the man know that he held nothing against him for being white and impatient. Then he refused to see the man any longer and stood pressing the button, the voices of the crowd reaching him like sounds in distant streets. Let them yell. All the Negroes down there were just ashamed because he was black like them. He smiled inwardly, knowing how it was. Most of the time he was ashamed of what Negroes did himself. Well, let them be ashamed for something this time. Like him. He was like a long thin black wire that was being stretched and wound upon the bingo wheel: wound until he wanted to scream; wound, but this time himself controlling the winding and the sadness and the shame, and because he did, Laura would be all right. Suddenly the lights flickered. He staggered backwards. Had something gone wrong? All this noise. Didn't they know that although he controlled the wheel, it also controlled him, and unless he pressed the button forever and forever and ever it would stop, leaving him high and dry, dry and high on this hard high slippery hill and Laura dead? There was only one chance; he had to do whatever the wheel demanded. And gripping the button in despair, he discovered with surprise that it imparted a nervous energy. His spine tingled. He felt a certain power.

Now he faced the raging crowd with defiance, its screams penetrating his eardrums like trumpets shrieking from a jukebox. The vague faces glowing in the bingo lights gave him a sense of himself that he had never known before. He was running the show, by God! They had to react to him, for he was their luck. This is *me*, he thought. Let the bastards yell. Then someone was laughing inside him, and he realized that somehow he had forgotten his own name. It was a sad, lost feeling to lose your name, and a crazy thing to do. That name had been given him by the white man who had owned his grandfather a long lost time ago down South. But maybe those wise guys knew his name.

"Who am I?" he screamed.

"Hurry up and bingo, you jerk!"

They didn't know either, he thought sadly. They didn't even know their own names, they were all poor nameless bastards. Well, he didn't need that old name; he was reborn. For as long as he pressed the button he was The-man-who-pressed-the-button-who-held-the-prize-who-was-the-King-of-Bingo. That was the way it was, and he'd have to press the button even if nobody understood, even though Laura did not understand.

"Live!" he shouted.

The audience quieted like the dying of a huge fan.

"Live, Laura baby. I got holt of it now, sugar. Live!"

He screamed it, tears streaming down his face. "I got nobody but YOU!"

The screams tore from his very guts. He felt as though the rush of blood to his head would burst out in baseball seams of small red droplets, like a head beaten by police clubs. Bending over he saw a trickle of blood splashing the toe of his shoe. With his free hand he searched his head. It was his nose. God, suppose something has gone wrong? He felt that the whole audience had somehow entered him and was stamping its feet in his stomach and he was unable to throw them out. They wanted the prize, that was it. They wanted the secret for themselves. But they'd never get it; he would keep the bingo wheel whirling forever, and Laura would be safe in the wheel. But would she? It had to be, because if she were not safe the wheel would cease to turn; it could not go on. He had to get away, *vomit* all, and his mind formed an image of himself running with Laura in his arms down the tracks of the subway just ahead of an A train, running desperately *vomit* with people screaming for him to come out but knowing no way of leaving the tracks because to stop would bring the train crushing down upon him and to attempt to leave across the other tracks would mean to run into a hot third rail as high as his waist which threw blue sparks that blinded his eyes until he could hardly see.

He heard singing and the audience was clapping its hands.

> Shoot the liquor to him, Jim boy!
> Clap-clap-clap
> Well a-calla the cop
> He's blowing his top!
> Shoot the liquor to him, Jim boy!

Bitter anger grew within him at the singing. They think I'm crazy. Well let 'em laugh. I'll do what I got to do.

He was standing in an attitude of intense listening when he saw that they were watching something on the stage behind him. He felt weak. But when he turned he saw no one. If only his thumb did not ache so. Now they were applauding. And for a moment he thought that the wheel had stopped. But that was impossible, his thumb still pressed the button. Then he saw them. Two men in uniform beckoned from the end of the stage. They were coming toward him, walking in step, slowly, like a tap-dance team returning for a third encore. But their shoulders shot forward, and he backed away, looking wildly about. There was nothing to fight them with. He had only the long black cord which led to a plug somewhere back stage, and he couldn't use that because it operated the bingo wheel. He backed slowly, fixing the men with his eyes as his lips stretched over his teeth in a tight, fixed grin; moved toward the end of the stage and realizing that he couldn't go much further, for suddenly the cord became taut and he couldn't afford to break the cord. But he had to do something. The audience was howling. Suddenly he stopped dead, seeing the men halt, their legs lifted as in an interrupted step of a slow-motion dance. There was nothing to do but run in the other direction and he dashed forward, slipping and sliding. The men fell back, surprised. He struck out violently going past.

"Grab him!"

He ran, but all too quickly the cord tightened, resistingly, and he turned and ran back again. This time he slipped them, and discovered by running in a circle before the wheel he could keep the cord from tightening. But this way he had to flail his arms to keep the men away. Why couldn't they leave a man alone? He ran, circling.

"Ring down the curtain," someone yelled. But they couldn't do that. If they did the wheel flashing from the projection room would be cut off. But they had him before he could tell them so, trying to pry open his fist, and he was wrestling and trying to bring his knees into the fight and holding on to the button, for it was his life. And now he was down, seeing a foot coming down, crushing his wrist cruelly, down, as he saw the wheel whirling serenely above.

"I can't give it up," he screamed. Then quietly, in a confidential tone, "Boys, I really can't give it up."

It landed hard against his head. And in the blank moment they had it away from him, completely now. He fought them trying to pull him up from the stage as he watched the wheel spin slowly to a stop. Without surprise he saw it rest at double-zero.

"You see," he pointed bitterly.

"Sure, boy, sure, it's O.K.," one of the men said smiling.

And seeing the man bow his head to someone he could not see, he felt very, very happy; he would receive what all the winners received.

But as he warmed in the justice of the man's tight smile he did not see the man's slow wink, nor see the bow-legged man behind him step clear of the swiftly descending curtain and set himself for a blow. He only felt the dull pain exploding in his skull, and he knew even as it slipped out of him that his luck had run out on the stage.

1. Describe the main character of the short story. What is he hoping to win by playing bingo? How does he feel about his current life? How does he feel about the South?

2. Why does he continue, even though "he knew that he stood on the slippery brink of some terrible embarrassment"? Why does he keep his grip on the button that controls the spinning wheel?

3. How do you respond to the main character's behavior? Is he insane, or is he truly experiencing an insight?

4. What is the story saying about luck? What is the meaning of the final sentence?

5. How have social conditions influenced the main character?

1. To what extent does the main character's dream foreshadow the conclusion of the story?

2. What is the symbolic significance of the wheel? Is it symbolic that the wheel finally rests at double-zero?

3. What is the role of the audience? Of the master of ceremonies?

 ANN PETRY

Like a Winding Sheet

He had planned to get up before Mae did and surprise her by fixing breakfast. Instead he went back to sleep and she got out of bed so quietly he didn't know she wasn't there beside him until he woke up and heard the queer soft gurgle of water running out of the sink in the bathroom.

He knew he ought to get up but instead he put his arms across his forehead to shut the afternoon sunlight out of his eyes, pulled his legs up close to his body, testing them to see if the ache was still in them.

Mae had finished in the bathroom. He could tell because she never closed the door when she was in there and now the sweet smell of talcum powder was drifting down the hall and into the bedroom. Then he heard her coming down the hall.

"Hi, babe," she said affectionately.

"Hum," he grunted, and moved his arms away from his head, opened one eye.

"It's a nice morning."

"Yeah," he rolled over and the sheet twisted round him, outlining his thighs, his chest. "You mean afternoon, don't ya?"

Mae looked at the twisted sheet and giggled. "Looks like a winding sheet," she said. "A shroud —." Laughter tangled with her words and she had to pause for a moment before she could continue. "You look like a huckleberry — in a winding sheet —"

"That's no way to talk. Early in the day like this," he protested.

He looked at his arms silhouetted against the white of the sheets. They were inky black by contrast and he had to smile in spite of himself and he lay there smiling and savoring the sweet sound of Mae's giggling.

"Early?" She pointed a finger at the alarm clock on the table near the bed, and giggled again. "It's almost four o'clock. And if you don't spring up out of there you're going to be late again."

"What do you mean 'again'?"

"Twice last week. Three times the week before. And once the week before and — "

"I can't get used to sleeping in the day time," he said fretfully. He pushed his legs out from under the covers experimentally. Some of the ache had gone out of them but they weren't really rested yet. "It's too light for good sleeping. And all that standing beats the hell out of my legs."

"After two years you oughtta be used to it," Mae said.

He watched her as she fixed her hair, powdered her face, slipping into a pair of blue denim overalls. She moved quickly and yet she didn't seem to hurry.

"You look like you'd had plenty of sleep," he said lazily. He had to get up but he kept putting the moment off, not wanting to move, yet he didn't dare let his legs go completely limp because if he did he'd go back to sleep. It was getting later and later but the thought of putting his weight on his legs kept him lying there.

When he finally got up he had to hurry and he gulped his breakfast so fast that he wondered if his stomach could possibly use food thrown at it at such a rate of speed. He was still wondering about it as he and Mae were putting their coats on in the hall.

Mae paused to look at the calendar. "It's the thirteenth," she said. Then a faint excitement in her voice. "Why it's Friday the thirteenth." She had one arm in her coat sleeve and she held it there while she stared at the calendar. "I oughtta stay home," she said. "I shouldn't go otta the house."

"Aw don't be a fool," he said. "Today's payday. And payday is a good luck day everywhere, any way you look at it." And as she stood hesitating he said, "Aw, come on."

And he was late for work again because they spent fifteen minutes arguing before he could convince her she ought to go to work just the same. He had to talk persuasively, urging her gently and it took time. But he couldn't bring himself to talk to her roughly or threaten to strike her like a lot of men might have done. He wasn't made that way.

So when he reached the plant he was late and he had to wait to punch the time clock because the day shift workers were streaming out in long lines, in groups and bunches that impeded his progress.

Even now just starting his work-day his legs ached. He had to force himself to struggle past the out-going workers, punch the time clock, and get the little cart he pushed around all night because he kept toying with the idea of going home and getting back in bed.

He pushed the cart out on the concrete floor, thinking that if this was his plant he'd make a lot of changes in it. There were too many standing up jobs for one thing. He'd figure out some way most of 'em could be done sitting down and he'd put a lot more benches around. And this job he had — this job that forced him to walk ten hours a night, pushing this little cart, well, he'd turn it into a sittin'-down job. One of those little trucks they used around railroad stations would be good for a job like this. Guys sat on a seat and the thing moved easily, taking up little room and turning in hardly any space at all, like on a dime.

He pushed the cart near the foreman. He never could remember to refer to her as the forelady even in his mind. It was funny to have a woman for a boss in a plant like this one.

She was sore about something. He could tell by the way her face was red and her eyes were half shut until they were slits. Probably been out late and didn't get enough sleep. He avoided looking at her and hurried a little, head down, as he passed her though he couldn't resist stealing a glance at her out of the corner of his eyes. He saw the edge of the light colored slacks she wore and the tip end of a big tan shoe.

"Hey, Johnson!" the woman said.

The machines had started full blast. The whirr and the grinding made the building shake, made it impossible to hear conversations. The men and women at the machines talked to each other but looking at them from just a little distance away they appeared to be simply moving their lips because you couldn't hear what they were saying. Yet the woman's voice cut across the machine sound—harsh, angry.

He turned his head slowly. "Good evenin', Mrs. Scott," he said and waited.

"You're late again."

"That's right. My legs were bothering me."

The woman's face grew redder, angrier looking. "Half this shift comes in late," she said. "And you're the worst one of all. You're always late. Whatsa matter with ya?"

"It's my legs," he said. "Somehow they don't ever get rested. I don't seem to get used to sleeping days. And I just can't get started."

"Excuses. You guys always got excuses," her anger grew and spread. "Every guy comes in here late always has an excuse. His wife's sick or his grandmother died or somebody in the family had to go to the hospital," she paused, drew a deep breath. "And the niggers are the worse. I don't care what's wrong with your legs. You get in here on time. I'm sick of you niggers — "

"You got the right to get mad," he interrupted softly. "You got the right to cuss me four ways to Sunday but I ain't letting nobody call me a nigger."

He stepped closer to her. His fists were doubled. His lips were drawn back in a thin narrow line. A vein in his forehead stood out swollen, thick.

And the woman backed away from him, not hurriedly but slowly — two, three steps back.

"Aw, forget it," she said. "I didn't mean nothing by it. It slipped out. It was an accident." The red of her face deepened until the small blood vessels in her cheeks were purple. "Go on and get to work," she urged. And she took three more slow backward steps.

He stood motionless for a moment and then turned away from the red lipstick on her mouth that made him remember that the foreman was a woman. And he couldn't bring himself to hit a woman. He felt a curious tingling in his fingers and he looked down at his hands. They were clenched tight, hard, ready to smash some of those small purple veins in her face.

He pushed the cart ahead of him, walking slowly. When he turned his head, she was staring in his direction, mopping her forehead with a dark blue handkerchief. Their eyes met and then they both looked away.

He didn't glance in her direction again but moved past the long work benches, carefully collecting the finished parts, going slowly and steadily up and down, back and forth the length of the building and as he walked he forced himself to swallow his anger, get rid of it.

And he succeeded so that he was able to think about what had happened without getting upset about it. An hour went by but the tension stayed in his hands. They were clenched and knotted on the handles of the cart as though ready to aim a blow.

And he thought he should have hit her anyway, smacked her hard in the face, felt the soft flesh of her face give under the hardness of his hands. He tried to make his hands relax by offering them a description of what it would have been like to strike her because he had the queer feeling that his hands were not exactly a part of him any more — they had developed a separate life of their own over which he had no control. So he dwelt on the pleasure his hands would have felt — both of them cracking at her, first one and then the other. If he had done that his hands would have felt good now — relaxed, rested.

And he decided that even if he'd lost his job for it he should have let her have it and it would have been a long time, maybe the rest of her life before she called anybody else a nigger.

The only trouble was he couldn't hit a woman. A woman couldn't hit back the same way a man did. But it would have been a deeply satisfying thing to have cracked her narrow lips wide open with just one blow, beautifully timed and with all his weight in back of it. That way he could have gotten rid of all the energy and tension his anger had created in him. He kept remembering how his heart had started pumping blood so fast he had felt it tingle even in the tips of his fingers.

With the approach of night fatigue nibbled at him. The corners of his mouth dropped, the frown between his eyes deepened, his shoulders sagged; but his hands stayed tight and tense. As the hours dragged by he noticed that the women workers had started to snap and snarl at each other. He couldn't hear what they said because of the sound of machines but he could see the quick lip movements that sent words tumbling from the sides of their mouth. They gestured irritably with their hands and scowled as their mouths moved.

Their violent jerky motions told him that it was getting close on to quitting time but somehow he felt that the night still stretched ahead of him, composed of endless hours of steady walking on his aching legs. When the whistle finally blew he went on pushing the cart, unable to believe that it had sounded. The whirring of the machines died away to a murmur and he knew then that he'd really heard the whistle. He stood still for a moment filled with a relief that made him sigh.

Then he moved briskly, putting the cart in the store room, hurrying to take his place in the line forming before the paymaster. That was another thing he'd change, he thought. He'd have the pay envelopes handed to the people right at their benches so there wouldn't be ten or fifteen minutes lost waiting for the pay. He always got home about fifteen minutes late on payday. They did it better in the plant where Mae worked, brought the money right to them at their benches.

He stuck his pay envelope in his pants' pocket and followed the line of workers heading for the subway in a slow moving stream. He glanced up at the sky. It was a nice night, the sky looked packed full to running over with stars. And he thought if he and Mae would go right to bed when they got home from work they'd catch a few hours of darkness for sleeping. But they never did. They fooled around — cooking and eating and listening to the radio and he always stayed in a big chair in the living room and went almost but not quite to sleep and when they finally got to bed it was five or six in the morning and daylight was already seeping around the edges of the sky.

He walked slowly, putting off the moment when he would have to plunge into the crowd hurrying toward the subway. It was a long ride to Harlem and tonight the thought of it appalled him. He paused outside an all-night restaurant to kill time, so that some of the first rush of workers would be gone when he reached the subway.

The lights in the restaurant were brilliant, enticing. There was life and motion inside. And as he looked through the window he thought that everything within range of his eyes gleamed — the long imitation marble counter, the tall stools, the white porcelain topped tables and especially the big metal coffee urn right near the window. Steam issued from its top and a gas flame flickered under it — a lively, dancing, blue flame.

A lot of the workers from his shift — men and women — were lining up near the coffee urn. He watched them walk to the porcelain topped tables carrying steaming cups of coffee and he saw that just the smell of the coffee lessened the fatigue lines in their faces. After the first sip their faces softened, they smiled, they began to talk and laugh.

On a sudden impulse he shoved the door open and joined the line in front of the coffee urn. The line moved slowly. And as he stood there the smell of coffee, the sound of the laughter and of the voices, helped dull the sharp ache in his legs.

He didn't pay any attention to the girl who was serving the coffee at the urn. He kept looking at the cups in the hands of the men who had been ahead of him. Each time a man stepped out of the line with one of the thick white cups the fragrant steam got in his nostrils. He saw that they walked carefully so as not to spill a single drop. There was a froth of bubbles at the top of each cup and he thought about how he would let the bubbles break against his lips before he actually took a big deep swallow.

Then it was his turn. "A cup of coffee," he said, just as he had heard the others say.

The girl looked past him, put her hands up to her head and gently lifted her hair away from the back of her neck, tossing her head back a little. "No more coffee for awhile," she said.

He wasn't certain he'd heard her correctly and he said, "What?" blankly.

"No more coffee for awhile," she repeated.

There was silence behind him and then uneasy movement. He thought someone would say something, ask why or protest, but there was only silence and then a faint shuffling sound as though the men standing behind him had simultaneously shifted their weight from one foot to the other.

He looked at her without saying anything. He felt his hands begin to tingle and the tingling went all the way down to his finger tips so that he glanced down at them. They were clenched tight, hard, into fists. Then he looked at the girl again. What he wanted to do was hit her so hard that the scarlet lipstick on her mouth would smear and spread over her nose, her chin, out toward her cheeks; so hard that she would never toss her head again and refuse a man a cup of coffee because he was black.

He estimated the distance across the counter and reached forward, balancing his weight on the balls of his feet, ready to let the blow go. And then his hands fell back down to his sides because he forced himself to lower them, to unclench them and make them dangle loose. The effort took his breath away because his hands fought against him. But he couldn't hit her. He couldn't even now bring himself to hit a woman, not even this one, who had refused him a cup of coffee with a toss of her head. He kept seeing the gesture with which she had lifted the length of her blonde hair from the back of her neck as expressive of her contempt for him.

When he went out the door he didn't look back. If he had he would have seen the flickering blue flame under the shiny coffee urn being extinguished. The line of men who had stood behind him lingered a moment to watch the people drinking coffee at the tables and then they left just as he had without having had the coffee they wanted so badly. The girl behind the counter poured water in the urn and swabbed it out and as she waited for the water to run out she lifted her hair gently from the back of her neck and tossed her head before she began making a fresh lot of coffee.

But he walked away without a backward look, his head down, his hands in his pockets, raging at himself and whatever it was inside of him that had forced him to stand quiet and still when he wanted to strike out.

The subway was crowded and he had to stand. He tried grasping an overhead strap and his hands were too tense to grip it. So he moved near the train door and stood there swaying back and forth with the rocking of the train. The roar of the train beat inside his head, making it ache and throb, and the pain in his legs clawed up into his groin so that he seemed to be bursting with pain and he told himself that it was due to all that anger-born energy that had piled up in him and not been used and so it had spread through him like a poison — from his feet and legs all the way up to his head.

Mae was in the house before he was. He knew she was home before he put the key in the door of the apartment. The radio was going. She had it turned up loud and she was singing along with it.

"Hello, Babe," she called out as soon as he opened the door.

He tried to say "hello" and it came out half a grunt and half a sigh.

"You sure sound cheerful," she said.

She was in the bedroom and he went and leaned against the door jamb. The denim overalls she wore to work were carefully draped over the back of a chair by the bed. She was standing in front of the dresser, tying the sash of a yellow housecoat around her waist and chewing gum vigorously as she admired her reflection in the mirror over the dresser.

"Whatsa matter?" she asid. "You get bawled out by the boss or somep'n?"

"Just tired," he said slowly. "For God's sake do you have to crack that gum like that?"

"You don't have to lissen to me," she said complacently. She patted a curl in place near the side of her head and then lifted her hair away from the back of her neck, ducking her head forward and then back.

He winced away from the gesture. "What you got to be always fooling with your hair for?" he protested.

"Say, what's the matter with you, anyway?" she turned away from the mirror to face him, put her hands on her hips. "You ain't been in the house two minutes and you're picking on me."

He didn't answer her because her eyes were angry and he didn't want to quarrel with her. They'd been married too long and got along too well and so he walked all the way into the room and sat down in the chair by the bed and stretched his legs out in front of him, putting his weight on the heels of his shoes, leaning way back in the chair, not saying anything.

"Lissen," she said sharply. "I've got to wear those overalls again tomorrow. You're going to get them all wrinkled up leaning against them like that."

He didn't move. He was too tired and his legs were throbbing now that he had sat down. Besides the overalls were already wrinkled and dirty, he thought. They couldn't help but be for she'd worn them all week. He leaned further back in the chair.

"Come on, get up," she ordered.

"Oh, what the hell," he said wearily and got up from the chair. "I'd just as soon live in a subway. There'd be just as much place to sit down."

He saw that her sense of humor was struggling with her anger. But her sense of humor won because she giggled.

"Aw, come on and eat," she said. There was a coaxing note in her voice. "You're nothing but a old hungry nigger trying to act tough and — " she paused to giggle and then continued, "You — "

He had always found her giggling pleasant and deliberately said things that might amuse her and then waited, listening fo the delicate sound to emerge from her throat. This time he didn't even hear the giggle. He didn't let her finish what she was saying. She was standing close to him and that funny tingling started in his finger tips, went fast up his arms and sent his fist shooting straight for her face.

There was the smacking sound of soft flesh being struck by a hard object and it wasn't until she screamed that he realized he had hit her in the mouth — so hard that the dark red lipstick blurred and spread over her full lips, reaching up toward the tip of her nose, down toward her chin, out toward her cheeks.

The knowledge that he had struck her seeped through him slowly and he was appalled but he couldn't drag his hands away from her face. He kept striking her and he thought with horror that something inside him was holding him, binding him to this act, wrapping and twisting about him so that he had to continue it. He had lost all control over his hands. And he groped for a phrase, a word, something to describe what this thing was like that was happening to him and he thought it was like being enmeshed in a winding sheet — that was it — like a winding sheet. And even as the thought formed in his mind his hands reached for her face again and yet again.

PROBING FOR
MEANING

1. Explain the meaning of Mae's statement in the beginning of the story, "You look like a huckleberry — in a winding sheet." What further significance does the phrase acquire when Johnson uses it at the end?

2. What role does color play in the relationships between the characters in the story: Johnson and Mrs. Scott; Johnson and the girl at the coffee shop; Johnson and Mae?

3. Discuss the social convention that men shouldn't strike women as it affects Johnson and as it operates in life in general. Why does he finally hit a woman?

4. What is the reasoning behind Johnson's behavior: that you can't hit *any* woman but you can hit your wife; or that you can't hit a white person but you can hit another black? In either case, is one justified in releasing one's frustrations on an innocent person?

PROBING FOR
METHOD

1. What is the effect of beginning the story with a nebulous "he" when the reader doesn't really discover who the "he" is until much later? Is the same effect also achieved by using "he" instead of "Johnson" (no first name is ever given) so often throughout the text?

2. What single effect is this story talking about? How does Petry organize the causes leading to that effect?

3. What is the author's attitude toward Mae? toward Johnson? How do the descriptive phrases and the thought patterns help you determine these differing attitudes?

4. The story is organized generally according to chronological sequence, but how does Petry keep it moving forward without making the time structure obtrusive?

GARY GILDNER

First Practice

After the doctor checked to see
we weren't ruptured,
the man with the short cigar took us
under the grade school,
where we went in case of attack
or storm, and said
he was Clifford Hill, he was
a man who believed dogs
ate dogs, he had once killed
for his country, and if
there were any girls present
for them to leave now.
                              No one
left. OK, he said, he said I take
that to mean you are hungry
men who hate to lose as much
as I do. OK. Then
he made two lines of us
facing each other,
and across the way, he said,
is the man you hate most
in the world,
and if we are to win
that title I wanted to see how.
But I don't want to see
any marks when you're dressed,
he said. He said, *Now.*

PROBING FOR
MEANING

1. What kind of person is the coach? What words and details convey the man's character?

2. What persuasive, even coercive devices does he use on the boys? Why doesn't he want to see any marks on them when they are dressed? What symbolic significance does the remark acquire?

3. The poem does not express in so many words the effects on the boys' lives of the forces put into motion by "the man with the short cigar." These effects, however, are the real subject of the poem. What are they?

PROBING FOR
METHOD
1. The poem bristles with tense drama. What are some of its dramatic effects? How does the poet achieve them?

2. What attitude does Gildner convey toward the entire incident? What was his attitude at the time? Why might it have changed?

 WALLACE STEVENS

Disillusionment of Ten O'Clock

The houses are haunted
By white night-gowns.
None are green,
Or purple with green rings,
Or green with yellow rings,
Or yellow with blue rings.
None of them are strange,
With socks of lace
And beaded ceintures.
People are not going
To dream of baboons and periwinkles.
Only, here and there, an old sailor,
Drunk and asleep in his boots,
Catches tigers
In red weather.

PROBING FOR
MEANING
1. Who is it that haunts the houses? To whom does the term "white night-gowns" refer?

2. What is the significance of there being no strange or colored night-gowns?

3. In what ways does the sailor contrast with the other dreamers in the poem?

4. Explain the poem's title. To whom does the title refer?

PROBING FOR
METHOD
1. What attitude does the poet convey toward the dreaming of "baboons and periwinkles"? How does his attitude toward such dreaming compare with his attitude toward the white nightgowns?

2. What use does the poet make of images of color? What do the colors symbolize in the poem?

YEVGENY YEVTUSHENKO

Colours

When your face
appeared over my crumpled life
at first I understood
only the poverty of what I have.
Then its particular light
on woods, on rivers, on the sea,
became my beginning in the coloured world
in which I had not yet had my beginning.
I am so frightened, I am so frightened,
of the unexpected sunrise finishing,
of revelations
and tears and the excitement finishing,
I don't fight it, my love is this fear,
I nourish it who can nourish nothing,
love's slipshod watchman.
Fear hems me in.
I am conscious that these minutes are short
and that the colours in my eyes will vanish
when your face sets.

PROBING FOR MEANING

1. Why is the poet's life "crumpled" and impoverished? How has the subject of the poem enriched his life?

2. Of what is the poet frightened? Why does he nourish his fear?

PROBING FOR METHOD

1. Explain the paradox of one's nourishing who "can nourish nothing." What other paradoxes appear in the poem? In what sense is the poem about a paradoxical emotion?

2. What metaphor is the entire poem based on? Explain the relationship between this metaphor and the poem's title.

Topics for Imitation

1. Sometimes we act in what seems to be an irrational manner. Yet the emotions that cause us to act this way are often understandable. Write an essay in which you discuss what one or more of the se-

lections in this chapter reveal about the causes and effects of irrational behavior.

2. In differing ways, Eiseley, Orwell, and Thomas all write about the effects of confronting death. Discuss the different emotions that each author suggests are aroused when a person confronts the reality of death and dying.

3. Several of the writers in this section analyze, to a greater or lesser extent, the causes of violence in the modern world. Write a cause-and-effect essay using violence as the effect and explaining its causes as presented by Orwell, Gold, Petry, and Gildner.

4. Poverty affects the lives of the characters in Ellison's and Petry's short stories. What are the effects of the family's poverty in each case? Are the effects similar or different?

5. Women's liberation has sent thirty million women into the labor force for both economic and ideological reasons. However, Marya Mannes believes that other factors still cause women to feel unequal. What are these factors? Do you agree that they exist? What other factors could you mention?

6. The competitive quality of American society has many effects apart from winning and losing. Discuss these side effects as Gold, Petry, Gildner, and Ralbovsky (Chapter 1) present them.

7. Many of the authors in this section attempt to evaluate highly emotional situations from a detached, objective, analytical point of view. Write an essay in which you compare the effect upon you of the most objective writer to the effect of the least objective writer. Explain why you find one writer more objective than the other.

8. Many emotional situations that exist in society have not been treated in this chapter: the crisis of belief in government, the increasing use of drugs or alcohol to escape from life's problems, the continual search for status, and so on. Choosing one of these or a topic of your own as either a cause or an effect, write an essay explaining the causes of the situation or the effects of it. Limit your topic to an aspect of the broader subject that you can discuss specifically.

FIVE

CHOICES

"And if a man lived in obscurity . . . obscurity is not uninteresting"

"Man is the only being who refuses to be what he is," writes Albert Camus, who believes that we can choose to become "fully human" — loving and peaceful — if we wish to do so. Other thinkers say our environment so shapes us that our freedom to choose that path is limited; if we are violent and unloving, environmental influences may prevent our breaking out of that pattern to something better.

While our ability to choose to be ourselves may be restricted, the selections in this chapter present many choices open to us. As a young boy Richard Rodriguez chose to learn English, although it meant sacrificing the emotional security he associated with Spanish, his family's language. In "The Necessary Enemy" Katherine Anne Porter presents the choice married people must make between romantic love and realistic love (which includes hate). In "Return to India," Santha Rama Rau discusses her preference for India over Russia. Alexander Petrunkevitch highlights the differences between behavior based on reasoning and behavior based on instinct, and William Golding discusses the consequences of choosing thinking as a hobby.

The short stories also emphasize the importance of choices. William Melvin Kelley suggests that if we choose security as our highest value, then it is unlikely that we will discover our most interesting self. Willa Cather's "A Wagner Matinée" is a poignant example of the ramifications of choosing to move

from a large cultural center in the East to a farm in a small
Nebraska village.

The major theme of the poems is also choice: Alastair Reid
contrasts people who choose the curiosity of cats with those
who choose the complacency of dogs; D. H. Lawrence points
out the consequences of choosing on the basis of education
rather than instinct; and Archibald MacLeish, in "Wildwest,"
contrasts Crazy Horse's love for his homeland with the crass-
ness of profiteers and "empire builders."

Comparing and Contrasting Alternatives and Selecting Vocabulary and Tone

If, in your prewriting stage of generating ideas about your
subject, you asked yourself "What is it like?" or "What can I
contrast it with?" then you may want to follow one of the
compare-and-contrast patterns in organizing your essay. Several patterns are presented on pp. 221–223 following William
Golding's essay "Thinking as a Hobby." What patterns do
the essayists in this chapter use?

Another part of the writing process is to determine what
your attitude toward your subject and your readers ought to
be and to choose words that convey this attitude clearly and
vividly. Some suggestions as to how to select both tone and
vocabulary follow Richard Rodriguez's essay on pp. 229–232.
As you read the other selections, make note of words that
"leap at you from the page" because of their peculiar appro-
priateness.

 WILLIAM GOLDING

Thinking as a Hobby

While I was still a boy, I came to the conclusion that there were
three grades of thinking; and since I was later to claim thinking as my
hobby, I came to an even stranger conclusion — namely, that I myself
could not think at all.

I must have been an unsatisfactory child for grownups to deal with. I remember how incomprehensible they appeared to me at first, but not, of course, how I appeared to them. It was the headmaster of my grammar school who first brought the subject of thinking before me — though neither in the way, nor with the result he intended. He had some statuettes in his study. They stood on a high cupboard behind this desk. One was a lady wearing nothing but a bath towel. She seemed frozen in an eternal panic lest the bath towel slip down any farther; and since she had no arms, she was in an unfortunate position to pull the towel up again. Next to her, crouched the statuette of a leopard, ready to spring down at the top drawer of a filing cabinet labeled A-AH. My innocence interpreted this as the victim's last, despairing cry. Beyond the leopard was a naked, muscular gentleman, who sat, looking down, with his chin on his fist and his elbow on his knee. He seemed utterly miserable.

Some time later, I learned about these statuettes. The headmaster had placed them where they would face delinquent children, because they symbolized to him the whole of life. The naked lady was the Venus of Milo. She was Love. She was not worried about the towel. She was just busy being beautiful. The leopard was Nature, and he was being natural. The naked, muscular gentleman was not miserable. He was Rodin's Thinker, an image of pure thought. It is easy to buy small plaster models of what you think life is like.

I had better explain that I was a frequent visitor to the headmaster's study, because of the latest thing I had done or left undone. As we now say, I was not integrated. I was, if anything, disintegrated; and I was puzzled. Grownups never made sense. Whenever I found myself in a penal position before the headmaster's desk, with the statuettes glimmering whitely above him, I would sink my head, clasp my hands behind my back and writhe one shoe over the other.

The headmaster would look opaquely at me, through flashing spectacles.

"What are we going to do with you?"

Well, what *were* they going to do with me? I would writhe my shoe some more and stare down at the worn rug.

"Look up, boy! Can't you look up?"

Then I would look up at the cupboard, where the naked lady was frozen in her panic and the muscular gentleman contemplated the hindquarters of the leopard in endless gloom. I had nothing to say to the headmaster. His spectacles caught the light so that you could see nothing human behind them. There was no possibility of communication.

"Don't you ever think at all?"

No. I didn't think, wasn't thinking, couldn't think — I was simply waiting in anguish for the interview to stop.

"Then you'd better learn — hadn't you?"

On one occasion the headmaster leaped to his feet, reached up and plonked Rodin's masterpiece on the desk before me.

"That's what a man looks like when he's really thinking."

I surveyed the gentleman without interest or comprehension.

"Go back to your class."

Clearly there was something missing in me. Nature had endowed the rest of the human race with a sixth sense and left me out. This must be so. I mused, on my way back to the class, since whether I had broken a window, or failed to remember Boyle's Law, or been late for school, my teachers produced me one, adult answer: "Why can't you think?"

As I saw the case, I had broken the window because I had tried to hit Jack Arney with a cricket ball and missed him; I could not remember Boyle's Law because I had never bothered to learn it; and I was late for school because I preferred looking over the bridge into the river. In fact, I was wicked. Were my teachers, perhaps, so good that they could not understand the depths of my depravity? Were they clear, untormented people who could direct their every action by this mysterious business of thinking? The whole thing was incomprehensible. In my earlier years, I found even the statuette of the Thinker confusing. I did not believe any of my teachers were naked, ever. Like someone born deaf, but bitterly determined to find out about sound, I watched my teachers to find out about thought.

There was Mr. Houghton. He was always telling me to think. With a modest satisfaction, he would tell me that he had thought a bit himself. Then why did he spend so much time drinking? Or was there more sense in drinking than there appeared to be? But if not, and if drinking were in fact ruinous to health — and Mr. Houghton was ruined, there was no doubt about that — why was he always talking about the clean life and the virtues of fresh air? He would spread his arms wide with the action of a man who habitually spent his time striding along mountain ridges.

"Open air does me good boy — I know it!"

Sometimes, exalted by his own oratory, he would leap from his desk and hustle us outside into a hideous wind.

"Now, boys! Deep breaths! Feel it right down inside you — huge draughts of God's good air!"

He would stand before us, rejoicing in his perfect health, an open-air man. He would put his hands on his waist and take a tremendous breath. You could hear the wind, trapped in the cavern of his chest and struggling with all the unnatural impediments. His body would reel with shock and his ruined face go white at the unaccustomed visitation. He would stagger back to his desk and collapse there, useless for the rest of the morning.

Mr. Houghton was given to high-minded monologues about the good life, sexless and full of duty. Yet in the middle of one of these monologues, if a girl passed the window, tapping along on her neat little feet, he would interrupt his discourse, his neck would turn of itself and he would watch her out of sight. In this instance, he seemed to me ruled not by thought but by an invisible and irresistible spring in his nape.

His neck was an object of great interest to me. Normally it bulged a bit over his collar. But Mr. Houghton had fought in the First World War alongside both Americans and French, and had come — by who knows what illogic? — to a settled detestation of both countries. If either country happened to be prominent in current affairs, no argument could make Mr. Houghton think well of it. He would bang the desk, his neck would bulge still further and go red. "You can say what you like," he would cry; "but I've thought about this — and I know what I think!"

Mr. Houghton thought with his neck.

There was Miss Parsons. She assured us that her dearest wish was our welfare, but I knew even then, with the mysterious clairvoyance of childhood, that what she wanted most was the husband she never got. There was Mr. Hands — and so on.

I have dealt at length with my teachers because this was my introduction to the nature of what is commonly called thought. Through them I discovered that thought is often full of unconscious prejudice, ignorance and hypocrisy. It will lecture on disinterested purity while its neck is being remorselessly twisted toward a skirt. Technically, it is about as proficient as most businessmen's golf, as honest as most politicians' intentions, or — to come near my own preoccupation — as coherent as most books that get written. It is what I came to call grade-three thinking, though more properly, it is feeling, rather than thought.

True, often there is a kind of innocence in prejudices, but in those days I viewed grade-three thinking with an intolerant contempt and an incautious mockery. I delighted to confront a pious lady who hated the Germans with the proposition that we should love our enemies. She taught me a great truth in dealing with grade-three thinkers; because of her, I no longer dismiss lightly a mental process which for nine-tenths of the population is the nearest they will ever get to thought. They have immense solidarity. We had better respect them, for we are outnumbered and surrounded. A crowd of grade-three thinkers, all shouting the same thing, all warming their hands at the fire of their own prejudices, will not thank you for pointing out the contradictions in their beliefs. Man is a gregarious animal, and enjoys agreement as cows will graze all the same way on the side of a hill.

Grade-two thinking is the detection of contradictions. I reached grade two when I trapped the poor, pious lady. Grade-two thinkers do not stampede easily, though often they fall into the other fault and lag behind. Grade-two thinking is a withdrawal, with eyes and ears open. It became my hobby and brought satisfaction and loneliness in either hand. For grade-two thinking destroys without having the power to create. It set me watching the crowds cheering His Majesty the King and asking myself what all the fuss was about, without giving me anything positive to put in the place of that heady patriotism. But there were compensations. To hear people justify the habit of hunting foxes and tearing them to pieces by claiming that the foxes liked it. To hear our Prime Minister talk about the great benefit we conferred on India by jailing people like Pandit Nehru and Gandhi. To hear American politicians talk about peace in one sentence and refuse to join the League of Nations in the next. Yes, there were moments of delight.

But I was growing toward adolescence and had to admit that Mr. Houghton was not the only one with an irresistible spring in his neck. I, too, felt the compulsive hand of nature and began to find that pointing out contradiction could be costly as well as fun. There was Ruth, for example, a serious and attractive girl. I was an atheist at the time. Grade-two thinking is a menace to religion and knocks down sects like skittles. I put myself in a position to be converted by her with an hypocrisy worth of grade three. She was a Methodist — or at least, her parents were, and Ruth had to follow suit. But, alas, instead of relying on the Holy Spirit to convert me, Ruth was foolish enough to open her pretty mouth in argument. She claimed that the Bible (King James Version) was literally inspired. I countered by saying that the Catholics believed in the literal inspiration of Saint Jerome's *Vulgate*, and the two books were different. Argument flagged.

At last she remarked that there were an awful lot of Methodists, and they couldn't be wrong, could they — not all those millions? That was too easy, said I restively (for the nearer you were to Ruth, the nicer she was to be near to) since there were more Roman Catholics than Methodists anyway; and they couldn't be wrong, could they — not all those hundreds of millions? An awful flicker of doubt appeared in her eyes. I slid my arm round her waist and murmured breathlessly that if we were counting heads, the Buddhists were the boys for my money. But Ruth had *really* wanted to do me good, because I was so nice. She fled. The combination of my arm and those countless Buddhists was too much for her.

That night her father visited my father and left, red-cheeked and indignant. I was given the third degree to find out what had happened. It was lucky we were both of us only fourteen. I lost Ruth and gained an undeserved reputation as a potential libertine.

So grade-two thinking could be dangerous. It was in this knowledge, at the age of fifteen, that I remember making a comment from the heights of grade two, on the limitations of grade three. One evening I found myself alone in the school hall, preparing it for a party. The door of the headmaster's study was open. I went in. The headmaster had ceased to thump Rodin's Thinker down on the desk as an example to the young. Perhaps he had not found any more candidates, but the statuettes were still there, glimmering and gathering dust on top of the cupboard. I stood on a chair and rearranged them. I stood Venus in her bath towel on the filing cabinet, so that now the top drawer caught its breath in a gasp of sexy excitement. "A-ah!" The portentous Thinker I placed on the edge of the cupboard so that he looked down at the bath towel and waited for it to slip.

Grade-two thinking, though it filled life with fun and excitement, did not make for content. To find out the deficiencies of our elders bolsters the young ego but does not make for personal security. I found that grade two was not only the power to point out contradictions. It took the swimmer some distance from the shore and left him there, out of his depth. I decided that Pontius Pilate was a typical grade-two thinker. "What is truth?" he said, a very common grade-two thought, but one that is used always as the end of an argument instead of the beginning. There is still a higher grade of thought which says, "What is truth?" and sets out to find it.

But these grade-one thinkers were few and far between. They did not visit my grammar school in the flesh though they were there in books. I aspired to them, partly because I was ambitious and partly because I now saw my hobby as an unsatisfactory thing if it went no further. If you set out to climb a mountain, however high you climb, you have failed if you cannot reach the top.

I *did* meet an undeniably grade-one thinker in my first year at Oxford. I was looking over a small bridge in Magdalen Deer Park, and a tiny mustached and hatted figure came and stood by my side. He was a German who had just fled from the Nazis to Oxford as a temporary refuge. His name was Einstein.

But Professor Einstein knew no English at that time and I knew only two words of German. I beamed at him, trying wordlessly to convey by my bearing all the affection and respect that the English felt for him. It is possible — and I have to make the admission — that I felt here were two grade-one thinkers standing side by side; yet I doubt if my face conveyed more than a formless awe. I would have given my Greek and Latin and French and a good slice of my English for enough German to communicate. But we were divided; he was as inscrutable as my headmaster. For perhaps five minutes we stood together on the bridge, undeniable grade-one thinker and breathless aspirant. With true greatness, Professor Einstein realized that any contact was better than none. He pointed to a trout wavering in midstream.

He spoke: *"Fisch."*

My brain reeled. Here I was, mingling with the great, and yet helpless as the veriest grade-three thinker. Desperately I sought for some sign by which I might convey that, I, too, revered pure reason. I nodded vehemently. In a brilliant flash I used up half my German vocabulary.

"*Fisch. Ja. Ja.*"

For perhaps another five minutes we stood side by side. Then Professor Einstein, his whole figure still conveying good will and amiability, drifted away out of sight.

I, too, would be a grade-one thinker. I was irreverent at the best of times. Political and religious systems, social customs, loyalties and traditions, they all came tumbling down like so many rotten apples off a tree. This was a fine hobby and a sensible substitute for cricket, since you could play it all the year round. I came up in the end with what must always remain the justification for grade-one thinking, its sign, seal and charter. I devised a coherent system for living. It was a moral system, which was wholly logical. Of course, as I readily admitted, conversion of the world to my way of thinking might be difficult, since my system did away with a number of trifles, such as big business, centralized government, armies, marriage. . . .

It was Ruth all over again. I had some very good friends who stood by me, and still do. But my acquaintances vanished, taking the girls with them. Young women seemed oddly contented with the world as it was. They valued the meaningless ceremony with a ring. Young men, while willing to concede the chaining sordidness of marriage, were hesitant about abandoning the organizations which they hoped would give them a career. A young man on the first rung of the Royal Navy, while perfectly agreeable to doing away with big business and marriage, got as red-necked as Mr. Houghton when I proposed a world without any battleships in it.

Had the game gone too far? Was it a game any longer? In those prewar days, I stood to lose a great deal, for the sake of a hobby.

Now you are expecting me to describe how I saw the folly of my ways and came back to the warm nest, where prejudices are so often called loyalties, where pointless actions are hallowed into custom by repetition, where we are content to say we think when all we do is feel.

But you would be wrong. I dropped my hobby and turned professional.

If I were to go back to the headmaster's study and find the dusty statuettes still there, I would arrange them differently. I would dust Venus and put her aside, for I have come to love her and know her for the fair thing she is. But I would put the Thinker, sunk in his desperate thought, where there were shadows before him — and at his back, I would put the leopard, crouched and ready to spring.

PROBING FOR
MEANING

1. Why was Golding "an unsatisfactory child for grownups to deal with"?

2. What did Golding learn about thought by observing Mr. Houghton? What is "grade-three thinking"?

3. What is the difference between grade-three thinking and grade-two thinking? Why is grade-two thinking "costly as well as fun"?

4. How does Golding distinguish grade-one thinking from grade-two? What effects did his attempt to be a grade-one thinker have upon him?

PROBING FOR
METHOD

1. To what extent are the similarities in Golding's relationships with Mr. Houghton, Ruth, and Einstein as important as the differences? What do the similarities illustrate about the act of thinking?

2. What is the difference between the way Golding rearranged the three statuettes in the headmaster's office when he was fifteen and the way he says he would like to rearrange them at the end of the essay? What do the contrasts between these two scenes reveal about him as a thinker?

3. In what way is the statement "Mr. Houghton thought with his neck" ironic? What other examples of irony can you point to in the essay? Under which grade of thinking should irony be classified?

4. Of what significance is the title of the essay?

5. Golding is obviously writing for a sophisticated audience. Define the following words:

penal	clairvoyance
opaquely	proficient
depravity	gregarious
oratory	skittles
visitation	portentous
discourse	inscrutable
detestation	aspirant

Comparing and Contrasting Alternatives

How does Golding develop his comparison-and-contrast essay? In comparing and contrasting the three types of thinkers, Golding discusses each one separately but compares and contrasts them as well. He presents grade-three thinking through the example of his teacher, Mr. Houghton, whose thinking is filled with "unconscious prejudice, ignorance and hypocrisy." He moves on to grade-two thinking that detects contradictions without attempting to solve them. He uses himself as an example in his years when he destroyed "without having the power to create."

At this point, he contrasts grade-two thinking with grade three by mentioning how, during his grade-two years, he contemptuously rearranged the statuettes to reflect the lust lurking in the mind of the grade-three thinker. He then proceeds to compare and contrast grade-two and grade-one thinking; the grade-two thinker asks cynically "What is truth?" whereas the grade-one thinker asks the same question with every intention of trying to answer it.

Golding then moves on to grade-one thinking. He compares himself to Albert Einstein, humorously implying that the contrast between himself and the physicist is greater than the similarity. Finally, returning to an earlier image in the essay, he once more rearranges the statuettes, this time dramatizing the danger inherent in the persistent pursuit of truth.

Comparing and contrasting alternatives.   Comparison and contrast is an organizational principle used by writers who wish to explain one item by reference to another, or are interested in measuring two items against a principle, or wish to explain a principle by comparing and contrasting two (or more) items. In this chapter, for example, Santha Rama Rau explains India by reference to Russia. Rodriguez, Porter, and Golding are interested in all of their items in reference to a principle (Rodriguez examines the value of bilingual education as measured against a child's emotional needs; Porter discusses hate as a necessary enemy of love; Golding evaluates three types of thinking against implied standards of truth and right). Petrunkevitch compares and contrasts intuition and intellect by comparing and contrasting the tarantula and the wasp.

In organizing a comparison-and-contrast essay, the writer may take one of three approaches: whole-by-whole, part-by-part, or a combination of the two. In the first method, the writer looks at all aspects of one item first and then examines all aspects of the other item or items, making continuous reference to points of comparison and contrast. Golding's essay is an illustration of this method.

In a part-by-part structure, the writer looks at one aspect of the first item and compares it to a corresponding aspect of the other item, and so on, working back and forth between the first and second items until all aspects have been covered. Examples of this method in the chapter are Rodriguez's, Porter's, and Rau's essays. Rodriguez contrasts several aspects of Spanish and English: the ease or difficulty with which his family spoke the language; his attitudes toward those who spoke Spanish and those who spoke English; the quality of sound of both languages; his association of Spanish with the private world and English with the public world. Rau contrasts Indian and Russian marketplaces, interpersonal relationships, public meeting places, and parades. Porter contrasts the role training plays in our attitudes toward and expression of love and hate; the nature of both love and hate; and the conditions under which they can peacefully coexist.

In the combination method, the writer fully presents item one and then compares and contrasts items one and two part·by part. Petrunkevitch uses this method: first, he introduces us to the tarantula with no mention of the wasp; then, he compares and contrasts the tarantula and the wasp part by part.

All items compared and contrasted must be in the same class; otherwise, the effort to relate them is meaningless. Rau compares two countries; Golding, three types of thinking; Rodriguez, two languages; Porter, two types of emotion; and Petrunkevitch, two forms of behavior.

Procedures to follow in comparing and contrasting alternatives.

  A. Ask yourself if your purpose in writing falls into one of the three categories discussed above: you wish to explain one item by reference to another; you are interested in both in reference to a principle; or you wish to explain a principle by comparing and contrasting the two items.

  B. Determine that both (or all) items are in the same class.

  C. Choose a method of development.

  1. The whole-by-whole method works well when the points to be made are broad and clear as in Golding's comparison and contrast of the three types of thinkers.

  2. The part-by-part method works when many details are involved, such as the many facets of languages in Rodriguez, the many aspects of life in a country as in Rau, and the great complexities in human emotions as in Porter.

  3. The combination approach can be used when one item converges on another only at one point, but the other is connected with the first at several points. The first item would be presented as a whole, and the second as it compares and contrasts with aspects of the first. In "The Spider and the Wasp" the tarantula is presented as a whole, but the wasp is compared and contrasted part-by-part with the spider. When comparing and contrasting traditional and contemporary views of a subject, the traditional would be discussed as a whole, the contemporary as it compares and contrasts part by part with the traditional. In comparing and contrasting women's attitudes toward fashion in the present with those of the past, for example, women's attitudes in the past three hundred years might be presented as a whole, while their attitudes of the last twenty years might be compared and contrasted part by part with those of the past.

RICHARD RODRIGUEZ

from Hunger of Memory

I remember to start with that day in Sacramento — a California now nearly thirty years past — when I first entered a classroom, able to understand some fifty stray English words.

The third of four children, I had been preceded to a neighborhood Roman Catholic school by an older brother and sister. But neither of them had revealed very much about their classroom experiences. Each afternoon they returned, as they left in the morning, always together, speaking in Spanish as they climbed the five steps of the porch. And their mysterious books, wrapped in shopping-bag paper, remained on the table next to the door, closed firmly behind them.

An accident of geography sent me to a school where all my classmates were white, many the children of doctors and lawyers and business executives. All my classmates certainly must have been uneasy on that first day of school — as most children are uneasy — to find themselves apart from their families in the first institution of their lives. But I was astonished.

The nun said, in a friendly but oddly impersonal voice, "Boys and girls, this is Richard Rodriguez." (I heard her sound out: *Rich-heard Road-ree-guess.*) It was the first time I had heard anyone name me in English. "Richard," the nun repeated more slowly, writing my name down in her black leather book. Quickly I turned to see my mother's face dissolve in a watery blur behind the pebbled glass door.

Many years later there is something called bilingual education — a scheme proposed in the late 1960s by Hispanic-American social activists, later endorsed by a congressional vote. It is a program that seeks to permit non-English-speaking children, many from lower-class homes, to use their family language as the language of school. (Such is the goal its supporters announce.) I hear them and am forced to say no: it is not possible for a child — any child — ever to use his family's language in school. Not to understand this is to misunderstand the public uses of schooling and to trivialize the nature of intimate life — a family's "language."

Memory teaches me what I know of these matters; the boy reminds the adult. I was a bilingual child, a certain kind — socially disadvantaged — the son of working-class parents, both Mexican immigrants.

In the early years of my boyhood, my parents coped very well in America. My father had steady work. My mother managed at home. They were nobody's victims. Optimism and ambition led them to a house (our home) many blocks from the Mexican south side of town. We lived among *gringos* and only a block from the biggest, whitest houses. It never occurred to my parents that they couldn't live wherever they chose. Nor was the Sacramento of the fifties bent on teaching them a contrary lesson. My mother and father were more annoyed than intimidated by those two or three neighbors who tried initially to make us unwelcome. ("Keep your brats away from my sidewalk!") But despite all they achieved, perhaps because they had so much to achieve, any deep feeling of ease, the confidence of "belonging" in public was withheld from them both. They regarded the people at work, the faces in crowds, as very distant from us. They were the others, *los gringos*. That term was interchangeable in their speech with another, even more telling, *los americanos*.

I grew up in a house where the only regular guests were my relations. For one day, enormous families of relatives would visit and there would be so many people that the noise and the bodies would spill out to the backyard and front porch. Then, for weeks, no one came by. (It was usually a salesman who rang the doorbell.) Our house stood apart. A gaudy yellow in a row of white bungalows. We were the people with the noisy dog. The people who raised pigeons and chickens. We were the foreigners on the block. A few neighbors smiled and waved. We waved back. But no one in the family knew the names of the old couple who lived next door; until I was seven years old, I did not know the names of the kids who lived across the street.

In public, my father and mother spoke a hesitant, accented, not always grammatical English. And they would have to strain — their bodies tense — to catch the sense of what was rapidly said by *los gringos*. At home they spoke Spanish. The language of their Mexican past sounded in counterpoint to the English of public society. The words would come quickly, with ease. Conveyed through those sounds was the pleasing, soothing, consoling reminder of being at home.

During those years when I was first conscious of hearing, my mother and father addressed me only in Spanish; in Spanish I learned to reply. By contrast, English (*inglés*), rarely heard in the house, was the language I came to associate with *gringos*. I learned my first words of English overhearing my parents speak to strangers. At five years of age, I knew just enough English for my mother to trust me on errands to stores one block away. No more.

I was a listening child, careful to hear the very different sounds of Spanish and English. Wide-eyed with hearing, I'd listen to sounds more than words. First, there were English (*gringos*) sounds. So many words were still unknown that when the butcher or the lady at the drugstore said something to me, exotic polysyllabic sounds would bloom in the midst of their sentences. Often, the speech of people in public seemed to me very loud, booming with confidence. The man behind the counter would literally ask, "What can I do for you?" But by being so firm and so clear, the sound of his voice said that he was a *gringo*; he belonged in public society.

I would also hear then the high nasal notes of middle-class American speech. The air stirred with sound. Sometimes, even now, when I have been traveling abroad for several weeks, I will hear what I heard as a boy. In hotel lobbies or airports, in Turkey or Brazil, some Americans will pass, and suddenly I will hear it again — the high sound of American voices. For a few seconds I will hear it with pleasure, for it is now the sound of *my* society — a reminder of home. But inevitably — already on the flight headed for home, the sound fades with repetition. I will be unable to hear it anymore.

When I was a boy, things were different. The accent of *los gringos* was never pleasing nor was it hard to hear. Crowds at Safeway or at bus stops would be noisy with sound. And I would be forced to edge away from the chirping chatter above me.

I was unable to hear my own sounds, but I knew very well that I spoke English poorly. My words could not stretch far enough to form complete thoughts. And the words I did speak I didn't know well enough to make into distinct sounds. (Listeners would usually lower their heads, better to hear what I was trying to say.) But it was one thing for *me* to speak English with difficulty. It was more troubling for me to hear my parents speak in public: their high-whining vowels and guttural consonants; their sentences that got stuck with "eh" and "ah" sounds; the confused syntax; the hesitant rhythm of sounds so different from the way *gringos* spoke. I'd notice, moreover, that my parents' voices were softer than those of *gringos* we'd meet.

I am tempted now to say that none of this mattered. In adulthood I am embarrassed by childhood fears. And, in a way, it didn't matter very much that my parents could not speak English with ease. Their linguistic difficulties had no serious consequences. My mother and father made themselves understood at the county hospital clinic and at government offices. And yet, in another way, it mattered very much — it was unsettling to hear my parents struggle with English. Hearing them, I'd grow nervous, my clutching trust in their protection and power weakened.

There were many times like the night at a brightly lit gasoline station (a blaring white memory) when I stood uneasily, hearing my father. He was talking to a teenaged attendant. I do not recall what they were saying, but I cannot forget the sounds my father made as he spoke. At one point his words slid together to form one word — sounds as confused as the threads of blue and green oil in the puddle next to my shoes. His voice rushed through what he had left to say. And, toward the end, reached falsetto notes, appealing to his listener's understanding. I looked away to the lights of passing automobiles. I tried not to hear anymore. But I heard only too well the calm, easy tone in the attendant's reply. Shortly afterward, walking toward home with my father, I shivered when he put his hand on my shoulder. The very first chance that I got, I evaded his grasp and ran on ahead into the dark, skipping with feigned boyish exuberance.

But then there was Spanish. *Español:* my family's language. *Español:* the language that seemed to me a private language. I'd hear strangers on the radio and in the Mexican Catholic church across town speaking in Spanish, but I couldn't really believe that Spanish was a public language, like English. Spanish speakers, rather, seemed related to me, for I sensed that we shared — through our language — the experience of feeling apart from *los gringos.* It was thus a ghetto Spanish that I heard and I spoke. Like those whose lives are bound by a barrio, I was reminded by Spanish of my separateness from *los otros, los gringos* in power. But more intensely than for most barrio children — because I did not live in a barrio — Spanish seemed to me the language of home. (Most days it was only at home that I'd hear it.) It became the language of joyful return.

A family member would say something to me and I would feel myself specially recognized. My parents would say something to me and I would feel embraced by the sounds of their words. Those sounds said: *I am speaking with ease in Spanish. I am addressing you in words I never use with* los gringos. *I recognize you as someone special, close, like no one outside. You belong with us. In the family.*

(*Ricardo.*)

At the age of five, six, well past the time when most other children no longer easily notice the difference between sounds uttered at home and words spoken in public, I had a different experience. I lived in a world magically compounded of sounds. I remained a child longer than most; I lingered too long, poised at the end of language — often frightened by the sounds of *los gringos,* delighted by the sounds of Spanish at home. I shared with my family a language that was startingly different from that used in the great city around us.

For me there were none of the gradations between public and private society so normal to a maturing child. Outside the house was public society; inside the house was private. Just opening or closing the screen door behind me was an important experience. I'd rarely leave home all alone or without reluctance. Walking down the sidewalk, under the canopy of tall trees, I'd warily notice the — suddenly — silent neighborhood kids who stood warily watching me. Nervously, I'd arrive at the grocery store to hear there the sounds of the *gringo* — foreign to me — reminding me that in this world so big, I was a foreigner. But then I'd return. Walking back toward our house, climbing the steps from the sidewalk, when the front door was open in summer, I'd hear voices beyond the screen door talking in Spanish. For a second or two, I'd stay, linger there, listening. Smiling, I'd hear my mother call out, saying in Spanish (words): "Is that you, Richard?" All the while her sounds would assure me: *You are home now; come closer; inside. With us.* "*Sí,*" I'd reply.

Once more inside the house I would resume (assume) my place in the family. The sounds would dim, grow harder to hear. Once more at home, I would grow less aware of that fact. It required, however, no more than the blurt of the doorbell to alert me to listen to sounds all over again. The house would turn instantly still while my mother went to the door. I'd hear her hard English sounds. I'd wait to hear her voice return to soft-sounding Spanish, which assured me, as surely as did the clicking tongue of the lock on the door, that the stranger was gone.

Plainly, it is not healthy to hear such sounds so often. It is not healthy to distinguish public words from private sounds so easily. I remained cloistered by sounds, timid and shy in public, too dependent on voices at home. And yet it needs to be emphasized: I was an extremely happy child at home. I remember many nights when my father would come back from work, and I'd hear him call out to my mother in Spanish, sounding relieved. In Spanish, he'd sound light and free notes he never could manage in English. Some nights I'd jump up just at hearing his voice. With *mis hermanos* I would come running into the room where he was with my mother. Our laughing (so deep was the pleasure!) became screaming. Like others who know the pain of public alienation, we transformed the knowledge of our public separateness and made it consoling — the reminder of intimacy. Excited, we joined our voices in a celebration of sounds. *We are speaking now the way we never speak out in public. We are alone — together,* voices sounded, surrounded to tell me. Some nights, no one seemed willing to loosen the hold sounds had on us. At dinner, we invented new words. (Ours sounded Spanish, but made sense only to us.) We pieced together new words by taking, say, an English verb and giving it Spanish endings. My mother's instructions at bedtime would be lacquered with mock-urgent tones. Or a word like *sí* would become, in several notes, able to convey added measures of feeling. Tongues explored the edges of words, especially the fat vowels. And we happily sounded that military drum roll, the twirling roar of the Spanish *r.* Family language: my family's sounds. The voices of my parents and sisters and brother. Their voices insisting: *You belong here. We are family members. Related. Special to one another. Listen!* Voices singing and sighing, rising, straining, then surging, teeming with pleasure that burst syllables into fragments of laughter. At times it

seemed there was steady quiet only when, from another room, the rustling whispers of my parents faded and I moved closer to sleep.

PROBING FOR
MEANING

1. Rodriguez says that he was "a listening child." What does he mean?

2. How did Rodriguez feel about the sounds of English when he was a
boy? How have his feelings changed now that he is grown?

3. What effect did his parents' halting English have upon Rodriguez
when he was a boy?

4. Why did Spanish seem "a private language" to Rodriguez? What
negative effects did his early feelings about Spanish have upon him? What
were the positive effects?

5. Do you get a sense from this short excerpt why Rodriguez is opposed to bilingual education?

PROBING FOR
METHOD

1. Rodriguez compares the way he felt about English as a child to the
way he felt about Spanish. To what extent does he organize his comparison by
focusing first on English, then on Spanish? What more specific comparisons
does he draw in the essay?

2. Rodriguez begins the essay by recalling how, on his first day in
public school, he watched his mother's face "dissolve in a watery blur behind
the pebbled glass door." In what sense is the image of the door symbolic?
Where else in the essay is the image of a door important? What other images
does Rodriguez employ to symbolize his thoughts and feelings?

3. What effect does the repeated use of the Spanish word *gringos* have
on a reader? What other Spanish words does Rodriguez introduce into the
essay, and to what effect?

4. Although Rodriguez's first language was Spanish, he has clearly acquired a mastery of English. Explain the meaning of the following words

trivialize	linguistic
counterpoint	falsetto
polysyllabic	gradations
guttural	cloistered
syntax	teeming

Selecting Vocabulary and Tone

What factors influenced Rodriguez in his selection of words?   Rodriguez's subject is
an emotional one, as he constantly reminds us. As a child he was "astonished,"
"frightened," "shy," "embarrassed," "delighted," or "happy," depending upon
the language he was hearing at the time. Even as an adult, he retains strong
emotions about his subject and wants his experiences to serve as an argument

against bilingual education. His tone therefore conveys great seriousness about his subject.

In order to express the strong, contrasting emotions that English and Spanish, respectively, awoke in him as a child, Rodriguez has chosen his vocabulary carefully. His word choice corresponds to three threads running through his essay: what Americans sounded like to him, what the efforts of his family to learn English sounded like, and what the sounds of their family language, Spanish, conveyed. We can chart the language in his essay in the following way:

American sounds	Efforts of his family to speak English	Spanish sounds
exotic, polysyllabic sounds would bloom		pleasing, soothing, consoling
very loud, booming with confidence	strain, tense	
firm, clear, high, nasal	high-whining vowels, guttural consonants	language of joyful return
The air stirred with sound.	confused syntax	soft-sounding
chirping chatter	hesitant rhythms	celebration of sounds
calm, easy tones	sounds as confused as the threads of blue and green oil in the puddle	Voices singing and sighing, rising, straining, then surging, teeming with pleasure that burst syllables into fragments of laughter

Rodriguez uses a vocabulary level that can be understood by the average person, and therefore he appears to be writing for a general audience.

Selecting vocabulary and tone.   In determining your word choice, you must consider who your audience is, your attitude toward that audience, and what you want to emphasize about your subject matter.

Vocabulary levels vary, even among adult audiences; a careful writer will not write "above the head" of the intended reader, nor insult the reader by aiming too low. The writers in this chapter use vocabularies of varying difficulty, some aiming for the educated audience and some for a general readership. Examining the vocabulary of writers like William Golding and Alexander Petrunkevitch, one assumes they are writing for the educated person.

Next, you must determine what attitude you will take toward your audience. The writers in this chapter establish various relationships with their audiences, from the intimate tone of Golding's essay ("I had better explain," "Now you are expecting me to describe how I saw the folly of my ways. . . . But you would be wrong"), to the trusting tone of Rodriguez who writes of very personal matters, to the informal but impersonal tone of Rau, to the increasingly formal tones of Porter and Petrunkevitch.

Once you have established your attitude toward your audience, you will want to decide what your tone should be in reference to your subject matter. We have already seen that Rodriguez's tone is serious. William Golding's tone is humorous and ironic, which is also in keeping with the education level of his audience. Petrunkevitch is writing on a scientific subject to the educated, perhaps scientific, reader, and his tone is correspondingly objective. Rau's tone is slightly sentimental toward India, a tone perhaps necessary to her purpose of advancing India over other cultures and also a tone frequently used when writing informally to the general reader. Porter, like Rau and Rodriguez, uses a vocabulary the general public can manage, but her attitude toward her subject, which combines sociological objectivity with personal involvement, suggests an educated reader.

Tone is conveyed through word choice. The writer chooses words that communicate a consistent attitude toward the subject. Selection of details also helps to transmit tone. Rodriguez, as we have seen, chooses words that convey his attitudes toward English, Spanish, and the effort of his family to learn English, and his anecdotes also support the same overall purpose. Golding, too, chooses words and examples that convey the humor and irony of his essay. But the absence of such emotional words and details in Petrunkevitch and Porter (Porter's words name emotions but do not evoke the emotions in the reader) creates the objective tone of their essays.

In choosing words to convey the tone you have adopted, it is wise to distinguish between the connotations and denotations of words. Words that have similar dictionary definitions (denotations) often have different cultural associations (connotations). Rodriguez, for example, uses the adjective "stray" in the first paragraph of his essay, a word that has the same denotation as "wandering" or "meandering." Why does Rodriguez use "stray"? Probably the reason is that it connotes more strongly than the two near-synonyms the purposelessness and lack of connection he feels toward his English vocabulary. He also chooses the word "mysterious" in reference to his brother's and sister's English-language textbooks. He could have used "unfamiliar" or "strange," but "mysterious" connotes a remoteness that the other two words do not. These words, occurring in the first two paragraphs, help to set the tone of his work.

Procedures to follow in choosing vocabulary.

    A. Audience considerations:

        1. Determine as precisely as possible who your audience will be. Is it your peers, your teacher, another designated relationship?

        2. Decide what your attitude toward your audience will be. Usually, in a classroom situation, you will adopt an informal but not familiar or colloquial tone toward your reader. Suit your tone toward your reader, and choose words that will convey this tone.

    B. Subject considerations: Decide next what attitude you will take toward your subject. Should you be serious or humorous, personally involved or impartial, sentimental or objective? Once you have chosen a tone toward your subject, choose words that will convey this tone.

    C. Word choice:

        1. Be precise in your choice of words. Aim for clarity in considering the connotations of words. Use a thesaurus for ideas, but be careful at the same time not to overwrite by using words you do not fully comprehend. Strive for words that convey your tone consistently and clearly.

        2. Avoid repetitiveness. Vary your vocabulary. Use your thesaurus along with your dictionary to find synonyms for words you use so frequently that they make your style boring.

        3. Avoid wordiness. Be concise. If your essay needs lengthening, add details about your topic, not unnecessary words.

ALEXANDER PETRUNKEVITCH

The Spider and the Wasp

    In the feeding and safeguarding of their progeny insects and spiders exhibit some interesting analogies to reasoning and some crass examples of blind instinct. The case I propose to describe here is that of the tarantula spiders and their archenemy, the digger wasps of the genus *Pepsis*. It is a classic example of what looks like intelligence pitted against instinct — a strange situation in which the victim, though fully able to defend itself, submits unwittingly to its destruction.

Most tarantulas live in the tropics, but several species occur in the temperate zone and a few are common in the southern U.S. Some varieties are large and have powerful fangs with which they can inflict a deep wound. These formidable-looking spiders do not, however, attack man; you can hold one in your hand, if you are gentle, without being bitten. Their bite is dangerous only to insects and small mammals such as mice; for man it is no worse than a hornet's sting.

Tarantulas customarily live in deep cylindrical burrows, from which they emerge at dusk and into which they retire at dawn. Mature males wander about after dark in search of females and occasionally stray into houses. After mating, the male dies in a few weeks, but a female lives much longer and can mate several years in succession. In a Paris museum is a tropical specimen which is said to have been living in captivity for 25 years.

A fertilized female tarantula lays from 20 to 400 eggs at a time; thus it is possible for a single tarantula to produce several thousand young. She takes no care of them beyond weaving a cocoon of silk to enclose the eggs. After they hatch, the young walk away, find convenient places in which to dig their burrows and spend the rest of their lives in solitude. The eyesight of tarantulas is poor, being limited to a sensing of change in the intensity of light and to the perception of moving objects. They apparently have little or no sense of hearing, for a hungry tarantula will pay no attention to a loudly chirping cricket placed in its cage unless the insect happens to touch one of its legs.

But all spiders, and especially hairy ones, have an extremely delicate sense of touch. Laboratory experiments prove that tarantulas can distinguish three types of touch: pressure against the body wall, stroking of the body hair, and riffling of certain very fine hairs on the legs called trichobothria. Pressure against the body, by the finger or the end of a pencil, causes the tarantula to move off slowly for a short distance. The touch excites no defensive reponse unless the approach is from above where the spider can see the motion, in which case it rises on its hind legs, lifts its front legs, opens its fangs and holds this threatening posture as long as the object continues to move.

The entire body of a tarantula, especially its legs, is thickly clothed with hair. Some of it is short and wooly, some long and stiff. Touching this body hair produces one of two distinct reactions. When the spider is hungry, it responds with an immediate and swift attack. At the touch of a cricket's antennae the tarantula seizes the insect so swiftly that a motion picture taken at the rate of 64 frames per second shows only the result and not the process of capture. But when the spider is not hungry, the stimulation of its hairs merely causes it to shake the touched limb. An insect can walk under its hairy belly unharmed.

The trichobothria, very fine hairs growing from disklike membranes on the legs, are sensitive only to air movement. A light breeze makes them vibrate slowly, without disturbing the common hair. When one blows gently on the trichobothria, the tarantula reacts with a quick jerk of its four front legs. If the front and hind legs are stimulated at the same time, the spider makes a sudden jump. This reaction is quite independent of the state of its appetite.

These three tactile responses — to pressure on the body wall, to moving of the common hair, and to flexing of the trichobothria — are so different from one another that there is no possibility of confusing them. They serve the tarantula adequately for most of its needs and enable it to avoid most annoyances and dangers. But they fail the spider completely when it meets its deadly enemy, the digger wasp *Pepsis*.

These solitary wasps are beautiful and formidable creatures. Most species are either a deep shiny blue all over, or deep blue with rusty wings. The largest have a wing span of about four inches. They live on nectar. When excited, they give off a pungent odor — a warning that they are ready to attack. The sting is much worse than that of a bee or common wasp, and the pain and swelling last longer. In the adult stage the wasp lives only a few months. The female produces but a few eggs, one at a time at intervals of two or three days. For each egg the mother must provide one adult tarantula, alive but paralyzed. The mother wasp attaches the egg to the paralyzed spider's abdomen. Upon hatching from the egg, the larva is many hundreds of times smaller than its living but helpless victim. It eats no other food and drinks no water. By the time it has finished its single Gargantuan meal and becomes ready for wasphood, nothing remains of the tarantula but it indigestible chitinous skeleton.

The mother wasp goes tarantula-hunting when the egg in her ovary is almost ready to be laid. Flying low over the ground late on a sunny afternoon, the wasp looks for its victim or for the mouth of a tarantula burrow, a round hole edged by a bit of silk. The sex of the spider makes no difference, but the mother is highly discriminating as to species. Each species of *Pepsis* requires a certain species of tarantula, and the wasp will not attack the wrong species. In a cage with a tarantula which is not its normal prey, the wasp avoids the spider and is usually killed by it in the night.

Yet when a wasp finds the correct species, it is the other way about. To identify the species the wasp apparently must explore the spider with her antennae. The tarantula shows an amazing tolerance to this exploration. The wasp crawls under it and walks over it without evoking any hostile response. The molestation is so great and so persistent that the tarantula often rises on all eight legs, as if it were on stilts. It may stand this way for several minutes. Meanwhile the wasp, having satisfied itself that the victim is of the right species, moves off a few inches to dig the spider's grave. Working vigorously with legs and jaws, it excavates a hole 8 to 10 inches deep with a diameter slightly larger than the spider's girth. Now and again the wasp pops out of the hole to make sure that the spider is still there.

When the grave is finished, the wasp returns to the tarantula to complete her ghastly enterprise. First she feels it all over once more with her antennae. Then her behavior becomes more aggressive. She bends her abdomen, protruding her sting, and searches for the soft membrane at the point where the spider's legs join its body — the only spot where she can penetrate the horny skeleton. From time to time, as the exasperated spider slowly shifts ground, the wasp turns on her back and slides along with the aid of her wings, trying to get under the tarantula for a shot at the vital spot. During all this maneuvering, which can last for several minutes, the tarantula makes no move to save itself. Finally the wasp corners it against some obstruction and grasps one of its legs in her powerful jaws. Now at last the harassed spider tries a desperate but vain defense. The two contestants roll over and over on the ground. It is a terrifying sight and the outcome is always the same. The wasp finally manages to thrust her sting into the soft spot and holds it there for a few seconds while she pumps in the poison. Almost immediately the tarantula falls paralyzed on its back. Its legs stop twitching; its heart stops beating. Yet it is not dead, as is shown by the fact that if taken from the wasp it can be restored to some sensitivity by being kept in a moist chamber for several months.

After paralyzing the tarantula, the wasp cleans herself by dragging her body along the ground and rubbing her feet, sucks the drop of blood oozing from the wound in the spider's abdomen, then grabs a leg of the flabby, helpless animal in her jaws and drags it down to the bottom of the grave. She stays there for many minutes, sometimes for several hours, and what she does all that time in the dark we do not know. Eventually she lays her egg and attaches it to the side of the spider's abdomen with a sticky secretion. Then she emerges, fills the grave with soil carried bit by bit in her jaws, and finally tramples the ground all around to hide any trace of the grave from prowlers. Then she flies away, leaving her descendant safely started in life.

In all this the behavior of the wasp evidently is qualitatively different from that of the spider. The wasp acts like an intelligent animal. This is not to say that instinct plays no part or that she reasons as man does. But her actions are to the point; they are not automatic and can be modified to fit the situation. We do not know for certain how she identifies the tarantula — probably it is by some olfactory or chemotactile sense — but she does it purposefully and does not blindly tackle a wrong species.

On the other hand, the tarantula's behavior shows only confusion. Evidently the wasp's pawing gives it no pleasure, for it tries to move away. That the wasp is not simulating sexual stimulation is certain because male and female tarantulas react in the same way to its advances. That the spider is not anesthetized by some odorless secretion is easily shown by blowing lightly at the tarantula and making it jump suddenly. What, then, makes the tarantula behave as stupidly as it does?

No clear, simple answer is available. Possibly the stimulation by the wasp's antennae is masked by a heavier pressure on the spider's body, so that it reacts as when prodded by a pencil. But the explanation may be much more complex. Initiative in attack is not in the nature of tarantulas; most species fight only when cornered so that escape is impossible. Their inherited patterns of behavior apparently prompt them to avoid problems rather than attack them. For example, spiders always weave their webs in three dimensions, and when a spider finds that there is insufficient space to attach certain threads in the third dimension, it leaves the place and seeks another, instead of finishing the web in a single plane. This urge to escape seems to arise under all circumstances, in all phases of life, and to take the place of reasoning. For a spider to change the pattern of its web is as impossible as for an inexperienced man to build a bridge across a chasm obstructing his way.

In a way the instinctive urge to escape is not only easier but often more efficient than reasoning. The tarantula does exactly what is most efficient in all cases except in an encounter with a ruthless and determined attacker dependent for the existence of her own species on killing as many tarantulas as she can lay eggs. Perhaps in this case the spider follows its usual pattern of trying to escape, instead of seizing and killing the wasp, because it is not aware of its danger. In any case, the survival of the tarantula species as a whole is protected by the fact that the spider is much more fertile than the wasp.

PROBING FOR
MEANING

1. How can the wasp's actions be described as intelligent? How can the tarantula's behavior be seen as instinctual? What possible explanations for the tarantula's confused behavior does Petrunkevitch present? (Remember that the tarantula is "fully able to defend itself.")

2. Petrunkevitch implies a comparison between animal behavior and human behavior. Can you think of any parallels between the digger wasp-tarantula interaction and situations in the human world?

3. How does the story of the spider and the wasp illustrate nature's way of maintaining balance?

PROBING FOR
METHOD

1. Where does the author present the central idea of the essay? How does he organize the essay around this central idea?

2. How successful is this attempt at presenting scientific material to lay readers? How does Petrunkevitch blend technical language and everyday speech? Cite examples of writing from the text that might not be suitable in a scientific journal.

3. Consult your dictionary for the meanings of the following words. Which would you describe as scientific terms?

progeny	evoking
analogy	molestation
formidable	qualitatively
riffling	olfactory
pungent	chemo-tactile
chitinous	ruthless

 SANTHA RAMA RAU

Return to India

During the three months that my husband and I and our small son were in the Soviet Union, we lost count of the number of times Russians asked us, "Don't you think our life here is very good?"

"Yes, very good," we always replied, politely refraining from adding "for the Russians."

Inevitably the point would be pressed a little further. Life in the Soviet Union was not only good, we would be assured, but was getting better every day. Certainly on the evidence of the past few years, this was no more than the truth. Usually after this kind of opening exchange, the Russians we met proved to be intensely inquisitive about life in America, my husband's country, and the questions ranged from the price of nylons to American intentions for nuclear war. Sometimes they even showed a faintly patronizing interest in my country, India.

On one such occasion I had a brief and uninspired conversation with a chance Russian acquaintance that I was to remember much later with quite a different feeling. A young man, noticing across a restaurant dining room that I wore a sari, came over to the table where my husband and I were sitting. "Hindi-Russki bhai-bhai!" he announced proudly — a phrase Russians learned when Prime Minister Nehru visited their country, a phrase they love to use, which means in Hindi, "Indians and Russians are brothers."

"Hindi-Russki bhai-bhai," I replied dutifully, and then, after the usual opening formalities, the young man started to ask me — or rather, to tell me — about life in India.

With my husband interpreting for us, he remarked, "The Indian people are very poor."

"Yes, they are."

"I have seen photographs. They have few clothes and many have no shoes."

"That's true.

"Most of them are uneducated."

"Yes."

"Many beggars on the streets."

"Yes."

"It must be very distressing to live in such a country."

"No — " I began, suddenly feeling very homesick.

But the young man was finished with the subject of India. "In Russia we have a very good life . . ."

After our stay in Russia, I returned with my son to visit my family in India. We flew from Uzbekistan in the far south of Russia, over the magnificent expanse of the Himalayas to New Delhi. The plane arrived after dark and by the time we reached my uncle's house it was quite late at night and we were too tired to do much talking or to pay much attention to our surroundings.

The next morning, with my first glimpse of the newspapers, I was sharply aware not so much that I was in India as that I was out of Russia. One paragraph was enough to convince me. It ran, as I remember, something like this: "Yesterday the Prime Minister opened the debate in parliament on the Second Five-Year Plan with a two-hour speech in his usual diffuse style." I read, and reread, and reread the words "his usual diffuse style," remembering the monotonously reverential tone of all Russian newspapers toward all Russian leaders — the ones in favor, that is.

This was trivial enough as an incident, but in the course of that first day a number of other moments — equally minor, equally transient — began to acquire a collective force. I had offered to help with the household shopping, partly because I always enjoy bazaars and partly because I wanted to show my son a little of the city. We started in the fruit market, which I'm afraid my Russian friends would have found hopelessly disorganized. No orderly queues, no rationing, no fixed prices, no stern-faced women with string shopping bags waiting in line, dutifully reading signs saying, "Drink fruit juices. They are good for you."

To me an Indian bazaar is a source of endless delight and excitement. It is usually a series of plain wooden stalls on which are piled, with unconscious artistry, brightly colored fruits, vegetables, spices, gleaming silver jewelry, brilliant silks and cottons, or charming, grotesque painted wooden toys. The vendors who can't afford a stall sit on the sidewalk outside the market, their baskets stacked behind them, their wives in vivid cotton saris crouching in the shade, and in front of them are spread carpets of scarlet chillies drying in the sun, small hills of saffron, tumeric, coriander, ginger, cinnamon — all the magical names from the old days of the spice trade with the Indies. With a worn stone mortar and pestle the vendor or his wife will grind your spices for you, blending them according to your particular taste, and weigh them in tiny brass scales strung on twine and balanced delicately in one hand. In all transactions you receive a pleasantly individual attention — nothing standardized.

The vegetable and fruit and flower merchants are surrounded by baskets of purple eggplant, green peppers, strings of tiny silvery onions, heads of bitter Indian spinach, and a dozen Indian vegetables for which I don't even know the English names. I had forgotten about the profusion of fruit in India — it is only during the brief, intense summer that you see much variety of fruit in Moscow. In Russia as winter approaches, all vegetables except for potatoes and the pervasive cabbage in soup seem to disappear from the menus.

My son was enjoying himself, pouncing on the stacks of bananas — unobtainable in Russia — regarding with some suspicion the papayas and chikus which he had not remembered from his last stay in India. He prodded a pile of the tiny, sharp Indian limes to see if they would collapse, an action for which he would have been severely reprimanded in Russia. I was reminded of the evening when we had run into an official of the Ministry of Culture in the lobby of the Metropole, our hotel in Moscow. He had come to the hotel to buy a lemon. It seemed like an extraordinary place to come for such an item, but he explained that there were too few lemons in the winter, so that they were saved for the tourists and the foreigners and could only be obtained, if you were lucky, at an Intourist hotel.

Flowers. This was something I missed very much in Russia, where flowers are a real luxury. I can remember standing at a street corner in Russia, astonished by the sight of a flower-woman sitting in the middle of a splash of color in those gray streets. The Russians stopped to look too. Not many of them bought the flowers — too costly — but a surprising number paused in the rush to get home from offices, factories, and shops in the shadowy autumn twilight just to feast for a moment on the rare color of a few stiff bunches of chrysanthemums on a street corner.

All around us, in Delhi, there were flowers. Yes, it is a tropical country, and yes, the climate makes this possible — but there was a personal pride and feminine joy in the countrywomen who tucked a marigold casually into their hair, who wove roses into small hoops to wear more formally around the knot of hair on the back of the head. I realized then that I had missed all this in Russia; the pleasure of women being women, a sense of decoration and unquestioned right of anyone to the small, cheap luxuries and gaieties.

But most impressive — to me, anyway — are the people in an

Indian bazaar. First of all there is the inquisitiveness that often embarrasses foreigners. When you are engaged on an errand as prosaic as buying potatoes, in the course of the transaction your vendor may well ask you any variety of what my American friends would call personal questions. How old are you? How many children do you have? Only one? (A commiserating shake of the head.) Better hurry and have another before you are too old. Where do you live? Is your mother-in-law alive? Inevitably I made the comparison with Russia, where this kind of passing, interested exchange (between Russians) is so suspect. The right to express ordinary human curiosity about a fellow countryman came to seem like an unusual privilege.

Meanwhile, the brisk, canny routine of bargaining would be going on, and the whole performance would be interspersed with jokes and cracks and comments. Next to me a man, bargaining for a basket of tangerines, remarked to the old woman standing behind the stall, "Clearly you believe in the soak-the-rich program." This was the popular description of India's new taxation policy. The woman looked amused and replied dryly, "Give me your income and I will gladly pay your taxes." And the bargaining went on without rancor — it was all very Indian, or rather, un-Russian.

We finished our shopping and summoned a boy to carry our purchases out of the bazaar — another small, cheap luxury.

On our way out of the market, we had to pass the familiar barrage of beggars on the sidewalk and, as usual, gave them the small change left over from shopping. Even my son was struck with the contrast to Moscow. "Why are they asking for money, Mummy?"

"Because they are poor, darling."

"Why are they poor, Mummy?"

"India is a poor country, darling. Too many people and not enough food."

"We could give them some of our fruit."

"Well, that's what we've done in another way. We've given them some money to buy whatever they choose."

Then I was left wondering, as so often in the past, about the ethics of begging and giving. It is easy to win approval from foreigners by deploring two elements of Indian life — the caste structure and begging for a livelihood. The best that can be said about either of them is that it is gradually disappearing. However, it would be less than honest to pretend that social malaise is all that is involved in either system. The goals in the Hindu view of life are not the same as those of Russia or the western world. Indeed, India's highest caste, the Brahmans, are traditionally sworn to poverty. Ambition, getting ahead, comfort, success are obstacles, not aims, in the Hindu concept of a good life. Enlightenment is reached, if it is reached, when you have detached yourself from worldly considerations and emotional drives of any sort, so it is not surprising that many of India's most respected "holy men" are, in fact, beggars, or perhaps live on unsolicited contributions from strangers, disciples, casual visitors.

What in the West is almost always a degrading occupation can, in India, be a high achievement. Not, of course, that all beggars are religious mendicants. Many are simply poor, or sick, or unemployed, or seeking a little extra income. If, to a westerner, they are an embarrassment or raise guilts about his own privileged life, to an Asian they are more likely to engender a down-to-earth recognition of conditions as they are and an urge to contribute in a small way to a social responsibility. This is combined with the knowledge that there is no society, including the Russian, in which privilege is unknown. Money, birth, education, accomplishment, something makes a class (or caste) structure. The Hindu view is not to rise to a higher level of privilege but to rise beyond the concern with privilege and levels altogether. It is hard enough to explain this attitude to a sympathetic, philosophic westerner; it is impossible to describe to the average Russian, to whom spiritual values seem to be mysterious, unacceptable, or discredited.

Could the Indian government, like the Russian or the Chinese, abolish beggars with a sweeping compulsory measure? I suppose it could. Would the cost in undemocratic forcefulness be too high? I think it might. We are committed to raising the standard of living in India, but by different methods, at a different pace — a pace designed to preserve other important aspects of our life. Although a number of these thoughts occurred to me that day at the bazaar, luckily I hadn't the time to try and explain many of them to my son because he was thirsty and was more concerned with demanding a *limonad* of the sort he had liked in Russia. We stopped at a nearby coffee shop.

An Indian coffeehouse, like an Indian bazaar, has its own peculiar atmosphere. It is a cheerful, unpretentious place in which to dawdle, encounter friends, talk, discuss, gossip. Students make fiery speeches to each other; women meet for a break in a morning's shopping; idlers stop by for a rest, to watch the world go by, to pick up a chance colleague. The actual drinking of coffee is the least important part of the whole affair. Looking around at the animated groups of uninhibited talkers at the tables, I couldn't help thinking that this particular sort of place doesn't exist in Moscow. There, one can find restaurants (mostly rather expensive by any standard), or "Parks of Culture and Rest," or hotel dining rooms, and several varieties of bar ranging from the *pivnaya,* where as a rule you can't even sit down, where women are seldom seen, and where the customers walk to the bar, order a drink, down it and leave, all within the space of five minutes, to the *stolovoye,* which is considered more refined, more suitable for women, and where ordinary vodka is not served, though wines and brandy are brought to your table. But India is not a drinking coun-

try — even in the states where there is no prohibition. The sight of
drunks being thrown out of restaurants with the offhand ruthlessness
that the Russians employ for such occasions is extremely rare in India.

Indians meet in public places for sociability, and though poor
housing contributes, as it does in Russia, to the life of cafés and restaurants and street corners, still Indians do not meet for the dedicated
purpose of getting drunk. They are incurable talkers. At the coffeehouse I found myself once again cozy and amused in the endless stream
of comments, criticism, scandal, anecdote, and analysis that accompanies one's day in an Indian society. I like the idea that one can be interested, amused, or disapproving of the activities or remarks of one's
neighbors, friends, and acquaintances, or of political figures, college
professors, taxi drivers, and artists. I like the idea that one's concern,
malicious or pleasant, in one's fellow countrymen cannot lead to their
political harassment.

Listening that morning in the coffeehouse to the flurry of debate that rose from the students' tables about the latest political contro-
versy, interspersed with the social chit-chat of the ladies or the shop
talk of secretaries, office workers, and clerks, I thought of the sad, sly
exchanges we had shared with our Russian acquaintances. I remembered the way conversation with a Russian in a restaurant would stop
cold whenever a waiter came to the table or strangers walked by. At
first I was astonished to find that Russians are much more willing to talk
than I had expected, that people will come up to you in parks, restaurants, on the street, drawn by curiosity to a foreigner, eager to ask and
answer questions. But we soon learned, after hearing some deeply intimate confidences from Russians we scarcely knew, that our relations
with them were very much in the nature of a shipboard romance. It can
be intimate because it is so brief. "I can talk to you frankly," one of our
friends said, not wistfully, merely as a statement of fact, "because you
are in Moscow only a short time. Soon you will go and we will never
meet again."

I remembered a waiter at the Metropole Hotel who had seen us
so often in the dining room that one day he drifted unobtrusively over
to our table to ask us in muttered conversation and scribbled notes
about foreign writers. In return for whatever fragments of information
we could give him, he told us about his favorite poet, Valery Byusov.
We had never heard of him, and then learned that he was banned in the
Soviet Union. "You see," the waiter whispered, "he is a symbolist." In
the rowdy air of the coffeehouse, it seemed incredible that there were
places where poetry, even symbolist poetry, was considered too dangerous for the fragile human intellect.

After those early days in India, both the novelty of being home
and the continual contrasts with Russia began to wear thin. Soon I
slipped back in the slow pace and familiar daily life of India. My son no

longer noticed beggars. I no longer thought of a trip to the bazaar or the coffeehouses as an occasion. I even remembered the cold blue evenings of Moscow with some nostalgia as the Indian climate warmed up to its early spring. But once during that time I had reason to think of my trip to Moscow and of India as a nation with a shock of rediscovery. It was during the Independence Day parade that takes place in New Delhi every January 26.

It is an immense celebration and villagers from all the surrounding areas of the city had been walking into the town or arriving in their bullock carts for days before. As the day grew closer all the open spaces of New Delhi were gradually filled with impromptu camps. Carts were unhitched, oxen grazed in the parks, the evening air was filled with the haze of open-air cooking fires for the scanty dinners of the travelers. On the streets you saw everywhere the brilliantly colored full ankle-length skirts and tight bodices of the village women. Each footstep (yes, barefoot, I would have had to admit to my Russian acquaintance) was emphasized by the metallic clink of silver anklets or toe rings. Every time a small child was hitched into a more comfortable position on his mother's hip, the sound of silver bracelets would accompany the movement. The fathers, proudly carrying sons on a tour of the city's sights or carefully washing their oxen at a public fountain, were less decorative but good-humored and ready for a festival. The streets were full of color and excitement and nobody checked the wanderings of the villagers as they looked around their capital.

In Russia you need a permit to travel even within the country, an identity card and an official permit before you may stay at a hotel. For most non-Muscovites, the only way to get to Moscow is to come, as a reward for outstanding service, on a brief "workers' tour" or as a member of some delegation. Chekhov's yearning phrase "To Moscow, to Moscow . . ." has just as intense a meaning now.

The day of the parade brought thousands of villagers and citizens of Delhi to the parade route, lining the roads in a dense, active crowd of mothers, fathers, children, babies, donkeys, oxen. Many families had their lunches tied up in pieces of cloth. Children clutched balloons or candy sticks. Little stalls selling nuts, tea, sweets, and fruit sprang up everywhere. I was lucky enough to have a seat on one of the bleachers outside the president's house where the procession started, and next to me was an old man in a worn khaki sweater and army trousers. A faded patch on his arm said "Engineers." He was obviously a veteran, obviously now retired, and obviously he had never been higher in rank than the equivalent of a sergeant.

When the procession began with the arrival of the Indian president, the old man stood up to get a better view. All the pomp and ceremony of viceregal days surrounded the appearance of the president — the outriders, the cavalry escort, the great coach drawn by matched horses, guarded by lancers. Out of the coach stepped a small thin man in a brown *achkan* (the Indian jacket), narrow trousers wrinkled at the ankles, a Gandhi cap on his head. He looked embarrassed by the flashy display that surrounded him. Smiling shyly, he brought his hands together in a *namaskar*, the Indian greeting, and hurried to his place on the reviewing platform. This in no way discouraged the old man next to me. He raised his hands in a *namaskar* above the heads of the people around him. With tears streaming down his face, he yelled (apparently convinced that the president could hear him), "Namaste ji! Jai Hind!" and continued with such fervor that the rest of us near him suddenly found ourselves joining in a tribute from an Indian who had spent all his life in the British Army to an Indian who represented, at last, the fact that all this and India itself belonged to all of us.

The parade was splendid as such things go — a vast cavalcade of camels, elephants, ski troops, horsemen, the tough Gurkhas, the bearded colorful Sikhs — all the diversity and pageantry of India. But I am not really very keen on parades. They worry and depress me, and while this fantastic procession was going on, in my mind I had slipped back to the day of the fortieth anniversary of the Russian Revolution in Moscow. Another parade. Of a very different sort. There were no crowds lining the sidewalks — the streets had been cleared for security reasons. There was none of the good-humored pushing and shoving and wriggling of small children to get to the front where they could see best. Color? Pageantry? No, a few people in the factory workers' groups in the procession carried paper flowers, and one realized in a moment how seldom one saw color on the streets in Moscow, how rarely the drab grays and browns of the city were ever lightened by even so much as a pretty shop window. Mostly the Russian parade was grimly military, tanks and guns and huge rockets, and ranks and ranks of marching soldiers.

At the end of our parade the tribesmen from the Naga hills came by to do a dance in the street in front of the president. Predictably (it couldn't happen in Russia), they were late in getting started. Consequently they clashed with the flypast of the new Indian jets. Watching the two performances simultaneously, I could only think I would never have been able to explain to that anonymous Russian acquaintance of mine the appeal of Indian casualness, of the need for color, ease, humor — the joy of an Indian festival.

Poor and undernourished and undereducated, yes. But in India, people turn out every election day in a larger percentage than anywhere else in the world to choose a government. They make a real holiday of it, decorating their oxcarts and dressing in their best clothes to go the polls. Certainly one cannot pretend that there is nothing in India that needs to be changed, but somewhere in all this is a confidence and pleasure in being Indian, and in the country's ways. And, yes, those ways are very different from Russian ways.

Well, it never fails: one always sounds sentimental in trying to say things like this. Perhaps it is just as well that I never got a chance to explain to that remote young man in Moscow how I feel about India.

PROBING FOR
MEANING

1. Santha Rama Rau has limited her discussion of Indian life to three aspects: the bazaar, the coffeehouse, and the parade. How does limiting her topic to these particular features of life in her native land help fulfill her purpose of showing why she prefers India to Russia?

2. At what points does she contrast India with Russia? Does she indicate any similarities? If so, what are they?

3. How does she answer foreigners' charges that Indian society creates beggars and maintains a caste system? Do you think her answer would silence India's accusers? Why or why not?

4. Which of her points of comparison and contrast are political? economic? aesthetic? social? intellectual? Does she indicate which are more important to her? Which do you feel carry more weight?

5. To what extent do her criticisms of Russia apply to America? Which of India's good points do we share? Which do we lack? What advantages and disadvantages do we have which neither India nor Russia shares?

PROBING FOR
METHOD

1. Rau describes three places in India and her experiences at these places. What other methods of development besides contrast and comparison does Rau use in her essay?

2. What effect was achieved by writing this essay in the first person?

3. In one sentence the author writes, "At the coffeehouse I found myself once again cozy and amused in the endless stream of comments, criticism, scandal, anecdote, and analysis that accompanies one's days in any Indian society." Find other sentences in the essay where she has also used alliteration this effectively.

 KATHERINE ANNE PORTER

The Necessary Enemy

She is a frank, charming, fresh-hearted young woman who married for love. She and her husband are one of those gay, good-looking pairs who ornament this modern scene rather more in profusion perhaps than ever before in our history. They are handsome, with a talent for finding their way in their world, they work at things that interest them, their tastes agree and their hopes. They intend in all good faith to spend their lives together, to have children and do well by them and each other — to be happy, in fact, which for them is the whole point of their marriage. And all in stride, keeping their wits about them. Nothing romantic, mind you; their feet are on the ground.

Unless they were this sort of person, there would be not much point to what I wish to say; for they would seem to be an example of the high-spirited, right-minded young whom the critics are always invoking to come forth and do their duty and practice all those sterling old-fashioned virtues which in every generation seem to be falling into disrepair. As for virtues, these young people are more or less on their own, like most of their kind; they get very little moral or other aid from their society; but after three years of marriage this very contemporary young woman finds herself facing the oldest and ugliest dilemma of marriage.

She is dismayed, horrified, full of guilt and forebodings because she is finding out little by little that she is capable of hating her husband, whom she loves faithfully. She can hate him at times as fiercely and mysteriously, indeed in terribly much the same way, as often she hated her parents, her brothers and sisters, whom she loves, when she was a child. Even then it had seemed to her a kind of black treacherousness in her, her private wickedness that, just the same, gave her her only private life. That was one thing her parents never knew about her, never seemed to suspect. For it was never given a name. They did and said hateful things to her and to each other as if by right, as if in them it was a kind of virtue. But when they said to her, "Control your feelings," it was never when she was amiable and obedient, only in the black times of her hate. So it was her secret, a shameful one. When they punished her, sometimes for the strangest of reasons, it was, they said, only because they loved her — it was for her own good. She did not believe this, but she thought herself guilty of something worse than ever they had punished her for. None of this really frightened her: the real fright came when she discovered that at times her father and mother hated each other; this was like standing on the doorsill of a familiar room and seeing in a lightning flash that the floor was gone, you were on the edge of a bottomless pit. Sometimes she felt that both of them hated her, but that passed, it was simply not a thing to be thought of, much less believed. She thought she had outgrown all this, but here it was again, an element in her own nature she could not control, or feared she could not. She would have to hide from her husband, if she could, the same spot in her feelings she had hidden from her parents, and for the same no doubt disreputable, selfish reasons: she wants to keep his love.

Above all, she wants him to be absolutely confident that she loves him, for that is the real truth, no matter how unreasonable it sounds, and no matter how her own feelings betray them both at times. She depends recklessly on his love; yet while she is hating him, he might very well be hating her as much or even more, and it would serve her right. But she does not want to be served right, she wants to be loved and forgiven — that is, to be sure he would forgive her anything, if he had any notion of what she had done. But best of all she would like not to have anything in her love that should ask for forgiveness. She doesn't mean about their quarrels — they are not so bad. Her feelings are out of proportion, perhaps. She knows it is perfectly natural for people to disagree, have fits of temper, fight it out; they learn quite a lot about each other that way, and not all of it disappointing either. When it passes, her hatred seems quite unreal. It always did.

Love. We are early taught to say it. I love you. We are trained to the thought of it as if there were nothing else, or nothing else worth having without it, or nothing worth having which it could not bring with it. Love is taught, always by precept, sometimes by example. Then hate, which no one meant to teach us, comes of itself. It is true that if we say I love you, it may be received with doubt, for there are times when it is hard to believe. Say I hate you, and the one spoken to believes it instantly, once for all.

Say I love you a thousand times to that person afterward and mean it every time, and still it does not change the fact that once we said I hate you, and meant that too. It leaves a mark on that surface love had worn so smooth with its eternal caresses. Love must be learned, and learned again and again; there is no end to it. Hate needs no instruction, but waits only to be provoked . . . hate, the unspoken word, the unacknowledged presence in the house, that faint smell of brimstone among the roses, that invisible tongue-tripper, that unkempt finger in every pie, that sudden oh-so-curiously *chilling* look — could it be boredom? — on your dear one's features, making them quite ugly. Be careful: love, perfect love, is in danger.

If it is not perfect, it is not love, and if it is not love, it is bound to be hate sooner or later. This is perhaps a not too exaggerated statement of the extreme position of Romantic Love, more especially in America, where we are all brought up on it, whether we know it or not. Romantic Love is changeless, faithful, passionate, and its sole end is to render the two lovers happy. It has no obstacles save those provided by the hazards of fate (that is to say, society), and such sufferings as the lovers may cause each other are only another word for delight: exacting jealousies, thrilling uncertainties, the ritual dance of courtship within the charmed close circle of their secret alliance; all *real* troubles come from without, they face them unitedly in perfect confidence. Marriage is not the end but only the beginning of true happiness, cloudless, changeless to the end. That the candidates for this blissful condition have never seen an example of it, nor ever knew anyone who had, makes no difference. That is the ideal and they will achieve it.

How did Romantic Love manage to get into marriage at last, where it was most certainly never intended to be? At its highest it was tragic: the love of Héloïse and Abélard.* At its most graceful, it was the homage of the trouvère† for his lady. In its most popular form, the adulterous strayings of solidly married couples who meant to stray for their own good reasons, but at the same time do nothing to upset the property settlements or the line of legitimacy; at its most trivial, the pretty trifling of shepherd and shepherdess.

This was generally condemned by church and state and a word of fear to honest wives whose mortal enemy it was. Love within the sober, sacred realities of marriage was a matter of personal luck, but in any case, private feelings were strictly a private affair having, at least in theory, no bearing whatever on the fixed practice of the rules of an institution never intended as a recreation ground for either sex. If the couple discharged their religious and social obligations, furnished forth a copious progeny, kept their troubles to themselves, maintained public civility and died under the same roof, even if not always on speaking terms, it was rightly regarded as a successful marriage. Apparently this testing ground was too severe for all but the stoutest spirits; it too was based on an ideal, as impossible in its way as the ideal Romantic Love. One good thing to be said for it is that society took responsibility for the conditions of marriage, and the sufferers within its bonds could always blame the system, not themselves. But Romantic Love crept into the marriage bed, very stealthily, by centuries, bringing its absurd notions about love as eternal springtime and marriage as a personal adventure meant to provide personal happiness. To a Western romantic such as I, though my views have been much modified by painful experience, it still seems to be a charming work of the human imagination, and it is a pity its central notion has been taken too literally and has hardened into a convention as cramping and enslaving as the older one. The refusal to acknowledge the evils in ourselves which therefore are implicit in any human situation is as extreme and unworkable a proposition as the doctrine of total depravity; but somewhere between them, or maybe beyond them, there does exist a possibility for reconciliation between our desires for impossible satisfactions and the simple unalterable fact that we also desire to be unhappy and that we create our own sufferings; and out of these sufferings we salvage our fragments of happiness.

* Pierre Abélard (1079–1142). Unorthodox French philosopher and theologian who seduced his student Héloïse whom he later secretly married. When the marriage was discovered by Héloïse's uncle, a conservative canon of Notre Dame Cathedral, he had Abélard emasculated. Héloïse became a nun and Abélard a monk.

† Trouvères — medieval poets of nothern France.

Our young woman who has been taught that an important part of her human nature is not real because it makes trouble and interferes with her peace of mind and shakes her self-love, has been very badly taught, but she has arrived at a most important stage of her re-education. She is afraid her marriage is going to fail because she has not love enough to face its difficulties; and this because at times she feels a painful hostility toward her husband, and cannot admit its reality because such an admission would damage in her own eyes her view of what love should be, an absurd view, based on her vanity of power. Her hatred is real as her love is real, but her hatred has the advantage at present because it works on a blind instinctual level, it is lawless; and her love is subjected to a code of ideal conditions, impossible by their very nature of fulfillment, which prevents its free growth and deprives it of its right to recognize its human limitations and come to grips with them. Hatred is natural in a sense that love, as she conceives it, a young person brought up in the tradition of Romantic Love, is not natural at all. Yet it did not come by hazard, it is the very imperfect expression of the need of the human imagination to create beauty and harmony out of chaos, no matter how mistaken its notion of these things may be, nor how clumsy its methods. It has conjured love out of the air, and seeks to preserve it by incantations; when she spoke a vow to love and honor her husband until death, she did a very reckless thing, for it is not possible by an act of the will to fulfill such an engagement. But it was the necessary act of faith performed in defense of a mode of feeling, the statement of honorable intention to practice as well as she is able the noble, acquired faculty of love, that very mysterious overtone to sex which is the best thing in it. Her hatred is part of it, the necessary enemy and ally.

PROBING FOR
MEANING

1. What sort of person is the woman described by Porter? What sort of dilemma does she face? What are the causes of her dilemma?

2. Why is it that hate needs no instruction? How is hate thus different from love, according to Porter?

3. What is romantic love? Why does Porter feel that it is too much an ideal to be taken seriously as the basis for a successful marriage? What, historically, has been taken as the basis for a successful marriage? Is it a more workable basis than romantic love?

4. Why is hate a "necessary" enemy of love? In what ways is it an ally?

PROBING FOR
METHOD

1. Porter suggests a definition of "hate" by explaining the ways in which it differs from love. What are the advantages of this strategy? What are the disadvantages?

2. What effect does Porter achieve by starting the essay with an illustrative example? Where does she actually introduce her thesis?

3. How important is it to know who Héloïse and Abélard were, or

what a trouvère was, in order to understand Porter's essay? What sort of audience does Porter seem most interested in addressing?

4. Define the following words as they are used in the context of the essay:

profusion   progeny
precept   incantations
copious

 WILLA CATHER

A Wagner Matinée

I received one morning a letter, written in pale ink on glassy, blue-lined note-paper, and bearing the postmark of a little Nebraska village. This communication, worn and rubbed, looking as if it had been carried for some days in a coat pocket that was none too clean, was from my uncle Howard, and informed me that his wife had been left a small legacy by a bachelor relative, and that it would be necessary for her to go to Boston to attend to the settling of the estate. He requested me to meet her at the station and render her whatever services might be necessary. On examining the date indicated as that of her arrival, I found it to be no later than tomorrow. He had characteristically delayed writing until, had I been away from home for a day, I must have missed my aunt altogether.

The name of my Aunt Georgiana opened before me a gulf of recollection so wide and deep that, as the letter dropped from my hand, I felt suddenly a stranger to all the present conditions of my existence, wholly ill at ease and out of place amid the familiar surroundings of my study. I became, in short, the gangling farmer-boy my aunt had known, scourged with chilblains and bashfulness, my hands cracked and sore from the corn husking. I sat again before her parlour organ, fumbling the scales with my stiff, red fingers, while she, beside me, made canvas mittens for the huskers.

The next morning, after preparing my landlady for a visitor, I set out for the station. When the train arrived I had some difficulty finding my aunt. She was the last of the passengers to alight, and it was not until I got her into the carriage that she seemed really to recognize me. She had come all the way in a day coach; her linen duster had become black with soot and her black bonnet grey with dust during her journey. When we arrived at my boarding-house the landlady put her to bed at once and I did not see her again until the next morning.

Whatever shock Mrs. Springer experienced at my aunt's appearance, she considerately concealed. As for myself, I saw my aunt's battered figure with that feeling of awe and respect with which we behold explorers who have left their ears and fingers north of Franz-Joseph-Land, or their health somewhere along the Upper Congo. My Aunt Georgiana had been a music teacher at the Boston Conservatory, somewhere back in the latter sixties. One summer, while visiting in the little village among the Green Mountains where her ancestors had dwelt for generations, she had kindled the callow fancy of my uncle, Howard Carpenter, then an idle, shiftless boy of twenty-one. When she returned to her duties in Boston, Howard followed her, and the upshot of this infatuation was that she eloped with him, eluding the reproaches of her family and the criticism of her friends by going with him to the Nebraska frontier. Carpenter, who, of course, had no money, took up a homestead in Red Willow County, fifty miles from the railroad. There they had measured off their land themselves, driving across the prairie in a wagon, to the wheel of which they had tied a red cotton handkerchief, and counting its revolutions. They built a dug-out in the red hillside, one of those cave dwellings whose inmates so often reverted to primitive conditions. Their water they got from the lagoons where the buffalo drank, and their slender stock of provisions was always at the mercy of bands of roving Indians. For thirty years my aunt had not been farther than fifty miles from the homestead.

I owed to this woman most of the good that ever came my way in my boyhood, and had a reverential affection for her. During the years when I was riding herd for my uncle, my aunt, after cooking the three meals — the first of which was ready at six o'clock in the morning — and putting the six children to bed, would often stand until midnight at her ironing-board, with me at the kitchen table beside her, hearing me recite Latin declensions and conjugations, gently shaking me when my drowsy head sank down over a page of irregular verbs. It was to her, at her ironing or mending, that I read my first Shakespeare, and her old textbook on mythology was the first that ever came into my empty hands. She taught me my scales and exercises on the little parlour organ which her husband had bought her after fifteen years during which she had not so much as seen a musical instrument. She would sit beside me by the hour, darning and counting, while I struggled with the "Joyous Farmer." She seldom talked to me about music, and I understood why. Once when I had been doggedly beating out some easy passages from an old score of *Euryanthe* I had found among her music books, she came up to me and, putting her hands over my eyes, gently drew my head back upon her shoulder, saying tremulously, "Don't love it so well, Clark, or it may be taken from you."

When my aunt appeared on the morning after her arrival in Boston, she was still in a semi-somnambulant state. She seemed not to realize that she was in the city where she had spent her youth, the place longed for hungrily half a lifetime. She had been so wretchedly train-sick throughout the journey that she had no recollection of anything but her discomfort, and, to all intents and purposes, there were but a few hours of nightmare between the farm in Red Willow County and my study on Newbury Street. I had planned a little pleasure for her that afternoon, to repay her for some of the glorious moments she had given me when we used to milk together in the straw-thatched cowshed and she, because I was more than usually tired, or because her husband had spoken sharply to me, would tell me of the splendid performance of the *Huguenots* she had seen in Paris, in her youth.

At two o'clock the Symphony Orchestra was to give a Wagner program, and I intended to take my aunt; though, as I conversed with her, I grew doubtful about her enjoyment of it. I suggested our visiting the Conservatory and the Common before lunch, but she seemed altogether too timid to wish to venture out. She questioned me absently about various changes in the city, but she was chiefly concerned that she had forgotten to leave instructions about feeding half-skimmed milk to a certain weakling calf, "old Maggie's calf, you know, Clark," she explained, evidently having forgotten how long I had been away. She was further troubled because she had neglected to tell her daughter about the freshly-opened kit of mackerel in the cellar, which would spoil if it were not used directly.

I asked her whether she had ever heard of the Wagnerian operas, and found that she had not, though she was perfectly familiar with their respective situations, and had once possessed the piano score of *The Flying Dutchman.* I began to think it would be best to get her back to Red Willow County without waking her, and regretted having suggested the concert.

From the time we entered the concert hall, however, she was a trifle less passive and inert, and for the first time seemed to perceive her surroundings. I had felt some trepidation lest she might become aware of her queer, country clothes, or might experience some painful embarrassment at stepping suddenly into the world to which she had been dead for a quarter of a century. But, again, I found how superficially I had judged her. She sat looking about her with eyes as impersonal, almost as stony, as those with which the granite Rameses in a museum watches the froth and fret that ebbs and flows about his pedestal. I have seen this same aloofness in old miners who drift into the Brown hotel at

Denver, their pockets full of bullion, their linen soiled, their haggard faces unshaven; standing in the thronged corridors as solitary as though they were still in a frozen camp on the Yukon.

The matinée audience was made up chiefly of women. One lost the contour of faces and figures, indeed any effect of line whatever, and there was only the colour of bodices past counting, the shimmer of fabrics soft and firm, silky and sheer; red, mauve, pink, blue, lilac, purple, écru, rose, yellow, cream, and white, all the colours that an impressionist finds in a sunlit landscape, with here and there the dead shadow of a frock coat. My Aunt Georgiana regarded them as though they had been so many daubs of tube-paint on a palette.

When the musicians came out and took their places, she gave a little stir of anticipation, and looked with quickening interest down over the rail at that invariable grouping, perhaps the first wholly familiar thing that had greeted her eye since she had left old Maggie and her weakling calf. I could feel how all those details sank into her soul, for I had not forgotten how they had sunk into mine when I came fresh from ploughing forever and forever between green aisles of corn, where, as in a treadmill, one might walk from daybreak to dusk without perceiving a shadow of change. The clean profiles of the musicians, the gloss of their linen, the dull black of their coats, the beloved shapes of the instruments, the patches of yellow light on the smooth, varnished bellies of the 'cellos and the bass viols in the rear, the restless, wind-tossed forest of fiddle necks and bows — I recalled how, in the first orchestra I ever heard, those long bow-strokes seemed to draw the heart out of me, as a conjurer's stick reels out yards of paper ribbon from a hat.

The first number was the *Tannhäuser* overture. When the horns drew out the first strain of the Pilgrim's chorus, Aunt Georgiana clutched my coat sleeve. Then it was I first realized that for her this broke a silence of thirty years. With the battle between the two motives, with the frenzy of the Venusberg theme and its ripping of strings, there came to me an overwhelming sense of the waste and wear we are so powerless to combat; and I saw again the tall, naked house on the prairie, black and grim as a wooden fortress; the black pond where I had learned to swim, its margin pitted with sun-dried cattle tracks; the rain-gullied clay banks about the naked house, the four dwarf-ash seedlings where the dish-cloths were always hung to dry before the kitchen door. The world there was the flat world of the ancients; to the east, a cornfield that stretched to daybreak; to the west, a corral that reached to sunset; between, the conquests of peace, dearer-bought than those of war.

The overture closed, my aunt released my coat sleeve, but she said nothing. She sat staring dully at the orchestra. What, I wondered, did she get from it? She had been a good pianist in her day, I knew, and her musical education had been broader than that of most music teachers of a quarter of a century ago. She had often told me of Mozart's operas and Meyerbeer's, and I could remember hearing her sing, years ago, certain melodies of Verdi. When I had fallen ill with a fever in her house she used to sit by my cot in the evening — when the cool, night wind blew in through the faded mosquito netting tacked over the window and I lay watching a certain bright star that burned red above the cornfield — and sing "Home to our mountains, O, let us return!" in a way fit to break the heart of a Vermont boy near dead of homesickness already.

I watched her closely through the prelude to *Tristan and Isolde*, trying vainly to conjecture what that seething turmoil of strings and winds might mean to her, but she sat mutely staring at the violin bows that drove obliquely downward, like the pelting streaks of rain in a summer shower. Had this music any message for her? Had she enough left to at all comprehend this power which had kindled the world since she had left it? I was in a fever of curiosity, but Aunt Georgiana sat silent upon her peak in Darien. She preserved this utter immobility throughout the number from *The Flying Dutchman*, though her fingers worked mechanically upon her black dress, as if, of themselves, they were recalling the piano score they had once played. Poor hands! They had been stretched and twisted into mere tentacles to hold and lift and knead with: — on one of them a thin, worn band that had once been a wedding ring. As I pressed and gently quieted one of those groping hands, I remembered with quivering eyelids their services for me in other days.

Soon after the tenor began the "Prize Song," I heard a quick drawn breath and turned to my aunt. Her eyes were closed, but the tears were glistening on her cheeks, and I think, in a moment more, they were in my eyes as well. It never really died, then — the soul which can suffer so excruciatingly and so interminably; it withers to the outward eye only; like that strange moss which can lie on a dusty shelf half a century and yet, if placed in water, grows green again. She wept so throughout the development and elaboration of the melody.

During the intermission before the second half, I questioned my aunt and found that the "Prize Song" was not new to her. Some years before there had drifted to the farm in Red Willow County a young German, a tramp cow-puncher, who had sung in the chorus at Bayreuth when he was a boy, along with the other peasant boys and girls. Of a Sunday morning he used to sit on his gingham-sheeted bed in the hands' bedroom which opened off the kitchen, cleaning the leather of his boots and saddle, singing the "Prize Song," while my aunt went about her work in the kitchen. She had hovered over him until she had prevailed upon him to join the country church, though his sole fitness for this step, in so far as I could gather, lay in his boyish face and his possession of this divine melody. Shortly afterward, he had gone to town on the Fourth of July, been drunk for several days, lost his money at a faro table, ridden a saddled Texas steer on a bet, and disappeared with a fractured collar-bone. All this my aunt told me huskily, wanderingly, as though she were talking in the weak lapses of illness.

"Well, we have come to better things than the old *Trovatore* at any rate, Aunt Georgie?" I queried, with a well-meant effort at jocularity.

Her lip quivered and she hastily put her handkerchief up to her mouth. From behind it she murmured, "And you have been hearing this ever since you left me, Clark?" Her question was the gentlest and saddest of reproaches.

The second half of the program consisted of four numbers from the *Ring*, and closed with Siegfried's funeral march. My aunt wept quietly, but almost continuously, as a shallow vessel overflows in a rain-storm. From time to time her dim eyes looked up at the lights, burning softly under their dull glass globes.

The deluge of sound poured on and on; I never knew what she found in the shining current of it; I never knew how far it bore her, or past what happy islands. From the trembling of her face I could well believe that before the last number she had been carried out where the myriad graves are, into the grey, nameless burying grounds of the sea; or into some world of death vaster yet, where, from the beginning of the world, hope has lain down with hope and dream with dream and, renouncing, slept.

The concert was over; the people filed out of the hall chattering and laughing, glad to relax and find the living level again, but my kinswoman made no effort to rise. The harpist slipped the green felt cover over his instrument; the flute-players shook the water from their mouthpieces; the men of the orchestra went out one by one, leaving the stage to the chairs and music stands, empty as a winter cornfield.

I spoke to my aunt. She burst into tears and sobbed pleadingly. "I don't want to go, Clark, I don't want to go!"

I understood. For her, just outside the concert hall, lay the black pond with the cattle-tracked bluffs; the tall, unpainted house, with weather-curled boards, naked as a tower; the crook-backed ash seedlings where the dishcloths hung to dry; the gaunt, moulting turkeys picking up refuse about the kitchen door.

PROBING FOR
MEANING

1. How did the narrator feel when he received the letter from his uncle? How did he feel upon seeing his aunt again?

2. What was Aunt Georgiana's life like in Nebraska? What was she like when the narrator was a boy? How had she changed?

3. Why did the narrator feel that he had judged his aunt "superficially" before they got to the concert hall?

4. What did Aunt Georgiana's reaction to the first number cause the

narrator to think about? How did her crying over the "Prize Song" change the narrator's thoughts? What did hearing the "Prize Song" remind her of?

5. According to the narrator, why didn't his aunt want to leave the concert hall?

PROBING FOR   1. How much does the narrator really know about his aunt's life? How
METHOD   objective a view does he have, for example, of her choice to marry and leave Boston? How would you characterize his tone, and hence his attitude, overall?

2. A central contrast in the story is that between the frontier life in Nebraska and the cultured life of Boston. What other contrasts are built into the story? Which is most important to an understanding of the tale's thematic focus?

3. Early in the story, the narrator compares his reaction to his aunt's appearance to "that feeling of awe and respect with which we behold explorers who have left their ears and fingers north of Franz-Joseph-Land." What do his other comparisons help us understand about him? What do they help us understand about his aunt?

WILLIAM MELVIN KELLEY

Saint Paul and the Monkeys

Standing just inside the metal door of her hospital room, Chig Dunford tried to decide if she was too sick to be kissed. "How are you, Avis?"

She opened her arms to him. "Come and kiss me."

He did, then inspected her again. She had the smooth face of a Polynesian. Her complexion, the rich brown of tarnished copper, seemed the slightest bit gray. Her large brown eyes looked tired. Her mouth was soft, a baby's. In her rust-colored hair were two small blue ribbons. Under her light blue pajamas, she wore no bra, and her small breasts were flat. "How are you?" He held her hand.

"I'm supposed to be pretty sick. The doctor at school said my blood was going crazy. He thought it was Mono, but he wanted me in the hospital to make sure." She had phoned him the night before to tell him she was in town and had been in the hospital since that morning.

He started to sit down, but instead kissed her again, lightly. She grabbed him around the neck and kissed him hard. He sat down, holding her hand. "Why didn't your parents want me to come last night?"

She turned away and did not answer. He thought he saw her shake with fighting tears, and reached to pat her back.

"Come on, now. You can tell me."

Suddenly, she was staring at him. "They don't want me to see you any more, Chig." As soon as she spoke, the threat of tears disappeared.

"They can't *do* that." He realized they could, felt desperate; and echoed himself softly. "They *can't* do that." Sensing what the answer would be, he asked: "What did you say?"

She turned away again. "I tried to, Chig. Honestly, I really wanted to — "

"But you didn't say anything." He sighed.

"I couldn't, Chig."

"But you could let them make us stop seeing each other?"

Her answer was flat and definite. "Yes." He knew what was coming next and hardened himself against it. "I'd do it just not to hurt them. You know how much I owe them. They've done an awful lot for me, put me through school and all."

"But they're your parents. They're supposed to do that kind of stuff."

"You always say that, Chig."

"Okay, if they're not supposed to, then they *wanted* to. They were happy doing it. Avis, you can only owe them so much."

"I owe them for everything." She was very calm now.

He did not want to argue about her parents, and changed the subject. "What's so bad about me anyway? Why don't they want me around any more?"

"They like you very much, Chig. It isn't that. But they don't think you're serious about me."

"Is going steady with you for three years not serious?"

"But you haven't spoken to them yet." It seemed almost as if she too doubted him. "You haven't asked my father for my hand or even mentioned it."

"What did you say to that?"

"I told them we were planning to get married some day. But . . ."

"Well?"

"But they said speaking to *me* wasn't enough. They said boys were apt to say anything to be intimate with a girl." When she spoke of her parents, she used their expressions. "Then they asked me if we had been intimate."

"What did you tell them?"

"You don't actually think I told them the truth, *do* you?"

"No, I guess not. But God, they should have enough sense to take it for granted. You're not a little girl any more, Avis."

She said nothing and he searched her face for a long moment. She had become timid and insecure. "Chig, will you . . . will you talk to Daddy about us getting married?"

He stared off into a dustless corner. "Avis, you know I want to marry you, but after I graduate in June, I still have three years of law school. I can't possibly support you. And you have to finish college too."

"But they don't even want us to set a date. They just want you to say something to them. You can do that."

"Sure I can. But I don't see why I should have to. I know they'll say Okay. Even if they didn't, wouldn't you marry me?"

"Of course I would." She believed it, but, for an instant, he did not. She leaned toward him. "But since they'll say Yes, it doesn't matter if you ask them or not. Aren't you sure of us?" Her face was troubled.

"Of course I am!" He decided quickly. "Okay, I'll ask him." It sounded right, but still he felt uncomfortable. He gripped her hand. "You know I want to marry you, don't you?"

Her eyes were a trifle pink. "I know that, Chig." She smiled.

"I'm only thinking of you. I want you to have everything."

"I will. I'll be marrying you."

He felt like sighing, but held it back. "When does he want me to speak to him?"

"Any time you feel like it. They really like you very much." She was trying to encourage him.

He had always hoped that their engagement would come about in a more romantic way. But her parents had robbed him of the perfect night and setting. He tried now to salvage a particle of his romantic dream. "You got an extra hairpin? The wire kind."

"Sure." She leaned over to the other side of the bed, opened a drawer, and handed it to him.

"Let me have your . . . right hand." She extended it to him, and he bent the hair pin around the knuckle of her ring finger.

"What are you doing?"

He searched her soft face to see if she was pretending ignorance, but could not tell. He put the hairpin into his pocket. "It's a surprise."

Before knocking, he inspected himself. This was a special day and he wanted his clothes in perfect order. He was not surprised to find his efforts had come to nothing. He still looked as if he had dressed in the panic of fleeing a burning house. As usual, his shirt was creeping out of his pants, his knees were bagging, his socks were sliding into his shoes. He sighed and knocked at the door.

Avis, propped on two pillows, was reading. In her hair, yellow ribbons had replaced yesterday's blue bows. She gave him her nicest smile. He asked her how she felt.

"Better. But I want to get out of here." She spoke as if he could do something about it.

He removed his overcoat, sneaking the ring box to his jacket pocket, and pulled up a chair.

"What kind of day did you have?"

"All right." He belittled the thrill of what he had done, and was about to do, trying to detect if she had any idea why he had wanted the hair pin. "Avis," he started, but bogged down in muddy nervousness.

She studied him. "Yes."

He tried again. "Avis, I always had a dream of how . . . I always thought I'd do this after something good happened to me that would sort of guarantee our security . . . and that it would be a surprise to you." He searched her face again. She knew now. "But none of that happened. So, anyway, it doesn't matter. Will you marry me?"

"Yes, Chig. I love you, Chig."

He reached into his pocket, produced the ring box, and handed it to her. She opened it, leaned toward him, and kissed him sweetly. Her tears were oily on his cheek. "It's beautiful, Chig. It didn't cost too much, did it?" She looked at it once more, then handed back the box.

A feeling like eating lemons spread through him. "What's wrong, Avis?" His voice cracked.

She did not notice. "*You* have to put it on me."

He did it; it was small and cold, and fit perfectly.

"*I'll never* take it off. Only you can take it off."

"Then you're stuck with it." Smiling, he sat back in his chair, tired. It was finished, settled; he was engaged. He began to think of the wonderful life that one day they would have with each other.

She interrupted his dreams. "I spoke to my parents, last night, Chig." The happiness in her eyes had fled while he was dreaming.

He leaned forward. "What did they say?"

She hesitated. "They want us to set a definite date. They want us to get married in August. They — "

"In August! What do they think I am?" He was standing, glaring down at her. "Didn't you tell them what I said?"

"Chig, don't shout."

He fell into his chair, and attempted to rein in his feelings by whispering. "Avis, how can I marry you in August? What'll we live on?"

She brightened. "That's no problem. Your parents are going to see you through law school, aren't they? And mine'll see me through college. I'll transfer to wherever you are."

He could not arrange all his different emotions, but one picture kept exploding in his mind — of a baby monkey he had seen once on television that shivered and whimpered in the corner of a wire cage, as lights flashed and the arms of a weird contrivance clawed and battered the air. The monkey had been part of a psychological experiment. Stress had destroyed its mind.

Avis was quite calm.

"Don't you see why it would be bad for us to get married so soon, Avis?"

"I know, Chig. But we don't have to worry about money. And I didn't think you minded *that* much." She looked down at the ring sparkling on her finger, and sighed. "Three years is a long time to wait, Chig."

"I know." He stared at the springs of the high bed. "But . . . I'm . . . You really want to get married in August, don't you?"

She answered with thoughts they had often expressed. "You always have to go home, go away from me, go back some place. It'd be nice to lock our door and say good-night to the world together."

He nodded. "Have you got enough time to transfer? How do you know you'll get into a school near me?"

"I'll just apply to all the places you do. I'll get in." Her face was beaming. "It can be so *nice*, Chig."

"Yes it can." He had forgotten about his cornered, frightened monkey, and begun to think now of a small attic apartment in a university town. He slapped the heel of his hand against his forehead. "God, how can I be so stupid! I worry about all the bad things when everything'll be so good."

"You just want it to be perfect, Chig. That's not bad." She smiled at him. "You're just a worrier."

"I'm stupid too." He shook his head and began to laugh, sensing, for an instant, that his laughter was not completely free or happy.

Avis did not laugh. "When are you going to ask my father?" Her voice was completely emotionless.

He was confused. "You just told me *he* wants us to get married."

"But he still expects you to ask him." She was annoyed with him. "He said he won't know you're sincere until you look him in the eye and ask him."

"Would I go out and buy a God-damned engagement ring if I wasn't sincere?" Again, he saw his monkey, shivering.

"It's the custom to ask him."

"Custom? Oh boy!" He rolled his eyes at the ceiling.

"Don't be disrespectful of my father!" She was too serious, and beginning to get red.

He did not want her angry at him. "I'll go see him right now. Is he in his office?"

She glared at him. "Yes, he is and you don't have to be sarcastic."

"I'm not being sarcastic," he whined.

"Look, do you really want to marry me?"

"Come on, don't be silly. I only want to get this junk out of the way."

"It is not junk. Why do you always have to be so disagreeable!"

"All right, Avis. I'm sorry." He sighed. "It's not junk. I'll go see him tonight — now."

"Don't go if you don't want to." She picked up the book she had been reading when first he came.

"I want to go." Suddenly he was so tired he could not hold up his head. The bones and muscles in his neck no longer existed.

"I'm sorry, Chig. I guess it's been a hard day for you." The tone of her voice made him feel better.

"It's just me. Look, I *will* go see him. Okay?"

She smiled. "Yes."

He put on his coat and came back to the edge of the bed. "I hope I didn't upset you. For a minute I forgot you were sick. I mean, that's taking advantage of you."

"Oh, Chig, I feel fine." She looked at her left hand, holding it before her proudly. "I'm engaged! It's a beautiful ring!"

He kissed her good-by. Closing the door, he turned back and found her gazing at the ring so intently she did not hear him whisper that he loved her.

The memory of the enchanted look on her face helped him survive his thirty-minute interview with her father, who finally consented to their August marriage.

At dinner, he told his parents and his sister he was engaged, and would be married in August if his parents would help financially as Avis's parents were planning to do. His father shook his hand. His mother kissed him. They said that of course they would help.

His sister, Connie, who was sixteen, sat across from him, silent for a while. "Are you really marrying Avis, Chig?"

At times, Connie asked ridiculous questions. "Sure." He nodded, puzzled.

Connie stared at him, unblinking. "Oh." She was disappointed.

Avis was dismissed from the hospital a week later. The doctors wanted her to stay at home and rest, rather than return to school. She and Chig planned an engagement party for the Friday before Christmas. He wanted to keep the party small and quiet, and to invite only their closest friends. Avis wanted it large and noisy. They compromised. He invited his two best friends; Avis invited sixty people and told them to bring their friends. This upset him. But finally he decided the act of getting married was, after all, by and for women. It would not hurt to let her have a gathering she would always remember.

The party, held at her house in Westchester, was to begin at eight, but Chig arrived in the early afternoon to help decorate. He began to drink immediately, but did not feel anything until well past nine. He discovered he was drunk when he mixed himself, instead of bourbon and soda, bourbon and scotch. He drank it anyway. He knew most of the people by sight, if not by name, but still felt lost, out of place, and began to lurk in the least crowded corners of the house.

Connie, feeling overmatched because of her age, found him on the enclosed porch, where, at the end of the day, there was a fine view of the sun being devoured by the rock cliffs on the western side of the Hudson. She sat beside him.

Chig squinted at her. "Having a good time?" He could not quite make out her face.

"All right." She smiled. "You look like you are. What gallon you drinking now?" She did not let him answer. "You shouldn't drink so much, Chig. You have to drive us home."

He raised his hand, pledging. "Promise to stop after this one. I know my limit." He took a swallow, and inspected his glass. "Good-by, last drink. You have served me well."

"What's wrong, Chig?" She had not dropped all her baby fat and her chubby face was more comic than earnest.

"What do you mean? God, was I like this when I was sixteen?" He was talking to his glass.

"Well, if you're so fine, what are you doing sitting out here when everybody else is having such a good time?"

"I'm having a good time."

"About as good a time as a rat in a cage."

He thought about that. Several times, sitting alone on the porch, he had thought about his monkey, wondering too why the stupid little creature clung to his thoughts. "Not a rat, sister dear, a monkey."

"What?"

"A baby monkey. Were you around that Sunday they had the monkey show?"

"What?"

"The Wisconsin monkey show." Her face was blank. He went on. "In Wisconsin . . . the University . . . they got these monkeys . . . in cages . . . away from their mothers. There was this one baby monkey in particular, sleeping on a blanket. Every day they took the blanket out to clean it and when they did the baby monkey would crawl into a corner and whimper and cry and shake." Connie did not understand. "Don't you see? The blanket was his mother!" The porch was lighted only by yellow party lamps from inside the house. Chig stared at his drink. "If the monkey has anything to do with people, they really showed what loneliness can do to you. People'll do anything not to be lonely, you know? I almost cried when they showed that monkey without his blanket." He shook his head.

Connie was staring at him. "Chig, you really love Avis?"

He shot her a glance. "Of course, I love her. Why do you ask such stupid questions?"

"You sure you love her?" She shifted toward him. Her voice seemed closer now. "No fooling?"

"What's wrong with you anyway?"

"How can you love her?"

"What do you mean?"

"She's all the things you don't like in anybody else. I've heard you make speeches about it." She stopped. "She's a phony, Chig."

He could not take her seriously. She was probably jealous of Avis. He and Connie had been very close up until three years before, when he started to go steady with Avis. "Why do you say that?" He heard himself being indulgent.

"It's clear as anything." She did not sound at all jealous. "Aren't you supposed to have a good time at your own engagement party?"

"I guess so."

She had a puzzled expression on her face. "You don't seem happy."

"I don't feel so hot."

She was silent for a while. "Chig, you better watch out. She'll eat you alive."

He was angry now and snapped at her. "What do you know about it?"

"I know you've changed a lot. You can't even blow your nose without wondering if you're doing it the right way. And you're getting to be a liar."

"What are you talking about?"

"You know you feel fine, but all this is making you feel bad. You can't even be honest with me any more."

Chig got up. "I want to see Avis." He left Connie sitting on the porch.

He went downstairs into the cellar playroom, carrying his glass and sloshing liquor on his shoes. He laughed to himself about it, then out loud, and several people turned around to greet him. "Where's Avis?"

Someone pointed to where people danced under soft lights to loud music.

Avis, in a billowing orange dress with long sleeves, spun around the floor. Chig could not identify her partner. An undirected jealousy hummed through him. Chig did not dance very well. At most parties they attended, he watched her stepping with someone else. Avis loved to dance and did so expertly.

He did not want to see her now, and returned to the porch. Connie had disappeared. He thought how nice it would be if Avis broke away from the people downstairs and came to sit quietly with him.

He did not know how long he brooded on the porch, but all at once people were thundering up from downstairs and filing into the dining room, talking and laughing.

Then Avis was standing by him, her hand on his shoulder. "Where have you been?"

"Right here." With her hair up, she was beautiful in the faint light. "You been looking for me?" He desperately hoped she had.

"Not until now. Come on." She grabbed his hand, attempting to pull him to his feet.

"Where?" He did not feel like moving.

"Daddy's going to announce our engagement." She tried again to rouse him. "You'll have to make a speech."

"Okay." He sighed and struggled to his feet. "Okay."

She led him to the dining room. The guests stood around a huge table upon which was a large square cake, small forks, pink napkins, and a stack of shining plates. Her father waited at the far end, his hands knit in front of him like a minister's. He was tall and lean, wore perfectly round spectacles, and a black suit. His hair was long, and brushed straight back in the style of a British diplomat.

Avis led Chig around the table, several people propelling him along with heavy smacks on the back. Her father took a step forward, as the murmuring guests quieted. He said he was proud to announce his daughter's engagement to Charles Dunford (only her father called him Charles), who he knew as a fine young man with a great future. Everyone applauded and the man shook Chig's hand for the first time since they had been introduced three years before.

Someone hollered for Chig to make a speech; the motion received a round of applause.

Chig lumbered forward. "Well, you know, I've been hanging around here for a long time. And I got to like Avis a lot." He looked at her and smiled. "But I have to say I was surprised when she asked me to marry her." Everyone laughed as Chig scanned faces.

"I didn't really know about that. But she put up a good fight . . ." There was more laughter. Connie stood far back on his right, her face grave. Chig went on. "So finally I told her Yes, and . . ." He became very serious now. "And I think it's the best decision I ever made in my life. Thanks very much for coming." He put his arm around Avis and kissed her high on the forehead. There was more applause. At that instant, he remembered that Connie had called him a liar. If he had not known before what she meant, he did now, and it frightened him.

*   *   *

At her house, slouching on a sofa, Chig watched Avis, who stood across the room, her back to him, looking at the river. "Avis, what would you say if I decided I didn't want to be a lawyer?" He tried to sound relaxed.

She did not turn around. "Okay. What do you want to be?"

He was delighted, wondering why he had expected opposition. "That's just it. I don't know. I'm not even sure I don't want to be a lawyer. But I'm . . ." He stopped.

She had turned to him, her lips parted. "You're actually serious?" She advanced on him.

Panic heated his body. "Well, I'm sort of serious."

She was standing in front of him, over him. He could not look her in the eye. The engagement ring winked on her finger. "How could you be serious?" Her voice was soft and baffled.

"Wouldn't it be wrong for me to do something I didn't really want to do? I mean, wouldn't it?" He tilted his head back, willed himself to look at her face, but quickly returned to the ring. "I mean, wrong for me?"

Her hands were knit in front of her. "Sure, it would. But you've always wanted to be a lawyer so much, ever since I've known you."

For an instant, he could not remember if he actually had stepped into her house wanting to be a lawyer. "I know that. But lately I've been having doubts. I don't even know why." He wished she would sit down beside him. He would feel less uncomfortable, more as if they were solving his problem together.

She smiled. He did not want her to smile just then. "Well, why all of sudden, do you —"

"Hell, I don't know." Her right hand hid her left and he could no longer see the ring. "Well, yes, I do. I was talking to my father a few nights ago and he told me how he felt about medicine — "

"What does medicine have to do with law?"

"Let me finish, will you?" His voice was whiny and high; his tone surprised him.

Her eyes became just the slightest bit cloudy. "All right, Chig."

"I'm sorry." He sighed. "I just realized how much a profession *can* mean to a person and that I don't look forward to being a lawyer nearly as much as he did to being a doctor. He said he doesn't even need people. He enjoys medicine as a . . . a body of knowledge. You know what I mean? Kind of abstract."

"He doesn't want to make people well?"

"Not exactly. I mean, that isn't his only consideration . . ." He wanted to say something more, but did not know what.

"I don't think that's right." She scowled. "He should care about them."

"He cares about them, Avis." He was impatient with her lack of understanding. He wanted her very much to understand. "It's like when you do something well, it gives you a good feeling whether anybody else benefits or not."

"That's a terrible attitude!" She was being huffy. "You can't just walk all over people."

He raised his voice. "He doesn't walk all over people, for God's sake. He just doesn't live or die on everything people say and think! He has private reasons for being a doctor."

"He can have them!" She was angry now. Chig was startled to discover he did not care, did not feel the urge to calm her.

"Look, does it make him any less a doctor? His patients still like and respect him. He still helps them."

"I can't see how — with his attitude."

"Avis, don't be so f---ing stupid!"

She was stunned; when she spoke her voice was wet. "My being stupid doesn't give you the right to curse at me."

"You're not stupid. I am. I can't make you understand." He was not trying to soothe her; he believed it. But realizing that if he did not stop it soon, it would go too far, he lost all taste for the discussion, and sighed. "Look, let's forget it now." He reached for her waist.

She stepped away, her back curled. "We can't forget it. If you're having doubts about . . . *things*, then we ought to find out . . . before it's too late."

He knew exactly what she meant, and thought it childish. "Avis, a minor difference between us doesn't all of a sudden mean I don't want to marry you. I asked a simple question: How would you feel if I decided not to be a lawyer? I wanted to know what you thought. Now you're making a big thing out of it."

"It *is* a big thing. It's important." She was standing too far from him. He could feel cold distance between them. "If you need time to think things over, I shouldn't push you into marrying me. Marriage is a big responsibility, Chig. I should give you time. There are things you have to decide a-*lone*."

This was crazy. He had never once said to her or even to himself that he definitely did not want to be a lawyer. It was simply that since the night of the party, when he realized he had lied, thanking the guests for coming, he had thought a great deal about himself, and had questioned many of his long-cherished goals. But now, it was getting out of hand.

He found himself staring at Avis. "How can I be so God-damned dense!" He started to laugh.

She was puzzled. She took a step toward him, but said nothing.

"I was getting set to botch up my whole life." He was still laughing. "God!"

"What happened?" She came a bit closer.

"Nothing. Not a God-damned thing!" He was serious now. "I read too many books. I just realized I want everything in my life to be like Saint Paul's Conversion." He started to giggle.

"What?" She smiled quizzically.

"Saint Paul's Conversion, Avis. Saint Paul was on his way to Damascus to suppress the Christians and God knocked him off his horse and made him see the light." Giggling overwhelmed him now.

Avis began to laugh too and collapsed beside him on the sofa. "Chig, you're so silly sometimes."

"I know. But most of the time I'm not even here." He hit his head to straighten out his brains. "Most of the time I'm not in real life. I'm living in a dream world of Saint Pauls and baby monkeys."

"What?"

"Forget it." He waved it all away. "Just remember I love you more than anything in the world." He put his arm around her shoulder. She turned to him and let him kiss her.

In January, Chig began to wonder again whether he actually wanted to be a lawyer, but he convinced himself that he was only doubting because he missed Avis so much. If he could see her, everything would be all right. He had not seen her since she returned to school after the holidays, a week or so after their discussion, which he had not been able to forget.

Early in March, Chig went up the Hudson River to visit Avis at school. On the train, he passed Sing Sing Prison. He wondered about prison life.

Avis had a single room and a key to her door. Chig was allowed in her room from twelve-thirty until seven in the evening. Behind the locked door, they made love.

She lived on the top floor of the tallest building on campus; they did not have to draw the blinds for privacy. The early afternoon sun warmed their bare feet and legs. She lay beside him, perfume mingling with sweat. They talked aimlessly about their marriage. Both were tired and happy.

"I found the nicest silverware." Avis babbled, whispering. "It's so simple and light and beautiful." She kissed him.

"Pull up the sheet. You'll catch cold." He reached down, untangled the bedclothes, and covered both of them. He smoothed her hair, which sweat had made kinky. "You'll have to do something about that."

"Does it look horrible?" She sounded worried.

"It looks beautiful. Don't get upset." He kissed the short baby hair that fringed her forehead.

"Are you sure?"

"Yes." He rolled onto his stomach.

On a bookcase beside the bed was a secondhand copy of *Huckleberry Finn*. Just to see it there made him feel good. He had read it five times since first discovering it. Reaching out, he took it in his hand and smiled to himself.

She felt him move. "What are you doing?" She rolled over and put her arm around his waist.

"I didn't know you had this." There was admiration for her in his voice.

"I had to read it for school." Her eyes closed lazily. "I wrote a paper on it."

"This is the greatest book ever — American anyway." He leafed through it, turning to his favorite chapter, and started to read aloud:

> . . . So I got a piece of paper and a pencil, all glad and excited, and set down and wrote:
>
> Miss Watson, your runaway nigger Jim is down here two mile below Pikesville, and Mr. Phelps has got him and he will give him up for the reward if you send.   Huck Finn.
>
> I felt good and all washed clean of sin for the first time I had ever felt so in my life, and I knowed I could pray now. But I didn't do it straight off, but laid the paper down and set there thinking — thinking how good it was all this happened so, and how near I came to being lost and going to hell. And went on thinking. And got to thinking over our trip down the river; and I see Jim before me all the time: in the day and in the night time, sometimes moonlight, sometimes storms, and we a-floating along, talking and singing and laughing. But somehow I couldn't seem to strike no places to harden me against him, but only the other kind.

Beside him, Avis yawned and stretched. He tried to ignore, forgive what she had done, and continued reading.:

> . . . and then I happened to look around and see that paper.
> It was a close place. I took it up, and held it in my hand. I was a-trembling, because I'd got to decide, forever, betwixt two things, and I knowed it. I studied a minute, sort of holding my breath, and then says to myself:
> "All right, then, I'll go to hell" — and tore it up.

Chig closed his eyes. It had always made him feel sightly melancholy, and warm. "That's great!" he sighed.

Avis was silent for a second. "It's nice how Twain spells out his own moral dilemma. Did you know he ran away to the West so as not to decide what side to fight on in the Civil War?"

"I don't mean it that way, Avis. I . . ." He did not know how to go on. He closed the book.

"Oh, you mean the way he sets up the conflict by having Huck do something he's been taught is wrong — the irony of it." She had propped herself on her elbows and her small breasts hung down between her arms.

He let his head fall on the pillow, turning away. "I mean, how does it make you feel?" He tried not to sound earnest.

"Okay, I guess. Chig, let's not talk about school any more. Not now."

He turned suddenly toward her and kissed her desperately, trying to chase away his own evil thoughts.

Later, they came out into the sun, onto mud-spongy ground. In shadowed corners, there was still snow crusted in dirty mounds. Other couples, holding mittened hands, ambled across the campus.

Avis was skipping. "Come on. I want to show you the lake."

There was still thin ice floating in the black water. Near the edges, dead leaves were frozen into the ice.

"Avis, I'm not going to law school."

"Oh, Chig, not again. I thought we had that settled."

"Does it really matter so much?"

"Of course it does." She stared at him. "You should want to be *something*. God, why do you have to be so melodramatic all the time?"

"I'm not being melodramatic, Avis. I just want to — "

"What's wrong with you anyway?" Tears popped into her eyes. She clenched her fists; her voice, louder now, bounced across the lake and back. There was no one else in sight. "What do you expect me to do?"

"I don't expect you to do anything but have some faith in me." He was pleading with her and did not mind.

"Chig, I'll have faith in you. You tell me you don't want to be a lawyer. All right! But what *do* you want to be?"

He felt foolish, put his hands in his pockets, and stared at the muddy toes of his shoes. "I don't know."

She pounced on that. "You don't know! And you're giving up . . . ? Chig, you're acting crazy. This isn't a movie. You have to know where you're going. You have to have some ambition and direction. Nobody gets anywhere without a goal, and ambition. Not my father . . . or even yours."

"But they love what they're doing. I wouldn't like being a lawyer."

"Suppose you wait and nothing hits you like your precious saint?" She had stopped crying now.

"I . . . I don't know." He realized he was defending an impossible position. He would defend it anyway.

"That's what I'm talking about. You don't know anything. You're like a girl who can't decide what dress to wear to a party and so she goes naked!"

Perhaps what she said was true. He hated the thought of it being true. "But, Avis, I have a right to want something to hit me like that. I'm asking you to have some faith in me. That's all."

"It's too much to ask." Her right hand covered her left. The fingers on her left hand were very straight as she slid off the engagement ring and held it in her right palm.

"Please, Avis, don't take it off." He stared at the ring. "Give me some space to breathe in."

"You mean, some space to be a *bum* in." She held out the ring.

He heard his voice crying. "I don't want to be a bum. I just want to be something I love being."

"Be a lawyer." Her arm, her hand holding the ring looked stiff and grotesque.

"I can't, Avis." He plucked up the ring. It was warm.

He had never actually seen a person faint before. His first impulse, not a cruel one, was to laugh — at the fluttering eyelids, at the sudden blue paleness that rushed into her baby's lips, at the buckling knees, at the comic, floating way she crumpled at his feet. She lay on her back, her arms spread wide, her feet twisted under her awkwardly.

Then he was angry. She was faking. People did not faint. She had threatened him, and now she was trying to keep him in line, using his own pity as a weapon.

"Come on, Avis, get up." He looked down, furious at her. "Get up." If she was awake and listening, she would know he was not being moved by her performance.

Still she remained, sprawled, mud in her hair. Avis would never have allowed mud to get in her hair.

He knelt beside her, frightened, not knowing what to do. He wanted now to gather her, like a dead child, into his arms. But if he touched her, he would kiss her. He knew that. And if he kissed her, he would slide the ring on her finger, and would go to law school.

He sat a short distance away from her, mud seeping through his wool pants, waiting patiently for her large brown eyes to open, hoping that when they did, he would have enough strength not to touch her when he walked her back to the dormitory.

PROBING FOR
MEANING

1. The story involves several conflicts between Avis and Chig. How does each arise and how is each resolved?

2. Chig's sister calls Avis a "phony" and Chig a "liar." What role do these remarks play in the story?

3. What significance do the stories of the baby monkey and of the conversion of Saint Paul have for Chig?

4. Explain the meaning of the scene from *Huckleberry Finn* in relation to Chig's growing awareness of a need to make a choice.

5. Will Chig be strong enough to sever his relationship with Avis? Compare and contrast the two kinds of life that Chig must choose between.

PROBING FOR
METHOD

1. Does the dialogue between Avis and Chig seem realistic to you? Why or why not?

2. Several sections of the story are physically identified by space breaks. What is the narrative function of these story sections? What devices bind them all together?

3. How does Kelley use chronology in this story? Are the chronological markers effective? Do they ever intrude too much into the story?

 ALASTAIR REID

Curiosity

may have killed the cat; more likely
the cat was just unlucky, or else curious
to see what death was like, having no cause
to go on licking paws, or fathering
litter on litter of kittens, predictably.

Nevertheless, to be curious
is dangerous enough. To distrust
what is always said, what seems,
to ask odd questions, interfere in dreams,
leave home, smell rats, have hunches
do not endear cats to those doggy circles
where well-smelt baskets, suitable wives, good lunches
are the order of things, and where prevails
much wagging of incurious heads and tails.

Face it. Curiosity
will not cause us to die —

only lack of it will.
Never to want to see
the other side of the hill
or that improbable country
where living is an idyll
(although a probable hell)
would kill us all.
Only the curious
have, if they live, a tale
worth telling at all.

Dogs say cats love too much, are irresponsible,
are changeable, marry too many wives,
desert their children, chill all dinner tables
with tales of their nine lives.
Well, they are lucky. Let them be
nine-lived and contradictory,
curious enough to change, prepared to pay
the cat price, which is to die
and die again and again,
each time with no less pain.
A cat minority of one
is all that can be counted on
to tell the truth. And what cats have to tell
on each return from hell
is this: that dying is what the living do,
that dying is what the loving do,
and that dead dogs are those who do not know
that dying is what, to live, each has to do.

PROBING FOR   1. The poet finds many instances in which to apply the old saying
MEANING   "Curiosity killed the cat" to human life. What kind of people are cats? Why is
curiosity dangerous for people?

      2. Why does the poet state, "Only the curious/have, if they live, a
tale/worth telling at all"?

      3. What kind of people are dogs? What criticism do they have of cats?
Why does the poet say dogs are dead? What does living entail?

      4. The poet uses paradox when he says, "Dying is what the living do."
What does this paradox mean?

PROBING FOR   1. What is the tone of the poem? How does the tone contribute to the
METHOD   meaning?

      2. The title of the poem also serves as the first line. Why might the
poet choose to structure the poem in this way?

      3. How does the line structure contribute to the poem's statement?

D. H. LAWRENCE

Snake

A snake came to my water-trough
On a hot, hot day, and I in pajamas for the heat,
To drink there.

In the deep, strange-scented shade of the great dark carob-tree
I came down the steps with my pitcher
And must wait, must stand and wait, for there he was at the
       trough before me.

He reached down from a fissure in the earth-wall in the gloom
And trailed his yellow-brown slackness soft-bellied down,
       over the edge of the stone trough
And rested his throat upon the stone bottom,
And where the water had dripped from the tap, in a small
       clearness,
He sipped with his straight mouth,
Softly drank through his straight gums, into his slack long
       body,
Silently.

Someone was before me at my water-trough,
And I, like a second comer, waiting.

He lifted his head from his drinking, as cattle do,
And looked at me vaguely, as drinking cattle do,
And flickered his two-forked tongue from his lips, and mused
       a moment,
And stooped and drank a little more,
Being earth-brown, earth-golden from the burning bowels of
       the earth
On the day of Sicilian July, with Etna smoking.

The voice of my education said to me
He must be killed,
For in Sicily the black, black snakes are innocent, the gold are
       venomous.

And voices in me said, If you were a man
You would take a stick and break him now, and finish him off.

But must I confess how I liked him,
How glad I was he had come like a guest in quiet, to drink at
        my water-trough

And depart peaceful, pacified, and thankless,
Into the burning bowels of this earth?

Was it cowardice, that I dared not kill him?
Was it perversity, that I longed to talk to him?
Was it humility, to feel so honored?
I felt so honored.

And yet those voices:
If you were not afraid, you would kill him!

And truly I was afraid, I was most afraid,
But even so, honored still more
That he should seek my hospitality
From out the dark door of the secret earth.

He drank enough
And lifted his head, dreamily, as one who has drunken,
And flickered his tongue like a forked night on the air, so
        black,
Seeming to lick his lips,
And looked around like a god, unseeing, into the air,
And slowly turned his head,
And slowly, very slowly, as if thrice adream,
Proceeded to draw his slow length curving round
And climb again the broken bank of my wall-face.

And as he put his head into that dreadful hole,
And as he slowly drew up, snake-easing his shoulders, and en-
        tered farther,
A sort of horror, a sort of protest against his withdrawing into
        that horrid black hole,
Deliberately going into the blackness, and slowly drawing
        himself after,
Overcame me now his back was turned.

I looked round, I put down my pitcher,
I picked up a clumsy log
And threw it at the water-trough with a clatter.

I think it did not hit him,
But suddenly that part of him that was left behind convulsed in
    undignified haste
Writhed like lightning, and was gone
Into the black hole, the earth-lipped fissure in the wall-front,
At which, in the intense still noon, I stared with fascination.

And immediately I regretted it.
I thought how paltry, how vulgar, what a mean act!
I despised myself and the voices of my accursed human
    education.

And I thought of the albatross
And I wished he would come back, my snake.

For he seemed to me again like a king,
Like a king in exile, uncrowned in the underworld,
Now due to be crowned again.

And so, I missed my chance with one of the lords
Of life.
And I have something to expiate;
A pettiness.

PROBING FOR
MEANING

1. What decision confronts the speaker of the poem? What are the two sides of the internal conflict the speaker experiences?

2. Why is he "honored" by the snake's actions? How does the snake respond to his presence? What characteristics of the snake are emphasized?

3. What causes the speaker to hurl a log at the snake? What must he "expiate"? Why is his action "a pettiness"?

PROBING FOR
METHOD

1. What does the snake symbolize? What is represented by the fact that the snake comes from the underworld, "the dark door of the secret earth"?

2. What is the biblical significance of the snake in the Garden of Eden? Does Lawrence's snake, "like a king in exile, uncrowned in the under-world," have any similarity to Satan? Are there any differences? Explain fully.

3. Notice how Lawrence uses repetition of meaning with a slight variation of form. Point out one example of this repetition and discuss its effect.

ARCHIBALD MACLEISH

Wildwest*

There were none of my blood in this battle:
There were Minneconjous, Sans Arcs, Brules,
Many nations of Sioux: they were few men galloping.

This would have been in the long days in June:
They were galloping well deployed under the plum-trees:
They were driving riderless horses: themselves they were few.

Crazy Horse had done it with few numbers.
Crazy Horse was small for a Lakota.
He was riding always alone thinking of something:

He was standing alone by the picket lines by the ropes:
He was young then, he was thirty when he died:
Unless there were children to talk he took no notice.

When the soldiers came for him there on the other side
On the Greasy Grass in the villages we were shouting
"Hoka Hey! Crazy Horse will be riding!"

They fought in the water: horses and men were drowning:
They rode on the butte: dust settled in sunlight:
Hoka Hey! they lay on the bloody ground.

No one could tell of the dead which man was Custer . . .
That was the end of his luck: by that river.
The soldiers beat him at Slim Buttes once:

They beat him at Willow Creek when the snow lifted:
The last time they beat him was the Tongue.
He had only the meat he had made and of that little.

Do you ask why he should fight? It was his country:
My God should he not fight? It was his.
But after the Tongue there were no herds to be hunting:

* Black Elk's memories of Crazy Horse recorded by Neihardt.

He cut the knots of the tails and he led them in:
He cried out "I am Crazy Horse! Do not touch me!"
There were many soldiers between and the gun glinting . . .

And a Mister Josiah Perham of Maine had much of the
land Mister Perham was building the Northern Pacific
railroad that is Mister Perham was saying at lunch that

forty say fifty millions of acres in gift and
government grant outright ought to be worth a
wide price on the Board at two-fifty and

later a Mister Cooke had relieved Mister Perham and
later a Mister Morgan relieved Mister Cooke:
Mister Morgan converted at prices current:

It was all prices to them: they never looked at it:
why should they look at the land? they were Empire Builders:
it was all in the bid and the asked and the ink on their
              books . . .

When Crazy Horse was there by the Black Hills
His heart would be big with the love he had for that country
And all the game he had seen and the mares he had ridden

And how it went out from you wide and clean in the sunlight.

PROBING FOR   1. What battle does the poem first describe? Why did the Indians
MEANING   drive riderless horses into the battle?
                      2. What sort of man was Crazy Horse? What do you make of the fact
               that "unless there were children to talk he took no notice"? Why did he fight?
               Why did he finally choose to surrender?
                      3. What contrast does the poem draw between Crazy Horse and those
               who conquered him?

PROBING FOR   1. Why does the poet interrupt his description of the battle in the
METHOD   fourth and fifth stanzas before concluding it in the sixth and seventh stanzas?
                      2. What is the predominant tone of the poem? Where does the
               speaker sound most bitter or angry? Where does he sound proudest? Where
               does his tone become sad and elegiac?
                      3. What effects does the speaker achieve by changing the pronoun
               reference from third person in the next-to-last stanza to second person in the
               final line of the poem?

Topics for Imitation

1. Compare and contrast D. H. Lawrence's treatment of the battle between instinct and reason in "Snake" with that of Petrunke-vitch in "The Spider and the Wasp."

2. How do "Hunger of Memory," "The Necessary Enemy," and "Snake" dramatize the relationship between social pressures and natural instincts? Compare and contrast their approaches.

3. Comment on one of the short stories or poems from the viewpoint that Alastair Reid expresses in "Curiosity." Which characters would Reid describe as "cat" people, and which would he describe as "dogs"?

4. How similar are Georgiana's and Chig's choices about mates in the Cather and Kelley short stories? How different?

5. How thoroughly different from one another are people of different cultural backgrounds? Compare and contrast the attitudes toward cultural differences expressed in the selections by Rodriguez, Rau, and MacLeish.

6. How important is the difference between our public and our private lives? Why is it necessary to have a private life? When can it be harmful to withdraw into a private world? Compare the contrasts drawn between public and the private lives in selections by two of the following authors: Rodriguez, Rau, Porter, Cather.

7. Many choices present themselves to us daily. Choose any one of the following pairs of alternatives and compare and contrast the choices. Be sure to devote equal space to each alternative; if you have a preference for one of the alternatives, indicate your choice only in your conclusion. In other words, use comparison and contrast rather than argumentation as your structure.

   a. Marrying or living together
   b. Giving either outside work or family priority
   c. Obtaining a college education or not
   d. Obtaining a liberal education or a professional/technical education
   e. Going away to school or commuting to school from home

SIX

PHILOSOPHIES

"Not people die but worlds die in them"

Plato, in his "Allegory of the Cave," compares man's search for sense and significance in life to his leaving the safe, dark but warm cave of illusions for the blinding light of the sun of truth. Most people prefer to remain in the cave and lead a life patterned for them by others, but some need the greater fulfillment resulting from the search for a personal philosophy of life.

"Techniques of living" is how Anne Morrow Lindbergh describes what she is looking for. Henry David Thoreau is in search of himself. Other writers use other phrases — "enlightened nature," "values of life" and "self-development" — but all are searching for a philosophy of existence.

Several writers, while searching, turn to nature: Thoreau moves to Walden Pond; E. M. Forster buys property in the country; Anne Morrow Lindbergh visits the seashore; and Daru, in Albert Camus's story, inhabits a barren Algerian plateau. Helen Keller, however, searches for meaning in New York City.

Each writer's truth is different. Keller finds significance in friendship; Thoreau, in solitude; Lindbergh, in simplicity; Camus, in brotherhood; Forster, in self-inspection; Garcia Márquez's Balthazar, in selflessness; Sexton, in God; Richard Wilbur's daughter, in art. Edna St. Vincent Millay finds no answer at all; for her, the question is more significant than the answer.

Illustrating Ideas

The best writing is vivid writing. As we have seen, your selection of words sharpens the fine points of your subject. So
do examples, illustrations, and comparisons, which support
your points and add a vital truthfulness to your writing. The
writing in this chapter achieves freshness and aliveness
through methods discussed on pp. 288–290 after Anne Morrow Lindbergh's essay "Channelled Whelk." The essays have
been selected for the lively, sharp illustrations the authors
have used. Do their examples, illustrations, and comparisons
indeed involve you in their subjects?

 ANNE MORROW LINDBERGH

Channelled Whelk

The shell in my hand is deserted. It once housed a whelk, a
snail-like creature, and then temporarily, after the death of the first oc-
cupant, a little hermit crab, who has run away, leaving his tracks behind
him like a delicate vine on the sand. He ran away, and left me his shell.
It was once a protection to him. I turn the shell in my hand, gazing into
the wide open door from which he made his exit. Had it become an en-
cumbrance? Why did he run away? Did he hope to find a better home, a
better mode of living? I too have run away, I realize, I have shed the
shell of my life, for these few weeks of vacation.

But his shell — it is simple; it is bare, it is beautiful. Small, only
the size of my thumb, its architecture is perfect, down to the finest detail. Its shape, swelling like a pear in the center, winds in a gentle spiral
to the pointed apex. Its color, dull gold, is whitened by a wash of salt
from the sea. Each whorl, each faint knob, each criss-cross vein in its
egg-shell texture, is as clearly defined as on the day of creation. My eye
follows with delight the outer circumstance of that diminutive winding
staircase up which this tenant used to travel.

My shell is not like this, I think. How untidy it has become!
Blurred with moss, knobby with barnacles, its shape is hardly recogniz-
able any more. Surely, it had a shape once. It has a shape still in my
mind. What is the shape of my life?

The shape of my life today starts with a family. I have a husband, five children and a home just beyond the suburbs of New York. I have also a craft, writing, and therefore work I want to pursue. The shape of my life is, of course, determined by many other things; my background and childhood, my mind and its education, my conscience and its pressures, my heart and its desires. I want to give and take from my children and husband, to share with friends and community, to carry out my obligations to man and to the world as a woman, as an artist, as a citizen.

But I want first of all — in fact, as an end to these other desires — to be at peace with myself. I want a singleness of eye, a purity of intention, a central core to my life that will enable me to carry out these obligations and activities as well as I can. I want, in fact — to borrow from the language of the saints — to live "in grace" as much of the time as possible. I am not using this term in a strictly theological sense. By grace I mean an inner harmony, essentially spiritual, which can be translated into outward harmony. I am seeking perhaps what Socrates asked for in the prayer from the *Phaedrus* when he said, "May the outward and inward man be at one." I would like to achieve a state of inner spiritual grace from which I could function and give as I was meant to in the eye of God.

Vague as this definition may be, I believe most people are aware of periods in their lives when they seem to be "in grace" and other periods when they feel "out of grace," even though they may use different words to describe these states. In the first happy condition, one seems to carry all one's tasks before one lightly, as if borne alone on a great tide; and in the opposite state one can hardly tie a shoestring. It is true that a large part of life consists in learning a technique of tying the shoe-string, whether one is in grace or not. But there are techniques of living too; there are even techniques in the search for grace. And techniques can be cultivated. I have learned by some experience, by many examples, and by the writings of countless others before me, also occupied in the search, that certain environments, certain modes of life, certain rules of conduct are more conducive to inner and outer harmony than others. There are, in fact, certain roads that one may follow. Simplification of life is one of them.

I mean to lead a simple life, to choose a simple shell I can carry easily — like a hermit crab. But I do not. I find that my frame of life does not foster simplicity. My husband and five children must make their way in the world. The life I have chosen as wife and mother entrains a whole caravan of complications. It involves a house in the suburbs and either household drudgery or household help which wavers between scarcity and non-existence for most of us. It involves food and shelter; meals, planning, marketing, bills, and making the ends meet in a thousand ways. It involves not only the butcher, the baker, the candlestickmaker but countless other experts to keep my modern house with its modern "simplifications" (electricity, plumbing, refrigerator, gas-stove, oil-burner, dish-washer, radios, car, and numerous other labor-saving devices) functioning properly. It involves health; doctors, dentists, appointments, medicine, cod-liver oil, vitamins, trips to the drugstore. It involves education, spiritual, intellectual, physical; schools, school conferences, carpools, extra trips for basket-ball or orchestra practice; tutoring; camps, camp equipment and transportation. It involves clothes, shopping, laundry, cleaning, mending, letting skirts down and sewing buttons on, or finding someone else to do it. It involves friends, my husband's, my children's, my own, and endless arrangements to get together; letters, invitations, telephone calls and transportation hither and yon.

For life today in America is based on the premise of everwidening circles of contact and communication. It involves not only family demands, but community demands, national demands, international demands on the good citizen, through social and cultural pressures, through newspapers, magazines, radio programs, political drives, charitable appeals, and so on. My mind reels with it. What a circus act we women perform every day of our lives. It puts the trapeze artist to shame. Look at us. We run a tight rope daily, balancing a pile of books on the head. Baby-carriage, parasol, kitchen chair, still under control. Steady now!

This is not the life of simplicity but the life of multiplicity that the wise men warn us of. It leads not to unification but to fragmentation. It does not bring grace; it destroys the soul. And this is not only true of my life, I am forced to conclude; it is the life of millions of women in America. I stress America, because today, the American woman more than any other has the privilege of choosing such a life. Woman in large parts of the civilized world has been forced back by war, by poverty, by collapse, by the sheer struggle to survive, into a smaller circle of immediate time and space, immediate family life, immediate problems of existence. The American woman is still relatively free to choose the wider life. How long she will hold this enviable and precarious position no one knows. But her particular situation has a significance far above its apparent economic, national or even sex limitations.

For the problem of the multiplicity of life not only confronts the American woman, but also the American man. And it is not merely the concern of the American as such, but of our whole modern civilization, since life in America today is held up as the ideal of a large part of the rest of the world. And finally, it is not limited to our present civilization, though we are faced with it now in an exaggerated form. It has always been one of the pitfalls of mankind. Plotinus was preaching the dangers of multiplicity of the world back in the third century. Yet, the problem is particularly and essentially woman's. Distraction is, always has been, and probably always will be, inherent in woman's life.

For to be a woman is to have interests and duties, raying out in all directions from the central mother-core, like spokes from the hub of a wheel. The pattern of our lives is essentially circular. We must be open to all points of the compass; husband, children, friends, home, community; stretched out, exposed, sensitive like a spider's web to each breeze that blows, to each call that comes. How difficult for us, then, to achieve a balance in the midst of these contradictory tensions, and yet how necessary for the proper functioning of our lives. How much we need, and how arduous of attainment is that steadiness preached in all rules for holy living. How desirable and distant is the ideal of the contemplative, artist, or saint — the inner inviolable core, the single eye.

With a new awareness, both painful and humorous, I begin to understand why the saints were rarely married women. I am convinced it has nothing inherently to do, as I once supposed, with chastity or children. It has to do primarily with distractions. The bearing, rearing, feeding and educating of children; the running of a house with its thousand details; human relationships with their myriad pulls — woman's normal occupations in general run counter to creative life, or contemplative life, or saintly life. The problem is not merely one of *Woman and Career, Woman and the Home, Woman and Independence.* It is more basically: how to remain whole in the midst of the distractions of life; how to remain balanced, no matter what centrifugal forces tend to pull one off center; how to remain strong, no matter what shocks come in at the periphery and tend to crack the hub of the wheel.

What is the answer? There is no easy answer, no complete answer. I have only clues, shells from the sea. The bare beauty of the channelled whelk tells me that one answer, and perhaps a first step, is in simplification of life, in cutting out some of the distractions. But how? Total retirement is not possible. I cannot shed my responsibilities. I cannot permanently inhabit a desert island. I cannot be a nun in the midst of family life. I would not want to be. The solution for me, surely, is neither in total renunciation of the world, nor in total acceptance of it. I must find a balance somewhere, or an alternating rhythm between these two extremes; a swinging of the pendulum between solitude and communion, between retreat and return. In my periods of retreat, perhaps I can learn something to carry back into my worldly life. I can at least practice for these two weeks the simplification of outward life, as a beginning. I can follow this superficial clue, and see where it leads. Here, in beach living, I can try.

One learns first of all in beach living the art of shedding; how little one can get along with, not how much. Physical shedding to begin with, which then mysteriously spreads into other fields. Clothes, first. Of course, one needs less in the sun. But one needs less anyway, one finds suddenly. One needs not need a closet-full, only a small suitcase-full. And what a relief it is! Less taking up and down of hems, less mending, and — best of all — less worry about what to wear. One finds one is shedding not only clothes — but vanity.

Next, shelter. One does not need the airtight shelter one has in winter in the North. Here I live in a bare sea-shell of a cottage. No heat, no telephone, no plumbing to speak of, no hot water, a two-burner oil stove, no gadgets to go wrong. No rugs. There were some, but I rolled them up the first day; it is easier to sweep the sand off a bare floor. But I find I don't bustle about with unnecessary sweeping and cleaning here. I am no longer aware of the dust. I have shed my Puritan conscience about absolute tidiness and cleanliness. Is it possible that, too, is a material burden? No curtains. I do not need them for privacy; the pines around my house are enough protection. I want the windows open all the time, and I don't want to worry about rain. I begin to shed my Martha-like anxiety about many things. Washable slipcovers, faded and old — I hardly see them; I don't worry about the impression they make on other people. I am shedding pride. As little furniture as possible; I shall not need much. I shall ask into my shell only those friends with whom I can be completely honest. I find I am shedding hypocrisy in human relationships. What a rest that will be! The most exhausting thing in life, I have discovered, is being insincere. That is why so much of social life is exhausting; one is wearing a mask. I have shed my mask.

I find I live quite happily without those things I think necessary in winter in the North. And as I write these words, I remember, with some shock at the disparity in our lives, a similar statement made by a friend of mine in France who spent three years in a German prison camp. Of course, he said, qualifying his remark, they did not get enough to eat, they were sometimes atrociously treated, they had little physical freedom. And yet, prison life taught him how little one can get along with, and what extraordinary spiritual freedom and peace such simplification can bring. I remember again, ironically, that today more of us in America than anywhere else in the world have the luxury of choice between simplicity and complication of life. And for the most part, we, who could choose simplicity, choose complication. War, prison, survival periods, enforce a form of simplicity on man. The monk and the nun choose it of their own free will. But if one accidentally finds it, as I have for a few days, one finds also the serenity it brings.

Is it not rather ugly, one may ask? One collects material possessions not only for security, comfort or vanity, but for beauty as well. Is your sea-shell house not ugly and bare? No, it is beautiful, my house. It is bare, of course, but the wind, the sun, the smell of the pines blow through its bareness. The unfinished beams in the roof are veiled by cobwebs. They are lovely, I think, gazing up at them with new eyes; they soften the hard lines of the rafters as grey hairs soften the lines on a middle-aged face. I no longer pull out grey hairs or sweep down cobwebs. As for the walls, it is true they looked forbidding at first. I felt cramped and enclosed by their blank faces. I wanted to knock holes in them, to give them another dimension with pictures or windows. So I dragged home from the beach grey arms of driftwood, worn satin-smooth by wind and sand. I gathered trailing green vines with floppy red-tipped leaves. I picked up the whitened skeletons of conchshells, their curious hollowed-out shapes faintly reminiscent of abstract sculpture. With these tacked to walls and propped up in corners, I am satisfied. I have a periscope out to the world. I have a window, a view, a point of flight from my sedentary base.

I am content. I sit down at my desk, a bare kitchen table with a blotter, a bottle of ink, a sand dollar to weight down one corner, a clam shell for a pen tray, the broken tip of a conch, pink-tinged, to finger, and a row of shells to set my thoughts spinning.

I love my sea-shell of a house. I wish I could live in it always. I wish I could transport it home. But I cannot. It will not hold a husband, five children and the necessities and trappings of daily life. I can only carry back my little channelled whelk. It will sit on my desk in Connecticut, to remind me of the ideal of a simplified life, to encourage me in the game I played on the beach. To ask how little, not how much, can I get along with. To say — is it necessary? — when I am tempted to add one more accumulation to my life, when I am pulled toward one more contrifugal activity.

Simplification of outward life is not enough. It is merely the outside. But I am starting with the outside. I am looking at the outside of a shell, the outside of my life — the shell. The complete answer is not to be found on the outside, in an outward mode of living. This is only a technique, a road to grace. The final answer, I know, is always inside. But the outside can give a clue, can help one to find the inside answer. One is free, like the hermit crab, to change one's shell.

Channelled whelk, I put you down again, but you have set my mind on a journey, up an inwardly winding spiral staircase of thought.

PROBING FOR   1. Why does Lindbergh compare the shell to her life? How is the shell
MEANING   different from the life she is living?

2. What does she mean by "being at peace" with herself? What does it mean to be "out of grace"? How serious a state is the latter?

3. What is the technique for living that she talks about? Do you agree with her that it is a very difficult technique to learn? What has contributed to this difficulty?

4. Do you agree with her that multiplicity leads to fragmentation? What evidence does she cite for this statement?

5. "Distraction is, always has been, and probably always will be, inherent in woman's life." Why is a woman's life more fragmented than a man's? Why is this particularly true in America? Why is it enviable, as Lindbergh claims it is, to be fragmented if fragmentation destroys the soul?

6. She discusses what she calls "the art of shedding." To what is this

analogous? Which people have perfected this art? How possible is it for most people to "shed"?

7. What stages in "shedding" does Lindbergh delineate? How did she avoid making shedding ugly?

8. What does she hope to accomplish in her cottage at the seashore? Why does she think her concentration on physical shedding will affect her spiritually or emotionally (in other words, that the "outside" will affect the "inside")?

PROBING FOR   1. What method does Lindbergh use in introducing her essay? Does
METHOD   her first paragraph include a thesis statement? If so, what is it?

2. What parallel exists between the whelk shell and her life? On how many levels does this parallel work? How does using the shell to refer to her life help convey her point? What other comparisons might she have used?

3. What techniques are employed in the conclusion? How effective is the conclusion?

4. What writing techniques does Lindbergh employ to achieve simplicity of style, thereby underscoring her theme of simplicity in life?

Illustrating Ideas

How does Lindbergh illustrate her essay?   Lindbergh uses many techniques of illustration, several of which are evident on the first page. *Simile,* a figure of speech in which one subject is likened to another not obviously similar (using "like" or "as"), is used in describing how the hermit crab ran away, "leaving his tracks behind him like a delicate vine on the sand." While we may not have seen the tracks of a hermit crab, we have seen a trailing vine; the picture is made much more vivid by the simile.

Metaphor, in which two unlike things are implicitly equated, forms the basis of another illustration: "I have shed the shell of my life." The phrase "the shell of my life" may imply that Lindbergh's life is a protective but burdensome and inelegant growth only partially related to the "real" person inside. A well-chosen metaphor can convey a great deal in a very few words. The author uses many other similes and metaphors in her essay. Can you find them?

Lindbergh also uses *example,* another illustrative device, in paragraph 7, where she lists all her involvements as a wife and mother providing food, shelter, health care, and education, maintaining household appliances, socializing, and so on. For each involvement, she lists several examples, thus making very specific her statement that her life is complex. Beyond these "local" examples she also uses extended example: seeking simplicity in a world of complexity, she uses her vacation at the seashore as an example of how one could live a simple life.

Her entire essay is organized around another illustrative device: *analogy,* which is an extended figurative comparison that uses a clear illustration to explain a difficult idea. As we have seen, her essay begins with a comparison of her life with the whelk's shell in a simple metaphor: "I have shed the shell of my life." This comparison is extended throughout the essay at various points: she compares their shapes, their simplicity, the shelter of shell and seaside cottage, the change both experience. What begins as a simple comparison extends throughout the essay to become an analogy that explains her sense of the meaning of her beach experiences. Lindbergh discusses an idea — the need for simplicity of life — using many concrete examples and comparisons to make her idea vivid.

Illustrating ideas.   As we saw in Chapters 1 and 5, specific topics and vivid language help forge the best writing. Specific illustration techniques further hone the abstract and general into the concrete and particular shape of good writing.

The writer may use example: "A luscious orange is an example of fruit." E. M. Forster's essay in this chapter is organized around examples.

Another logical method of illustrating an abstract principle is to tell a story or create a hypothetical situation which through its narrative qualities makes the abstract concrete: "The cycle of fruit from seed to ripening can be illustrated through the story of the orange." See Helen Keller's essay for the use of extended example.

Or the writer may, as in metaphor or simile, use a totally unrelated illustration which still offers some information about the subject: "A poem is palpable and mute as globed fruit" ("Ars Poetica," Archibald MacLeish). Metaphors and similes bound in "The Village" by Henry David Thoreau.

Analogy and allegory, which also form unrelated comparisons, extend throughout a paragraph or an essay. An analogy explains a difficult concept by comparing it to a more accessible one. Analogy can be used to describe a poem at various junctures in an essay as having many properties of fruit — beauty, nourishment, sweetness, and so on. Anne Morrow Lindbergh uses analogy as we have seen.

In allegory the writer "camouflages" his true subject with another, more innocent-looking one. Two levels of meaning exist simultaneously: the literal level (the "camouflage") and the abstract level (the true subject). Allegory extends throughout a paragraph or essay, and makes an abstraction concrete. See Plato's "Allegory of the Cave" in this chapter as an example of allegory. Compare and contrast the Plato and Lindbergh selections to distinguish between allegory and analogy.

Procedures to follow in using illustration.

A. Any topic can be successfully developed through the use of one or more illustrative devices. In Chapter 2, Eldridge Cleaver describes the jailer's keys as sounding like Christmas bells when the jailer brings him mail. Loren Eiseley's essay in Chapter 4, "The Brown Wasp," is developed with analogous examples from nature and human nature. Santha Rama Rau's essay on India in Chapter 5 is based on illustrations from Indian life. William Golding's essay in the same chapter uses example and illustration.

B. Metaphors and similes can be included in any writing. Whenever you are making a point ask yourself what comparisons might make your point more vivid. Be sure to avoid clichés, however; comparisons too often used lose their effectiveness. Strive for a fresh effect.

C. A major method of paragraph development (see Chapter 3) is the use of examples. Almost any paragraph topic can be developed through the use of examples. As you write each paragraph of your essay, ask yourself what example can be cited to support that paragraph topic and make it concrete. An extended example or illustration may form the foundation of your entire essay (see Helen Keller's essay in this chapter).

D. Analogy and allegory refer to the entire structure of an essay and require careful planning. While allegory is in a certain sense an outmoded literary form, it has occasionally been used in modern writing; Orwell's *Animal Farm* is probably the best-known example. Analogy is much more useful; a physiologist, for example, wishing to explain the workings of the nervous system, might compare it with something in the reader's experience such as the telephone network. Writers often look to the insect or animal world for illustrative material; they use familiar things to give the reader new insights into the unfamiliar.

 HELEN KELLER

Three Days to See

All of us have read thrilling stories in which the hero had only a limited and specified time to live. Sometimes it was as long as a year; sometimes as short as twenty-four hours. But always we were interested in discovering just how the doomed man chose to spend his last days or his last hours. I speak, of course, of free men who have a choice, not condemned criminals whose sphere of activities is strictly delimited.

Such stories set us thinking, wondering what we should do under similar circumstances. What events, what experiences, what associations should we crowd into those last hours as mortal beings? What happiness should we find in reviewing the past, what regrets?

Sometimes I have thought it would be an excellent rule to live each day as if we should die tomorrow. Such an attitude would empha-

size sharply the values of life. We should live each day with a gentleness, a vigor, and a keenness of appreciation which are often lost when
time stretches before us in the constant panorama of more days and
months and years to come. There are those, of course, who would
adopt the epicurean motto of "Eat, drink, and be merry," but most
people would be chastened by the certainty of impending death.

In stories, the doomed hero is usually saved at the last minute
by some stroke of fortune, but almost always his sense of values is
changed. He becomes more appreciative of the meaning of life and its
permanent spiritual values. It has often been noted that those who live,
or have lived, in the shadow of death bring a mellow sweetness to
everything they do.

Most of us, however, take life for granted. We know that one
day we must die, but usually we picture that day as far in the future.
When we are in buoyant health, death is all but unimaginable. We seldom think of it. The days stretch out in an endless vista. So we go about
our petty tasks, hardly aware of our listless attitude toward life.

The same lethargy, I am afraid, characterizes the use of all our
faculties and senses. Only the deaf appreciate hearing, only the blind
realize the manifold blessings that lie in sight. Particularly does this
observation apply to those who have lost sight and hearing in adult life.
But those who have never suffered impairment of sight or hearing seldom make the fullest use of these blessed faculties. Their eyes and ears
take in all sights and sounds hazily, without concentration and with little appreciation. It is the same old story of not being grateful for what
we have until we lose it, of not being conscious of health until we are ill.

I have often thought it would be a blessing if each human being
were stricken blind and deaf for a few days at some time during his
early adult life. Darkness would make him more appreciative of sight;
silence would teach him the joys of sound.

Now and then I have tested my seeing friends to discover what
they see. Recently I was visited by a very good friend who had just returned from a long walk in the woods, and I asked her what she had
observed. "Nothing in particular," she replied. I might have been in-
credulous had I not been accustomed to such responses, for long ago I
became convinced that the seeing see little.

How was it possible, I asked myself, to walk for an hour
through the woods and see nothing worthy of note? I who cannot see
find hundreds of things to interest me through mere touch. I feel the
delicate symmetry of a leaf. I pass my hands lovingly about the smooth
skin of a silver birch, or the rough shaggy bark of a pine. In spring I
touch the branches of trees hopefully in search of a bud, the first sign of
awakening Nature after her winter's sleep. I feel the delightful, velvety
texture of a flower, and discover its remarkable convolutions; and
something of the miracle of Nature is revealed to me. Occasionally, if I

am fortunate, I place my hand gently on a small tree and feel the happy quiver of a bird in full song. I am delighted to have the cool waters of a brook rush through my open fingers. To me a lush carpet of pine needles or spongy grass is more welcome than the most luxurious Persian rug. To me the pageant of seasons is a thrilling and unending drama, the action of which streams through my finger tips.

At times my heart cries out with longing to see all these things. If I can get so much pleasure from mere touch, how much more beauty must be revealed by sight. Yet, those who have eyes apparently see little. The panorama of color and action which fills the world is taken for granted. It is human, perhaps, to appreciate little that which we have and to long for that which we have not, but it is a great pity that in the world of light the gift of sight is used only as a mere convenience rather than as a means of adding fullness to life.

If I were the president of a university I should establish a compulsory course in "How to Use Your Eyes." The professor would try to show his pupils how they could add joy to their lives by really seeing what passes unnoticed before them. He would try to awake their dormant and sluggish faculties.

Perhaps I can best illustrate by imagining what I should most like to see if I were given the use of my eyes, say, for just three days. And while I am imagining, suppose you, too, set your mind to work on the problem of how you would use your own eyes if you had only three more days to see. If with the oncoming darkness of the third night you knew that the sun would never rise for you again, how would you spend those three precious intervening days? What would you most want to let your gaze rest upon?

I, naturally, should want most to see the things which have become dear to me through my years of darkness. You, too, would want to let your eyes rest long on the things that have become dear to you so that you could take the memory of them with you into the night that loomed before you.

If by some miracle I were granted three seeing days, to be followed by a relapse into darkness, I should divide the period into three parts.

On the first day, I should want to see the people whose kindness and gentleness and companionship have made my life worth living. First I should like to gaze long upon the face of my dear teacher, Mrs. Anne Sullivan Macy, who came to me when I was a child and opened the outer world to me. I should want not merely to see the outline of her face, so that I could cherish it in my memory, but to study that face and find in it the living evidence of the sympathetic tenderness and patience with which she accomplished the difficult task of my education. I should like to see in her eyes that strength of character which has enabled her to stand firm in the face of difficulties, and that compassion for all humanity which she has revealed to me so often.

I do not know what it is to see into the heart of a friend through that "window of the soul," the eye. I can only "see" through my finger tips the outline of a face. I can detect laughter, sorrow, and many other obvious emotions. I know my friends from the feel of their faces. But I cannot really picture their personalities by touch. I know their personalities, of course, through other means, through the thoughts they express to me, through whatever of their actions are revealed to me. But I am denied that deeper understanding of them which I am sure would come through sight of them, through watching their reactions to various expressed thoughts and circumstances, through noting the immediate and fleeting reactions of their eyes and countenance.

Friends who are near to me I know well, because through the months and years they reveal themselves to me in all their phases; but of casual friends I have only an incomplete impression, an impression gained from a handclasp, from spoken words which I take from their lips with my finger tips, or which they tap into the palm of my hand.

How much easier, how much more satisfying it is for you who can see to grasp quickly the essential qualities of another person by watching the subtleties of expression, the quiver of a muscle, the flutter of a hand. But does it ever occur to you to use your sight to see into the inner nature of a friend or acquaintance? Do not most of you seeing people grasp casually the outward features of a face and let it go at that?

For instance, can you describe accurately the faces of five good friends? Some of you can, but many cannot. As an experiment, I have questioned husbands of long standing about the color of their wives' eyes, and often they express embarrassed confusion and admit that they do not know. And, incidentally, it is a chronic complaint of wives that their husbands do not notice new dresses, new hats, and changes in household arrangements

The eyes of seeing persons soon become accustomed to the routine of their surroundings, and they actually see only the startling and spectacular. But even in viewing the most spectacular sights the eyes are lazy. Court records reveal every day how inaccurately "eyewitnesses" see. A given event will be "seen" in several different ways by as many witnesses. Some see more than others, but few see everything that is within the range of their vision.

Oh, the things that I should see if I had the power of sight for just three days!

The first day would be a busy one. I should call to me all my dear friends and look long into their faces, imprinting upon my mind the outward evidences of the beauty that is within them. I should let my eyes rest, too, on the face of a baby, so that I could catch a vision of the eager, innocent beauty which precedes the individual's consciousness of the conflicts which life develops.

And I should like to look into the loyal, trusting eyes of my dogs — the grave, canny little Scottie, Darkie, and the stalwart, understanding Great Dane, Helga, whose warm, tender, and playful friendships are so comforting to me.

On that busy first day I should also view the small simple things of my home. I want to see the warm colors in the rugs under my feet, the pictures on the walls, the intimate trifles tht transform a house into home. My eyes would rest respectfully on the books in raised type which I have read, but they would be more eagerly interested in the printed books which seeing people can read, for during the long night of my life the books I have read and those which have been read to me have built themselves into a great shining lighthouse, revealing to me the deepest channels of human life and the human spirit.

In the afternoon of that first seeing day, I should take a long walk in the woods and intoxicate my eyes on the beauties of the world of Nature, trying desperately to absorb in a few hours the vast splendor which is constantly unfolding itself to those who can see. On the way home from my woodland jaunt my path would lie near a farm so that I might see the patient horses plowing in the field (perhaps I should see only a tractor!) and the serene content of men living close to the soil. And I should pray for the glory of a colorful sunset.

When dusk had fallen, I should experience the double delight of being able to see by artificial light, which the genius of man has created to extend the power of his sight when Nature decrees darkness.

In the night of that first day of sight, I should not be able to sleep, so full would be my mind of the memories of the day.

The next day — the second day of sight — I should arise with the dawn and see the thrilling miracle by which night is transformed into day. I should behold with awe the magnificent panorama of light with which the sun awakens the sleeping earth.

This day I should devote to a hasty glimpse of the world, past and present. I should want to see the pageant of man's progress, the kaleidoscope of the ages. How can so much be compressed into one day? Through the museums, of course. Often I have visited the New York Museum of Natural History to touch with my hands many of the objects there exhibited, but I have longed to see with my eyes the condensed history of the earth and its inhabitants displayed there — animals and the races of men pictured in their native environment; gigantic carcasses of dinosaurs and mastodons which roamed the earth long before man appeared, with his tiny stature and powerful brain, to conquer the animal kingdom; realistic presentations of the processes of evolution in animals, in man, and in the implements which man has used to fashion for himself a secure home on this planet; and a thousand and one other aspects of natural history.

I wonder how many readers of this article have viewed this panorama of the face of living things as pictured in that inspiring museum. Many, of course, have not had the opportunity, but I am sure that many who *have* had the opportunity have not made use of it. There, indeed, is a place to use your eyes. You who see can spend many fruitful days there, but I, with my imaginary three days of sight, could only take a hasty glimpse, and pass on.

My next stop would be the Metropolitan Museum of Art, for just as the Museum of Natural History reveals the material aspects of the world, so does the Metropolitan show the myriad facets of the human spirit. Throughout the history of humanity the urge to artistic expression has been almost as powerful as the urge for food, shelter, and procreation. And here, in the vast chambers of the Metropolitan Museum, is unfolded before me the spirit of Egypt, Greece, and Rome, as expressed in their art. I know well through my hands the sculptured gods and goddesses of the ancient Nile-land. I have felt copies of Parthenon friezes, and I have sensed the rhythmic beauty of charging Athenian warriors. Apollos and Venuses and the Winged Victory of Samothrace are friends of my finger tips. The gnarled, bearded features of Homer are dear to me, for he, too, knew blindness.

My hands have lingered upon the living marble of Roman sculpture as well as that of later generations. I have passed my hands over a plaster cast of Michelangelo's inspiring and heroic Moses; I have sensed the power of Rodin; I have been awed by the devoted spirit of Gothic wood carving. These arts which can be touched have meaning for me, but even they were meant to be seen rather than felt, and I can only guess at the beauty which remains hidden from me. I can admire the simple lines of a Greek vase, but its figured decorations are lost to me.

So on this, my second day of sight, I should try to probe into the soul of man through his art. The things I knew through touch I should now see. More splendid still, the whole magnificent world of painting would be opened to me, from the Italian Primitives, with their serene religious devotion, to the Moderns, with their feverish visions. I should look deep into the canvases of Raphael, Leonardo da Vinci, Titian, Rembrandt. I should want to feast my eyes upon the warm colors of Veronese, study the mysteries of El Greco, catch a new vision of Nature from Corot. Oh, there is so much rich meaning and beauty in the art of the ages for you who have eyes to see!

Upon my short visit to this temple of art I should not be able to review a fraction of that great world of art which is open to you. I should be able to get only a superficial impression. Artists tell me that for a deep and true appreciation of art one must educate the eye. One must learn through experience to weigh the merits of line, of composition, of form and color. If I had eyes, how happily would I embark upon so fascinating a study! Yet I am told that, to many of you who have eyes to see, the world of art is a dark night, unexplored and unilluminated.

It would be with extreme reluctance that I should leave the Metropolitan Museum, which contains the key to beauty — a beauty so neglected. Seeing persons, however, do not need a Metropolitan to find this key to beauty. The same key lies waiting in smaller museums, and in books on the shelves of even small libraries. But naturally, in my limited time of imaginary sight, I should choose the place where the key unlocks the greatest treasures in the shortest time.

The evening of my second day of sight I should spend at a theater or at the movies. Even now I often attend theatrical performances of all sorts, but the action of the play must be spelled into my hand by a companion. But how I should like to see with my own eyes the fascinating figure of Hamlet, or the gusty Falstaff amid colorful Elizabethan trappings! How I should like to follow each movement of the graceful Hamlet, each strut of the hearty Falstaff! And since I could see only one play, I should be confronted by a many-horned dilemma, for there are scores of plays I should want to see. You who have eyes can see any you like. How many of you, I wonder, when you gaze at a play, a movie, or any spectacle, realize and give thanks for the miracle of sight which enables you to enjoy its color, grace, and movement?

I cannot enjoy the beauty of rhythmic movement except in a sphere restricted to the touch of my hands. I can envision only dimly the grace of a Pavlova, although I know something of the delight of rhythm, for often I can sense the beat of music as it vibrates through the floor. I can well imagine that cadenced motion must be one of the most pleasing sights in the world. I have been able to gather something of this by tracing with my fingers the lines in sculptured marble; if this static grace can be so lovely, how much more acute must be the thrill of seeing grace in motion.

One of my dearest memories is of the time when Joseph Jefferson allowed me to touch his face and hands as he went through some of the gestures and speeches of his beloved Rip Van Winkle. I was able to catch thus a meager glimpse of the world of drama, and I shall never forget the delight of that moment. But, oh, how much I must miss, and how much pleasure you seeing ones can derive from watching and hearing the interplay of speech and movement in the unfolding of a dramatic performance! If I could see only one play, I should know how to picture in my mind the action of a hundred plays which I have read or had transferred to me through the medium of the manual alphabet.

So, through the evening of my second imaginary day of sight, the great figures of dramatic literature would crowd sleep from my eyes.

*   *   *

The following morning, I should again greet the dawn, anxious to discover new delights, for I am sure that, for those who have eyes which really see, the dawn of each day must be a perpetually new revelation of beauty.

This, according to the terms of my imagined miracle, is to be my third and last day of sight. I shall have no time to waste in regrets or longings; there is too much to see. The first day I devoted to my friends, animate and inanimate. The second revealed to me the history of man and Nature. Today I shall spend in the workaday world of the present, amid the haunts of men going about the business of life. And where can one find so many activities and conditions of men as in New York? So the city becomes my destination.

I start from my home in the quiet little suburb of Forest Hills, Long Island. Here, surrounded by green lawns, trees, and flowers, are neat little houses, happy with the voices and movements of wives and children, havens of peaceful rest for men who toil in the city. I drive across the lacy structure of steel which spans the East River, and I get a new and startling vision of the power and ingenuity of the mind of man. Busy boats chug and scurry about the river — racy speed boats, stolid, snorting tugs. If I had long days of sight ahead, I should spend many of them watching the delightful activity upon the river.

I look ahead, and before me rise the fantastic towers of New York, a city that seems to have stepped from the pages of a fairy story. What an awe-inspiring sight, these glittering spires, these vast banks of stone and steel — structures such as the gods might build for themselves! This animated picture is a part of the lives of millions of people every day. How many, I wonder, give it so much as a second glance? Very few, I fear. Their eyes are blind to this magnificent sight because it is so familiar to them.

I hurry to the top of one of those gigantic structures, the Empire State Building, for there, a short time ago, I "saw" the city below through the eyes of my secretary. I am anxious to compare my fancy with reality. I am sure I should not be disappointed in the panorama spread out before me, for to me it would be a vision of another world.

Now I begin my rounds of the city. First, I stand at a busy corner, merely looking at people, trying by sight of them to understand something of their lives. I see smiles, and I am happy. I see serious determination, and I am proud. I see suffering, and I am compassionate.

I stroll down Fifth Avenue. I throw my eyes out of focus so that I see no particular object but only a seething kaleidoscope of color. I am certain that the colors of women's dresses moving in a throng must be a gorgeous spectacle of which I should never tire. But perhaps if I had sight I should be like most other women — too interested in styles and the cut of individual dresses to give much attention to the splendor of color in the mass. And I am convinced, too, that I should become an inveterate window shopper, for it must be a delight to the eye to view the myriad articles of beauty on display.

From Fifth Avenue I make a tour of the city — to Park Avenue, to the slums, to factories, to parks where children play. I take a stay-at-home trip abroad by visiting the foreign quarters. Always my eyes are open wide to all the sights of both happiness and misery so that I may probe deep and add to my understanding of how people work and live. My heart is full of the images of people and things. My eye passes lightly over no single trifle; it strives to touch and hold closely each thing its gaze rests upon. Some sights are pleasant, filling the heart with happiness; but some are miserably pathetic. To these latter I do not shut my eyes, for they, too, are part of life. To close the eye on them is to close the heart and mind.

My third day of sight is drawing to an end. Perhaps there are many serious pursuits to which I should devote the few remaining hours, but I am afraid that on the evening of that last day I should again run away to the theater, to a hilariously funny play, so that I might appreciate the overtones of comedy in the human spirit.

At midnight my temporary respite from blindness would cease, and permanent night would close in on me again. Naturally in those three short days I should not have seen all I wanted to see. Only when darkness had again descended upon me should I realize how much I had left unseen. But my mind would be so crowded with glorious memories that I should have little time for regrets. Thereafter the touch of every object would bring a glowing memory of how that object looked.

Perhaps this short outline of how I should spend three days of sight does not agree with the program you would set for yourself if you knew that you were about to be stricken blind. I am, however, sure that if you actually faced that fate your eyes would open to things you had never seen before, storing up memories for the long night ahead. You would use your eyes as never before. Everything you saw would become dear to you. Your eyes would touch and embrace every object that came within your range of vision. Then, at last, you would really see, and a new world of beauty would open itself before you.

I who am blind can give one hint to those who see — one admonition to those who would make full use of the gift of sight: Use your eyes as if tomorrow you would be stricken blind. And the same method can be applied to the other senses. Hear the music of voices, the song of a bird, the mighty strains of an orchestra, as if you would be stricken deaf tomorrow. Touch each object you want to touch as if tomorrow your tactile sense would fail. Smell the perfume of flowers, taste with relish each morsel, as if tomorrow you could never smell and taste again. Make the most of every sense; glory in all the facts of pleasure and beauty which the world reveals to you through the several means of contact which Nature provides. But of all the senses, I am sure that sight must be the most delightful.

PROBING FOR
MEANING

1. Do you agree with Keller's statement that "most people would be chastened by the certainty of impending death" rather than adopting the motto of "Eat, drink, and be merry"? Is it true that the only people who appreciate life are those who live or have lived near death, either their own or someone else's?

2. Do we take our senses for granted as well as our life? Do only the deaf and blind appreciate hearing and seeing? What would be the curriculum of a college course in "How to Use Your Eyes"?

3. What priorities does Keller establish for what she would like to see in her three allotted days of sight? She says others would not agree with her program. How would your priorities compare with hers?

4. Do you agree that you have to see people really to know them? Why does she think so? Do you agree that we are as unobservant about even our close friends as she claims?

5. Why would she visit museums on her second day of sight? Why does she say that our "urge to artistic expression has been almost as powerful as the urge for food, shelter, and procreation"? How does her desire to visit the theater relate to her visit to the museums?

6. How would your tour of New York or any other large city differ from hers? Why does she choose a city?

7. Helen Keller was both deaf and blind, yet she chose sight as "the most delightful" of all the senses. Do you agree with her choice?

PROBING FOR
METHOD

1. Where does Keller's introduction end? Where does her thesis statement occur? What technique does she employ in this rather lengthy introduction?

2. Why does she choose three days rather than two, four, or any other number?

3. What is her purpose in constantly referring to and asking questions of the reader?

4. Her illustration of how to appreciate life grows very naturally out of her own experience as a person blind from infancy. What other illustrations of her theme does she mention? Can you think of illustrations other than those she mentioned of having only three days to live or see?

5. To what extent does her conclusion build a frame around her essay? Does it refer to the introduction in any way?

PLATO

The Allegory of the Cave

Next, said I, here is a parable to illustrate the degrees in which our nature may be enlightened or unenlightened. Imagine the condition of men living in a sort of cavernous chamber underground, with an entrance open to the light and a long passage all down the cave. Here they have been from childhood, chained by the leg and also by the neck, so that they cannot move and can see only what is in front of them, because the chains will not let them turn their heads. At some distance higher up is the light of a fire burning behind them; and between the prisoners and the fire is a track with a parapet built along it, like the screen at a puppet-show, which hides the performers while they show their puppets over the top.

I see, said he.

Now behind this parapet imagine persons carrying along various artificial objects, including figures of men and animals in wood or stone or other materials, which project above the parapet. Naturally, some of these persons will be talking, others silent.

It is a strange picture, he said, and a strange sort of prisoners.

Like ourselves, I replied; for in the first place prisoners so confined would have seen nothing of themselves or of one another, except the shadows thrown by the firelight on the wall of the Cave facing them, would they?

Not if all their lives they had been prevented from moving their heads.

And they would have seen as little of the objects carried past.

Of course.

Now, if they could talk to one another, would they not suppose that their words referred only to those passing shadows which they saw?

Necessarily.

And suppose their prison had an echo from the wall facing them? When one of the people crossing behind them spoke, they could only suppose that the sound came from the shadow passing before their eyes.

No doubt.

In every way, then, such prisoners would recognize as reality nothing but the shadows of those artificial objects.

Inevitably.

Now consider what would happen if their release from the chains and the healing of their unwisdom should come about in this way. Suppose one of them were set free and forced suddenly to stand up, turn his head, and walk with eyes lifted to the light; all these movements would be painful, and he would be too dazzled to make out the objects whose shadows he had been used to see. What do you think he would say, if someone told him that what he had formerly seen was meaningless illusion, but now, being somewhat nearer to reality and turned towards more real objects, he was getting a truer view? Suppose further that he were shown the various objects being carried by and were made to say, in reply to questions, what each of them was. Would he not be perplexed and believe the objects now shown him to be not so real as what he formerly saw?

Yes, not nearly so real.

And if he were forced to look at the fire-light itself, would not his eyes ache, so that he would try to escape and turn back to the things which he could see distinctly, convinced that they really were clearer than these other objects now being shown to him?

Yes.

And suppose someone were to drag him away forcibly up the steep and rugged ascent and not let him go until he had hauled him out into the sunlight, would he not suffer pain and vexation at such treatment, and, when he had come out into the light, find his eyes so full of its radiance that he could not see a single one of the things that he was now told were real?

Certainly he would not see them all at once.

He would need, then, to grow accustomed before he could see things in that upper world. At first it would be easiest to make out shadows, and then the images of men and things reflected in water, and later on the things themselves. After that, it would be easier to watch the heavenly bodies and the sky itself by night, looking at the light of the moon and stars rather than the Sun and the Sun's light in the daytime.

Yes, surely.

Last of all, he would be able to look at the Sun and contemplate its nature, not as it appears when reflected in water or any alien medium, but as it is in itself in its own domain.

No doubt.

And now he would begin to draw the conclusion that it is the Sun that produces the seasons and the course of the year and controls everything in the visible world, and moreover is in a way the cause of all that he and his companions used to see.

Clearly he would come at last to that conclusion.

Then if he called to mind his fellow prisoners and what passed for wisdom in his former dwelling-place, he would surely think himself

happy in the change and be sorry for them. They may have had a practice of honouring and commending one another, with prizes for the
man who had the keenest eye for the passing shadows and the best
memory for the order in which they followed or accompanied one another, so that he would make a good guess as to which was going to
come next. Would our released prisoner be likely to covet those prizes
or to envy the men exalted to honour and power in the Cave? Would he
not feel like Homer's Achilles, that he would far sooner be on earth as a
hired servant in the house of a landless man or endure anything rather
than go back to his old beliefs and live in the old way?

Yes, he would prefer any fate to such a life.

Now imagine what would happen if he went down again to
take his former seat in the Cave. Coming suddenly out of the sunlight,
his eyes would be filled with darkness. He might be required once more
to deliver his opinion on those shadows, in competition with the prisoners who had never been released, while his eyesight was still dim and
unsteady; and it might take some time to become used to the darkness.
They would laugh at him and say that he had gone up only to come
back with his sight ruined; it was worth no one's while even to attempt
the ascent. If they could lay hands on the man who was trying to set
them free and lead them up, they would kill him.

Yes, they would.

Every feature in this parable, my dear Glaucon, is meant to fit
our earlier analysis. The prison dwelling corresponds to the region revealed to us through the sense of sight, and the fire-light within it to the
power of the Sun. The ascent to see the things in the upper world you
may take as standing for the upward journey of the soul into the region
of the intelligible; then you will be in possession of what I surmise,
since that is what you wish to be told. Heaven knows whether it is true;
but this, at any rate, is how it appears to me. In the world of knowledge,
the last thing to be perceived and only with great difficulty is the essential Form of Goodness. Once it is perceived, the conclusion must follow
that, for all things, this is the cause of whatever is right and good; in the
visible world it gives birth to light and to the lord of light, while it is
itself sovereign in the intelligible world and the parent of intelligence
and truth. Without having had a vision of this Form no one can act with
wisdom, either in his own life or in matters of state.

PROBING FOR   1. An allegory or parable is a concrete story on one level and an ex-
MEANING   plication of abstract, moral truths on another. Plato explains at the end what
each part of his story symbolizes on the oral level. What correspondences does
he establish?

2. If we assume that the people in the cave represent humankind, why
does Plato call them "prisoners"? Plato is not specific as to who placed the

people in chains, but who seems to be the jailer when the freed prisoner returns to free the others?

    3. Plato equates making the "ascent to see the things in the upper world" on the story level with gaining knowledge on the abstract level. Why, instead of making the ascent, would people prefer to remain in the cave with illusions of what is real? Do you agree with Plato's analysis of human nature here? Explain.

    4. Plato says of the man who returns to the cave after seeing the sun, "If they could lay hands on [him] . . . they would kill him." Are there historical or contemporary situations that fulfill this prediction?

PROBING FOR METHOD

    1. Plato's essay is presented as a dialogue between teacher and student. What contribution to structure and theme is made by the brief comments of the student?

    2. What logical plan of organization can be seen at work within this essay?

    3. Why is Plato's language so simple? How does it compare with Lindbergh's in "Channelled Whelk"? What purpose does his language serve?

    4. Is Plato's final comment upon the allegory necessary, or would you have been able to fit together its features without this ending?

 HENRY DAVID THOREAU

The Village

    After hoeing, or perhaps reading and writing, in the forenoon, I usually bathed again in the pond, swimming across one of its coves for a stint, and washed the dust of labor from my person, or smoothed out the last wrinkle which study had made, and for the afternoon was absolutely free. Every day or two I strolled to the village to hear some of the gossip which is incessantly going on there, circulating either from mouth to mouth, or from newspaper to newspaper, and which, taken in homœopathic doses, was really as refreshing in its way as the rustle of leaves and the peeping of frogs. As I walked in the woods to see the birds and squirrels, so I walked in the village to see the men and boys; instead of the wind among the pines I heard the carts rattle. In one direction from my house there was a colony of muskrats in the river

meadows; under the grove of elms and buttonwoods in the other horizon was a village of busy men, as curious to me as if they had been
prairie-dogs, each sitting at the mouth of its burrow, or running over to
a neighbor's to gossip. I went there frequently to observe their habits.

The village appeared to me a great news room; and on one side,
to support it, as once at Redding & Company's on State Street, they
kept nuts and raisins, or salt and meal and other groceries. Some have
such a vast appetite for the former commodity, that is, the news, and
such sound digestive organs, that they can sit forever in public avenues
without stirring, and let it simmer and whisper through them like the
Etesian winds, or as if inhaling ether, it only producing numbness and
insensibility to pain, — otherwise it would often be painful to hear, —
without affecting the consciousness. I hardly ever failed, when I ram-
bled through the village, to see a row of such worthies, either sitting on
a ladder sunning themselves, with their bodies inclined forward and
their eyes glancing along the line this way and that, from time to time,
with a voluptuous expression, or else leaning against a barn with their
hands in their pockets, like caryatides, as if to prop it up. They, being
commonly out of doors, heard whatever was in the wind. These are the
coarsest mills, in which all gossip is first rudely digested or cracked up
before it is emptied into finer and more delicate hoppers within doors.

I observed that the vitals of the village were the grocery, the
bar-room, the post-office, and the bank; and, as a necessary part of the
machinery, they kept a bell, a big gun, and a fire-engine, at convenient
places; and the houses were so arranged as to make the most of mankind, in lanes and fronting one another, so that every traveller had to
run the gauntlet, and every man, woman, and child might get a lick at
him. Of course, those who were stationed nearest to the head of the
line, where they could most see and be seen, and have the first blow at
him, paid the highest prices for their places; and the few straggling inhabitants in the outskirts, where long gaps in the line began to occur,
and the traveller could get over walls or turn aside into cow-paths, and
so escape, paid a very slight ground or window tax. Signs were hung
out on all sides to allure him; some to catch him by the appetite, as the
tavern and victualling cellar; some by the fancy, as the dry goods store
and the jeweller's; and others by the hair or the feet or the skirts, as the
barber, the shoemaker, or the tailor. Besides, there was a still more terrible standing invitation to call at every one of these houses, and company expected about these times.

For the most part I escaped wonderfully from these dangers,
either by proceeding at once boldly and without deliberation to the
goal, as is recommended to those who run the gauntlet, or by keeping
my thoughts on high things, like Orpheus, who "loudly singing the
praises of the gods to his lyre, drowned the voices of the Sirens, and
kept out of danger." Sometimes I bolted suddenly, and nobody could

tell my whereabouts, for I did not stand much about gracefulness, and never hesitated at a gap in a fence. I was even accustomed to make an irruption into some houses, where I was well entertained, and after learning the kernels and very last sievefull of views, — what had subsided, the prospects of war and peace, and whether the world was likely to hold together much longer, — I was let out through the real avenues, and so escaped to the woods again.

It was very pleasant, when I stayed late in town, to launch myself into the night, especially if it was dark and tempestuous, and set sail from some bright village parlor or lecture room, with a bag of rye or Indian meal upon my shoulder, for my snug harbor in the woods, having made all tight without and withdrawn under hatches with a merry crew of thoughts, leaving only my outer man at the helm, or even tying up the helm when it was plain sailing. I had many a genial thought by the cabin fire "as I sailed." I was never cast away nor distressed in any weather, though I encountered some severe storms. It is darker in the woods, even in common nights, than most suppose. I frequently had to look up at the opening between the trees above the path in order to learn my route, and, where there was no cartpath, to feel with my feet the faint track which I had worn, or steer by the known relation of particular trees which I felt with my hands, passing between two pines for instance, not more than eighteen inches apart, in the midst of the woods, invariably, in the darkest night. Sometimes, after coming home thus late in a dark and muggy night, when my feet felt the path which my eyes could not see, dreaming and absent-minded all the way, until I was aroused by having to raise my hand to lift the latch, I have not been able to recall a single step of my walk, and I have thought that perhaps my body would find its way home if its master should forsake it, as the hand finds its way to the mouth without assistance.

Several times, when a visitor chanced to stay into evening, and it proved a dark night, I was obliged to conduct him to the cartpath in the rear of the house, and then point out to him the direction he was to pursue, and in keeping which he was to be guided rather by his feet than his eyes. One very dark night I directed thus on their way two young men who had been fishing in the pond. They lived about a mile off through the woods, and were quite used to the route. A day or two after one of them told me that they wandered about the greater part of the night, close by their own premises, and did not get home till toward morning, by which time, as there had been several heavy showers in the meanwhile, and the leaves were very wet, they were drenched to their skins. I have heard of many going astray even in the village streets, when the darkness was so thick that you could cut it with a knife, as the saying is. Some who live in the outskirts, having come to town a-shopping in their wagons, have been obliged to put up for the night; and gentlemen and ladies making a call have gone half a mile out of their way, feeling the sidewalk only with their feet, and not knowing when they turned.

It is a surprising and memorable, as well as valuable experience, to be lost in the woods any time. Often in a snow-storm, even by day, one will come out upon a well-known road and yet find it impossible to tell which way leads to the village. Though he knows that he has travelled it a thousand times, he cannot recognize a feature in it, but it is as strange to him as if it were a road in Siberia. By night, of course, the perplexity is infinitely greater. In our most trivial walks, we are constantly, though unconsciously, steering like pilots by certain well-known beacons and headlands, and if we go beyond our usual course we still carry in our minds the bearing of some neighboring cape; and not till we are completely lost, or turned round, — for a man needs only to be turned round once with his eyes shut in this world to be lost, — do we appreciate the vastness and strangeness of nature. Every man has to learn the points of compass again as often as he awakes, whether from sleep or any abstraction. Not till we are lost, in other words not till we have lost the world, do we begin to find ourselves, and realize where we are and the infinite extent of our relations.

One afternoon, near the end of the first summer, when I went to the village to get a shoe from the cobbler's, I was seized and put into jail, because, as I have elsewhere related, I did not pay a tax to, or recognize the authority of, the State which buys and sells men, women, and children, like cattle, at the door of its senate-house. I had gone down to the woods for other purposes. But, wherever a man goes, men will pursue and paw him with their dirty institutions, and, if they can, constrain him to belong to their desperate odd-fellow society. It is true, I might have resisted forcibly with more or less effect, might have run "amok" against society; but I preferred that society should run "amok" against me, it being the desperate party. However, I was released the next day, obtained my mended shoe, and returned to the woods in season to get my dinner of huckleberries on Fair Haven Hill. I was never molested by any person but those who represented the State. I had no lock nor bolt but for the desk which held my papers, not even a nail to put over my latch or windows. I never fastened my door night or day, though I was to be absent several days; not even when the next fall I spent a fortnight in the woods of Maine. And yet my house was more respected than if it had been surrounded by a file of soldiers. The tired rambler could rest and warm himself by my fire, the literary amuse himself with the few books on my table, or the curious, by opening my closet door, see what was left of my dinner, and what prospect I had of a supper. Yet, though many people of every class came this way to the pond, I suffered no serious inconvenience from these sources, and I never missed anything but one small book, a volume of Homer, which perhaps was improperly gilded, and this I trust a soldier of our camp has found by this time.

I am convinced, that if all men were to live as simply as I then did, thieving and robbery would be unknown. These take place only in communities where some have got more than is sufficient while others have not enough. The Pope's Homers would soon get properly distributed.

> "Nec bella fuerunt,
> Faginus astabat dum scyphus ante dapes."

> "Nor wars did men molest,
> When only beechen bowls were in request."

"You who govern public affairs, what need have you to employ punishments? Love virtue, and the people will be virtuous. The virtues of a superior man are like the wind; the virtues of a common man are like the grass; the grass, when the wind passes over it, bends."

PROBING FOR MEANING

1. What impression of life in his cabin in the woods around Walden Pond does Thoreau give in the first sentence of the essay?

2. What comparisons and contrasts does he make between the pond and the village? What does *homœopathic* mean? How does its meaning further convey his attitudes toward woods and village?

3. What characteristics of the village does he mention? Why does he say he "escaped" to the woods again?

4. How is he able to find his way through the woods in the dark? Many travellers, he says, lose their way at night. How does this relate to Helen Keller's theory about not using all our senses?

5. "Not till we are lost, in other words not till we have lost the world, do we begin to find ourselves, and realize where we are and the infinite extent of our relations." Could this be the thesis statement of Thoreau's essay? How does it relate to the thesis statement of Helen Keller's essay? Is Thoreau hinting at a profounder meaning in his essay that was not at first obvious?

6. Notice that near the end of the essay, when Thoreau recounts his imprisonment for not paying his taxes, he equates the village with "the State." To what extent is the essay an allegory of civilization versus nature, with the village representing civilization and the woods near Walden Pond symbolizing nature? What is Thoreau saying about civilization? about living apart from it?

7. What major complaint does Thoreau have against the village? Why did the village become "the desperate party" in its dealings with him? How and why is the pond (or woods) life preferable?

8. How similar are Thoreau's and Anne Morrow Lindbergh's notions of simplicity?

PROBING FOR METHOD

1. Thoreau uses many comparisons to convey more vividly his various points. What comparisons, for example, does he make in describing the similarities between the village and his house near the pond?

2. Locate the story of Orpheus and the Sirens from Greek mythology. How does this myth help to convey Thoreau's attitude toward the village?

3. Thoreau uses two metaphors in describing his jaunts through the village and later his journey home through the woods. What are these metaphors? How successful are they?

4. Compare his introduction with his conclusion. Are they similar in theme? What accounts for their dissimilarity in tone?

 E. M. FORSTER

My Wood

A few years ago I wrote a book which dealt in part with the difficulties of the English in India. Feeling that they would have no difficulties in India themselves, the Americans read the book freely. The more they read it the better it made them feel, and a cheque to the author was the result. I bought a wood with the cheque. It is not a large wood — it contains scarcely any trees, and it is intersected, blast it, by a public footpath. Still, it is the first property that I have owned, so it is right that other people should participate in my shame, and should ask themselves, in accents that will vary in horror, this very important question: What is the effect of property upon the character? Don't let's touch economics; the effect of private ownership upon the community as a whole is another question — a more important question, perhaps, but another one. Let's keep to psychology. If you own things, what's their effect on you? What's the effect on me of my wood?

In the first place, it makes me feel heavy. Property does have this effect. Property produces men of weight, and it was a man of weight who failed to get into the Kingdom of Heaven. He was not wicked, the unfortunate millionaire in the parable, he was only stout; he stuck out in front, not to mention behind, and as he wedged himself this way and that in the crystalline entrance and bruised his well-fed flanks, he saw beneath him a comparatively slim camel passing through the eye of a needle and being woven into the robe of God. The Gospels all through couple stoutness and slowness. They point out what is perfectly obvious, yet seldom realized: that if you have a lot of things you cannot move about a lot, that furniture requires dusting, dusters require servants, servants require insurance stamps, and the whole tangle of them makes you think twice before you accept an invitation to dinner or go for a bathe in the Jordan. Sometimes the Gospels proceed further and say with Tolstoy that property is sinful; they approach the difficult ground of asceticism here, where I cannot follow them. But as to the immediate effects of property on people, they just show straightforward logic. It produces men of weight. Men of weight cannot, by definition, move like the lightning from the East unto the West, and the ascent of a fourteen-stone bishop into a pulpit is thus the exact antithesis of the coming of the Son of Man. My wood makes me feel heavy.

In the second place, it makes me feel it ought to be larger.

The other day I heard a twig snap in it. I was annoyed at first, for I thought that someone was blackberrying, and depreciating the value of the undergrowth. On coming nearer, I saw it was not a man who had trodden on the twig and snapped it, but a bird, and I felt pleased. My bird. The bird was not equally pleased. Ignoring the relation between us, it took fright as soon as it saw the shape of my face, and flew straight over the boundary hedge into a field, the property of Mrs. Henessy, where it sat down with a loud squawk. It had become Mrs. Henessy's bird. Something seemed grossly amiss here, something that would not have occurred had the wood been larger. I could not afford to buy Mrs. Henessy out, I dared not murder her, and limitations of this sort beset me on every side. Ahab did not want that vineyard — he only needed it to round off his property, preparatory to plotting a new curve — and all the land around my wood has become necessary to me in order to round off the wood. A boundary protects. But — poor little thing — the boundary ought in its turn to be protected. Noises on the edge of it. Children throw stones. A little more, and then a little more, until we reach the sea. Happy Canute! Happier Alexander! And after all, why should even the world be the limit of possession? A rocket containing a Union Jack, will, it is hoped, be shortly fired at the moon. Mars. Sirius. Beyond which . . . But these immensities ended by saddening me. I could not suppose that my wood was the destined nucleus of universal dominion — it is so very small and contains no mineral wealth beyond the blackberries. Nor was I comforted when Mrs. Henessy's bird took alarm for the second time and flew clean away from us all, under the belief that it belonged to itself.

In the third place, property makes its owner feel that he ought to do something to it. Yet he isn't sure what. A restlessness comes over him, a vague sense that he has a personality to express — the same sense which, without any vagueness, leads the artist to an act of creation. Sometimes I think I will cut down such trees as remain in the wood, at other times I want to fill up the gaps between them with new trees. Both impulses are pretentious and empty. They are not honest movements towards money-making or beauty. They spring from a foolish desire to express myself and from an inability to enjoy what I have got. Creation, property, enjoyment form a sinister trinity in the human mind. Creation and enjoyment are both very, very good, yet they are often unattainable without a material basis, and at such moments property pushes itself in as a substitute, saying, "Accept me instead — I'm good enough for all three." It is not enough. It is, as Shakespeare said of lust, "The expense of spirit in a waste of shame"; it is "Before, a joy proposed; behind, a dream." Yet we don't know how to shun it. It is forced on us by our economic system as the alternative to starvation. It is also forced on us by an internal defect in the soul, by the feeling that in property may lie the germs of self-development and of exquisite or heroic deeds. Our life on earth is, and ought to be, material and carnal. But we have not yet learned to manage our materialism and carnality properly; they are still entangled with the desire for ownership, where (in the words of Dante) "Possession is one with loss."

And this brings us to our fourth and final point: the blackberries.

Blackberries are not plentiful in this meagre grove, but they are easily seen from the public footpath which traverses it, and all too easily gathered. Foxgloves, too — people will pull up the foxgloves, and ladies of an educational tendency even grub for toadstools to show them on the Monday in class. Other ladies, less educated, roll down the bracken in the arms of their gentlemen friends. There is paper, there are tins. Pray, does my wood belong to me or doesn't it? And, if it does, should I not own it best by allowing no one else to walk there? There is a wood near Lyme Regis, also cursed by a public footpath, where the owner has not hesitated on this point. He has built high stone walls each side of the path, and has spanned it by bridges, so that the public circulate like termites while he gorges on the blackberries unseen. He really does own his wood, this able chap. Dives in Hell did pretty well, but the gulf dividing him from Lazarus could be traversed by vision, and nothing traverses it here. And perhaps I shall come to this in time. I shall wall in and fence out until I really taste the sweets of property. Enormously stout, endlessly avaricious, pseudo-creative, intensely selfish, I shall weave upon my forehead the quadruple crown of possession until those nasty Bolshies come and take it off again and thrust me aside into the outer darkness.

PROBING FOR-
MEANING

1. Why does Forster say that the effect of private ownership upon the community is another, perhaps more important, issue than its effect is upon character?

2. How do the examples Forster uses in his second paragraph illustrate the first effect of property on character? Do you agree that property produces men of weight? Are people more virtuous if they have fewer possessions?

3. Who are Ahab, Canute, and Alexander? From what you know or can learn about their lives, why are they good examples of Forster's second effect? Does ownership always make one more greedy?

4. What effect does the last sentence in the fourth paragraph have on the meaning of the paragraph?

5. "Creation, property, enjoyment form a sinister trinity in the human mind." What does Forster mean by this statement? What examples does he give to explain it? What examples can you add of your own? Is property in your opinion a substitute for creativity?

6. Explain Dante's words, "Possession is one with loss."

7. What point does Forster make with the example of the blackberries? Do you agree that property generally has this effect?

8. Who are the "nasty Bolshies" mentioned in the last paragraph? What does this sentence contribute to the essay?

PROBING FOR METHOD

1. Forster leads into his introduction by commenting that Americans provided him with the money to purchase his wood. For what reason does Forster mention Americans in an introduction to an essay on materialism? What attitude does he have toward them?

2. What attitude toward his wood does Forster have? Do the words "shame" and "horror" used in paragraph 1 desribe his tone in any way? How does the last sentence of the essay contribute to tone?

3. Forster's organization is perfectly clear. What devices does he use to convey the movement of the essay? Is this device effective? Why don't all writers mark each section of their essays as clearly?

4. What would the essay have been like without all the examples Forster uses? Would it have been as effective?

5. While Forster's essay uses concrete examples throughout, his thesis is the abstract one that property affects us adversely. Much of his language is also abstract; what, for example, do the words *antithesis, trinity, carnality, avaricious,* and *pseudo-creative* mean? How, in each case, do they relate either to his thesis or to his example?

 ALBERT CAMUS

The Guest

The schoolmaster was watching the two men climb toward him. One was on horseback, the other on foot. They had not yet tackled the abrupt rise leading to the schoolhouse built on the hillside. They were toiling onward, making slow progress in the snow, among the stones, on the vast expanse of the high, deserted plateau. From time to time the horse stumbled. Without hearing anything yet, he could see the breath issuing from the horse's nostrils. One of the men, at least, knew the region. They were following the trail although it had disappeared days ago under a layer of dirty white snow. The schoolmaster calculated that it would take them half an hour to get onto the hill. It was cold; he went back into the school to get a sweater.

He crossed the empty, frigid classroom. On the blackboard the four rivers of France, drawn with four different colored chalks, had been flowing toward their estuaries for the past three days. Snow had suddenly fallen in mid-October after eight months of drought without the transition of rain, and the twenty pupils, more or less, who lived in the villages scattered over the plateau had stopped coming. With fair weather they would return. Daru now heated only the single room that was his lodging, adjoining the classroom and giving also onto the plateau to the east. Like the class windows, his window looked to the south too. On that side the school was a few kilometers from the point where the plateau began to slope toward the south. In clear weather could be seen the purple mass of the mountain range where the gap opened onto the desert.

Somewhat warmed, Daru returned to the window from which he had first seen the two men. They were no longer visible. Hence they must have tackled the rise. The sky was not so dark, for the snow had stopped falling during the night. The morning had opened with a dirty light which had scarcely become brighter as the ceiling of clouds lifted. At two in the afternoon it seemed as if the day were merely beginning. But still this was better than those three days when the thick snow was falling amidst unbroken darkness with little gusts of wind that rattled the double door of the classroom. Then Daru had spent long hours in his room, leaving it only to go to the shed and feed the chickens or get some coal. Fortunately the delivery truck from Tadjid, the nearest village to the north, had brought his supplies two days before the blizzard. It would return in forty-eight hours.

Besides, he had enough to resist a siege, for the little room was cluttered with bags of wheat that the administration left as a stock to distribute to those of his pupils whose families had suffered from the drought. Actually they had all been victims because they were all poor. Every day Daru would distribute a ration to the children. They had missed it, he knew, during these bad days. Possibly one of the fathers or big brothers would come this afternoon and he could supply them with grain. It was just a matter of carrying them over to the next harvest. Now shiploads of wheat were arriving from France and the worst was over. But it would be hard to forget that poverty, that army of ragged ghosts wandering in the sunlight, the plateaus burned to a cinder month after month, the earth shriveled up little by little, literally scorched, every stone bursting into dust under one's foot. The sheep had died then by thousands and even a few men, here and there, sometimes without anyone's knowing.

In contrast with such poverty, he who lived almost like a monk in his remote schoolhouse, nonetheless satisfied with the little he had and with the rough life, had felt like a lord with his white-washed walls, his narrow couch, his unpainted shelves, his well, and his provision of water and food. And suddenly this snow, without warning, without the foretaste of rain. This is the way the region was, cruel to live in, even without men — who didn't help matters either. But Daru had been born here. Everywhere else, he felt exiled.

He stepped out onto the terrace in front of the schoolhouse. The two men were now halfway up the slope. He recognized the horseman as Balducci, the old gendarme he had known for a long time. Balducci was holding on the end of a rope an Arab who was walking behind him with hands bound and head lowered. The gendarme waved a greeting to which Daru did not reply, lost as he was in contemplation of the Arab dressed in a faded blue jellaba, his feet in sandals but covered with socks of heavy raw wool, his head surmounted by a narrow, short *chèche*. They were approaching. Balducci was holding back his horse in order not to hurt the Arab and the group was advancing slowly.

Within earshot, Balducci shouted: "One hour to do the three kilometers from El Ameur!" Daru did not answer. Short and square in his thick sweater, he watched them climb. Not once had the Arab raised his head. "Hello," said Daru when they got up onto the terrace. "Come in and warm up." Balducci painfully got down from his horse without letting go the rope. From under his bristling mustache he smiled at the schoolmaster. His little dark eyes, deep-set under a tanned forehead, and his mouth surrounded with wrinkles made him look attentive and studious. Daru took the bridle, led the horse to the shed, and came back to the two men, who were now waiting for him in the school. He led them into his room. "I am going to heat up the classroom," he said. "We'll be more comfortable there." When he entered the room again, Balducci was on the couch. He had undone the rope tying him to the Arab, who had squatted near the stove. His hands still bound, the *chèche* pushed back on his head, he was looking toward the window. At first Daru noticed only his huge lips, fat, smooth, almost Negroid; yet his nose was straight, his eyes were dark and full of fever. The *chèche* revealed an obstinate forehead and, under the weathered skin now rather discolored by the cold, the whole face had a restless and rebellious look that struck Daru when the Arab, turning his face toward him, looked him straight in the eyes. "Go into the other room," said the schoolmaster, "and I'll make you some mint tea." "Thanks," Balducci said. "What a chore! How I long for retirement." And addressing his prisoner in Arabic: "Come on, you." The Arab got up and, slowly, holding his bound wrists in front of him, went into the classroom.

With the tea, Daru brought a chair. But Balducci was already enthroned on the nearest pupil's desk and the Arab had squatted against the teacher's platform facing the stove, which stood between the desk and the window. When he held out the glass of tea to the prisoner, Daru hesitated at the sight of his bound hands. "He might perhaps be untied." "Sure," said Balducci. "That was for the trip." He started to get to his feet. But Daru, setting the glass on the floor, had knelt beside the Arab. Without saying anything, the Arab watched him with his feverish eyes. Once his hands were free, he rubbed his swollen wrists against each other, took the glass of tea, and sucked up the burning liquid in swift little sips.

"Good," said Daru. "And where are you headed?"

Balducci withdrew his mustache from the tea. "Here, son."

"Odd pupils! And you're spending the night?"

"No. I'm going back to El Ameur. And you will deliver this fellow to Tinguit. He is expected at police headquarters."

Balducci was looking at Daru with a friendly little smile.

"What's this story?" asked the schoolmaster. "Are you pulling my leg?"

"No, son. Those are the orders."

"The orders? I'm not . . ." Daru hesitated, not wanting to hurt the old Corsican. "I mean, that's not my job."

"What! What's the meaning of that? In wartime people do all kinds of jobs."

"Then I'll wait for the declaration of war!"

Balducci nodded.

"O.K. But the orders exist and they concern you too. Things are brewing, it appears. There is talk of a forthcoming revolt. We are mobilized, in a way."

Daru still had his obstinate look.

"Listen, son," Balducci said. "I like you and you must understand. There's only a dozen of us at El Ameur to patrol throughout the whole territory of a small department and I must get back in a hurry. I was told to hand this guy over to you and return without delay. He couldn't be kept there. His village was beginning to stir; they wanted to take him back. You must take him to Tanguit tomorrow before the day is over. Twenty kilometers shouldn't faze a husky fellow like you. After that, all will be over. You'll come back to your pupils and your comfortable life."

Behind the wall the horse could be heard snorting and pawing the earth. Daru was looking out the window. Decidedly, the weather was clearing and the light was increasing over the snowy plateau. When all the snow was melted, the sun would take over again and once more would burn the fields of stone. For days, still, the unchanging sky would shed its dry light on the solitary expanse where nothing had any connection with man.

"After all," he said, turning around toward Balducci, "what did he do?" And, before the gendarme had opened his mouth, he asked: "Does he speak French?"

"No, not a word. We had been looking for him for a month, but they were hiding him. He killed his cousin."

"Is he against us?"

"I don't think so. But you can never be sure."

"Why did he kill?"

"A family squabble, I think. One owed the other grain, it seems. It's not at all clear. In short, he killed his cousin with a billhook. You know, like a sheep, *kreezk!*"

Balducci made the gesture of drawing a blade across his throat and the Arab, his attention attracted, watched him with a sort of anxiety. Daru felt a sudden wrath against the man, against all men with their rotten spite, their tireless hates, their blood lust.

But the kettle was singing on the stove. He served Balducci more tea, hesitated, then served the Arab again, who, a second time, drank avidly. His raised arms made the jellaba fall open and the schoolmaster saw his thin, muscular chest.

"Thanks, kid," Balducci said. "And now, I'm off."

He got up and went toward the Arab, taking a small rope from his pocket.

"What are you doing?" Daru asked dryly.

Balducci, disconcerted, showed him the rope.

"Don't bother."

The old gendarme hesitated. "It's up to you. Of course, you are armed?"

"I have my shotgun."

"Where?"

"In the trunk."

"You ought to have it near your bed."

"Why? I have nothing to fear."

"You're crazy, son. If there's an uprising, no one is safe, we're all in the same boat."

"I'll defend myself. I'll have time to see them coming."

Balducci began to laugh, then suddenly the mustache covered the white teeth.

"You'll have time? O.K. That's just what I was saying. You have always been a little cracked. That's why I like you, my son was like that."

At the same time he took out his revolver and put it on the desk.

"Keep it; I don't need two weapons from here to El Ameur."

The revolver shone against the black paint of the table. When the gendarme turned toward him, the schoolmaster caught the smell of leather and horseflesh.

"Listen, Balducci," Daru said suddenly, "every bit of this disgusts me, and first of all your fellow here. But I won't hand him over. Fight, yes, if I have to. But not that."

The old gendarme stood in front of him and looked at him severely.

"You're being a fool," he said slowly. "I don't like it either. You don't get used to putting a rope on a man even after years of it, and you're even ashamed — yes, ashamed. But you can't let them have their way."

"I won't hand him over," Daru said again.

"It's an order, son, and I repeat it."

"That's right. Repeat to them what I've said to you: I won't hand him over."

Balducci made a visible effort to reflect. He looked at the Arab and at Daru. At last he decided.

"No, I won't tell them anything. If you want to drop us, go ahead; I'll not denounce you. I have an order to deliver the prisoner and I'm doing so. And now you'll just sign this paper for me."

"There's no need. I'll not deny that you left him with me."

"Don't be mean with me. I know you'll tell the truth. You're from hereabouts and you are a man. But you must sign, that's the rule."

Daru opened his drawer, took out a little square bottle of purple ink, the red wooden penholder with the "sergeant-major" pen he used for making models of penmanship, and signed. The gendarme carefully folded the paper and put it into his wallet. Then he moved toward the door.

"I'll see you off," Daru said.

"No," said Balducci. "There's no use being polite. You insulted me."

He looked at the Arab, motionless in the same spot, sniffed peevishly, and turned away toward the door. "Good-by, son," he said. The door shut behind him. Balducci appeared suddenly outside the window and then disappeared. His footsteps were muffled by the snow. The house stirred on the other side of the wall and several chickens fluttered in fright. A moment later Balducci reappeared outside the window leading the horse by the bridle. He walked toward the little rise without turning around and disappeared from sight with the horse following him. A big stone could be heard bouncing down. Daru walked back toward the prisoner, who, without stirring, never took his eyes off him. "Wait," the schoolmaster said in Arabic and went toward the bedroom. As he was going through the door, he had a second thought, went to the desk, took the revolver, and stuck it in his pocket. Then, without looking back, he went into his room.

For some time he lay on his couch watching the sky gradually close over, listening to the silence. It was this silence that had seemed painful to him during the first days here, after the war. He had requested a post in the little town at the base of the foothills separating the upper plateaus from the desert. There, rocky walls, green and black to the north, pink and lavender to the south, marked the frontier of eternal summer. He had been named to a post farther north, on the plateau itself. In the beginning, the solitude and the silence had been hard for him on those wastelands peopled only by stones. Occasionally, furrows suggested cultivation, but they had been dug to uncover a certain kind of stone good for building. The only plowing here was to harvest rocks. Elsewhere a thin layer of soil accumulated in the hollows would be scraped out to enrich paltry village gardens. This is the way it was: bare rock covered three quarters of the region. Towns sprang up, flourished, then disappeared; men came by, loved one another or fought bitterly, then died. No one in this desert, neither he nor his guest, mattered. And yet, outside this desert neither of them, Daru knew, could have really lived.

When he got up, no noise came from the classroom. He was amazed at the unmixed joy he derived from the mere thought that the Arab might have fled and that he would be alone with no decision to make. But the prisoner was there. He had merely stretched out between the stove and the desk. With eyes open, he was staring at the ceiling. In that position, his thick lips were particularly noticeable, giving him a pouting look. "Come," said Daru. The Arab got up and followed him. In the bedroom, the schoolmaster pointed to a chair near the table under the window. The Arab sat down without taking his eyes off Daru.

"Are you hungry?"

"Yes," the prisoner said.

Daru set the table for two. He took flour and oil, shaped a cake in a frying-pan, and lighted the little stove that functioned on bottled gas. While the cake was cooking, he went out to the shed to get cheese, eggs, dates, and condensed milk. When the cake was done he set it on the window sill to cool, heated some condensed milk diluted with water, and beat up the eggs into an omelette. In one of his motions he knocked against the revolver stuck in his right pocket. He set the bowl down, went into the classroom, and put the revolver in his desk drawer. When he came back to the room, night was falling. He put on the light and served the Arab. "Eat," he said. The Arab took a piece of the cake, lifted it eagerly to his mouth, and stopped short.

"And you?" he asked.

"After you. I'll eat too."

The thick lips opened slightly. The Arab hesitated, then bit into the cake determinedly.

The meal over, the Arab looked at the schoolmaster. "Are you the judge?"

"No, I'm simply keeping you until tomorrow."

"Why do you eat with me?"

"I'm hungry."

The Arab fell silent. Daru got up and went out. He brought back a folding bed from the shed, set it up between the table and the stove, perpendicular to his own bed. From a large suitcase which, upright in a corner, served as a shelf for papers, he took two blankets and arranged them on the camp bed. Then he stopped, felt useless, and sat down on his bed. There was nothing more to do or to get ready. He had to look at this man. He looked at him, therefore, trying to imagine his face bursting with rage. He couldn't do so. He could see nothing but the dark yet shining eyes and the animal mouth.

"Why did you kill him?" he asked in a voice whose hostile tone surprised him.

The Arab looked away.

"He ran away. I ran after him."

He raised his eyes to Daru again and they were full of a sort of woeful interrogation. "Now what will they do to me?"

"Are you afraid?"

He stiffened, turning his eyes away.

"Are you sorry?"

The Arab stared at him openmouthed. Obviously he did not understand. Daru's annoyance was growing. At the same time he felt awkward and self-conscious with his big body wedged between the two beds.

"Lie down there," he said impatiently. "That's your bed."

The Arab didn't move. He called to Daru:

"Tell me!"

The schoolmaster looked at him.

"Is the gendarme coming back tomorrow?"

"I don't know."

"Are you coming with us?"

"I don't know. Why?"

The prisoner got up and stretched out on top of the blankets, his feet toward the window. The light from the electric bulb shone straight into his eyes and he closed them at once.

"Why?" Daru repeated, standing beside the bed.

The Arab opened his eyes under the blinding light and looked at him, trying not to blink.

"Come with us," he said.

*   *   *

In the middle of the night, Daru was still not asleep. He had gone to bed after undressing completely; he generally slept naked. But when he suddenly realized that he had nothing on, he hesitated. He felt vulnerable and the temptation came to him to put his clothes back on. Then he shrugged his shoulders; after all, he wasn't a child and, if need be, he could break his adversary in two. From his bed he could observe him, lying on his back, still motionless with his eyes closed under the harsh light. When Daru turned out the light, the darkness seemed to coagulate all of a sudden. Little by little, the night came back to life in the window where the starless sky was stirring gently. The schoolmaster soon made out the body lying at his feet. The Arab still did not move, but his eyes seemed open. A faint wind was prowling around the schoolhouse. Perhaps it would drive away the clouds and the sun would reappear.

During the night the wind increased. The hens fluttered a little and then were silent. The Arab turned over on his side with his back to Daru, who thought he heard him moan. Then he listened for his guest's breathing; it became heavier and more regular. He listened to that breath so close to him and mused without being able to go to sleep. In this room where he had been sleeping alone for a year, this presence bothered him. But it bothered him also by imposing on him a sort of brotherhood he knew well but refused to accept in the present circumstances. Men who share the same rooms, soldiers or prisoners, develop a strange alliance as if, having cast off their armor with their clothing, they fraternized every evening, over and above their differences, in the ancient community of dream and fatigue. But Daru shook himself; he didn't like such musings, and it was essential to sleep.

A little later, however, when the Arab stirred slightly, the schoolmaster was still not asleep. When the prisoner made a second move, he stiffened, on the alert. The Arab was lifting himself slowly on his arms with almost the motion of a sleepwalker. Seated upright in bed, he waited motionless without turning his head toward Daru, as if he were listening attentively. Daru did not stir; it had just occurred to him that the revolver was still in the drawer of his desk. It was better to act at once. Yet he continued to observe the prisoner, who, with the same slithery motion, put his feet on the ground, waited again, then began to stand up slowly. Daru was about to call out to him when the Arab began to walk, in a quite natural but extraordinarily silent way. He was heading toward the door at the end of the room that opened into the shed. He lifted the latch with precaution and went out, pushing the door behind him but without shutting it. Daru had not stirred. "He is running away," he merely thought. "Good riddance!" Yet he listened attentively. The hens were not fluttering; the guest must be on the plateau. A faint sound of water reached him, and he didn't know what it was until the Arab again stood framed in the doorway, closed the door carefully, and came back to bed without a sound. Then Daru turned his back on him and fell asleep. Still later he seemed, from the depths of his sleep, to hear furtive steps around the schoolhouse. "I'm dreaming! I'm dreaming!" he repeated to himself. And he went on sleeping.

When he awoke, the sky was clear; the loose window let in a cold, pure air. The Arab was asleep, hunched up under the blankets now, his mouth open, utterly relaxed. But when Daru shook him, he started dreadfully, staring at Daru with wild eyes as if he had never seen him and such a frightened expression that the schoolmaster stepped back. "Don't be afraid. It's me. You must eat." The Arab nodded his head and said yes. Calm had returned to his face, but his expression was vacant and listless.

The coffee was ready. They drank it together on the folding bed as they munched their pieces of the cake. Then Daru led the Arab under the shed and showed him the faucet where he washed. He went back into the room, folded the blankets and the bed, made his own bed and put the room in order. Then he went through the classroom and out onto the terrace. The sun was already rising in the blue sky; a soft, bright light was bathing the deserted plateau. On the ridge the snow was melting in spots. The stones were about to reappear. Crouched on the edge of the plateau, the schoolmaster looked at the deserted expanse. He thought of Balducci. He had hurt him, for he had sent him off in a way as if he didn't want to be associated with him. He could still hear the gendarme's farewell and, without knowing why, he felt strangely empty and vulnerable. At that moment, from the other side of the schoolhouse, the prisoner coughed. Daru listened to him almost despite himself and then, furious, threw a pebble that whistled through the air before sinking in the snow. That man's stupid crime revolted him, but to hand him over was contrary to honor. Merely thinking of it made him smart with humiliation. And he cursed at one and the same time his own people who had sent him this Arab and the Arab too who had dared to kill and not managed to get away. Daru got up, walked in a circle on the terrace, waited motionless, and then went back into the schoolhouse.

The Arab, leaning over the cement floor of the shed, was washing his teeth with two fingers. Daru looked at him and said: "Come." He went back into the room ahead of the prisoner. He slipped a hunting-jacket on over his sweater and put on walking-shoes. Standing, he waited until the Arab had put on his *chèche* and sandals. They went into the classroom and the schoolmaster pointed to the exit, saying: "Go head." The fellow didn't budge. "I'm coming," said Daru. The Arab went out. Daru went back into the room and made a package of pieces of rusk, dates, and sugar. In the classroom, before going out, he hesitated a second in front of his desk, then crossed the threshold and locked the door. "That's the way," he said. He started toward the east, followed by the prisoner. But, a short distance from the schoolhouse, he thought he heard a slight sound behind them. He retraced his steps and examined the surroundings of the house; there was no one there. The Arab watched him without seeming to understand. "Come on," said Daru.

They walked for an hour and rested beside a sharp peak of limestone. The snow was melting faster and faster and the sun was drinking up the puddles at once, rapidly cleaning the plateau, which gradually dried and vibrated like the air itself. When they resumed walking, the ground rang under their feet. From time to time a bird rent the space in front of them with a joyful cry. Daru breathed in deeply the fresh morning light. He felt a sort of rapture before the vast familiar expanse, now almost entirely yellow under its dome of blue sky. They walked an hour more, descending toward the south. They reached a level height made up of crumbly rocks. From there on, the plateau sloped down, eastward, toward a low plain where there were a few spindly trees and, to the south, toward outcroppings of rock that gave the landscape a chaotic look.

Daru surveyed the two directions. There was nothing but the sky on the horizon. Not a man could be seen. He turned toward the Arab, who was looking at him blankly. Daru held out the package to him. "Take it," he said. "There are dates, bread, and sugar. You can hold out for two days. Here are a thousand francs too." The Arab took the package and the money but kept his full hands at chest level as if he didn't know what to do with what was being given him. "Now look," the schoolmaster said as he pointed in the direction of the east, "there's the way to Tinguit. You have a two-hour walk. At Tinguit you'll find the administration and the police. They are expecting you." The Arab looked toward the east, still holding the package and the money against his chest. Daru took his elbow and turned him rather roughly toward the south. At the foot of the height on which they stood could be seen a faint path. "That's the trail across the plateau. In a day's walk from here you'll find pasturelands and the first nomads. They'll take you in and shelter you according to their law." The Arab had now turned toward Daru and a sort of panic was visible in his expression. "Listen," he said. Daru shook his head: "No, be quiet. Now I'm leaving you." He turned his back on him, took two long steps in the direction of the school, looked hesitantly at the motionless Arab, and started off again. For a few minutes he heard nothing but his own step resounding on the cold ground and did not turn his head. A moment later, however, he turned around. The Arab was still there on the edge of the hill, his arms hanging now, and he was looking at the schoolmaster. Daru felt something rise in his throat. But he swore with impatience, waved vaguely, and started off again. He had already gone some distance when he again stopped and looked. There was no longer anyone on the hill.

Daru hesitated. The sun was now rather high in the sky and was beginning to beat down on his head. The schoolmaster retraced his steps, at first somewhat uncertainly, then with decision. When he reached the little hill, he was bathed in sweat. He climbed it as fast as he could and stopped, out of breath, at the top. The rock-fields to the south stood out sharply against the blue sky, but on the plain to the east a steamy heat was already rising. And in that slight haze, Daru, with heavy heart, made out the Arab walking slowly on the road to prison.

A little later, standing before the window of the classroom, the schoolmaster was watching the clear light bathing the whole surface of the plateau, but he hardly saw it. Behind him on the blackboard, among the winding French rivers, sprawled the clumsily chalked-up words he had just read: "You handed over our brother. You will pay for this." Daru looked at the sky, the plateau, and, beyond, the invisible lands stretching all the way to the sea. In this vast landscape he had loved so much, he was alone.

PROBING FOR
MEANING

1. "Cruel to live in" is the way the narrator describes this part of Algeria. What details indicate the truth of the description? Why doesn't Daru leave? Where in the story does he indicate his attitude toward the land?

2. What does Daru think of humanity? What connection exists between his attitude toward people and his profession?

3. Describe the relationship between Balducci and Daru. What does this relationship further reveal about Daru's attitude toward others?

4. Daru, the French Algerian, must play host to an Arab. What kind of host is he? How would you describe his behavior toward, and thoughts about, the Arab?

5. How does the guest respond to the host? What details of conversation and action indicate this response?

6. "That man's stupid crime revolted him, but to hand him over was contrary to honor." Why does Daru's philosophy make it dishonorable to turn in a murderer?

7. Why does Daru give the Arab a choice, rather than setting him on the path to freedom? Why does the Arab choose to walk to prison? Daru observes the Arab's choice "with heavy heart." Why?

8. "In this vast landscape he had loved so much, he was alone." For what reason does Camus add the ironic touch of the Arab threat scrawled on the blackboard? Was Daru ever not alone? Does he want to be alone?

PROBING FOR
METHOD

1. To what extent do we see the action through Daru's eyes? Do we enter the mind of any characters other than Daru? Could the story have been written in the first person? What different effect would a first-person narration create?

2. Why is the natural setting so appropriate for a story dramatizing the author's philosophy that life is meaningless except as people choose to make it meaningful?

3. How do the snowstorm and sunlight — dark and light — serve as an ironic symbolic background to the actions of Daru and the Arab?

GABRIEL GARCÍA MÁRQUEZ

Balthazar's Marvelous Afternoon

The cage was finished. Balthazar hung it under the eave, from force of habit, and when he finished lunch everyone was already saying that it was the most beautiful cage in the world. So many people came to see it that a crowd formed in front of the house, and Balthazar had to take it down and close the shop.

"You have to shave," Ursula, his wife, told him. "You look like a Capuchin."

"It's bad to shave after lunch," said Balthazar.

He had two weeks' growth, short, hard, and bristly hair like the mane of a mule, and the general expression of a frightened boy. But it was a false expression. In February he was thirty; he had been living with Ursula for four years, without marrying her and without having children, and life had given him many reasons to be on guard but none to be frightened. He did not even know that for some people the cage he had just made was the most beautiful one in the world. For him, accustomed to making cages since childhood, it had been hardly any more difficult than the others.

"Then rest for a while," said the woman. "With that beard you can't show yourself anywhere."

While he was resting, he had to get out of his hammock several times to show the cage to the neighbors. Ursula had paid little attention to it until then. She was annoyed because her husband had neglected the work of his carpenter's shop to devote himself entirely to the cage, and for two weeks had slept poorly, turning over and muttering incoherencies, and he hadn't thought of shaving. But her annoyance dissolved in the face of the finished cage. When Balthazar woke up from his nap, she had ironed his pants and a shirt; she had put them on a chair near the hammock and had carried the cage to the dining table. She regarded it in silence.

"How much will you charge?" she asked.

"I don't know," Balthazar answered. "I'm going to ask for thirty pesos to see if they'll give me twenty."

"Ask for fifty," said Ursula. "You've lost a lot of sleep in these two weeks. Furthermore, it's rather large. I think it's the biggest cage I've ever seen in my life."

Balthazar began to shave.

"Do you think they'll give me fifty pesos?"

"That's nothing for Mr. Chepe Montiel, and the cage is worth it," said Ursula. "You should ask for sixty."

The house lay in the stifling shadow. It was the first week of April and the heat seemed less bearable because of the chirping of the cicadas. When he finished dressing, Balthazar opened the door to the patio to cool off the house, and a group of children entered the dining room.

The news had spread. Dr. Octavio Giraldo, an old physician, happy with life but tired of his profession, thought about Balthazar's cage while he was eating lunch with his invalid wife. On the inside terrace, where they put the table on hot days, there were many flowerpots and two cages with canaries. His wife liked birds, and she liked them so much that she hated cats because they could eat them up. Thinking about her, Dr. Giraldo went to see a patient that afternoon, and when he returned he went by Balthazar's house to inspect the cage.

There were a lot of people in the dining room. The cage was on display on the table: with its enormous dome of wire, three stories inside, with passageways and compartments especially for eating and sleeping and swings in the space set aside for the birds' recreation, it seemed like a small-scale model of a gigantic ice factory. The doctor inspected it carefully, without touching it, thinking that in effect the cage was bettter than its reputation, and much more beautiful than any he had ever dreamed of for his wife.

"This is a flight of the imagination," he said. He sought out Balthazar among the group of people and, fixing his maternal eyes on him, added, "You would have been an extraordinary architect."

Balthazar blushed.

"Thank you," he said.

"It's true," said the doctor. He was smoothly and delicately fat, like a woman who had been beautiful in her youth, and he had delicate hands. His voice seemed like that of a priest speaking Latin. "You wouldn't even need to put birds in it," he said, making the cage turn in front of the audience's eyes as if he were auctioning it off. "It would be enough to hang it in the trees so it could sing by itself." He put it back on the table, thought a moment, looking at the cage, and said:

"Fine, then I'll take it."

"It's sold," said Ursula.

"It belongs to the son of Mr. Chepe Montiel," said Balthazar. "He ordered it specially."

The doctor adopted a respectful attitude.

"Did he give you the design?"

"No," said Balthazar. "He said he wanted a large cage, like this one, for a pair of troupials."

The doctor looked at the cage.

"But this isn't for troupials."

"Of course it is, Doctor," said Balthazar, approaching the table. The children surrounded him. "The measurements are carefully calculated," he said, pointing to the different compartments with his forefinger. Then he struck the dome with his knuckles, and the cage filled with resonant chords.

"It's the strongest wire you can find, and each joint is soldered outside and in," he said.

"It's even big enough for a parrot," interrupted one of the children.

"That it is," said Balthazar.

The doctor turned his head.

"Fine, but he didn't give you the design," he said. "He gave you no exact specifications, aside from making it a cage big enough for troupials. Isn't that right?"

"That's right," said Balthazar.

"Then there's no problem," said the doctor. "One thing is a cage big enough for troupials, and another is this cage. There's no proof that this one is the one you were asked to make."

"It's this very one," said Balthazar, confused. "That's why I made it."

The doctor made an impatient gesture.

"You could make another one," said Ursula, looking at her husband. And then, to the doctor: "You're not in any hurry."

"I promised it to my wife for this afternoon," said the doctor.

"I'm very sorry, Doctor," said Balthazar, "but I can't sell you something that's sold already."

The doctor shrugged his shoulders. Drying the sweat from his neck with a handkerchief, he contemplated the cage silently with the fixed, unfocused gaze of one who looks at a ship which is sailing away.

"How much did they pay you for it?"

Balthazar sought out Ursula's eyes without replying.

"Sixty pesos," she said.

The doctor kept looking at the cage. "It's very pretty." He sighed. "Extremely pretty." Then, moving toward the door, he began to fan himself energetically, smiling, and the trace of that episode disappeared forever from his memory.

"Montiel is very rich," he said.

In truth, José Montiel was not as rich as he seemed, but he would have been capable of doing anything to become so. A few blocks from there, in a house crammed with equipment, where no one had ever smelled a smell that couldn't be sold, he remained indifferent to the news of the cage. His wife, tortured by an obsession with death, closed the doors and windows after lunch and lay for two hours with her eyes opened to the shadow of the room, while José Montiel took his siesta. The clamor of many voices surprised her there. Then she opened the door to the living room and found a crowd in front of the house, and Balthazar with the cage in the middle of the crowd, dressed in white, freshly shaved, with that expression of decorous candor with which the poor approach the houses of the wealthy.

"What a marvelous thing!" José Montiel's wife exclaimed, with a radiant expression, leading Balthazar inside. "I've never seen anything like it in my life," she said, and added, annoyed by the crowd which piled up at the door:

"But bring it inside before they turn the living room into a grandstand."

Balthazar was no stranger to José Montiel's house. On different occasions, because of his skill and forthright way of dealing, he had been called in to do minor carpentry jobs. But he never felt at ease among the rich. He used to think about them, about their ugly and argumentative wives, about their tremendous surgical operations, and he always experienced a feeling of pity. When he entered their houses, he couldn't move without dragging his feet.

"Is Pepe home?" he asked.

He had put the cage on the dining-room table.

"He's at school," said José Montiel's wife. "But he shouldn't be long," and she added, "Montiel is taking a bath."

In reality, José Montiel had not had time to bathe. He was giving himself an urgent alcohol rub, in order to come out and see what was going on. He was such a cautious man that he slept without an electric fan so he could watch over the noises of the house while he slept.

"Adelaide!" he shouted. "What's going on?"

"Come and see what a marvelous thing!" his wife shouted.

José Montiel, obese and hairy, his towel draped around his neck, appeared at the bedroom window.

"What is that?"

"Pepe's cage," said Balthazar.

His wife looked at him perplexedly.

"Whose?"

"Pepe's," replied Balthazar. And then, turning toward José Montiel, "Pepe ordered it."

Nothing happened at that instant, but Balthazar felt as if someone had just opened the bathroom door on him. José Montiel came out of the bedroom in his underwear.

"Pepe!" he shouted.

"He's not back," whispered his wife, motionless.

Pepe appeared in the doorway. He was about twelve, and had the same curved eyelashes and was as quietly pathetic as his mother.

"Come here," José Montiel said to him. "Did you order this?"

The child lowered his head. Grabbing him by the hair, José Montiel forced Pepe to look him in the eye.

"Answer me."

The child bit his lip without replying.

"Montiel," whispered his wife.

José Montiel let the child go and turned toward Balthazar in a fury. "I'm very sorry, Balthazar," he said. "But you should have consulted me before going on. Only to you would it occur to contract with a minor." As he spoke, his face recovered its serenity. He lifted the cage without looking at it and gave it to Balthazar.

"Take it away at once, and try to sell it to whomever you can," he said. "Above all, I beg you not to argue with me." He patted him on the back and explained, "The doctor has forbidden me to get angry."

The child had remained motionless, without blinking, until Balthazar looked at him uncertainly with the cage in his hand. Then he emitted a gutteral sound, like a dog's growl, and threw himself on the floor screaming.

José Montiel looked at him, unmoved, while the mother tried to pacify him. "Don't even pick him up," he said. "Let him break his head on the floor, and then put salt and lemon on it so he can rage to his heart's content." The child was shrieking tearlessly while his mother held him by the wrists.

"Leave him alone," José Montiel insisted.

Balthazar observed the child as he would have observed the death throes of a rabid animal. It was almost four o'clock. At that hour, at his house, Ursula was singing a very old song and cutting slices of onion.

"Pepe," said Balthazar.

He approached the child, smiling, and held the cage out to him. The child jumped up, embraced the cage which was almost as big as he was, and stood looking at Balthazar through the wirework without knowing what to say. He hadn't shed one tear.

"Balthazar," said José Montiel softly. "I told you already to take it away."

"Give it back," the woman ordered the child.

"Keep it," said Balthazar. And then, to José Montiel: "After all, that's what I made it for."

José Montiel followed him into the living room.

"Don't be foolish, Balthazar," he was saying, blocking his path. "Take your piece of furniture home and don't be silly. I have no intention of paying you a cent."

"It doesn't matter," said Balthazar. "I made it expressly as a gift for Pepe. I didn't expect to charge anything for it."

As Balthazar made his way through the spectators who were blocking the door, José Montiel was shouting in the middle of the living room. He was very pale and his eyes were beginning to get red.

"Idiot!" he was shouting. "Take your trinket out of here. The last thing we need is for some nobody to give orders in my house. Son of a bitch!"

In the pool hall, Balthazar was received with an ovation. Until that moment, he thought that he had made a better cage than ever before, that he'd had to give it to the son of José Montiel so he wouldn't keep crying, and that none of these things was particularly important. But then he realized that all of this had a certain importance for many people, and he felt a little excited.

"So they give you fifty pesos for the cage."

"Sixty," said Balthazar.

"Score one for you," someone said. "You're the only one who has managed to get such a pile of money out of Mr. Chepe Montiel. We have to celebrate."

They bought him a beer, and Balthazar responded with a round for everybody. Since it was the first time he had ever been out drinking, by dusk he was completely drunk, and he was talking about a fabulous project of a thousand cages, at sixty pesos each, and then of a million cages, till he had sixty million pesos. "We have to make a lot of things to sell to the rich before they die," he was saying, blind drunk. "All of them are sick, and they're going to die. They're so screwed up they can't even get angry any more." For two hours he was paying for the jukebox, which played without interruption. Everybody toasted Balthazar's health, good luck, and fortune, and the death of the rich, but at mealtime they left him alone in the pool hall.

Ursula had waited for him until eight, with a dish of fried meat covered with slices of onion. Someone told her that her husband was in the pool hall, delirious with happiness, buying beer for everyone, but she didn't believe it, because Balthazar had never got drunk. When she went to bed, almost at midnight, Balthazar was in a lighted room where there were little tables, each with four chairs, and an outdoor dance floor, where the plovers were walking around. His face was smeared with rouge, and since he couldn't take one more step, he thought he wanted to lie down with two women in the same bed. He had spent so much that he had had to leave his watch in pawn, with the promise to pay the next day. A moment later, spread-eagled in the street, he realized that his shoes were being taken off, but he didn't want to abandon the happiest dream of his life. The women who passed on their way to five-o'clock Mass didn't dare look at him, thinking he was dead.

1. Characterize Balthazar. Is he an artist? Why doesn't he sell the cage to Dr. Giraldo and build another one for Pepe? Why does Balthazar "contract with a minor"?

2. Why does Balthazar give the cage to Pepe when José Montiel refuses to pay for it? Why does José react to this with anger?

3. Why does Balthazar let the patrons of the pool hall believe that he has sold the cage for a considerable profit? What exactly does Balthazar celebrate? Why does the story conclude with Balthazar, drunk and broke, lying in the street, yet having the "happiest dream of his life"?

4. What does the story express about the differences between the rich and the poor in this South American village?

1. What is the symbolic significance of the cage?

2. What philosophies (for instance, spiritualism, materialism, idealism, and so forth) do the various characters represent?

3. The narrative style is simple. No motives are examined and few comments are made about the characters' actions. Why not? How objective is the narrator?

 RICHARD WILBUR

The Writer

In her room at the prow of the house
Where light breaks, and the windows are tossed with linden,
My daughter is writing a story.

I pause in the stairwell, hearing
From her shut door a commotion of typewriter-keys
Like a chain hauled over a gunwale.

Young as she is, the stuff
Of her life is a great cargo, and some of it heavy:
I wish her a lucky passage.

But now it is she who pauses,
As if to reject my thought and its easy figure.
A stillness greatens, in which

The whole house seems to be thinking,
And then she is at it again with a bunched clamor
Of strokes, and again is silent.

I remember the dazed starling
Which was trapped in that very room, two years ago;
How we stole in, lifted a sash

And retreated, not to affright it;
And how for a helpless hour, through the crack of the door,
We watched the sleek, wild, dark

And iridescent creature
Batter against the brilliance, drop like a glove
To the hard floor, or the desk-top,

And wait then, humped and bloody,
For the wits to try it again; and how our spirits
Rose when, suddenly sure,

It lifted off from a chair-back,
Beating a smooth course for the right window
And clearing the sill of the world.

It is always a matter, my darling,
Of life or death, as I had forgotten. I wish
What I wished you before, but harder.

PROBING FOR
MEANING

1. What has changed during the course of the poem? The speaker says, "I wish/what I wished you before, but harder." Why does he now wish harder?

2. What is "always a matter of life or death"? Why? What does the poem say about the creative process?

3. Who is "the writer"?

PROBING FOR
METHOD

1. The beginning of the poem draws an elaborate comparison between the daughter's writing and a sea voyage. Review the poem and explain each of the sea images.

2. When does the speaker drop the sea imagery and "its easy figure"? Why?

3. What is the similarity between the daughter's efforts to write and the starling's efforts to escape? What does the speaker learn from the example of the starling?

ANNE SEXTON

The Rowing Endeth

I'm mooring my rowboat
at the dock of the island called God.
This dock is made in the shape of a fish
and there are many boats moored
at many different docks.
"It's okay," I say to myself,
with blisters that broke and healed
and broke and healed —
saving themselves over and over.
And salt sticking to my face and arms like
a glue-skin pocked with grains of tapioca.
I empty myself from my wooden boat
and onto the flesh of The Island.

"On with it!" He says and thus
we squat on the rocks by the sea
and play —— can it be true ——
a game of poker.
He calls me.
I win because I hold a royal straight flush.
He wins because He holds five aces.
A wild card had been announced
but I had not heard it
being in such a state of awe
when He took out the cards and dealt.
As He plunks down His five aces
and I sit grinning at my royal flush,
He starts to laugh,
and laughter rolling like a hoop out of His mouth
and into mine,
and such laughter that He doubles right over me
laughing a Rejoice-Chorus at our two triumphs.
Then I laugh, the fishy dock laughs
the sea laughs. The Island laughs.
The Absurd laughs.

Dearest dealer,
I wish my royal straight flush,
love you so for your wild card,
that untamable, eternal, gut-driven *ha-ha*
and lucky love.

1. What has the poet evidently gone through to moor "at the dock of the island called God"? What does her rowing to God symbolize?

2. What effect is created by her representation of God as a gambler whose announcement of a wild card is not heard by his opponent? What is her image of God? What does God's attitude toward her seem to be?

3. Despite her loss in the poker game, the poet seems quite happy with her royal straight flush and shares in God's laughter at their "two triumphs." In what sense has the poet won? Why is she not resentful about God's wild card? How do the last two lines contribute to the reader's understanding of her attitude?

4. Can you paraphrase the poem? What is its religious meaning? What is the "Absurd"?

1. How effective is the poet's comparison of God with an island to which we must row? Why is the dock shaped like a fish?

2. The poet uses unusual combinations of words. What do the expressions "glue-skin" and "gut-driven" mean? Can you find any other unusual uses of words?

3. How would you categorize the poet's vocabulary? Is it formal? informal? colloquial? slangy? Select words from the poem to defend your answer. What effect does her vocabulary have on the meaning of the poem?

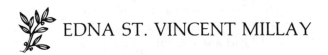 EDNA ST. VINCENT MILLAY

Spring

To what purpose, April, do you return again?
Beauty is not enough.
You can no longer quiet me with the redness
Of little leaves opening stickily.
I know what I know.
The sun is hot on my neck as I observe

The spikes of the crocus.
The smell of the earth is good.
It is apparent that there is no death.
But what does that signify?
Not only under ground are the brains of men
Eaten by maggots.
Life in itself
Is nothing,
An empty cup, a flight of uncarpeted stairs.
It is not enough that yearly, down this hill,
April
Comes like an idiot, babbling and strewing flowers.

PROBING FOR
MEANING

1. What characteristics usually associated with April does the poet mention?

2. What does the line "It is apparent that there is no death" mean?

3. Why, despite the beauty of April, is the poet angry? Why does she say, "Beauty is not enough"?

4. Why is the poet deliberately reversing the usual attitude toward spring?

PROBING FOR
METHOD

1. Observe the comparisons in the poem. What do they contribute to your understanding of the meaning?

2. Why has the poet formed line length as she has? What is the effect, for example, of the shorter lines? Why, near the end of the poem, does the poet make the word *April* a separate line? What relationship exists between content and line length?

Topics for Imitation

1. Property "makes me feel heavy," says Forster in "My Wood." Lindbergh and Thoreau also write about materialism in this chapter. Discuss their attitudes toward possessions or, in Thoreau's case, commercialism.

2. Many writers discuss our reluctance to confront reality. What do Keller, Plato, and Millay contribute to this discussion?

3. The poems of Sexton and Millay express their attitudes about death. How do their views differ?

4. Both Balthazar in "Balthazar's Marvelous Afternoon" and Richard Wilbur's daughter are artists. Balthazar elevates his carpentry to an art, and Wilbur's daughter writes stories. How are their experiences similar? different?

5. "Sometimes I have thought it would be an excellent rule to live each day as if we should die tomorrow. Such an attitude would

emphasize sharply the values of life." Thoreau in "The Village" and Daru in "The Guest" share Helen Keller's keen awareness that people should utilize their freedom to appreciate life. Discuss what each of these writers values in life.

6. Plato, Thoreau, and Daru chose to live apart from society. How did their philosophies affect them?

7. Write an essay of your own using one of the methods of illustration to make an abstract idea concrete. The following are some possible approaches.

  a. Choose an object of nature, as Wilbur chose the starling and Lindbergh chose the channelled whelk, and use it to illustrate an idea of your own.

  b. Think of an illustration other than Plato's cave to represent truth versus illusion, and develop it either as an analogy or as an allegory.

  c. Find your own way of illustrating Helen Keller's idea of the necessity of living life in the present moment.

  d. Write about an idea of yours, including many metaphors and similes, as Thoreau does. Be sure not to use clichés but to create fresh comparisons.

  e. Use a possession of yours to illustrate your attitude toward possessions. Try using Forster's essay as a model.

Biographies

JAMES AGEE (1909–1955)   American novelist and film critic, born and raised in the Cumberland Mountain area of Tennessee, which is the setting for his two novels: *The Morning Watch* (1954) and *Death in the Family*. The latter, published posthumously in 1957, was awarded the Pulitzer Prize. Alabama sharecroppers were the subject of his nonfiction work *Let Us Now Praise Famous Men* (1941). The first volume of *Agee on Film* was published in 1958; the second volume (1960) contains five of his screen plays.

SHERWOOD ANDERSON (1876–1941)   American novelist and short-story writer who was born in a small town in Ohio and spent most of his life there. His collection of short stories, *Winesburg, Ohio* (1919), reflects life in a small Midwestern town. Although these stories are fictional, Anderson's early life experiences are obvious influences in his writing as he has captured the details of small-town life so well. Anderson was convinced that the growth of urban centers would result in the disintegration of the personal life. His interest both in small-town life and its effect on people is evident in his autobiographical essay "Discovery of a Father."

MAYA ANGELOU (b. 1928)   Black American author, poet, playwright, stage and screen performer, and singer born in St. Louis, Missouri. After a tragic childhood ("from a broken family, raped at eight, unwed mother at sixteen"), Angelou first joined a dance company and then went on to star in an off-Broadway play. She wrote three books of poetry, produced a series on Africa for PBS-TV, and served as a coordinator for the Southern Christian Leadership Conference. Angelou has been awarded three honorary doctorates. She is best known for the four books that comprise her autobiography, the first of which is *I*

Know Why the Caged Bird Sings (1970) and the most recent volume *The Heart of a Woman* (1981).

W. H. AUDEN (1907–1973)   British poet and dramatist who often expressed the hope that socialism would help cure society's political and economic problems. During World War II, Auden turned to Christianity as his central preoccupation. His later works reflect both his early political beliefs and his later spiritual concerns, although he gradually abandoned his belief in Marxism; his later poems are essentially humanistic reflections on the importance of all aspects of human love. Auden's works include *Poems* (1930), *On This Island* (1936), *Another Time* (1940), *The Quest* (1941), *The Age of Anxiety* (1951), *The Shield of Achilles* (1955), and *Homage to Clio* (1960).

SAUL BELLOW (b. 1915)   Jewish American writer who was born in Quebec but has spent most of his life in Chicago. He deals in his novels with "intelligent beings in a complex society struggling with absurdity, meaning, ignominy, and their own emotions." In 1976 he won the Nobel Prize for Literature. Bellow writes: "As human isolation increases, while education and abilities multiply, the most vital questions and answers become the internal ones." Bellow believes strongly in the primacy of the emotions. His most important works include *Dangling Man* (1944), *The Victim* (1947), *The Adventures of Augie March* (1953), *Seize the Day* (1956), *Henderson the Rain King* (1959), *Herzog* (1964), *Humboldt's Gift* (1975), and *To Jerusalem and Back* (1976).

ARNA BONTEMPS (1902–1973)   Black American writer and university professor who was born in Louisiana and died in Tennessee. His writings include *God Sends Sunday* (1931), *Black Thunder* (1936), *We Have Tomorrow* (1945), *Story of the Negro* (1948), *Lonesome Boy* (1955), *One Hundred Years of Negro Freedom* (1961), and *The Harlem Renaissance Remembered* (1972). Bontemps was raised in California, but he returned to Louisiana "to write something about the changes [he had] seen in [his] lifetime, and about the Negro's awakening and regeneration."

ALBERT CAMUS (1913–1960)   French novelist, dramatist, essayist, and journalist whose work had a great impact on his contemporaries. He was a member of the French Resistance movement during World War II and was the editor of *Combat*, an underground publication. Although he has been identified with existentialism, Camus's profound humanism distinguishes him from existentialist purists. Convinced of the absurdity of life,

Camus nevertheless struggled, in his art and in his life, with the paradoxical aspirations of personal freedom and social justice, solitude and solidarity, and reason and passion. He was awarded the Nobel Prize in 1957 for his philosophical essays, which include *The Myth of Sisyphus* (1942) and *The Rebel* (1953), and for his fiction which includes *The Stranger* (1942), *The Plague* (1948), and *The Fall* (1957). He was killed in an automobile accident at the height of his literary career.

WILLA CATHER (1873–1941)   Born in Gore, Virginia, but taken as a child to Nebraska, which later provided the setting for much of her fiction. She was a journalist for many years, taught English for a brief period, and then became editor of *McClure's Magazine*. The life of immigrant farmers in Nebraska was the focal point of two of her most successful novels, *O Pioneers!* (1913) and *My Ántonia* (1918). Her later fiction, however, including "A Wagner Matinée," reflects the struggle of the sensitive artist in an unsympathetic environment.

ELDRIDGE CLEAVER (b. 1935)   Black American writer and political activist who spent most of the years from 1947 to 1966 in reformatories and prisons. During his time in San Quentin, he educated himself and after his release became an editor of *Ramparts*. In 1968 he published *Soul on Ice*, a collection of essays and letters, many of which (including "A Day in Folsom Prison") were written while he was in prison. In the mid-1960s Cleaver became a leader of the Black Panther party, and in 1968 he ran for president as the candidate of the Peace and Freedom party. In November 1968 Cleaver left America, settling first in Havana and then in Algeria, but he returned to America in 1976, disillusioned. He served a prison sentence for his former activities with the Black Panthers. He is currently very interested in religion.

EMILY DICKINSON (1830–1886)   American poet who spent practically her entire life in Amherst, Massachusetts. After attending Amherst Institute and Mount Holyoke Female Seminary as a young woman, Dickinson became a recluse and rarely even left her room to greet visitors. Although only two of the nearly 2000 poems she wrote were published in her lifetime, Dickinson is considered a major poet and an important influence in modern poetry. She believed, as is evident in her poetry, that spirit is manifested in nature.

JOAN DIDION (b. 1934)   Born in Sacramento, California, she earned her reputation as a fine essayist for her collection *Slouching Towards*

Bethlehem, a description of and critical commentary on the psychological, cultural, and political turmoil of the 1960s. Didion's works include *Play It As It Lays* (1971), *A Book of Common Prayer* (1977), and *The White Album* (1979). Most of her writing concerns the cultural environment of California and the West. In 1983, she published *Salvador,* an account of the conditions she observed in El Salvador the previous year.

LOREN EISELEY (1907–1977) American educator, anthropologist, poet, and author born in Lincoln, Nebraska. He was best known for his ability to combine a poetic style with scientific subject matter. He believed that reason by itself, without vision and imagination, would destroy mankind. His best-known works are *The Immense Journey* (1957), *Darwin's Century* (1958), and *The Unexpected Universe* (1969).

RALPH ELLISON (b. 1914) Black American novelist, essayist, and teacher born in Oklahoma City, Oklahoma. During the Depression, he moved to New York City and began to work for the New York Federal Writers' Project. His widely acclaimed novel *Invisible Man* (1952), which won the National Book Award in 1953, reflects the complex struggle of black people for identity in the post–World War II era. *Shadow and Act* (1964), his other major work, is a collection of essays dealing with various aspects of American culture. Ellison writes: "If our black writers are going to become more influential in the broader community, they will do it in terms of style; by imposing a style upon a sufficient area of American life to give other readers a sense that this is true, that here is a revelation of reality."

E. M. FORSTER (1879–1970) English novelist, short-story writer, and essayist. He wrote six novels, all of which deal with the class concerns of his era. In the early 1900s Forster lived in Greece and Italy, and during these years, he wrote his first four novels: *Where Angels Fear to Tread* (1905), *The Longest Journey* (1907), *A Room with a View* (1908) and *Howards End* (1910). After World War I, Forster moved to India where he wrote his best-known novel, *A Passage to India* (1924), which exemplifies the liberal humanism so pervasive in his work and so much a part of his philosophy.

   A Passage to India exposes the prejudices and injustices that existed under British domination in colonial India. With subtle irony, he reveals the moral and emotional emptiness of British middle-class life. He believed that the bourgeoisie buries their capacity for passion and intuition and have to recapture those qualities for their lives to have meaning. Forster also wrote seven books of literary criticism, and in 1951 he published a collection of sociological essays entitled *Two Cheers for Democracy.*

GARY GILDNER (b. 1938)   American poet whose collected works include *First Practice* (1969), *Digging for Indians* (1971), *Letters from Vicksburg* (1976), and *The Runner and Other Poems* (1978). He currently teaches creative writing at the University of Iowa and is working on a collection of short stories.

HERBERT GOLD (b. 1924)   American novelist with existentialist leanings, insofar as he is concerned with our capacity for creating values. That Gold is essentially an optimist, unlike other existentialists, is revealed most clearly in his novels *Birth of a Hero* (1951) and *The Prospect Before Us* (1954). Gold's other works include *The Man Who Was Not With It* (1956), *First Person Singular: Essays for the Sixties* (1963), *The Magic Will: Short Stories and Essays of a Decade* (1971), *My Last Two Thousand Years* (1972), *Waiting For Cordelia* (1977), and *Slave Trade* (1979).

WILLIAM GOLDING (b. 1911)   English novelist, the author of *The Inheritors* (1955), *Lord of the Flies* (1954), *Pincher Martin* (1956), *Free Fall* (1959), and *The Spire* (1964). Golding referred to his books as fables, and he used them as a vehicle to express his dark view of the world — that people are basically evil and that life is a game of war. He has said that his experiences in World War II and his years spent teaching young boys greatly influenced his philosophical stance.

RICHARD GOLDSTEIN (b. 1944)   American journalist born in New York City. His writings include *One in Seven: Drugs on Campus* (1966), *The Poetry of Rock* (1969), and *Goldstein's Greatest Hits: A Book Mostly About Rock 'n Roll* (1970), and he has written numerous columns for *Vogue*, *New York* magazine, and *The Village Voice.*

TED HUGHES (b. 1930)   British poet and playwright born in Yorkshire, England. His volumes of poetry include *The Hawk in the Rain* (1957), *Lupercal* (1957), *Selected Poems, 1957–1967, Cave Birds* (1977), and *Moortown* (1980). His children's books include *The Earth-Owl and Other Moon-People* (1963), *How the Whale Became* (1963), *Nessie the Mannerless Monster* (1963), *Season Songs* (1974), and *Remains of Elmet* (1979). Hughes's later works contain violent animal symbolism suggestive of a savage world confronting a hostile God.

HELEN KELLER (1880–1968)   American memoirist, essayist, and counselor on international relations for the American Foundation of the Blind. She was deaf and blind from the age of nineteen months. The story of how her teacher, Annie Sullivan, broke through the barrier of silence to reach her has been dramatized as "The Miracle Worker." Through Sullivan, Keller learned to communicate, first by using sign language and later through voice lessons. Despite her physical handicaps, Keller had a keen awareness and insight into human nature and the world around her. She graduated with honors from Radcliffe and received critical acclaim for her autobiography *Story of My Life* (1902). Among her other works are *Optimism* (1903), *The World I Live In* (1908), and *Out of the Dark* (1913).

WILLIAM MELVIN KELLEY (b. 1937)   Black American writer born in New York City. His works include *A Different Drummer* (1962), his best-known novel; *Dancers on the Shore* (1964), a short-story collection; and his novels *A Drop of Patience* (1965), *Dem* (1967), and *Dunford's Travels Everywhere* (1970). A belief in the worth of the individual and his basic rights is the basis for all of Kelley's writings. Kelley is interested, among other things, in "the plight of Negroes, *as individual human beings,* in America."

D. H. LAWRENCE (1885–1930)   English novelist, essayist, and poet born in Eastwood, Nottinghamshire. Lawrence's fiction presents the conflict caused by his father's working-class background and his mother's aspirations toward gentility and social refinement. Lawrence explored the depth of human passion and emotion in such novels as *Sons and Lovers* (1912), *The Rainbow* (1915), *Women in Love* (1921), and *Lady Chatterley's Lover* (1928). His several volumes of poetry include *Birds, Beasts and Flowers* (1923) and *Last Poems* (1932). Lawrence has also written universally respected critical essays.

DENISE LEVERTOV (b. 1923)   Born in Ilford, Essex, England, she came to live in the United States in 1956. Best known for her poetry, Levertov initiated the Writers' and Artists' Protest Against the War in Vietnam in 1965. Her numerous volumes of poetry include *The Double Image* (1946), *The Jacob's Ladder* (1961), *The Sorrow Dance* (1967), *To Stay Alive* (1971), and *Life in the Forest* (1978). Levertov has written: "I do not believe that a violent imitation of the horrors of our times is the concern of poetry. . . . I long for poems of an inner harmony in utter contrast to the chaos in which they exist. Insofar as poetry has a social function it is to awaken sleepers by other means than shock."

ANNE MORROW LINDBERGH (b. 1906)   American writer best known for "The Wave of the Future" (1940), a controversial essay that was regarded as a defense of fascism. In 1955, she wrote *Gift from the Sea*, which was addressed especially to women. Lindbergh's novel *Dearly Beloved* (1962) comments on marriage; *Earth Shine* (1969) depicts the launching of the Apollo moon mission. She has also written several volumes of letters and diaries.

ARCHIBALD MACLEISH (1892–1982)   American poet and playwright who became an expatriate in Paris after his first volume of poetry *Tower of Ivory* was published in 1917. During his stay in Paris from 1917 through 1928, MacLeish was greatly influenced by T. S. Eliot, Ezra Pound, and the French symbolists. In 1932, MacLeish was awarded the Pulitzer Prize for *Conquistador*. Throughout the 1930s he continued to publish volumes of poetry, but he was also recognized for his verse plays, each of which presented a "political" message generalized into a universal problem of human nature. During World War II, MacLeish became more involved in politics and the state of the world. He held several governmental positions, and his poetry of this period is political and patriotic. In 1952 MacLeish won his second Pulitzer Prize with the publication of *Collected Poems 1917–1952* and a third Pulitzer for his major postwar work, the play *J.B.* (1959). Among other important works are *Hypocrite Anteus* (1952), *The Trojan Horse* (1952), and *Poetry and Experience* (1961).

BERNARD MALAMUD (b. 1914)   Jewish American writer born in Brooklyn, New York. "The Jews are absolutely the very *stuff* of drama," writes Bernard Malamud. Although he does often write about Jews and Jewish life, Malamud also strives for universality: "All men are Jews," as Malamud wrote. His best-known works are *The Assistant* (1957), *The Magic Barrel* (1958), *The Fixer* (1966), and *Dubin's Lives* (1979); his most recent is *God's Grace* (1982).

MARYA MANNES (b. 1904)   American novelist, essayist, and journalist born in New York City. She has been a contributor to various publications such as *Vogue, Glamour, McCall's,* and *The New York Times.* Her major works inlude *Message from a Stranger* (1948), a novel; and *Out of My Time* (1971), an autobiography.

GABRIEL GARCÍA MÁRQUEZ (b. 1928)   Novelist and writer born in Aracataca, Colombia. After studying in Bogotá, he became a journalist and lived in Paris, Mexico, and Spain for several years. His publications include *Los Funerales de la Mama Grande* (1962), a collection of short stories; *La Mala Hora* (1962), a novel; *The Autumn of the Patriarch* (1968); and *No One Writes to the Colonel and Other Stories* (1960), which contains "Balthazar's Marvelous Afternoon." One critic said of his novel *One Hundred Years of Solitude* (1970) that it is "the first piece of literature since the Book of Genesis that should be required reading for the entire race. It takes up not long after Genesis left off and carries through to the air age, reporting on everything that happened in between with more lucidity, wit, wisdom, and poetry than is expected from 100 years of novelists, let alone one man." Márquez received the Nobel Prize in 1982. His most recent novel, *Chronicle of a Death Foretold*, was published in 1983.

JOYCE MAYNARD (b. 1954)   Born in Durham, New Hampshire. At eighteen she was one of the youngest writers to be published in *The New York Times*. In her freshman year at Yale she wrote an autobiography, *Looking Back: A Chronicle of Growing Up Old in the Sixties* (1973), from which "The Lion Tamers" is taken. She currently lives in New York and in 1981 published a novel, *Baby Love*. She is also a frequent contributor to the weekly "Hers" column of *The New York Times*.

CARSON McCULLERS (1917–1967)   American writer born in Columbus, Georgia. Her first novel, *The Heart is a Lonely Hunter* (1940), won her immediate critical acclaim. Her fiction, focusing on the alienated, has been praised for its sensitive characterization and effective communication of impressions. "The Sojourner" is taken from a collection entitled *The Ballad of the Sad Café* (1951).

EDNA ST. VINCENT MILLAY (1892–1950)   Born in Austerlitz, New York, she has often been referred to as "the female Byron," as much of her early poetry is comprised of sonnets celebrating love and life. Her later work was more concerned with social issues. Millay's volume *The Harp Weaver and Other Poems* won her the Pulitzer Prize in 1923. Her use of traditional poetic forms creates an interesting juxtaposition with her radical ideas as exemplified in her poem "Spring."

GEORGE ORWELL (1903–1950)   English novelist, essayist, and critic born in India. He was considered to be a free-thinking socialist, and his works are largely comprised of studies of working-class life and culture. Orwell's works deal directly with the question of human freedom, and his best known novels *Animal Farm* (1946) and *1984* (1949) are both horrifying journeys into the world of totalitarianism.

FRANK O'CONNOR (1903–1966)   The pen name of Michael O'Donovan, an Irish short-story writer and translator of poetry from Gaelic. Born in Cork, Ireland, and virtually self-educated, he was imprisoned during the civil war in 1923 and used his time to read extensively in Irish literature. His first collection of short stories, *Guests of the Nation*, was published in 1931, and for a few years following he worked as director of the Abbey Theatre in Dublin. Although all of his stories have an Irish background, his subsequent fiction, including *Stories of Frank O'Connor* (1953) and *My Oedipus Complex* (1963), was written in America, where he spent much of the latter part of his life.

WILFRED OWEN (1893–1918)   English poet widely recognized as the best poet of World War I. Owen wrote passionately of his hatred for war, and he savagely and ironically depicted the cruelty and horrors he saw around him at the battlefront. Among his best known poems are "Dulce Et Decorum Est," "Anthem for Doomed Youth," and "Strange Meeting."

ALEXANDER PETRUNKEVITCH (1875–1964)   Russian zoologist who gained recognition as an authority on spiders. His books include *Index Catalogue of Spiders of North, Central and South America* (1911) and *Principles of Classification* (1952). He taught for many years at several American universities, and in his later life became a well-known translator of Russian poetry.

ANN PETRY (b. 1912)   Born and raised in Old Saybrook, Connecticut, she has spent most of her life in Harlem. A black novelist, journalist, and short-story writer, Petry's first novel, *The Street* (1946), met with striking literary acclaim. Other novels are *Country Place* (1947) and *The Narrows* (1953). A collection of short stories, *Miss Muriel and Other Stories*, was published in 1971. Her fiction reflects the naturalist school, and in keeping with this tradition, many of her works are drawn from her experience in the urban setting.

PLATO (427–348 B.C.)   Greek philosopher and writer who became actively involved in the politics of the Athenian state. He vehemently protested the corruption that had permeated Athenian democracy. The death of his teacher and friend Socrates impelled him to search for an alternative life-style. He is best known for his philosophic dialogues. His thinking has had a lasting impact on Western thought.

KATHERINE ANNE PORTER (1890–1980)   American short-story writer and novelist born in Indian Creek, Texas. Her most famous works include *Flowering Judas* (1935), *The Leaning Tower, and Other Stories* (1944), *A Defense of Circe* (1954), and *Ship of Fools* (1962). "My whole attempt," Porter wrote, "has been to discover and understand human motives, human feelings, to make a distillation of what human relations and experiences my mind has been able to absorb. I have never known an uninteresting human being, and I have never known two alike. . . ."

MARTIN RALBOVSKY (b. 1942)   Born in Schenectady, New York, he has been a sportswriter for numerous periodicals and newspapers including *New York* magazine, *TV Guide, Sport* magazine, *The Atlantic Monthly,* and *The New York Times.* Ralbovsky studies arena sports from a moral and sociological view. He writes: "I have seen the dark side of life, and the dark side of American sports particularly. . . . Somebody, too, has to question whether or not the manufactured violence in sports contributes to this society's acceptance of real violence as being a commonplace thing. That's what I do, lonely voice in the night that I am." Ralbovsky feels that most writers choose to take a Pollyanna view of the sports scene in America.

SANTHA RAMA RAU (b. 1923)   Indian memoirist, travel writer, and novelist. She was educated in England and America and has traveled widely in Europe and Asia. *Home to India* (1944) describes Rau's return to her native country after ten formative years in England, and reflects Rau's total commitment to Indian nationalism. Rau's other works include a dramatization of E. M. Forster's 1924 novel *A Passage to India* (1956), and several collections of essays including *My Russian Journey* (1959), *Gift of Passage* (1961), and *A Princess Remembers: The Memories of the Maharani of Jaipur* (1974).

ALASTAIR REID (b. 1926)   Poet, translator, essayist, and author of books for children. Born in Scotland, he currently lives in Spain. He has taught at Sarah Lawrence College in New York and has published several volumes of poetry including, most recently, *Weathering: New and Selected Poems* (1978). Reid is also a frequent contributor to periodicals including *The Atlantic Monthly, Encounter,* and *The New Yorker,* and has written for television.

ADRIENNE RICH (b. 1928)   American poet born in Baltimore. She has received many honors for her poetry, including Guggenheim fellowships in 1952 and 1961; National Institute of Arts and Letters award for poetry (1961); and the National Book Award for her volume *Diving Into the Wreck* (1973). Her poetry expresses the conflicts she confronted as she sought to express herself artistically, while struggling with her roles as wife and mother. Her keen insights on the changing world around her and her changing self are revealed in such volumes of poetry as *Snapshots of a Daughter-in-Law* (1962), *Necessities of Life* (1966), and *A Wild Patience Has Taken Me This Far* (1981), from which "Hattie Rice Rich" was taken.

RICHARD RODRIGUEZ (b. 1944)   Mexican-American writer who grew up in Sacramento, California. As a child, Rodriguez struggled in parochial school with the task of learning his "public" language — English. He subsequently studied at Stanford and Columbia and did graduate work at the Warburg Institute in London and the University of California at Berkeley. In 1981 he wrote *Hunger of Memory: The Education of Richard Rodriguez* in which he describes the complexities and contradictions — personal and political — of growing up bilingual in America.

RICHARD H. ROVERE (1915–1979)   Writer and historian born in Jersey City, New Jersey. He is best known for his keen insights into American civilization and politics as he revealed them in such books as *The General and the President* (1951), *Affairs of State: The Eisenhower Years* (1956), *The American Establishment and Other Conceits, Enthusiasms, and Hostilities* (1962), and *Waist Deep in the Big Muddy: Personal Reflections on 1968* (1968).

RICHARD SELZER (b. 1928)   Maintains a private practice with a specialty in general surgery as well as teaching surgery at Yale University Medical School. He has written on various aspects of medicine for such journals as *Esquire, Harper's, Mademoiselle,* and *Redbook.* In 1975 Selzer won the National Magazine Award from Columbia University School of Journalism for his essays published in *Esquire.* His books include a volume of short stories, *Rituals of Surgery* (1974), and *Mortal Lessons* (1977), a collection of essays on the life of a doctor.

ANNE SEXTON (1928–1974)   American poet born in Newton, Massachusetts, where she spent most of her life. She published sev-

eral volumes of poetry and, in 1966, won the Pulitzer Prize for
Live or Die. Sexton is a confessional poet; her work is a poignant
expression of her personal struggle. Her poetry, full of concrete
and vivid images, reflects the relationship between the personal
and metaphysical. Her most famous volumes of poetry include
All My Pretty Ones (1962), *To Bedlam and Part Way Back* (1963),
Live or Die (1966), and *The Awful Rowing Toward God* (1975).
Sexton committed suicide in 1974.

GARY SNYDER (b. 1930)   American poet born in San Francisco, California. He writes of himself: "As poet I hold the most archaic
values on earth. They go back to the Neolithic: the fertility of
the soil, the magic of animals, the power vision in solitude, the
terrifying initiation and rebirth, the love and ecstasy of the
dance, the common work of the tribe." Among the honors and
awards Snyder has won are the National Academy of Arts and
Letters poetry award (1966), Bollinger Foundation grant
(1966–1967), and the Pulitzer Prize for poetry (1974). His volumes of poetry include *Myths and Texts* (1960), *Six Sections from
Mountains and Rivers Without End* (1965), *The Back Country*
(1967), and *Turtle Island* (1974).

WALLACE STEVENS (1879–1955)   American poet born in Reading,
Pennsylvania. He is regarded by critics as one of the most important American poets of the twentieth century. Stevens was
an avowed agnostic who sought philosophical reassurance in
what he called "supreme fiction." He strongly believed that the
only way to understand a universe in constant change was
through the use of the creative imagination. His works include
Harmonium (1923), *Ideas of Order* (1935), *Notes Toward a Supreme
Fiction* (1942), and *Opus Posthumous* (1957).

LEWIS THOMAS (b. 1913)   American physician, researcher, and essayist,
born in Flushing, New York. He is currently director of the
Memorial Sloane-Kettering Cancer Center. Thomas's first
book, *Lives of a Cell* (1974) brought him wide acclaim as an essayist. In addition to writing frequently for the *New England
Journal of Medicine,* Thomas has published a second essay collection, *The Medusa and the Snail* (1979).

HENRY DAVID THOREAU (1817–1862)   American essayist, naturalist,
and poet born in Concord, Massachusetts. He is best remembered for his impassioned argument against the powers of the
state as he described them in his essay *On Civil Disobedience*
(1849). As recorded in this essay, Thoreau was a nonviolent ac-

tivist: he helped escaped slaves flee to Canada, and he went to prison rather than pay his poll tax to a government that made war against Mexico. This nonviolent activism influenced both Mahatma Gandhi and Martin Luther King, Jr. In 1845, Thoreau built a one-room cabin at Walden Pond in Massachusetts where he lived for the next two years. In *Walden* (1854), from which "The Village" is taken, he describes his daily experiences and the natural life around him. He is recognized today not only for his prose style but for his individualism, which challenged the social status quo of his contemporaries and ours today as well.

JAMES THURBER (1894–1961) Born in Columbus, Ohio, he is best known for his humorous and satirical essays, stories, and cartoons depicting the follies of men and women. Of humor, Thurber has written that it is "emotional chaos remembered in tranquility." Thurber's works include *Is Sex Necessary?* (1929), a self-help manual he wrote with E. B. White; *My Life and Hard Times* (1933), autobiographical essays; and *My World and Welcome to It* (1942), which he illustrated himself and from which "The Secret Life of Walter Mitty" is excerpted. "Walter Mitty" has been made into a film.

JOHN UPDIKE (b. 1932) Born in Shillington, Pennsylvania, Updike began his writing career in 1955 as a "Talk of the Town" reporter at *The New Yorker*. Later he turned to fiction, publishing his first collection of short stories, *The Poorhouse Fair* (1960). For his novel *The Centaur* (1963) he received the National Book Award. His major novels are concerned with the rather nondescript hero of *Rabbit Run* (1960), *Rabbit Redux* (1971), and *Rabbit Is Rich* (1981). His most recent novel is *Beck Is Back* (1983). Of having chosen writing as a career Updike says, "I'm still running on energy laid down in childhood. Writing is a way of keeping up that childhood."

HANA WEHLE (b. 1917) Born in Prague, Czechoslovakia. She spent several years in Terezin/Theresienstadt, Birkenau-Auschwitz, and Stutthof. Her first husband was killed by the SS in Terezin. When she returned to Prague after the defeat of the Nazis in 1945, she met and married a fellow survivor. Wehle now lives in New York and has four children.

E. B. WHITE (b. 1899) Born in Mount Vernon, New York. His keen wit and succinct, highly refined prose style earned him a reputation as one of America's finest essayists. His essays and short stories are primarily social commentaries on contemporary life. In his acceptance speech for the National Medal for Literature, White remarked: "I fell in love with the sound of an early typewriter and have been stuck with it ever since. I believed then, as I do now, in the goodness of the published word: it seemed to contain an essential goodness, like the smell of leaf mold." White's books include *Charlotte's Web* (1952), a beloved children's story, *The Second Tree From the Corner* (1954), and *The Points of My Compass* (1962).

ELIE WIESEL (b. 1928)   Born in Sighet, Hungary. As a Jewish prisoner in a Nazi concentration camp at a very young age, Wiesel saw his family perish. He has dedicated much of his adult life to memorializing those who died and bearing witness to destruction, past and present. His most famous novels in which we see the plight of the Jews depicted are *Night* (1959), *Dawn* (1960), *The Town Beyond the Wall* (1961), *The Accident* (1962), and *The Gates of the Forest* (1966). Wiesel writes poignantly, always with a sense of urgency: "What torments me most is not the Jews of silence I met in Russia, but the silence of the Jews I live among today." He goes on to say that the Jew must "cry out, cry out, . . . enlist public opinion, . . . turn to those with influence, . . . involve the governments — the hour is late."

RICHARD WILBUR (b. 1921)   American poet, translator, and literary critic born in New York City. His many volumes of poetry include *The Beautiful Changes and Other Poems* (1947), *Advice to a Prophet* (1961), *Walking to Sleep* (1969), and *The Mind-Reader* (1976). He also wrote lyrics for the Broadway musical *Candide*. Wilbur is considered an excellent literary critic, and he has also been a major translator of the dramas of Molière. He has won many awards for poetry, including the Pulitzer Prize and the National Book Award.

JAMES WRIGHT (1927–1980)   American poet and translator born in Martins Ferry, Ohio. His poems are filled with images of loneliness, alienation, and separation. A *New York Times* critic once noted that while Wright's "mood was sometimes very dark, . . . one of his great strengths . . . was the life-affirming quality of his work." His works include *The Green Wall* (1957), *The Branch Will Not Break* (1963), *Collected Poems* (1971), *Moments of the Indian Summer* (1976), and *To A Blossoming Pear Tree* (1978).

YEVGENY YEVTUSHENKO (b. 1933)   Russian poet and author born in Siberia. Yevtushenko first became prominent in the Soviet Union with the publication of his poem "Babi Yar" (1962). He was criticized by the Soviet regime for his censure of its anti-Semitic actions. He has subsequently toured the United States and Europe, drawing record audiences to his poetry readings. His collections include *City Lights* (1961), *Selected Poems* (1963), and *Stolen Apples* (1971). In his later work he has shifted his thematic emphasis from the political to the personal.

(*Continued from page iv*)

Edward Mendelson, by permission of Random House, Inc. and Faber and Faber Ltd, London.

Saul Bellow, "On a Kibbutz." From *To Jerusalem and Back* by Saul Bellow, © 1977 by Saul Bellow; reprinted by permission of the publisher, Viking Penguin Inc.

Arna Bontemps, "Southern Mansions." From *Personals* by Arna Bontemps. Copyright © 1963 by Arna Bontemps. Reprinted by permission of Harold Ober Associates, Incorporated.

Albert Camus, "The Guest." From *Exile and the Kingdom,* by Albert Camus, translated by Justin O'Brien. Copyright © 1957, 1958 by Alfred A. Knopf, Inc. Reprinted by permission of the publisher.

Willa Cather, "A Wagner Matinee." Reprinted from *Youth and the Bright Medusa,* by Willa Cather, courtesy of Alfred A. Knopf, Inc.

Eldridge Cleaver, "A Day in Folsom Prison." From *Soul on Ice,* by Eldridge Cleaver. Copyright © 1968 by Eldridge Cleaver. Reprinted by permission of McGraw-Hill Book Company.

Emily Dickinson, "I Taste a Liquor Never Brewed." From *The Poems of Emily Dickinson.* Reprinted by permission of the publishers and the Trustees of Amherst College from *The Poems of Emily Dickinson,* edited by Thomas H. Johnson, Cambridge, Mass.: The Belknap Press of Harvard Univesity Press, Copyright © 1951, © 1955, 1979 by the President and Fellows of Harvard College.

Joan Didion, "Marrying Absurd." From *Slouching Towards Bethlehem* by Joan Didion. Copyright © 1967, 1968 by Joan Didion. Reprinted by permission of Farrar, Straus & Giroux, Inc.

Loren Eiseley, "The Brown Wasps." In *The Night Country.* Copyright © 1971 Loren Eiseley. Reprinted with the permission of Charles Scribner's Sons.

Ralph Ellison, "King of the Bingo Game." Copyright © 1944 by Ralph Ellison. Reprinted by permission of William Morris Agency, Inc. on behalf of the author.

E. M. Forster, "My Wood." From *Abinger Harvest* by E. M. Forster, copyright 1936, 1964 by Edward Morgan Forster. Reprinted by permission of Harcourt Brace Jovanovich, Inc. and Edward Arnold (Publishers) Ltd., London.

Gary Gildner, "First Practice." Reprinted from *First Practice* by Gary Gildner by permission of the University of Pittsburgh Press. © 1969 by Gary Gildner.

Herbert Gold, "Let's Kill the First Red-Haired Man We See." Copyright © 1970 by Herbert Gold. Reprinted from *The Magic Will,* by Herbert Gold, by permission of Random House, Inc.

William Golding, "Thinking As a Hobby." Copyright © 1961 by William Golding. First printed in *Holiday* Magazine. Reprinted by permission of Curtis Brown Ltd.

Richard Goldstein, "Gear." Copyright © The Village Voice, Inc., 1976. Reprinted by permission of The Village Voice.

Ted Hughes, "Secretary." From *The Hawk in the Rain* by Ted Hughes. Copyright © 1957 by Ted Hughes. Reprinted by permission of Harper & Row Publishers, Inc.

Helen Keller, "Three Days to See." Courtesy American Foundation for the Blind, New York.

William Melvin Kelley, "St. Paul and the Monkeys." From *Dancers on the Shore.* Copyright © 1963 by William Melvin Kelley. Reprinted by permission of Doubleday & Company, Inc.

D. H. Lawrence, "Snake." Reprinted from *The Complete Poems of D. H. Lawrence,* © 1964 by Angelo Ravagli and C. M. Weekley, by permission of the publisher, Viking Penguin Inc.

Denise Levertov, "From the Roof." From *The Jacob's Ladder.* Copyright © 1961 by Denise Levertov Goodman. Reprinted by permission of New Directions Publishing Corporation.

Anne Morrow Lindbergh, "Channelled Whelk." From *Gift of the Sea,* by Anne Morrow Lindbergh. Copyright © 1965 by Anne Morrow Lindbergh. Reprinted by permission of Pantheon Books, a division of Random House, Inc.

Archibald MacLeish, "Wild West." From *Collected Poems* by Archibald MacLeish. Copyright © 1952 by Archibald MacLeish. Reprinted by permission of Houghton Mifflin Company.

Carson McCullers, "The Sojourner." From *The Ballad of the Sad Cafe and Collected Short Stories* by Carson McCullers. Copyright © 1936, 1941, 1950, 1955 by Carson McCullers. Reprinted by permission of Houghton Mifflin Company.

Bernard Malamud, "The Prison." From *The Magic Barrel* by Bernard Malamud. Copyright © 1950, 1958, 1978 by Bernard Malamud. Reprinted permission of Farrar, Straus & Giroux, Inc.

Marya Mannes, "Television: The Splitting Image." From *The Saturday Review of Literature,* November 1970. Reprinted by permission of David J. Blow.

Gabriel García Márquez, "Balthazar's Marvelous Afternoon." From *No One Writes to the Colonel,* by Gabriel García Márquez, translated by J. S. Berstein. Copyright © 1968 in the English translation by Harper & Row, Publishers, Inc. Used by permission.

Joyce Maynard, "The Lion Tamers." From *Looking Back* by Joyce Maynard (New York: Doubleday and Company, 1973). Copyright © 1973 by Joyce Maynard. Reprinted by permission.

Edna St. Vincent Millay, "Spring." From *Collected Poems,* Harper & Row. Copyright 1921, 1948 by Edna St. Vincent Millay and Norma Millay Ellis.

Frank O'Connor, "First Confession." Copyright 1951 by Frank O'Connor. Reprinted from *Collected Stories* by Frank O'Connor, by permission of Alfred A. Knopf, Inc. and Joan Daves, New York.

George Orwell, "Paddy the Tramp." From *Down and Out in Paris and London,* copyright 1933 by George Orwell; renewed 1961 by Sonia Pitt-Rivers. Reprinted by permission of Harcourt Brace Jovanovich, Inc. and the estate of the late Sonia Brownell Orwell and Martin Secker & Warburg Ltd. "Revenge Is Sour." From *The Collected Essays, Journalism and Letters of George Orwell,* Volume Four, copyright © 1968 by Sonia Brownell Orwell. Reprinted by permission of Harcourt Brace Jovanovich, Inc. and the estate of the late Sonia Brownell Orwell and Martin Secker & Warburg Ltd.

Wilfred Owen, "Disabled." From *The Collected Poems of Wilfred Owen.* Copyright © Chatto & Windus, Ltd. 1963. Reprinted by permission of New Directions Publishing Corporation, the Owen Estate, and Chatto & Windus.

Alexander Petrunkevitch, "The Spider and the Wasp." From *Scientific American,* August 1952. Copyright © 1952 by Scientific American, Inc. All rights reserved. Reprinted with permission.

Ann Petry, "Like a Winding Sheet." From *Miss Muriel and Other Stories* by Ann Petry. Copyright © 1971 by Ann Petry. Copyright 1945, 1947, 1958, 1963, 1965, 1967 by Ann Petry. Reprinted by permission of Houghton Mifflin Company.

Katherine Anne Porter, "The Necessary Enemy." Excerpted from the book *The Collected Essays and Occasional Writings of Katherine Anne Porter.* Copyright © 1948 by Katherine Anne Porter. Originally published in *Mademoiselle.* Reprinted by permission of Delacorte Press/Seymour Lawrence.

Martin Ralbovsky, "A Little Foul Play the Coach's Way." Copyright © 1974 by Martin Ralbovsky. From the book *Lords of the Locker Room,* published by Peter H. Wyden, a division of David McKay Co., Inc. Reprinted by permission of the publisher.

Santha Rama Rau, "Return to India." Reprinted by permission of William Morris Agency, Inc., on behalf of Santha Rama Rau. Copyright © 1960 by Reporter Magazine Co.

Alastair Reid, "Curiosity." Reprinted by permission; © 1959 The New Yorker Magazine, Inc.

Adrienne Rich, "Hattie Rice Rich" from "Grandmothers" is reprinted from *A Wild Patience Has Taken Me This Far,* Poems 1978–1981, by Adrienne Rich, by permission of W. W. Norton & Company, Inc. Copyright © 1981 by Adrienne Rich.

Richard Rodriguez, from *Hunger of Memory* by Richard Rodriguez. Copyright © 1982 by Richard Rodriguez. Reprinted by permission of David R. Godine, Publisher, Boston.

Richard Rovere, "Wallace." Reprinted with permission of Macmillan Publishing Company from *Arrivals and Departures* by Richard H. Rovere. Copyright © 1950, 1976 by Richard H. Rovere. Originally appeared in *The New Yorker.*

Richard Selzer, "An Absence of Windows." From *Confessions of a Knife,* by Richard Selzer. Copyright © 1979 by David Goldman and Janet Selzer, trustees. Reprinted by permission of Simon & Schuster, a Division of Gulf & Western Corportion.

Anne Sexton, "The Rowing Endeth." From *The Awful Rowing Toward God* by Anne Sexton, Copyright © 1975 by Loring Conant, Jr., Executor of the Estate of Anne Sexton. Reprinted by permission of Houghton Mifflin Company.

Gary Snyder, "Mid-August At Sourdough Mountain Lookout." From *Riprap and Cold Mountain Poems* by Gary Snyder. Copyright © 1965 by Gary Snyder. Reprinted by permission of the author.

Wallace Stevens, "Disillusionment of Ten O'Clock." Copyright 1923 and renewed 1957 by Wallace Stevens. Reprinted from *The Collected Poems of Wallace Stevens,* by Wallace Stevens, by permission of Alfred A. Knopf, Inc.

Lewis Thomas, "Death in the Open." From *The Lives of a Cell* by Lewis Thomas, © 1974 by Lewis Thomas, reprinted by permission of the publisher, Viking Penguin, Inc.

James Thurber, "The Secret Life of Walter Mitty." Copyright © 1942 by James Thurber; © 1970 by Helen Thurber. From *My World—and Welcome to It,* published by Harcourt Brace Jovanovich. Originally printed in *The New Yorker.*

John Updike, "A & P." Copyright © 1962 by John Updike. Reprinted from *Pigeon Feathers and Other Stories,* by John Updike, by permission of Alfred A. Knopf, Inc. Originally appeared in *The New Yorker.*

Hana Wehle, "The Return." Reprinted by permission of the author.

E. B. White. "Once More to the Lake." Copyright 1941, 1969 by E. B. White. "The Geese." Copyright © 1971 by E. B. White. Originally appeared in *The New Yorker.* Both reprinted by permission of Harper & Row, Publishers, Inc.

Elie Wiesel, "The Watch." Copyright © 1965 by Elie Wiesel. Reprinted from *One Generation After,* by Elie Wiesel, by permission of Random House, Inc.

Richard Wilbur, "The Writer." © 1971 by Richard Wilbur. Reprinted by permission of Harcourt Brace Jovanovich, Inc., from the volume *The Mind Reader.*

James Wright, "A Blessing." Copyright © 1961 by James Wright. Reprinted from *The Branch Will Not Break* by permission of Wesleyan University Press. This poem first appeared in *Poetry.*

Yevgeny Yevtushenko, "People." From Yevtushenko: *Selected Poems,* translated by Robin Milner–Gulland and Peter Levi (Penguin Modern European Poets 1962). Copyright © Robin Milner–Guilland and Peter Levi, 1962. "Colours" from Yevtushenko: *Selected Poems,* translated by Robin Milner–Gulland and Peter Levi (Penguin Modern European Poets, 1962). Copyright © Robin Milner–Gulland and Peter Levi, 1962. Both reprinted by permission of Penguin Books Ltd.

Index of authors

To the Student:

Part of our job as educational publishers is to try to improve the textbooks we publish. Thus, when revising a book, we take into account the experience of both instructors and students with the previous edition. At some time your instructor may be asked to comment extensively on *Someone Like Me*, Fifth Edition, but right now we want to hear from you. After all, though your instructor assigned this book, you are the one who paid for it.

Please help us by completing this questionnaire and returning it to College English Development Group, Little, Brown & Company, 34 Beacon Street, Boston, Massachusetts 02106.

School _____ Course title _____

Instructor's name _____

Please rate the selections:	Liked best				Liked least	Didn't read
ONE: PEOPLE "No people are uninteresting"						
Sherwood Anderson, "Discovery of a Father"	5	4	3	2	1	____
Maya Angelou, "Sister Flowers"	5	4	3	2	1	____
Martin Ralbovsky, "A Little Foul Play, the Coach's Way"	5	4	3	2	1	____
George Orwell, "Paddy the Tramp"	5	4	3	2	1	____
Richard Goldstein, "Gear"	5	4	3	2	1	____
Richard Rovere "Wallace"	5	4	3	2	1	____
James Thurber, "The Secret Life of Walter Mitty"	5	4	3	2	1	____
Adrienne Rich, "Hattie Rice Rich"	5	4	3	2	1	____
Ted Hughes, "Secretary"	5	4	3	2	1	____
W. H. Auden, "The Unknown Citizen"	5	4	3	2	1	____
TWO: PLACES ". . . planet is dissimilar from planet"						
Saul Bellow, "On a Kibbutz"	5	4	3	2	1	____
E. B. White, "Once More to the Lake"	5	4	3	2	1	____
James Agee, "Knoxville Summer: 1915"	5	4	3	2	1	____
Eldridge Cleaver, "A Day in Folsom Prison"	5	4	3	2	1	____
Joan Didion, "Marrying Absurd"	5	4	3	2	1	____
John Updike, "A & P"	5	4	3	2	1	____
Bernard Malamud, "The Prison"	5	4	3	2	1	____
Arna Bontemps, "Southern Mansion"	5	4	3	2	1	____
Gary Snyder, "Mid-August at Sourdough Mountain Lookout"	5	4	3	2	1	____
Denise Levertov, "From the Roof"	5	4	3	2	1	____
THREE: EVENTS AND EXPERIENCES ". . . first snow and kiss and fight"						
E. B. White, "The Geese"	5	4	3	2	1	____
Joyce Maynard, "The Lion Tamers"	5	4	3	2	1	____
Richard Selzer, "An Absence of Windows"	5	4	3	2	1	____
Hanna Wehle, "Return"	5	4	3	2	1	____
Elie Wiesel, "The Watch"	5	4	3	2	1	____
Carson McCullers, "The Sojourner"	5	4	3	2	1	____
Frank O'Connor, "First Confession"	5	4	3	2	1	____
Emily Dickinson, "I Taste a Liquor Never Brewed"	5	4	3	2	1	____
Wilfred Owen, "Disabled"	5	4	3	2	1	____
James Wright, "A Blessing"	5	4	3	2	1	____
FOUR: EMOTIONS "To each his world is private"						
Loren Eiseley, "The Brown Wasps"	5	4	3	2	1	____
George Orwell, "Revenge is Sour"	5	4	3	2	1	____
Marya Mannes, "Television Advertising: The Splitting Image"	5	4	3	2	1	____
Herbert Gold, "Let's Kill the First Red-haired Man We See"	5	4	3	2	1	____
Lewis Thomas, "Death in the Open"	5	4	3	2	1	____
Ralph Ellison, "King of the Bingo Game"	5	4	3	2	1	____
Ann Petry, "Like a Winding Sheet"	5	4	3	2	1	____

Please rate the selections:

	Liked best				Liked least	Didn't read
Gary Gildner, "First Practice"	5	4	3	2	1	——
Wallace Stevens, "Disillusionment of Ten O'Clock"	5	4	3	2	1	——
Yevgeny Yevtushenko, "Colours"	5	4	3	2	1	——

FIVE: CHOICES "And if a man lived in obscurity . . . obscurity is not uninteresting"

William Golding, "Thinking as a Hobby"	5	4	3	2	1	——
Richard Rodreguez, from "A Hunger of Memory"	5	4	3	2	1	——
Alexander Petrunkevitch, "The Spider and the Wasp"	5	4	3	2	1	——
Santha Rama Rau, "Return to India"	5	4	3	2	1	——
Katherine Anne Porter, "The Necessary Enemy"	5	4	3	2	1	——
Willa Cather, "A Wagner Matinee"	5	4	3	2	1	——
William Melvin Kelley, "Saint Paul and the Monkeys"	5	4	3	2	1	——
Alastair Reid, "Curiosity"	5	4	3	2	1	——
D. H. Lawrence, "Snake"	5	4	3	2	1	——
Archibald MacLeish, "Wild West"	5	4	3	2	1	——

SIX: PHILOSOPHIES "Not people die but worlds die in them"

Anne Morrow Lindbergh, "Channelled Whelk"	5	4	3	2	1	——
Helen Keller, "Three Days to See"	5	4	3	2	1	——
Plato, "The Allegory of the Cave"	5	4	3	2	1	——
Henry David Thoreau, "The Village"	5	4	3	2	1	——
E. M. Forster, "My Wood"	5	4	3	2	1	——
Albert Camus, "The Guest"	5	4	3	2	1	——
Gabriel Garcia Marquez, "Balthazar's Marvelous Afternoon"	5	4	3	2	1	——
Richard Wilbur, "The Writer"	5	4	3	2	1	——
Anne Sexton, "The Rowing Endeth"	5	4	3	2	1	——
Edna St. Vincent Millay, "Spring"	5	4	3	2	1	——

What did you think of the exercises following the readings?

_____

_____

Did you read the biographical material on the authors? _____

Did it help in your reading? _____

Please add any comments or suggestions on how we might improve this book. _____

_____

_____

_____

Your name _____ Date _____

Mailing address _____

May we quote you either in promotion for this book or in future publishing ventures?

Yes _____ No _____

Thank you.